Disability and the Sociological Imagination

Allison C. Carey
Shippensburg University of Pennsylvania

$SAGE

Los Angeles | London | New Delhi
Singapore | Washington DC | Melbourne

$SAGE

FOR INFORMATION:

SAGE Publications, Inc.
2455 Teller Road
Thousand Oaks, California 91320
E-mail: order@sagepub.com

SAGE Publications Ltd.
1 Oliver's Yard
55 City Road
London, EC1Y 1SP
United Kingdom

SAGE Publications India Pvt. Ltd.
B 1/I 1 Mohan Cooperative Industrial Area
Mathura Road, New Delhi 110 044
India

SAGE Publications Asia-Pacific Pte. Ltd.
18 Cross Street #10-10/11/12
China Square Central
Singapore 048423

Acquisitions Editor: Jeff Lasser
Product Associate: Kenzie Offley
Production Editor: Vijayakumar
Copy Editor: Christobel Colleen Hopman
Typesetter: TNQ Technologies
Proofreader: Benny Willy Stephen
Indexer: TNQ Technologies
Cover Designer: Candice Harman
Marketing Manager: Jennifer Jones

Copyright © 2023 by SAGE Publications, Inc.

All rights reserved. Except as permitted by U.S. copyright law, no part of this work may be reproduced or distributed in any form or by any means, or stored in a database or retrieval system, without permission in writing from the publisher.

All third-party trademarks referenced or depicted herein are included solely for the purpose of illustration and are the property of their respective owners. Reference to these trademarks in no way indicates any relationship with, or endorsement by, the trademark owner.

Printed in the United States of America

Library of Congress Cataloging-in-Publication Data

Names: Carey, Allison C., author.

Title: Disability and the sociological imagination / Allison C. Carey.

Identifiers: LCCN 2022007509 | ISBN 9781071818152 (paperback) | ISBN 9781071818190 (adobe pdf) | ISBN 9781071818169 (epub) | ISBN 9781071818176 (epub)

Subjects: LCSH: Sociology of disability. | People with disabilities—Social conditions.

Classification: LCC HV1568 .C36 2023 | DDC 362.4—dc23/eng/20220222

LC record available at https://lccn.loc.gov/2022007509

This book is printed on acid-free paper.

22 23 24 25 26 10 9 8 7 6 5 4 3 2 1

Brief Contents

List of Figures	xi
List of Tables	xiii
Preface	xv
Acknowledgments	xvii
About the Author	xix

PART I: BUILDING BLOCKS OF THE SOCIOLOGY OF DISABILITY — 1

1 Introducing the Sociology of Disability and Theoretical Perspectives — 2

2 Researching Disability — 24

3 Social Constructions of Disability Through Time and Place: A Brief History — 44

PART II: THE COMPLEX EXPERIENCE OF DISABILITY — 71

4 Inequality and Ableism — 72

5 Culture and Disability — 93

6 Disability Identity and Socialization — 115

7 Intersectionality: Gender, Sexuality, and Race — 137

PART III: MACRO SOCIAL STRUCTURES AND DISABILITY   **165**

8   Family Through the Life Course   166

9   Economy and Politics   189

10   Health Care   211

11   Education and Criminal Justice   234

12   Social Movements and Social Change   262

Glossary   283

References   292

Index   323

Detailed Contents

List of Figures	xi
List of Tables	xiii
Preface	xv
Acknowledgments	xvii
About the Author	xix

PART I: BUILDING BLOCKS OF THE SOCIOLOGY OF DISABILITY — 1

1 Introducing the Sociology of Disability and Theoretical Perspectives — 2

Chapter Synopsis	2
Learning Outcomes	2
Disability and the Sociological Imagination	2
Sociology of Disability: An Emerging Field	3
Common Definitions of Disability	5
The Social Construction of Disability	6
The Medical and Social Models of Disability	8
Explaining the Production and Experience of Disability	11
The Construction of Meaning and Culture on the Micro and Macro Levels	12
Materialist Theories	13
Political and State-Centered Theories	15
Stratification, Intersectionality, and Relationality	16
Embodiment	18
Crip Theories	19
Theory Overview	20
Conclusion	21
Key Terms	22
Resources	22
Activities	23

2 Researching Disability — 24

Chapter Synopsis	24
Learning Outcomes	24
Why Study Disability?	24
Measuring Disability	26
Quantitative Approaches to Measuring Disability	26
Qualitative Approaches to Measure Disability	32
Considering Data Literacy	34
Ethical Issues in Researching Disability	34
Harm to Research Participants	34
Exclusion from Research and the Silencing of Disabled Voices	35
Power and the Research Process	38
Conclusion	40
Key Terms	41
Resources	41
Activities	42

3 Social Constructions of Disability Through Time and Place: A Brief History — 44

Chapter Synopsis	44	Colonial Caribbean	57
Learning Outcomes	44	1850–1950	58
Historical Comparative Analysis	44	The United States	58
Early Civilizations in the Ancient World: Egypt, Greece, and Rome	45	India	61
		1950 to the Present Day	64
Ancient Egypt	45	The United States	64
Ancient Greece and Rome	46	Brazil	67
Medieval Era—5th Century to 1400	48	Conclusion	69
Medieval Europe	48	Key Terms	69
China	50	Resources	69
Early Modern Period to 1850	51	Activities	70
Early Modern Europe	51		
Early America	53		

PART II: THE COMPLEX EXPERIENCE OF DISABILITY — 71

4 Inequality and Ableism — 72

Chapter Synopsis	72	Ableism and Inaccessibility	86
Learning Outcomes	72	Ableism and Segregation, Invisibility and Violence	88
Stratification Systems: Caste Versus Class	72		
People With Disabilities as a Minority Group	75	Conclusion	90
Ableism	77	Key Terms	90
Prejudice	79	Resources	90
Discrimination	81	Activities	91
Institutional Ableism	84		

5 Culture and Disability — 93

Chapter Synopsis	93	Representation	105
Learning Outcomes	93	Habitus and the Reproduction of Inequality	109
Culture and the Elements of Culture	93		
American Values and Disability	94	Cultural Resistance and Disability Culture	110
Symbols and Language	98		
Norms and Rituals	101	Conclusion	112
Material Culture	102	Key Terms	113
Cultural Oppression and Inequality	102	Resources	113
Narratives and Discourses	103	Activities	114

6 Disability Identity and Socialization — 115

Chapter Synopsis	115
Learning Outcomes	115
Disability Identity and the Self	115
Disability, Status, and Roles	116
Disability as a Status and the Sick Role	117
Disability, Stigma, and the Invalidation of Access to Other Statuses	118
Collective Disability Identity and Disability Pride	120
Darling's Typology of Disability Orientations	123
Socialization	125
Embodiment, Impression Management, and Performativity	128
Navigating the Concealment or Display of Disability Identity	129
Performativity	131
Disability Identity as Fluid	131
The Meaning of the Body: Cyborgs, Transhumanism, and Inequality	132
Conclusion	134
Key Terms	134
Resources	134
Activities	135

7 Intersectionality: Gender, Sexuality, and Race — 137

Chapter Synopsis	137
Learning Outcomes	137
Gender	137
Prevalence of Disability by Gender	137
Feminist and Intersectional Frameworks	139
Constructions of Disability and Gender	140
Gender, Disability, and Unequal Outcomes	144
Disability and the Feminist Movement	147
Sexuality	147
Barriers to Sexuality	148
Disability as an Opportunity for Sexual Exploration	150
Contested Sexual Politics	151
Activism, Sexual Rights, and the Politics of Pleasure	153
Race	153
Prevalence of Disability by Race and Outcomes	154
Racialization of Diagnosis	155
Disability and Racial Stereotypes	157
Disability, Race, and Identity	158
African American Civil Rights Activism and Disability Activism	160
Conclusion	161
Key Terms	162
Resources	162
Activities	163

PART III: MACRO SOCIAL STRUCTURES AND DISABILITY — 165

8 Family Through the Life Course — 166

Chapter Synopsis	166
Learning Outcomes	166
Disability, the Family, and Demographics	167
Disability, Family, and the Life Course	169

Pregnancy and Birth	169
Parenting a Child With a Disability	171
Transition to Adulthood	176
Forming (and Dissolving) New Families	178
Parenting Among People With Disabilities	181
Aging and the Family	184
Conclusion	186
Key Terms	186
Resources	186
Activities	188

9 Economy and Politics 189

Chapter Synopsis	189
Learning Outcomes	189
Materialist and Political Economy Theories	189
The Production of Disability	190
Capitalism and the Production of Disability	190
The Production of Disability and the State	193
The Production of Disability Through Economic Inequality	194
The Production of Disability Through Economic Inequality on a Global Scale	197
Political Economy and National Responses to Disability	199
Response 1: Legal and Social Exclusion	199
Response 2: Benefits and Protections	200
Response 3: Civil Rights, Employment, and Inclusion	202
Balancing Responses Based on Productivity	204
The Disability Industry	206
Alternative Approaches	207
Human Rights	208
Disability Justice	208
Conclusion	209
Key Terms	209
Resources	209
Activities	210

10 Health Care 211

Chapter Synopsis	211
Learning Outcomes	211
Conceptualizations of Health, Illness, and Disability	211
Distinguishing Illness and Disability	212
Mental Illness and Disability	213
The Growing Dominance of the Medical Model	216
Treatment and Rehabilitation	217
Institutionalization	219
Deinstitutionalization	221
The Incomplete Process of Deinstitutionalization	222
Home- and Community-Based Services	223
Access to Health Care and Health Equity	226
Health Differentials	226
Determinants of Health and Disability	226
Disability and Health Through the Lens of COVID-19	229
Conclusion	231
Key Terms	231
Resources	231
Activities	233

11 Education and Criminal Justice — 234

Learning Outcomes	234	Ableism in Higher Education	253
Education	234	Wrapping Up Education	254
The Rise of Special Education	235	Criminal Justice and Carceral Responses to Disability	254
Educational Achievements and Concerns	236	Why Incarcerate People With Disabilities?	255
Labeling Theory, Rising Rates, and Shifting Diagnoses	239	The School-to-Prison Pipeline	258
Labeling and Stigma	240	Therapeutic Jurisprudence, Alternative Sentencing, Social Services, and Disability Justice	259
Inclusion and Segregation	240		
Building an Intersectional Analysis of Special Education	243	Conclusion	259
"Promising" and Less Promising Diagnoses	244	Key Terms	260
Bringing in SES	246	Resources	260
Bringing in Race	248	Activities	261
Higher Education	251		
Differences in the Disability Services and Accommodations in High School and College	251		

12 Social Movements and Social Change — 262

Chapter Synopsis	262	Barriers to Activism	272
Learning Outcomes	262	Inequality in Activism	273
Introduction	262	The Never-Ending Cycle of Activism	275
Examples of Social Change and Stasis	263	Structural Change and Stasis	276
Explaining Social Change: Social Movements and Disability Activism	263	Structural Changes	276
		Social Stasis	277
The Disability Rights Movement and Disability Activism	264	Conclusion	279
		Key Terms	279
The Emergence of the Disability Activism	265	Resources	280
Tactics of Disability Activism	269	Activities	281
Becoming a Disability Activist	270		

Glossary	283
References	292
Index	323

List of Figures

2.1 ICF Model	27
4.1 Average (Mean) Earnings 1988–2014 for Working-Age People Using Current Population Survey Data	76
4.2 Average Percentage Employed 1988–2014 for Working-Age People Using Current Population Survey Data	77
5.1 Accessibility Symbols	99
7.1 Prevalence of Disability Type by Gender and Age, 2018	138
7.2 Percentage of Adult Disabled Respondents by Disability Type and Gender, 2014	139
7.3 Rates of Poverty and Employment by Disability and Gender, 2020 (Ages 25–54)	145
7.4 Percentage of Sexual Violence Victimization in One's Lifetime and in the Past Year by Gender and Disability, 2005–2007	146
7.5 Prevalence of Disability by Race, 2019	154
7.6 Percentage in Poverty by Race and Disability Status, 2015	155
7.7 Employment Rates by Disability & Race	156
7.8 Education Rates by Disability & Race	156
9.1 Global Rates of Poverty for People With Disabilities, 2010 (Schur et al., 2013)	195
9.2 US Federal Budget Allocation, 2019	196
9.3 GNI per Capita and DALY Loss, 2012	198
9.4 The Influences of Productivism on Disability Policy	204
10.1 Depression by Gender, 2007–2017 (Geiger & Davis, 2019)	215
10.2 Growth of ADHD Rates, 1997–2017	217
10.3 Total Populations in State-Funded Public Institutions, 1967–2014	221
10.4 Prevalence of Secondary Conditions, 2017	227
11.1 Percentage of Students in Special Education, 1976–2018	237
11.2 Percentage of Students With Disabilities Served Under the IDEA Graduating With a Regular High School Diploma, 1995–2015	238
11.3 Percentage of Adults Ages 25–32 Without a High School Diploma, 2008–2018	238
11.4 Percentage of Adults Ages 25–32 With a Bachelor's Degree or Higher, 2008–2018	239
11.5 Considering Success and Failure in the Inclusive Classroom	242

11.6 Number of Special Education Students (in Thousands) in Diagnosis Categories, 1976–2018   244

11.7 Percentage of Students in Inclusive Settings by Diagnosis, 2015–2016   245

11.8 Percentage of Students Served by IDEA in 2015–2016 by Race and Exit Path for High School   248

11.9 Percentage of Students Included in General Education at Least 80% of Class-Time by Race, 2015–2016   249

11.10 Mental Health of Inmates, 2011–2012   255

List of Tables

1.1 Medical and Social Models	9
1.2 Overview of Theoretical Perspectives	20
2.1 Approaches to Measuring Disability	33
3.1 Social Structure in Ancient Egypt	46
3.2 Social Structure in Ancient Rome and Greece	48
3.3 Social Structure in Medieval Europe	50
3.4 Social Structure in Medieval China	51
3.5 Social Structure in Early Modern—1850 Europe	54
3.6 Social Structure in Early America	56
3.7 Social Structure in Colonial Caribbean	58
3.8 Social Structure in America, 1850–1950	62
3.9 Social Structure in Colonial India	63
3.10 Social Structure in the United States 1950 to the Present Day	66
3.11 Social Structure in Brazil 1950 to the Present	68
4.1 Stereotype Content Model	80
5.1 Involvement in Social Activities for People With and Without Disabilities, 2010	109
6.1 Darling's Typology of Disability Orientations	124
8.1 Type of Disability in American Families, 2000	168
8.2 Median Income by for Families With and Without Disabled Members, 2000	168
8.3 Family Characteristics and Poverty, 2000	169
8.4 The Disability Marriage Penalty	180
8.5 Economic Marginality of Parents With and Without Disabilities, 2008	182
9.1 Positive and Negative Consequences of the Commodification of Disability Services	207
10.1 Advantages and Disadvantages of Medicalization	216
10.2 Comparison on Institutional Settings and Person-Centered Settings	225
11.1 The Provisions of the Individuals With Disabilities Education Act	236
11.2 Disability Services in High School and College	252

Preface

Although 19% of Americans experience disability (US Census Bureau, 2017), disability has received little attention in Sociology. Fortunately, this is beginning to change. *Disability and the Sociological Imagination* meets a pressing need by providing a cutting-edge, accessible text in the Sociology of Disability designed for undergraduate students and for graduate students new to the field. *Disability and the Sociological Imagination* introduces students to a wide array of sociological concepts, theories, and empirical research foundational to the field. Moreover, it connects the subfield to the broader discipline of Sociology by building connections to classical and contemporary theories in varied fields such as social movements and cultural sociology.

The Sociology of Disability broadly conceptualizes disability as a product of social interaction and the social environment, rather than as simply an objective, biological fact. It examines the macro structural issues relevant to people with disabilities, such as the ways that capitalism's demand for standardized and highly productive workers may exclude some people from employment, the effects of war and global poverty on producing disability, and the role of cultural discourse in determining what is and is not seen as disability. It examines micro social factors, such as the creation of meanings of disabilities and the lived experiences of disability as embedded in social contexts. And, it examines the connections and causal pathways between the macro and micro levels. In its breadth and range of foci, the Sociology of Disability is akin to other stratification subfields such as race and ethnicity, gender, and class.

This book is ideal for courses in the Sociology of Disability, as well as courses in Medical Sociology to examine a disability perspective, in inequality and diversity courses to address disability as an axis of inequality, and in Disability Studies courses that wish to teach sociology as one of many fields contributing to the interdisciplinary inquiry into disability.

Guiding Principles

The guiding principles for the organization and content of this work include the following:

- Encouraging the sociological imagination by firmly rooting the examination of disability to the discipline of sociology, including key sociological concepts, theories, and methods.
- Fostering data literacy and scientific skills by explaining the complexity of conceptualizing and measuring disability and grounding the discussion of disability in empirical research.
- Providing both micro- and macro-level theories while stressing a macro, structural approach that examines the ways in which major social structures such as the economy, political system, stratification system, and culture produce and reproduce disability and the inequalities associated with disability.

- Emphasizing the centrality of inequality and ableism in the understanding of disability and the consideration of social justice strategies.
- Examining a diversity of experiences and intersectional axes of inequality to showcase the complexity of the disability experience.
- Ensuring that the writing style and information is engaging and presented in an accessible format.

Pedagogical Features

Each chapter contains pedagogical features to aid students in learning and exploring the information and faculty in presenting it. These include the following:

- **Chapter synopses** at the outset of each chapter summarize and provide an overview of the material.
- **Learning objectives** highlight the key knowledge and skills students will build.
- **Key terms** focus students on central ideas while reading. They are bolded in text, listed at the end of the chapter, and compiled into a glossary to assist students in organizing the material and remembering concepts across chapters.
- **Figures, tables, and charts** present complex material, especially quantitative material, graphically to make it more readily understandable for students.
- **Recommended supplemental material**, including academic readings, memoirs, videos and films, podcasts, and internet sites, are listed at the end of each chapter with short summaries. This aids instructors in considering how to further develop the material and engage students and assists students in building additional knowledge.
- **Suggested activities** provide thoughtful tips for structuring student engagement.
- **Global focus text boxes** are featured in many chapters. The text focuses on disability in America, and the Global Focus text boxes offer a means for international comparison and contrast related to significant themes and concepts.

Acknowledgments

In the construction of any textbook, there are many people who contribute to the end product. The team at Sage Press, including Jeff Laser and Lauren Younker, provided guidance and facilitated the processes of writing, developing the pedagogical features, gathering reviews, and ultimately strengthening the text. I am thrilled to have the opportunity to work with the amazing team at Sage. The reviewers provided thoughtful feedback and productive suggestions to improve the text, and I am indebted to them.

Shippensburg University provided support in several ways. The College of Arts and Sciences of Shippensburg University provided funding for student involvement, and Shippensburg University funded a sabbatical so that I could focus on organizing material and writing. Undergraduate students, including Darin Warfield and Casey Zimmerman, provided student feedback and assisted with editing. Furthermore, students in my Sociology of Disability class read the first draft as part of their course material, which offered me the opportunity to see what aspects of the draft worked well and what did not, and I greatly appreciate their patience and enthusiasm.

My husband, Blyden Potts, offered feedback on the chapters and pedagogy, and he assisted in identifying relevant data. Several friends and colleagues provided input at various stages of the project development, including Richard Scotch, Sara Green, Brian Grossman, Carol Marfisi, and Cheryl Najarian Souza. Cheryl Najarian Souza and I collaborated on a study of syllabi in the Sociology of Disability, a project which provided a window into faculty priorities and approaches to the field. Engaging conversations with Cheryl molded my priorities, and I thank her and all of the instructors who contributed syllabi for that project, which is published in *Teaching Sociology*. Chapter 4 on Ableism and Inequality was first published in *On Inequality and Freedom*, edited by Lawrence Eppard and Henry Giroux (Oxford University Press, 2021), and I thank Oxford University Press for permission to include a similar version as part of this work.

More generally, the members and officers of the Disability and Society section of the American Sociological Association and the Disability Interest Group of the Society for the Study of Social Problems provided access to cutting-edge research and avenues to engage with members in the field. The Society for Disability Studies fosters interdisciplinary engagement and always expands my thinking about disability. The many activists, scholars, and students in the field offer a vibrant community that I deeply love and appreciate. I hope that this text is a way to give back to this amazing community and to help it further grow. Finally, my family has provided immeasurable love and support as I have pursued my academic passions.

About the Author

Allison C. Carey is Professor of Sociology and Chair of the Sociology Department at Shippensburg University. In collaboration with other faculty members at Shippensburg University, she helped found Shippensburg University's Interdisciplinary Minor in Disability Studies and served as its founding director for six years. Her areas of specialization are the social construction of intellectual disability, eugenics, civil rights and disability rights, and disability activism. She authored *On the Margins of Citizenship: Intellectual Disability and Civil Rights in Twentieth Century America* (Temple University Press, 2009), and coauthored *Allies and Obstacles: Disability Activism and Parents of Children with Disabilities* (Temple University Press, 2020), both of which were awarded the North Central Sociological Association's Scholarly Achievement Award. She is a series co-editor of *Research in Social Science and Disability* with Emerald Press and has coedited several volumes including *Disability and Community* (Volume 6, with Richard Scotch, 2006), *Disability Alliances and Allies: Opportunities and Challenges* (Volume 12, with Joan Ostrove and Tara Fannon, 2020), and *Disability in the Time of Pandemic* (Volume 13, with Sara Green and Laura Mauldin, forthcoming). She also co-edited *Disability Incarcerated: Disability and Imprisonment in the United States and Canada* (with Liat Ben-Moshe and Chris Chapman, Palgrave Macmillan, 2014). She has served as chair of the ASA Disability in Society section, as chair of the Committee on the Status of Persons with Disabilities, and as an officer on the Board of Directors of the Society for Disability Studies. In 2021, she was awarded the Outstanding Career in the Sociology of Disability award by the Disability in Society section of the American Sociological Association (ASA).

Building Blocks of the Sociology of Disability

PART I

CHAPTER 1

Introducing the Sociology of Disability and Theoretical Perspectives

Learning Outcomes

1.1 Explain the sociological imagination as it relates to disability.

1.2 Trace the development of sociological thinking concerning disability.

1.3 Identify common definitions of disability.

1.4 Articulate the significance of disability as a social construct.

1.5 Apply the medical and social models of disability.

1.6 Describe and apply the key theoretical paradigms.

Chapter Synopsis

Chapter 1 introduces the field of the Sociology of Disability, explains the Medical and Social Models of Disability, and familiarizes the reader with a range of theoretical traditions that inform the field. Although diverse, the theories share the idea that disability is a social construct which can be explained through social forces and processes such as culture, economy, and power. As such, a sociological lens is essential to understanding disability.

Disability and the Sociological Imagination

People with disabilities constitute one of America's largest minority groups. The 2010 US Census estimated that 19% of the American population has a disability (United States Census Bureau, 2012). Looking only at adults (who are more likely to have disabilities than children), in 2016 the Centers for Disease Control and Prevention (CDC) estimated that one in four American adults—61 million Americans—have a disability that impacts major life activities (CDC, 2018). That's a lot of Americans!

Not only do people with disabilities make up a sizable portion of the population, but they face numerous social disadvantages. Among working-age adults in 2016, only 35.9% of people with disabilities were employed, compared to 76.6% of people without disabilities, a difference of 40.7 percentage points. Of those employed, people with disabilities earned only two-thirds of what people without disabilities earned ($22,047 vs. $32,479). Not surprisingly then, people with disabilities were almost eight percentage points more likely to live in poverty (20.9% vs. 13.1%) (Kraus et al., 2018). Across measures of quality of life and satisfaction (e.g., marriage, social activity, education), people with disabilities fare less well than people without disabilities. They are less likely to socialize or eat out, and, when asked to rate their life satisfaction, only 34% reported being very satisfied compared to 61% of people without disabilities (Krane & Hanson, 2004).

To resist these social disadvantages, people with disabilities at times join together, forming powerful social organizations to fight for rights, services, and access. Many artists and scholars with disabilities embrace disability culture, leading to a range of cultural products (e.g., art, dance, books, film) that illuminate and prioritize the lived experiences of people with disabilities and celebrate their value in society (Brown, 2002).

Thus, people with disabilities are a large group who disproportionately experience social disadvantage, many of whom work collaboratively toward social change. These qualities make disability an area ripe for sociological study. Sociology, though, has been slow to incorporate disability into its theories and research (Gerschick & Stevens, 2016; Green & Barnartt, 2016). For too long, sociologists have **essentialized** disability—or, in other words, viewed disability as a biological, individual-level trait and the social disadvantages that accrue to disabled people as the natural outcomes of biological traits.

The Sociology of Disability aims to change that oversight. In doing so, sociologists take up the call issued by C. Wright Mills (1959) to develop the **Sociological Imagination**—the process by which we recognize the broader social context shaping individual experiences. According to Mills, many concerns experienced as *personal troubles* are better understood as *public issues* shaped by social institutions and historical trends. Disability may feel like a personal trouble that one copes with individually, but the experience of disability is deeply shaped by the social and historical context. These social factors include, for instance, cultural beliefs about disability, policies that may support or demean people with disabilities, and economic systems that provide avenues for participation or sideline people with disabilities. Disability is not simply a biological or medical fact. Instead, society—via social institutions like education and government, relationships, expectations and opportunity structures, and belief systems—shapes what disability means and the effects of it. Understanding disability is fundamentally a sociological task, requiring the use of the sociological imagination.

Sociology of Disability: An Emerging Field

For most of the history of sociology, disability was primarily discussed in specific subfields, especially medical sociology and the study of deviance (Green & Barnartt, 2016). **Medical sociology** studies the social constructions and institutional practices related to health, illness, and well-being. Within this framework, sociologists position disability primarily in the context of health and health care, examining issues like the perceptions and expectations of sick and disabled people, the interaction of patients with the medical system, and inequality in accessing health care. The subfield of **deviance** examines the establishment and violation of social norms. Classical sociologists, including Talcott Parsons (1951) and Erving Goffman (1963), considered sickness and disability to be a kind of deviance insofar as they preclude one from exercising expected roles in society and give rise to a stigmatized identity. Within a deviance framework, sociologists explore issues like the stigmatization of people with disabilities and how stigmatized people manage their interactions with others.

While both fields are relevant to understanding disability, disability as a social phenomenon and the social experience of people with disabilities cannot be reduced to these realms. Such a reductionist view would be like discussing women only when we study family or childbirth; these are relevant topics, but women's lives are not solely defined by family and childbirth. By considering disability only within the confines of medical sociology and deviance, sociology further stigmatizes people with disabilities, reaffirming the idea that people with disabilities are only relevant as objects of medical practice and/or as deviants. However, this is not an accurate representation of the experience of people with disabilities.

Sociologist Irving Zola was among the pioneers who thought more expansively about disability (Bell, 2016; Welsh, 2016). In his 1982 "socio-autobiography" *Missing Pieces: A Chronicle of Living with a Disability*, Zola examined life with a disability and the broader social context shaping the experience of disability. In doing so, he shed light on how the fixation on health, youth, and beauty devalues people seen as frail or broken, leading to segregation and exclusion from the range of human experiences. Other scholars also began approaching disability in new ways. In *The Politics of Disablement*, Mike Oliver, a British sociologist, theorized the economic and social processes by which society produces disability. And, Richard Scotch, in his book *From Good Will to Civil Rights* (1984), examined the shift in disability policy from a charity approach to a civil rights approach that guaranteed accessibility and rights for people with disabilities as equal citizens. These new sociological approaches used and created theories related to the state, culture, and stratification, breaking free from the confines of disability as only medical or deviant. These scholars, and many others, forged a new subfield of sociology—the Sociology of Disability.

The **Sociology of Disability**, like the Sociology of Gender or the Sociology of Race and Ethnicity, seeks to examine a broad range of social experiences, processes, and outcomes in relation to a social concept and identity category—in this case, disability.

As a field within sociology, disability sociologists use scientific methods to develop social explanations (rather than, for example, biological, psychological, or religious explanations) for social phenomena. They study, among other things:

- the ways that disability is socially constructed and given meaning, and as such the variation in the meaning of disability across time and place;
- the social consequences of disability;
- the social position of people with disabilities within the larger stratification structure, the processes through which disability oppression operates, and the intersection of disability oppression with oppression based on race, gender, sexuality, class, and other bases of inequality;

- the ways in which disability is produced and made relevant in and through various social institutions (e.g., education, media, politics);
- the social processes of identity formation and disability as an identity category;
- the ways that disability influences and is shaped by micro processes such as small-group interaction and conversation; and
- the dynamics of social change affecting and led by people with disabilities

Common Definitions of Disability

The first question disability sociologists usually encounter is: What is disability? This is a harder question to answer than you might think! Harlan Hahn (1987, p. 182) famously stated, "Disability is essentially whatever public laws and programs say it is."

There are many ways that people think about and define disability. Below we offer a few definitions that are commonly used in American society. These will be explored at greater length in Chapter 2, which focuses on researching and measuring disability. Disability may be defined as:

- *The experience of limitations or difficulties due to biological conditions and environmental constraints.* One of the most common definitions of disability is the experience of limitations or difficulties in performing important tasks due to biological conditions as experienced in particular environmental contexts. These tasks are often called Activities of Daily Living (ADLs) and Instrumental Activities of Daily Living (IADLs). ADLs include basic self-care activities such as bathing, toileting, feeding oneself, and dressing. IADLs include higher-order tasks like managing money, food shopping, managing medications, and doing housework. According to this definition, if one experiences limitations/difficulties in tasks due to biological conditions, one has a disability.
- *A set of significant and chronic health conditions.* Another approach to defining disability is to determine a list of chronic conditions associated with physical/mental limitations. For example, a study might consider blind people to be disabled, regardless of whether they experience difficulties in particular tasks or not.
- *The inability to work due to a biological condition.* The Social Security Administration defines disability quite narrowly, as "the inability to engage in any substantial gainful activity (SGA) by reason of any medically determinable physical or mental impairment(s) which can be expected to result in death or which has lasted or can be expected to last for a continuous period of not less than 12 months." For the Social Security Administration, disability is only meaningful in relation to the ability to work.
- *The experience of social disadvantage, prejudice, and discrimination associated with physical or mental impairment or the perception of*

impairment. To offer one last example, the Americans with Disabilities Act of 1990 (ADA) is the centerpiece of American legislation prohibiting discrimination against people with disabilities. It provides one of the most important legal definitions of disability. In this law, disability includes persons with a physical or mental impairment that substantially limits one or more major life activities, those who have a history or record of such an impairment, and/or those who are perceived by others as having such an impairment. This definition recognizes that disability is not simply rooted in individual biology or limitations but is also shaped by social views and discrimination.

We could list additional definitions embedded in varied laws, service systems, or cultural frameworks. The key point that we wish to make, though, is that definitions of disability vary widely. These definitions vary in their criteria, who is included, and the percentage of the population that likely falls under any given definition. If we look across time and place, it becomes clear there is no single definition of disability. Disability is what people say it is, especially when those people have power to confer or deny resources based on labels. Disability is a social construct.

The Social Construction of Disability

Although the definitions and approaches used to study disability vary, sociologists tend to understand disability as produced via social processes. To explore this idea, let's start with the idea of social construction. **Social construction** is the process by which people create the meaning of the world around them through social interaction. According to phenomenologists Peter Berger and Thomas Luckmann (1966), humans experience the world through our senses. We cannot discern "objective reality"; we can only know our own awareness of it. Through social interaction, we build consensus to some degree about the meaning of the things around us and establish a sense of a shared social reality. We decide things like what range of shades will be called "red," what animals are appropriate to eat and what foods are "breakfast foods," and what traits make someone "beautiful." These shared meanings get institutionalized; for example, certain shades of lipsticks are marketed as red, General Mills sells "breakfast" cereals, and the media promotes particular looks as beautiful. Once institutionalized, these shared meanings seem real and objective, like fixed reality. Meanings seem even more fixed when we are born into a culture and taught meanings as if they represent objective reality. Yet, we know that meanings can and do vary by time and culture, and they change all the time. If you've ever felt culture shock, you probably have realized that the ideas that you hold as "true" are simply cultural beliefs.

So, what does it mean to say that disability is a social construction? Through social interaction, people create meanings related to different bodies/minds. For example, people identify some bodies/minds as preferable to others. These labels then shape interactions and the opportunities available to people with different bodies/minds. **Disability**, therefore, is constructed via the *social processes* by which some bodies/minds are identified, categorized, and treated as "disabled."

Let's develop an example in greater depth using intellectual disability. Intellectual disability is usually understood as an individual-level impairment characterized by subaverage intelligence, rooted in one's biology, that causes difficulties in meeting the demands of one's environment. In contrast, sociologists point out that intellectual disability must be understood as a social construct. Intelligence itself is socially constructed; debates have raged for decades about what it means to be intelligent, what kinds of intelligences are valued, and how to measure intelligence. Furthermore, the beliefs, expectations, and attitudes surrounding intellectual disability vary dramatically across time and place (Carey, 2009; Trent, 1994). The very same intellectual capacities may be considered severe disability in one culture, mild disability in another culture, and not disability at all in another culture. Furthermore, the consequences of intellectual disability vary. Historically in America, a diagnosis of intellectual disability led to institutionalization, compulsory sterilization, and exclusion from public education. Now, these outcomes are less common, but people with intellectual disabilities still experience higher levels of social isolation, poverty, and social control.

Saying that intellectual disability is a social construct does not mean there is no biological basis underlying disability. There may be, or there may not be. Some sociologists distinguish between **impairment** (physical and mental traits determined to be atypical and often perceived as undesirable) and **disability** (the social processes by which some bodies/minds are identified, categorized, and treated as disabled). This distinction is similar to the common sociological practice of distinguishing sex and gender. Sex is determined by the presence of particular sex organs and traits, whereas gender constitutes the broad set of social meanings, expectations, norms, and consequences associated with being male or female. A woman may have a uterus (sex), but having a uterus does not determine the meaning and consequences of being female such as standards of dress or employment opportunities (gender).

Similarly, some people may have physical or mental traits, such as Down syndrome, which affect their intelligence; however, even if the biology of Down syndrome (impairment) affects intelligence, it does not explain the meanings and consequences that flow from it such as the variation in the marginalization of people with Down syndrome over time and across cultures (disability). Furthermore, people may be *regarded* as disabled in the absence of impairment. Women, for example, historically were thought to be physically and mentally unable to engage in high-order reasoning. Scientists declared their bodies/minds were too disabled for learning, and women were excluded from higher education on this basis, although now we know that women can achieve intellectually.

Other sociologists reject a sharp distinction between impairment and disability. They argue that even impairments, one's body, and the experience of one's body are shaped by social experiences and processes. For example, intelligence is a social construct, and Down syndrome cannot be understood without recognizing that people created the construct of intelligence and measures for it. Moreover, social factors, such as exposure to toxins and lack of exposure to positive stimulation, also affect intelligence. Thus, even biology is *a product of social processes*. Regardless of whether sociologists distinguish between impairment and disability or not, to say intellectual disability is a social construction means that there are vast social meanings and consequences tied to the label of intellectual disability which are not clearly caused by biology.

As a social construct, disability is, most simply, whatever people say it is. **Labeling theory** (Becker, 1966) argues that social phenomena are best understood through the process by which a label is socially created and applied to a group of people, often resulting in various consequences. Drawing on this theory, disability is a label created and applied to a group of people, a label that can be institutionalized in various ways and that results in various consequences. Across societies and times, various bodies and minds were understood differently. People are "disabled" when they are defined and treated as such.

Because disability is a social construction, we should not be surprised that ideas about disability and what constitutes disability vary by time and place. The same physical or mental condition may or may not be understood as "disability" depending on how common it is, the cultural beliefs in a society, and the extent of the disadvantages that flow from a condition. The very idea of "disability"—an umbrella term uniting an array of physical and mental conditions and experiences—is actually a relatively modern concept (Nielsen, 2012). Definitions of disability depend on who is doing the defining and why they are defining it. For example, educators might want to cast a broad net to deliver supports to all those who need them, while administrators might want a narrow definition of disability that identifies fewer people and thereby saves money by delivering services to fewer people. Moreover, disability is fluid. Both physical abilities and environmental contexts shift, leading to greater or lesser experiences of disablement.

The Medical and Social Models of Disability

The competing ideas of disability as biological versus disability as a social construct are often referred to as the medical model versus the social model. A model is a way of representing something and putting it in relationship with other things. The **medical model** regards disability as an individual deficit or limitation rooted in individual biology. The **social model** regards disability as a social construct rooted in the physical and social environment.

The most important difference between these models is the understanding of where disability lies—in the person or in the environment. To use blindness as an example, the *medical model* roots disability in physical defects that limit vision and seeks to remedy these defects through medical and therapeutic interventions to enable the blind person to achieve sight, or to approximate the behaviors and abilities of a sighted person as much as possible. Doctors, for example, typically use the medical model. When they encounter blindness, they assume it is an unfortunate defect of an individual's body that ideally will be fixed through medical intervention. Many nonmedical professionals share this view.

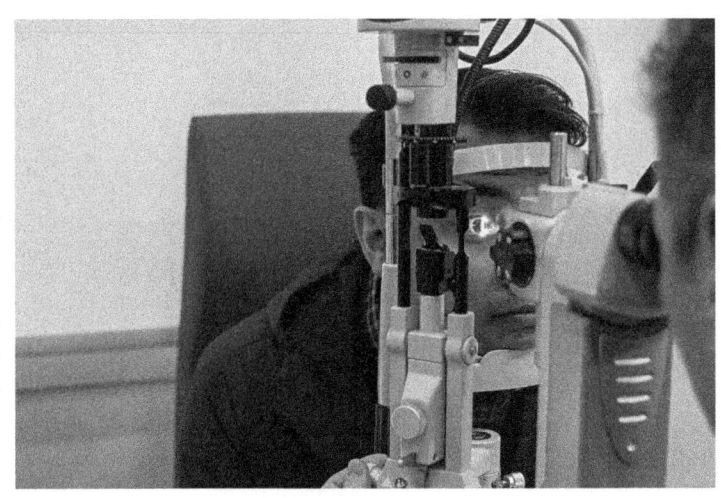

PHOTO 1.1
A doctor relies on the medical model, examining patients to identify illnesses and problems.

The *social model* (Oliver, 1990), on the other hand, asserts that the biology of blindness does not need to be cured or fixed. It locates disability, instead, in the social and environmental barriers that deny opportunities and rights to people with different bodies/minds, thereby disabling them. The social model emerged in Britain in the 1970s as a way for disabled activists to call attention to the social barriers—including physical barriers, prejudice, and social policies that create social disadvantage and to demand that we *fix society* (UIPAS, 1976). In this view, the biological difference is usually far less limiting than the social response to the difference.

Returning to the example of blindness, blind activists argue that the key barriers they face are not due to the physicality of blindness. Rather, the key barriers are low expectations, discrimination, and inaccessibility. Blind scholar and activist Jacobus tenBroek (1966) famously wrote that blind people have "a right to live in this world." To achieve this right, society needs to rectify problematic stereotypes, such as that blind people are incapable of participating in activities like work or travel, should be segregated for their own safety, and should hide their blindness from view.

In the social model, *society creates the key social, environmental, and policy barriers that disable people,* and, in turn, society can create inclusive and accessible environments that enable people. When blind people are in accessible environments, they successfully learn, attend college, work, marry, have children, and live self-determined lives. In accessible environments, blindness is not disabling.

Table 1.1 summarizes the differences between the medical and social models.

PHOTO 1.2 According to the social model, blindness is not disabling when society provides access, such as this student using a Braille textbook.

TABLE 1.1 Medical and Social Models

	Medical Model	Social Model
Disability is	An individual defect or abnormality resulting in functional limitations	A disadvantage produced by the social environment, including attitudes, architecture, and policies
Disability is rooted in	One's individual biology	The social environment; a poor fit between individual biology and one's environment
Disability manifests in	Individual limitations in functionality or activities of daily life (e.g., I can't walk, inability to hear)	Blocked opportunities for valued participation (e.g., this business has no ramp so I cannot work here, this event has no ASL interpreter so I cannot attend)

(Continued)

TABLE 1.1 Medical and Social Models *(Continued)*

	Medical Model	**Social Model**
Disability is identified by	Identifying individual deficits and their biological reasons: Why can't you see? Why can't you walk?	Identifying social barriers that prevent opportunity: Why is public transportation inaccessible? Why do schools teach Spanish but not ASL?
Disability is addressed via	Individual-level "fixes" (e.g., medical intervention and therapy to "normalize" the person) and charity	Changes in the environment to increase access and empowerment (build ramps, provide education to reduce stigma); Rights to access and participation
Expertise lies in	Medical and the helping professions	People with disabilities
Advantages of the model	Promotes medical research May cure or ameliorate painful or even deadly conditions	Identifies social barriers and changes them to make the world more just; Confers respect and power to people with disabilities
Disadvantages of the model	May increase stigma for people who cannot be or choose not to be fixed; May assume people want or need to be "fixed"; May naturalize anti-disability social values	May overlook important physical differences; May overlook pain, suffering, and negative experiences rooted in biology; May stigmatize decision to seek medical cure

While scholarship often treats the medical and social model as mutually exclusive, they are not (Morris, 1991; Shakespeare, 2010; Thomas, 1999). The experience of disability may be rooted in both biology and society. People with disabilities often use both models (i.e., they consider disability from both perspectives). They may draw on medical expertise to attain optimal health *and* demand rights and the removal of social barriers.

Also, keep in mind that sociologists often recognize that the medical model itself is a social construction. In other words, although the people who adhere to the medical model believe that disability is "natural," sociologists argue that the *belief* in disability as a natural, biological, objective state is itself a cultural belief system, one most commonly held in highly industrialized societies. It is *the* dominant belief system currently in America related to disability. Although particular groups believe that biology and medicine are based on objective facts, medicine is actually a value system, and medical practitioners and those who rely on a medical perspective have a symbolic, constructed culture. This culture celebrates a very particular body that adheres to the statistical norm. It often presents the nonnormative body, such as bodies that shake, drool, falter, or show other signs of "weakness," as the enemy. Medical culture celebrates the fight for a cure and praises those who overcome their sickness or disability to attain "normality" (Katz, 1998).

Once the social and medical model are framed as belief systems (i.e., social constructions) by which people *construct and understand* disability, it may not be surprising that there are more models/belief systems representing other ways that people and cultures understand and explain disability. For example, scholars have shown the importance of the Moral/Religious Model—the belief that disability is conferred purposefully from god(s/esses) as a punishment, a moral challenge or test, or a gift (Wheatley, 2010). If one understands disability to be caused by supernatural causes, then the responses to disability will likely also be spiritual in nature, such as prayer, strengthening one's faith, and cleansing/healing ceremonies. There is also a Charity Model in which people with disabilities are primarily seen as dependent, helpless, and in need of financial and moral rescue from "good" people. While charity accomplishes positive goals of redistributing important resources and acknowledging human need and suffering, it can have negative consequences when it is the primary way in which we understand disability. Charity can lead, for example, to the objectification of people with disabilities, the perpetuation of the stereotype that all people with disabilities want or need charity, and the constant evaluation of people with disabilities in terms of their deservedness of charity (Longmore, 2016).

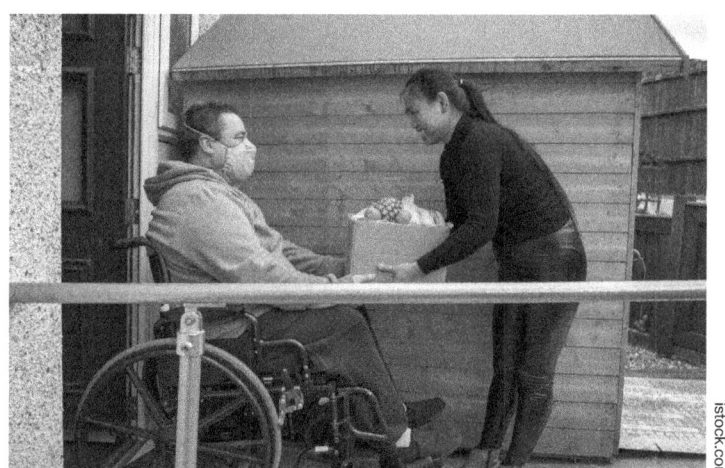

PHOTO 1.3
People with disabilities may benefit from charity, such as this man receiving a food delivery during COVID Quarantine, but few people want to be defined only as charity recipients.

Credit: Green (2020). Reproduced with permission from istock.com.

Explaining the Production and Experience of Disability

The models already discussed describe the worldviews by which groups of people understand disability. But the social model is very broad, arguing simply that the environment produces and shapes disability. What does this mean? How and why does this happen? Sociologists focus their explanations—or theories—on causal social forces and structures. In each chapter of the book, we will encounter theories to help explain disability, along with the evidence supporting those theories. In this chapter, we offer a foundation of several broad categories of sociological theory that can be used to explain and explore disability. It is not a complete list, and the theories intertwine and overlap. The goal is for you to gain exposure to a broad range of theories that sociologists use, highlighting the varied social forces that may explain disability.

The Construction of Meaning and Culture on the Micro and Macro Levels

We begin our discussion of theories with those that focus on the construction of meaning and the role of culture. This set of theories argues that, to understand disability, we must examine how people *create* disability by defining and responding to some phenomena *as* disability.

Max Weber, one of the founders of Sociology, introduced the term **verstehen** (the German word for understanding) to explain the unique task of sociologists. Sociologists must understand the world from the point of view of those being studied. Humans, unlike rocks or plants, create the world by producing and organizing their own understanding of it—the process of social construction that we have already discussed.

George Herbert Mead (1934) and Charles Horton Cooley ([1902] 1983) then developed the theory of **symbolic interactionism** to explain how we create meaning. They argue that, on a micro level, people interact with each other, and through our everyday social interactions, we create and share symbols and meanings. These symbols and meanings are repeated, enacted, preserved, and eventually come to feel "real." We forget, for instance, that we created the idea of "autism" to represent a very broad and complex set of behaviors and over time come to imagine that autism is a real, objective fact. As we accept these meanings, we also shape our behavior in relation to them.

The meaning of disability is created and negotiated in micro settings like family and school. For example, Melvin Juette (Juette & Berger, 2008) was paralyzed in a gang-related dispute. His local context and social relationships—including his peers in the gang, an uninspiring high school counselor, and later access to a competitive wheelchair basketball team and a rousing coach—shaped the way he came to think about his acquired disability and his new identity. In the book *Wheelchair Warrior: Gangs, Disability and Basketball* (p. 3), Juette explained that disability was "both the worst and best thing that happened" to him. Disability cut short his opportunities in his gang, while opening other opportunities to recreate himself as a wheelchair athlete, college student, and later as a professional. While disability opened valuable opportunities for Juette, for others, the shift in status more clearly threatens their established jobs and roles.

While some sociologists look at how meaning is constructed at a micro level, others examine the production and impact of macro cultural discourses in shaping disability. A **discourse** involves the organization of meaning in ways that constitute knowledge and inform our behavior. **Dominant discourses** are organized systems of meaning embedded in and manifest through relations of power and social institutions such as politics, law, medicine, and education. More simply, dominant discourses are the grand stories that are widely told by those in power and are widely believed. Michel Foucault (1980) famously argued that discourse, power, and knowledge intertwine as people with institutional power gain the authority to position their discourse as "truth." Discourse then not only describes what people believe, but it creates, shapes, and constrains people's ideas and behaviors. Discourse reinforces the power of some groups, while legitimating the oppression of others.

The dominant discourse of disability in modern America is the medical model, and this shapes and constrains the opportunities of people with disabilities. This discourse encourages research into cure, the use of therapy, and the pursuit of the perfect, or at least the normative, body/mind. In doing so, it values the "norm," defines people outside of the norm as disabled, and demands they seek cure and strive to become as "normal" as possible. For those outside of the range of acceptable normality, their exclusion is seen as justified. Thus, the medical model as a discourse encourages some behaviors and confers some opportunities while discouraging other behaviors and blocking access to other opportunities.

Culture on the macro and micro levels intertwine. Sociologist Pierre Bourdieu (1984) famously theorizes how macro cultural systems shape our identities and behaviors and vice versa. Discussed at greater length in Chapter 5 on culture, Bourdieu argues that each social space or "field" produces a complex set of social relations where people engage in everyday practices and create meaning. One's "capital"—a range of resources used to accrue more resources—effects one's access to and position within a field. As one engages in any given field, one develops dispositions, or as Bourdieu explained it, "a sense of the game." Over time, people accrue experiences and develop dispositions across fields. Some of these become deeply ingrained or habitual. Bourdieu referred to these "deeply ingrained habits, skills, and dispositions that we possess due to our life experiences" as **habitus**. The habitus one develops tends to reflect one's social position across fields and thereby reproduces inequality.

Alan Santinele Martino's work (2020, 2021) offers a compelling example of Bourdieu's theory as related to disability. He shows that people with intellectual disabilities are often excluded from sexual fields (places and interactions where sexuality is discussed, learned about and performed), and as such they lack a "sense of the game." Despite their interest in forming romantic and intimate relationships, they lack the social, cultural, or economic capital (resources) to engage in the practices of sexuality, such as identifying sexual partners or going to places like parties and clubs where romantic/sexual relationships form and advance. Without the opportunity to engage in these social practices, people with disabilities may develop low sexual self-esteem and constricted sexual identities. In a reinforcing cycle, their inferior social access and constricted sexual identities then inform the views others have of them and their own behaviors. As such, macro cultural beliefs about the asexuality of people with disabilities become incorporated into the identities and behaviors of individuals with disabilities and the views of others, which in turn reinforce the macro cultural belief about the asexuality of people with disabilities.

Materialist Theories

Materialist theories prioritize the role of the economy and the resources people need to survive (the material environment) as the primary systems which determine our social relationships, culture, and disability. Karl Marx ([1845] 1978) proposed that the way a society produces the things its members need and use—its **means of production**—creates and corresponds to a particular set of **relations of production**, the patterns of social relationships characterized most simply by who owns/controls the means of production (the "haves") and who does not (the "have nots"). Since the advent of capitalism, the "haves" have been capitalists and the "have nots" primarily have been the working class, also known as the proletariat.

Capitalism is characterized by private ownership of the means of production, mass production, expansive commodification of resources for sale in the marketplace (i.e., almost all things we need must be purchased), profit motive, and exploitation of the working class by the capitalists. Since the working class do not own the means of production, other than their own bodies, they must sell their labor power to survive. In the drive for greater and greater profit, capitalists exploit the workers more and more, forcing them to work longer hours, work faster, live with fewer benefits/securities, and work in poorer conditions.

The imperative for profit is a defining feature of capitalism and operates in a context of competition among capitalists. This means that capitalists have little choice but to exploit their laborers. If they do not, other companies will reap greater profits, their own company will ultimately fail, and they will be pushed into the growing ranks of the proletariat. Thus, benevolence by capitalists cannot be sustained. Marx described the conditions of capitalism as brutal, a system in which naked economic transactions erase all sense of social or human obligation on the part of the capitalist class to care for the working class who actually produce the goods and wealth of the society on which the capitalists live.

For Marx, other social institutions such as politics, media, culture, and education serve as **superstructure**—institutions which are structured to support and legitimate capitalism and the needs of the capitalists. For example, according to Marx, political systems may be superstructure, catering to the needs of capitalists and ensuring that resources and profit flow to this increasingly small class of people. The media also could be superstructure. It celebrates the trappings of capitalism—unabashed consumerism, the pursuit of wealth, the idolization of the rich—while devaluing the working class. In materialist theories, culture plays a role, but its role is largely *shaped by* the economic system and the class interests of capitalists.

The centrality of capitalism and other economic systems in producing and shaping disability is key to many sociological theories of disability. British sociologist Michael Oliver, one of the earliest proponents of the social model, developed a materialist theory in his pioneering work, *The Politics of Disablement* (1990). He argues that the "cultural production of disability is dependent upon a variety of factors including the type of economy, the size of the economic surplus, and the values that influence the redistribution of this surplus" (p. 24). In other words, capitalism produces much of disability, causes many of the social disadvantages (e.g., exclusion and oppression) experienced by people with disabilities, and shapes the social response to disability.

The role of the economy generally and capitalism specifically will be explored in greater depth in Chapter 9. Here, let's briefly consider some of the ways that capitalism shapes disability.

Capitalism produces disability though unsafe and grueling work conditions, the mental onslaught of constant competition with little social safety net, and the devastation of communities with high poverty rates. These negative effects are uneven, as global systems of labor exploitation disproportionately disabled people from impoverished nations and people of color (Erevelles, 2011).

Capitalism disadvantages people with disabilities. The standardization of the work process (e.g., assembly lines, predetermined "efficient" production methods) excludes atypical bodies and minds. The focus on profit demands the fastest, most efficient, or smartest laborers, and the fierce competition for jobs removes the need for capitalists to utilize less profitable laborers or those even imagined to possibly be less profitable. Capitalist culture supports the priorities of capitalism, celebrating individualism and productivity while vilifying dependence and disablement (Charlton, 2000; Oliver, 1990; Russell, 1998).

Capitalism shapes our response to disability. According to Bernard Farber (1968) and Andrew Scull (2015), capitalism creates "surplus labor"—those who are perceived by capitalists to be undesirable or unfit workers—and then must invent solutions for how to deal with these populations. Compulsory education emerges to provide workplace training and supervision for children whose parents are now working away from home; institutions emerge for people increasingly defined as biologically unfit because their bodies do not adequately match the demands of capitalists; nursing homes supervise aging people who have grown less productive and have heightened care demands; and prisons grow larger and larger to contain and control a range of bodies/people, often people of color, deemed deviant and threatening to capitalists (Ben-Moshe et al., 2014).

Capitalism commodifies disability and the needs of people with disabilities, treating care and needs as opportunities for profit. As Gary Albrecht documents in his 1992 work *The Disability Business*, disability-specific "services" come to operate as profit-generating industries. Care is commodified (placed on the market for a price), and people with disabilities become central to these arenas of commodification (e.g., pharmaceuticals, medical equipment, medical services, nursing homes, therapies, home health and personal aides). Through this process of commodification, people with disabilities potentially gain value in society via their role in producing profit as consumers (DePoy & Gilson, 2018). However, due to economic exclusion and the resultant poverty of many people with disabilities, they rarely control the purchase of commodities, and this potential source of power rarely materializes.

PHOTO 1.4 Industrial assembly lines require standardized bodies and speed of work.

Political and State-Centered Theories

Whereas some theories focus on culture and the economy as causal factors shaping disability, **state-centered theories** examine the role of the state in defining and affecting disability. In her classic work *The Disabled State*, sociologist Deborah Stone (1984) analyzes the creation of disability as an administrative category used by the state to distribute resources/benefits, especially to differentiate between citizens worthy or unworthy of assistance. People with disabilities are often judged as a category of people worthy of aid, in contrast to the "able-bodied" poor who are denied aid. State laws then must define and distinguish disability to determine eligibility for aid.

Definitions of disability are embedded in other laws and state programs as well. Because the government operates on multiple levels and through many systems, the definitions, policies, and laws regarding disability do not always align, leading to bizarre inconsistencies in who is defined as disabled and the consequences of that label. Brian Grossman's (2019) work, for example, showcases the problems of interstate variation in state policy. Because Medicaid (one of America's public national health insurance systems) is implemented on a state-by-state basis, people with disabilities experience sharply different access to services and supports across states. This affects not only their services in any given state, but also restricts their ability to move across state lines because their benefits and services do not transfer across state lines. Therefore, people with disabilities may not have the same freedom as others to pursue educational, employment, or even romantic opportunities across state (or even county) lines. In contrast, some people with disabilities find that they *must* move to a different state, away from their families and natural supports, to access necessary state-funded supports.

This theoretical approach is at times rooted in Weber's ([1922] 1968) classic work on bureaucracy and authority which highlights the growth of bureaucratic organizations focused on efficiency. In contrast with Marx's view in which capitalists hold most of the power, for Weber many people exercise authority, often based on their position within bureaucracies. State officials hold such power, as do lots of people who work in agencies that exercise power over people with disabilities. This theory highlights the broad range of people who might exert power over people with disabilities, such as nursing home administrators, teachers, social workers, and employers. It also suggests ways that people with disabilities might approach making social change through occupying positions of authority, influencing people in positions of authority, and reconfiguring the bureaucracies that affect their lives.

Culture, economy, and the state intertwine, often in ways that confer significant power to a few people and usually disadvantage people with disabilities. **Political economy** approaches explain how economic and political systems interact to shape resource distribution and class stratification. For example, James Charlton's (2000) political economy approach prioritizes the role of capitalism and documents how state policies serve the interests of capitalists, leading to the oppression of people with disabilities internationally.

Stratification, Intersectionality, and Relationality

Social stratification is the way in which a society groups people and creates a social hierarchy. Stratification is, simply put, the processes by which inequality occurs in a society. Societies have different stratification systems and offer different ideologies to legitimate inequality. Inequality might be justified through claims like meritocracy (those who work hardest and are the most talented rise to the top), religion (some group is god-ordained to have power), or birth-right (some group is born into positions of power). To note, the justification for inequality is not necessarily true, but it is often widely accepted as true by those who live within that society.

The study of stratification is central to Sociology and has historically focused on class, race, and gender; however, people with disabilities are among the poorest people both in America and globally. Their poverty is often naturalized, seen as a consequence of physical or mental biology rather than as a product of economic, political, and cultural systems. The Sociology of Disability seeks to remedy this oversight.

Some disability scholars have posited a **minority model** of disability (Asch & Fine, 1988; Barnartt & Seelman, 1988; Barnes, 2016; Hahn, 1985; Scotch, 2000), which argues that people with disabilities are a minority group with systemically inferior access to power and resources. Overwhelmingly, research documents that people with disabilities are disproportionately poor, unemployed, underrepresented in politics, segregated, and incarcerated (Schur et al., 2013). People with disabilities are less likely to graduate from college, and a college degree leads to less economic gain for people with disabilities than for others. Compared to people with disabilities in other industrialized nations, people with disabilities in the United States have higher rates of poverty and are less likely to be employed (Schur et al., 2013). This variation shows that the inferior social position of people with disabilities is produced, not natural.

Increasingly theories of stratification look at **intersectionality**, the ways in which multiple systems of oppression intersect, often in complex ways (Collins, 1990; Crenshaw, 1989). As a simple example, scholars point out the double disadvantage of women with disabilities or the triple disadvantage of Black women with disabilities. Rather than simply assuming an additive effect, however, intersectional work examines the ways that one system of oppression is constitutive of and influential for another system of oppression. To consider Black women with disabilities as an example, not only are Black women with disabilities more disadvantaged in the workplace than White men without disabilities (an additive effect), but the stereotypes around disability, femininity, and African Americans intersect and reinforce each other. All three groups (people with disabilities, women, and African Americans) suffer from stereotypes suggesting that they are intellectually incompetent and irrational, and these stereotypes reinforce each other when someone is an African American disabled woman. While there may be similarities, the patterns and stereotypes may also differ across groups. Disabled Black men, for example, are particularly likely to face stereotypes that their disability is related to violence, gang-behavior, and criminality. Thus, intersectional scholarship looks at the complicated ways that disability intertwines with other social statuses to shape stratification.

To aid in the study of intersectional oppression, intersectional frameworks such as feminist disability studies, critical race and disability studies, and crip queer studies have emerged. Each looks at how disability interacts with

PHOTO 1.5
Disabled Black Lives Matter Actvist- the intersection of race and disability increases vulnerability to police violence.

other forms of oppression and vice versa and imagines social justice from this intersectional perspective. For example, feminist disability scholars examine, among other things, how gender shapes the experience of disability, how disability shapes the experience of gender, and how social justice requires addressing sexism and ableism.

Relational models of disability potentially enable both an understanding of inequality and the intersectional dynamics across varied groups. Relational models examine the complicated composition and impact of relationships and relational patterns on disability and the lives of people with disabilities. Alison Kafer (2013, p. 8) argues that a relational model of disability is essential because "disability is experienced in and through relationships; it does not occur in isolation."

Embodiment

We have two more sets of theory to discuss! Hang in there.

Sociology and the social model of disability turn our gaze toward the social context. While very valuable, more recently sociologists have brought the body back into our work, considering how the body itself is produced by social forces and how diverse bodies lead to different social experiences. **Embodiment** argues that our bodies matter for how we experience the world. Our engagement with and interpretation of the world is mediated through our senses and bodies. People in different bodies will experience the world differently. For example, blind people may have a different relationship to spatial organization, smells, and vibrations than sighted people. People who walk with ease may not even notice a step, whereas those who use wheelchairs may feel excluded. Due to the different ways children process information, some may perform well sitting in rows listening to a teacher, whereas others may not.

PHOTO 1.6
The experience of inaccessible environments - such as this female wheelchair user blocked by steps - shapes one's opportunities and outlook.

Credit: XiXinXing (2015). Reproduced with permission from istock.com.

Not only do we experience the world through our bodies, but the world—and inequality in particular—is written and imposed on our bodies. Poverty, war, lack of access to clean water, and exposure to toxins *cause* impairments. The experience of racism leads to disability, as racial minorities experience higher levels of stress, violence, and poverty. The effects of social inequality are not simply social; they are physical.

The bodies of disabled people are also subjected to social control. In addition to violence, people with disabilities often live in institutional settings in which they experience intense surveillance, physical regulation, and systems of rewards/punishments to ensure normative conformity (Ben-Moshe et al., 2014; Foucault, 1965, 1975). While most people are encouraged to follow the rules more or less, people who reside within the social service system (e.g., group homes) live under constant surveillance. Their lives are often dominated by therapeutic regimes, even when they are trying to relax at home. They face punishments like the denial of leisure time if they "act out." Their bodies are constantly under watch and regulated.

Sociologists also consider the ways in which the body is central to identity formation (e.g., our sense of who we are). Judith Butler's (1990) theory of **performativity** argues that identity is constituted through repeated, enacted performances. Gender, Butler argues, is learned and performed, and our gender identity develops over time through our performances. Because of this, gender identity is fundamentally fluid and dynamic insofar as we have access to learn, enact, and be recognized for different performances. Disability and ableness are also enacted embodied performances. We learn over time how to act "able" and/or what it means to interact as a disabled person. Moreover, disability may affect our ability to perform particular identities and the perception by others of those performances (Siebers, 2008).

In the poem "The Magic Wand," for example, African American blind artist Lynn Manning (2009) explores his control over his identity as well as the constraints he faces in how people perceive him. Manning describes the different stereotypes of Black men and blind men, stereotypes which he encounters based on whether or not he displays his white cane (to note, a white cane is used for mobility purposes among people who are blind). Without the cane, his Black body provokes one set of reactions. People assume he is a gangster or an athlete and he reacts to these stereotypes. With the cane, his blind body now takes priority in how people interact with him. People assume he needs charity or that he has almost supernatural wisdom. As he moves through the world in his body, he must confront the ways in which people react to him as a blind or a Black man. Manning's poetry shows the ways in which the body one inhabits shapes one's interactions with society and how the world is experienced and understood.

Crip Theories

Crip theories center the experience of disability and explain the world from the perspective of disability. They draw on the tradition of standpoint theory, developed by feminist and race scholars. In classical social theory, W. E. B. Du Bois ([1903] 1994) argued that African Americans occupy a particular social position in society and experience the world and build knowledge from that position—an idea referred to as **standpoint theory**. He drew upon his standpoint as an African American to identify the economic and cultural processes used by Whites to enforce racism. Drawing on standpoint theory as applied to women, Dorothy Smith (2007) advocated a sociology for and by women which would examine women's experiences of the social world and retheorize all social phenomenon (e.g., work, family, violence, war, politics) to consider how gender is constitutive of it and affected by it. Crip theories prioritize the world from the perspective and experience of people with disabilities.

Moreover, crip theory encourages a liberatory commitment to redesign the world in ways that are accessible and inclusive of the broad range of human diversity. "To crip" (e.g., to crip sexuality theory, to crip the arts) becomes a political and academic verb, meaning to recognize the imposition of ableist worldviews and to reimagine a world that values and includes people with disabilities (McRuer, 2006). Crip theories of physical and social geography, for example, identify the ways in which architectural designs exclude people with disabilities and offer new designs that are welcoming to all (Titchkosky, 2011).

One of my favorite examples of crip theory is the discussion of "crip time." Scholars including Alison Kafer (2013) and Ellen Samuels (2017) have pointed out that time is not simply naturally occurring. In the United States, we experience time in a particular way: the relentless demands of production schedules (e.g., you have one week to meet this goal, 45 minutes to take this test); the standardization of daily schedules through education and beyond (everyone must be ready to start at 7:45, must learn in 50-minute blocks, must navigate the halls in 10 minutes, must eat lunch in only 30 minutes and need no more than two quick bathroom breaks); and the developmental and lifespan timeline (children should walk by age 1½, learn their ABCs by age 5, begin algebra in middle school, engage in productive work from their 20s–60s). This imposition of *normative time* ignores and constrains human variation; it creates disability among those who cannot meet these specific norms. Crip theory not only reveals the social and oppressive forces in the imposition of normative time, but also offers a liberatory framework. By centering the perspectives of people with disabilities, it encourages us to imagine a world that uses crip time, a world in which we have time to be sick and to rest, to perform paid work on our own timeline, to provide care for others and to engage in self-care, and to recognize the varied human experience of development across the lifespan (Samuels, 2017).

Theory Overview

While exposure to all of these theories may feel overwhelming, the key point here is that disability is a social phenomenon and, as such, needs to be explained through examining social processes and structures, such as social interaction, culture, the economy, and the state. In doing so, sociologists take into account systems of inequality, intersectional oppression, and the ways in which our bodies affect and are affected by society. Embodiment and crip theory offer theoretical perspectives that prioritize the lived experiences and perspectives of people with disabilities. Sociologists draw on this rich range of theories, and others, to examine disability in society. Table 1.2 provides a synopsis of the theoretical perspectives.

TABLE 1.2 Overview of Theoretical Perspectives

Theories	Main Idea	Embedded Ideas	Example
Symbolic Interactionism and Cultural Theories	Disability is created through social interaction. We create the meaning of disability, which then shapes our experience of disability.	Verstehen Discourse Habitus	Medical model is a discourse that shapes the way we think about and experience disability.
Materialist Theories	Disability is created through and affected by unequal access to resources.	Capitalism Means of production Relations of production Superstructure	In its drive for profit, capitalism exploits workers and excludes those who are not productive enough. Harsh working conditions create disability.

TABLE 1.2   Overview of Theoretical Perspectives *(Continued)*

Theories	Main Idea	Embedded Ideas	Example
Political/ State-Centered Theories	The state creates disability as an administrative category. More broadly, those who exercise authority in a variety of settings define and enforce disability.	Interstate variation Political Economy	State and county governments create different definitions of disability, leading to vastly different experiences of disability.
Stratification/ Intersectionality/ Relationality	Each society is composed of groups, with differential access (or lack of access) to resources. Disability, often in combination with other axes of inequality, shapes relationships and access to resources	Minority Model Intersectionality	People with disabilities have access to far fewer resources. This situation is often made worse when combined with other minority statuses.
Embodiment	One's body shapes one's experiences of the world, and therefore mediates one's disability experience.	Performativity	If one uses a wheelchair and confronts steps, one experiences the world in a different way than others. People also *use* their bodies to perform certain roles.
Crip Theories	A liberatory perspective that envisions the world from the standpoint of people with disabilities and pursues a world in which people with disabilities are empowered and valued	Standpoint To crip	Society constructs normative ways of doing things, like learning in 50-minute blocks, and these norms disadvantage some people. To crip education is to reconfigure it in ways that are inclusive and center students with disabilities.

Conclusion

In this chapter, we introduced the Sociology of Disability, presented some common definitions of disability, explained the ideas of the social construction of disability and the social and medical models, and reviewed several of the theories used by sociologists of disability. In doing so, we established some of the key foundations of the Sociology of Disability and provided the tools for students to begin to explore the social construction of disability across time and place and to uncover the social factors that produce and shape disability.

KEY TERMS

Crip theories 19
Deviance 4
Disability 6
Discourse 12
Dominant discourses 12
Embodiment 18
Essentialized 3
Habitus 13
Impairment 7
Intersectionality 17
Labeling theory 7
Materialist theories 13
Means of production 13
Medical model 8
Medical sociology 3
Minority model 17
Performativity 19
Political economy 16
Relations of production 13
Social construction 6
Sociological imagination 3
Social model 8
Social stratification 16
Sociology of disability 4
Standpoint theory 19
State-centered theories 15
Superstructure 14
Symbolic interactionism 12
Verstehen 12

RESOURCES

Classic Readings in the Sociology of Disability

Oliver, Mike. 1993. *What's so wonderful about walking?* A lecture delivered at the University of Greenwich, available in text (25 pages) at https://disability-studies.leeds.ac.uk/wp-content/uploads/sites/40/library/Oliver-PROFLEC.pdf. Oliver offers a sociological analysis of walking, including its cultural meaning and the value accorded to it in rehabilitation.

Zola, Irving Kenneth. 1982. "Chapter 11: Four steps on the road to invalidity: The denial of sexuality, anger, vulnerability and potential." In *Missing pieces: A chronicle of living with a disability*, 212–237. Philadelphia, PA: Temple University Press. This chapter concludes Zola's thoughts on his experience at a residence designed for people with physical disabilities in the Netherlands called Het Dorp. One of the earliest writings in the Sociology of Disability.

Example of Contemporary Theory

Samuels, Ellen. 2017. "Six ways of looking at crip time." *Disability Studies Quarterly* 37, no. 3, https://dsq-sds.org/article/view/5824/468424/4684. An accessible essay discussing crip theory and crip time.

Memoirs Useful for Discussing the Medical and Social Models

Greely, Lucy. 1994. *Autobiography of a face*. Boston, MA: Houghton Mifflin. Documents Grealy's experience with cancer and disfigurement and offers the potential to discuss the medical and the social model.

Heumann, Judith and Kristen Joiner. 2020. *Being Heumann: An unrepentant memoir of a disability rights activist*. Beacon Press. Heumann's activism is on the forefront of the shift from a medical to a social model and imaging how to recreate an accessible and empowered world.

YouTube

"Social Model of Disability With Mike Oliver." https://www.youtube.com/watch?v=gDO6U0-uaoM&t=186s. A discussion of the creation of the social model by one of its original proponents, Michael Oliver (7:41).

"What is the Social Model?" https://www.youtube.com/watch?v=0e24rfTZ2CQ. A very short explanation of the social model expressed by prominent members of the disability community (2 minutes).

Poetry

Manning, Lynn. Reading of his poem "*The Magic Wand*." http://lynnmanning.com/images/26.The_Magic_Wand.mp3 (2 minutes).

ACTIVITIES

1. **Using the Medical and Social Models**
   Judy Heumann was born in 1947 and contracted polio when 18 months old. With the help of doctors, she underwent treatment and recovered from the polio, but had life-long effects including becoming a wheelchair user. At the time it was legal for public schools to exclude students with disabilities, and her school did so, calling her a "fire hazard." She eventually graduated from college but was denied her teacher's license because the board believed she could not protect children in an emergency situation. She sued and won her case. She emerged as a leading disability rights activist, fighting against discrimination and for policies that increase access.

   If one is using the medical model, what is the problem and the solution?

   If one is using the social model, what is the problem and the solution?

   What might be useful for each model?

   What might be limiting about each model?

2. **Exploring theories of disability**
   Sociology seeks to explain social patterns by looking at macro social factors. This chapter provides a range of theories about the macro social factors that might affect disability in society, including cultural theories, materialist theories, political/state-centered theories, stratification and intersectionality, embodiment, and crip theories.

   a. For each theory, summarize in a few bullet points what factors or processes produce and/or affect disability in society. (e.g., Cultural theories start by looking at how meanings are created and shift to produce certain social effects.)

   b. Theory allows us to brainstorm possible explanations for social phenomena, and research then provides a way for us to test these explanations. So, let's take a social phenomenon and brainstorm the factors that each theory would call attention to. Let's consider the rapidly increasing rates of autism diagnosis in the United States. Autism was first identified in the 1940s, and the diagnosis was very rare. By 2000, 1 in 150 children was identified as autistic. By 2008 diagnosis increased to 1 in 88 and by 2017 1 in 68. This is an incredibly rapid change, leading some to declare an "autism epidemic." Sociologists look at how social factors might create this rapid increase in autism and/or autism diagnosis.

   Read the following short article "The Real Reasons Autism Rates are Up in the United States" at https://www.scientificamerican.com/article/the-real-reasons-autism-rates-are-up-in-the-u-s/. What explanations are offered for the rise in autism rates? Relate these explanations to at least one of the theories discussed in the chapter. For those theories that you haven't connected to the article, brainstorm how each theory might explain or think about this trend.

CHAPTER 2

Researching Disability

Learning Outcomes

2.1 Articulate why sociologists conduct research.

2.2 Evaluate the varied approaches to measuring disability.

2.3 Explain the ethical concerns raised by including and excluding people with disabilities as research participants.

2.4 Identify methodologies that empower people with disabilities in the research process.

Chapter Synopsis

Chapter 2 examines the conduct of sociological research on the topic of disability and doing research with people with disabilities. The chapter discusses the difficulties of measuring disability, the history of harm to people with disabilities by researchers, the underrepresentation of people with disabilities as research subjects, and methodologies developed that seek to upend traditional power relations and challenge disability oppression. Students in the field need to be mindful of these issues to increase their data literacy and to inform their own research practices.

Why Study Disability?

Sociology is a science committed to producing knowledge about our social world. Let's take a quick look at some of what we know about people with disabilities in America by looking at findings from the 2018–2019 American Community Survey (Houtenville & Rafal, 2020):

- Prevalence: The overall disability prevalence rate is 13.2%.
- Employment: Of adults 18–64 living in the community, 38.9% of people with disabilities are employed compared to 78.6% of people without disabilities, a gap of 39.7 percentage points.

- Earnings: Of those 16+ years of age who work full-time and year-round, the median annual earnings of people with disabilities is $40,360, compared to $48,406 for people without disabilities, a difference of $8,046.

- Poverty: 25.9% of people with disabilities live in poverty, compared to 11.4% of people without disabilities, a gap of 14.5 percentage points.

- Education: Of Americans 25–34 years old, 16.1% of people with disabilities have a bachelor's degree or more, compared to 39.2% of people without disabilities, a gap of 23.1 percentage points.

- Health Insurance: 89.9% of people with disabilities have some form of health insurance, compared to 86.9% of people without disabilities, a positive gap of +3 percentage points. If we look at private insurance though, only 46% of people with disabilities have private insurance compared to 75.8% of people without disabilities, a gap of 29.8 percentage points.

What stands out to you about these findings? Was any of the information surprising to you?

Sociologists collect data for many reasons. They may want to *describe* a social phenomenon, in this case the experiences of people with disabilities. Data reveal, among other things, the way people experience the world, what challenges they confront, and what successes they enjoy. Descriptive information also allows sociologists to distinguish fact from myth. There are many myths about disability. One myth is that employment has increased steadily among people with disabilities, especially since the 1990 passage of the Americans with Disabilities Act (ADA); however, statistics over time reveal that employment rates have not increased since 1990, and unemployment continues to be a significant problem among people with disabilities (Maroto & Pettinicchio, 2015).

Sociologists also conduct research to *evaluate or build theories*. As discussed in Chapter 1, theories offer explanations. Continuing with the issue of employment, if a sociologist wants to know *why* employment rates have not increased, they might, for example, use the deductive method of science in which they propose testable hypotheses, gather data, and confirm or refute their hypotheses. Research expands knowledge base by identifying broad patterns and causal relationships.

Research findings are often used to *inform action*, such as establishing and modifying policies and programs. For example, we might propose different employment policies depending on whether obtaining employment is challenging for all groups, for people with disabilities specifically, or for subsets of people with disabilities (e.g., people with less education, racial minorities). Data also provide a way to assess the effectiveness of established policies and practices. For example, the American Community Survey indicates that, whereas three-quarters of people without disabilities have private health insurance, only 46% of people with disabilities do. This is likely because private insurance is largely secured through employment. Given the current disparities in employment, the public health care system (e.g., Medicaid, Medicare) provides an essential safety net for many people with disabilities who would otherwise be left without necessary care. Politicians, policy makers, and/or activists may use this knowledge to build policy initiatives or enact social change. Across these purposes (description, assessing theory, and informing action), conducting research is a very important job of sociologists.

Although researching disability is very important, it is not easy. In the following sections, we explore several challenges and opportunities related to researching disability, starting with the challenges of measuring disability.

Measuring Disability

If you google the question "what is the rate of disability in the United States?," you will find a tremendous array of numbers. Page one of my quick search yielded rates ranging from 12.6% to 26%. Relying on the 2018–2019 American Community Survey, 13.2% of Americans have a disability. In contrast, according to the 2010 Census, 19% of Americans have a disability. You may wonder, how could the numbers be so different? Which number is right? The better question is: what does each number represent? Different studies use different definitions of disability and research methods, leading to different findings.

In deductive science, concepts are transformed—or **operationalized**—into variables that are measurable and used in the collection of empirical data. In other words, when sociologists study social phenomena like gender, juvenile delinquency, unemployment, or disability (concepts), they must decide how they are going to actually define and measure these ideas (creating variables). If a sociologist wants to measure juvenile delinquency, they must decide if their definition will include all actions performed by minors that are against the rules (a definition which would yield *a lot* of delinquency), only actions that are against the law (yielding fewer instances), or only illegal actions for which minors are officially convicted (yielding far fewer instances). In the process of operationalization, there is always a gap, so to speak, between the concept and how it is defined and measured.

The process of operationalization is fraught for disability. Because definitions of disability vary widely by time, place, and culture, there are a wide variety of measures of disability (Altman, 2001; Mont, 2007). The continued stigma of disability and diverse language conventions further complicate measurement (US Census Bureau, 2017a). Each measure yields different rates of disability and provides different information about disability. The discussion below offers several ways that sociologists measure disability. It is not a complete list. Rather, it is meant to help you see a variety of measures and the implications of how one measures disability.

Quantitative Approaches to Measuring Disability

Quantitative research gathers data in a way that transforms data into numbers. For disability, this often means identifying and counting the number of people with disabilities. Within quantitative research, there are many approaches to disability measurement, of which we will discuss five.

1. **Disability as limitations and difficulties in activities due to health conditions and embedded within environments.**

One of the most common definitions asserts that disability is the experience of limitations or difficulties due to health conditions or impairments within certain environments. This definition is elaborated upon in the **International Classification of Functioning, Disability and Health Model (ICF)**. According to the ICF, disability is not defined as a medical condition/impairment. Rather, it is the experience of limitations or difficulties in body structure and function, activity, and/or social participation (Mont, 2007). *Body structure and function* refer to specific impairments in the functioning of one's body systems, such as the inability to move one's legs or to see. *Activity limitations* refer to limitations in performing basic actions, such as getting dressed or feeding oneself. *Participation limitations* refer to difficulties performing higher-order social activities, such as working and attending school. In the model, limitations in these three domains are potentially affected by environmental factors (e.g., job market, accessibility of the school) and personal factors (e.g., age, gender). Thus, this model defines disability as the limitations resulting from a condition, not the presence of a condition or its cause.

Figure 2.1 offers an example of these factors, using a case study of a woman with cerebral palsy (CP). CP is an impairment but having CP does not mean that she is disabled. People with CP vary tremendously in their skills, experiences, and resources. Disability—represented in the second row—is the set of limitations which result from CP as she experiences it, such as her inability to grasp with her hands, inability to self-transfer to a toilet, and limitations in attending social events without a personal assistant. The third row indicates that these limitations may also be affected by her environment and her personal characteristics. Greater accessibility, for example, might enable her to attend social events and self-transfer. Thus, environmental changes can reduce/erase disability even if the biological impairment is stable.

To research disability, sociologists move from this definition to specific measures of disability. Given the ICF's definition of disability, the corresponding measurement tends to be a set of questions assessing limitations and difficulties rooted in impairment.

FIGURE 2.1 **ICF Model**

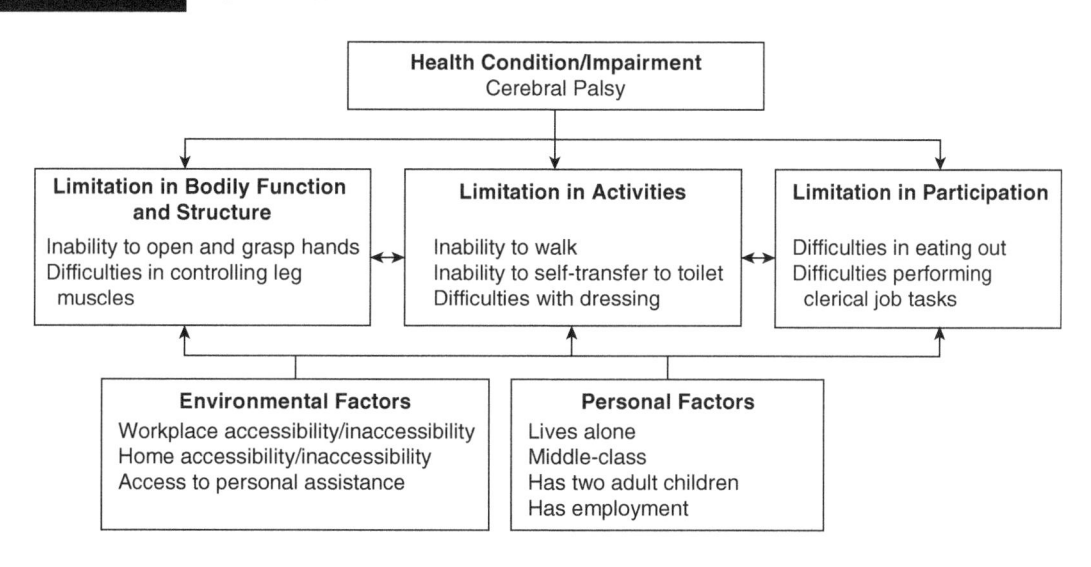

```
                    ┌─────────────────────────────┐
                    │  Health Condition/Impairment │
                    │        Cerebral Palsy        │
                    └─────────────────────────────┘
                                   │
        ┌──────────────────────────┼──────────────────────────┐
        ▼                          ▼                          ▼
┌───────────────────┐   ┌───────────────────────┐   ┌────────────────────────┐
│ Limitation in     │   │ Limitation in         │   │ Limitation in          │
│ Bodily Function   │◄─►│ Activities            │◄─►│ Participation          │
│ and Structure     │   │                       │   │                        │
│                   │   │ Inability to walk     │   │ Difficulties in eating │
│ Inability to open │   │ Inability to self-    │   │   out                  │
│   and grasp hands │   │   transfer to toilet  │   │ Difficulties performing│
│ Difficulties in   │   │ Difficulties with     │   │   clerical job tasks   │
│   controlling leg │   │   dressing            │   │                        │
│   muscles         │   │                       │   │                        │
└───────────────────┘   └───────────────────────┘   └────────────────────────┘
          ▲                      ▲    ▲                       ▲
          │                      │    │                       │
   ┌──────────────────────────────┐   ┌──────────────────────────┐
   │   Environmental Factors      │   │   Personal Factors       │
   │                              │   │                          │
   │ Workplace accessibility/     │   │ Lives alone              │
   │   inaccessibility            │   │ Middle-class             │
   │ Home accessibility/          │   │ Has two adult children   │
   │   inaccessibility            │   │ Has employment           │
   │ Access to personal assistance│   │                          │
   └──────────────────────────────┘   └──────────────────────────┘
```

Source: Adapted from Mont (2007).

The 2000 US Census (US Census Bureau, n.d.a) used this approach when it asked:

> *Because of a physical, mental or emotional condition lasting 6 months or more, does this person have any difficulty in doing any of the following activities: (a) Learning, remembering or concentrating (b) dressing, bathing, or getting around inside the home (c) (if the person is 16 years or over) going outside the home alone to shop or visit a doctor's office and (d) (if the person is 16 years or over) working at a job or business?*

The American Community Survey (remember, the data presented at the beginning of this chapter are from the ACS) also defines disability as difficulties and limitations, but it asks six questions covering the following areas (US Census Bureau, n.d.b):

> Hearing difficulty—Is this person deaf or does he/she have serious difficulty hearing?
>
> Vision difficulty—Is this person blind or does he/she have serious difficulty seeing even when wearing glasses?
>
> Cognitive difficulty—Because of a physical, mental, or emotional problem, does this person have serious difficulty remembering, concentrating, or making decisions?
>
> Ambulatory difficulty—Does this person have serious difficulty walking or climbing stairs?
>
> Self-care difficulty—Does this person have difficulty bathing or dressing?
>
> Independent living difficulty—Because of a physical, mental, or emotional problem, does this person have difficulty doing errands alone such as visiting a doctor's office or shopping?

19 a. Because of a physical, mental, or emotional condition, does this person have serious difficulty concentrating, remembering, or making decisions?
☐ Yes
☐ No

b. Does this person have serious difficulty walking or climbing stairs?
☐ Yes
☐ No

c. Does this person have difficulty dressing or bathing?
☐ Yes
☐ No

PHOTO 2.1
One of the American Community Survey Disability Questions.

Credit: U.S. Census Bureau (2022). Obtained from https://www.census.gov/acs/www/about/why-we-ask-each-question/disability/

Respondents who report any of the six difficulties are usually considered to have a disability (US Census Bureau, 2017b). Note that even though both the Census and ACS drew on a definition of disability as limitations and difficulties, the questions from the 1990 Census and the 2019 ACS were different and yielded significantly different counts.

There are several advantages to measurements of disability based on difficulties. These measures make an important distinction between the impairment and the experience of difficulty. Information on difficulties may be more relevant for decisions regarding policy and service delivery than the presence of impairments. Compared with some other measures, like self-identity, this approach yields higher rates. This approach has also been more widely adopted internationally, allowing for some global comparisons (Pettinicchio & Maroto, 2021).

However, there are important disadvantages. Critics argue that, because this approach reduces disability to a set of difficulties, it represents an individual-level deficit orientation. In other words, disability is measured by what one cannot do, rather than the environmental barriers that produce disability. Moreover, the ACS measures tend to be biased toward physical and sensory disability and offer a less accurate count of intellectual, behavioral, and mental disability.

2. **Disability as biophysiological conditions/impairments**.

Drawing on the medical model, some research defines disability as the presence of significant impairments. Disability is conflated with (seen as the same as) impairment. Given this definition, researchers may measure disability by asking respondents to report their impairments or offer them a checklist of chronic and significant health conditions.

Using this strategy, the US National Medical Expenditure Survey, which provides national data on access to and cost of health care, asks respondents to list all "health problems, physical conditions, accidents, or injuries that affect any part of the body as well as mental or emotional health conditions, such as feeling sad, blue, or anxious about something." As another example, the National Institute on Mental Health collects data on the prevalence of all conditions listed in the Diagnostic Statistical Manual (DSM, the reference manual that lists and defines mental illnesses). Excluding developmental and substance use disorders, they state that one in five Americans (46.6 million in 2017) live with mental illness (National Institute on Mental Health, 2019).

As an advantage, this strategy provides details about the prevalence of specific conditions, which can be very useful. We learn, for example, how many people have been diagnosed with depression or autism. However, it also has an important disadvantage. Impairments are not necessarily disabling. In other words, they may not result in a functional limitation or social disadvantage. Thus, there seems to be a significant gap between a list of conditions and the concept of "disability." There is also tremendous variation in the rates of disability produced based on the list of impairments provided to respondents.

3. **Disability as an identity**.

Disability may be defined as a personal identity. Some people define themselves as disabled and others do not. The decision to identify as disabled is shaped by numerous factors. Disability as identity may be measured, for example, by asking people whether they identify as a person with a disability or whether they have a disability. Many surveys ask a simple question like: "Do you have a disability?" Zambia's 2000 Census, for instance, asked, "Are you disabled in any way?" (Washington Group on Disability Statistics, 2009).

The primary advantage of measures based on self-identity is that they reveal the extent to which people actively identify as a person with a disability at that moment in time. It also tends to be a single question, which is attractive to those designing and taking surveys. There are many disadvantages to this approach though. Although self-identification is a common technique for measuring race and gender, its use for disability is far more problematic (Washington Group, 2009). The likelihood of disability identification is complicated by stigma; many people avoid the term "disabled," as well as related labels like mentally ill. Diverse belief systems about disability and language conventions across cultures further complicates the use of self-identification. Disability is a broad umbrella category encompassing varied impairments and experiences, but many cultures do not have a word, or a belief system for that matter, that corresponds conceptually to "disability" as it is intended in American surveys. They may have only narrower terms that relate to specific impairments (e.g., words for blindness, deafness, mental illness) or broader, vaguer terms like "unfortunates" (Groce, 2006). Disability is also fluid in its manifestation, its sociocultural relevance, and its salience for one's identity. In other words, someone may have multiple sclerosis, but the extent to which they feel or identify as disabled may vary by factors like fluctuations in symptoms; the social environment, its expectations, and accessibility; and their own values, conceptions of disability, dispositions, and identity composition.

Due to the reasons listed above, self-identification typically yields low rates of disability. This is especially true in low-income nations where people with disabilities tend to experience significant stigma and social isolation, and where the idea of "disability" is uncommon (Me & Mbogoni, 2006). In Zambia, measures based on self-identification found a disability rate of 2.7% (Washington Group, 2009), whereas measures based on functional limitations yielded a rate of 13% (Üstün et al., 2010).

4. Disability as social disadvantage related to impairment or perception of impairment.

The social model argues that the environment creates disablement. Building on the social model, some researchers try to measure the environmental barriers that disable. Kenjiro Sakakibara (2018), for example, created a disablement score in which respondents rank from 0 to 100 the level of social adversity and exclusion (e.g., the negative effect on finding a job, marriage, joining social clubs) associated with a variety of conditions (0 = no adverse effect, 100 = completely adverse effect). The disablement score, therefore, assesses the *social* constraints faced by people with varied conditions, presenting the context as more or less disabling depending on your body/mind. He found, using a relatively small sample in Japan, sensory disabilities like deaf-blindness and blindness received the highest "disablement" scores, while being a person of short stature received one of the lowest scores. Other researchers may examine the experience of inaccessibility and exclusion, asking questions such as: In the last six months, have you had difficulty in doing activities or interacting with others due to the inaccessibility of communication systems, physical environments, or transportation, or due to negative attitudes, beliefs, or policies related to disability?

There are several advantages of this approach. It is aligned with the social model, which is one of the most common sociological definitions of disability. As such, it moves away from the individual deficit-model and instead documents environmental barriers/problems that disable people. Because it focuses attention on the environment, findings rooted in this approach may better inform social reform.

CHAPTER 2   Researching Disability

There are important disadvantages, though. The social model suggests that the barriers *create* disability; therefore, disability is only present to the degree that the barriers are present. This means that one's status as a disabled person shifts as the environment shifts; if the environments are not disabling, the people are not disabled. Hence, the unit of analysis is the person/environment interaction, not the person, which is far more complex to measure. For example, a blind person is not disabled by the lack of sight, or the personal difficulties of mobility, but only when they experienced situations like a lack of Braille menus, websites that do not work with software that reads the website aloud, stigma against the white cane, or prejudice in the workplace. In one setting or interaction, a person may be disabled, and in another the same person is not disabled. This is very fluid, dynamic, and difficult to count.

Furthermore, many researchers argue that there is good reason to keep disability and the experience of barriers conceptually distinct. Keeping these concepts distinct allows for the analysis of the rates of inclusion/exclusion and the factors that promote each. If researchers define disability *as* the experience of social disadvantage, they cannot see *if* people with disabilities are advantaged or disadvantaged because they have defined disability as disadvantage. Thus, it becomes more difficult to examine for whom or how exclusion or inclusion increases.

5. **Disability as the receipt of disability benefits or program eligibility.**

A final definition and measure that we will discuss (we could discuss more!) ties disability to the definitions and eligibility requirements embedded within disability policies and programs. In this approach, one is disabled if one is eligible for and/or enrolled in some program for people with disabilities. For example, we might measure disability as anyone who receives disability benefits through Social Security or has an Individualized Education Program (IEP) at school.

PHOTO 2.2
Form for Disability Benefits.

Credit: Designer491 (2018). Reproduced with permission from istock.com.

The key advantage to this approach is its direct policy relevance. It informs us how many people are eligible for and/or participating in particular programs, and we can then examine their profile and needs. It is also a relatively convenient measure since a program has already identified a group of people as disabled. As a disadvantage, though, while it is useful to know how many people are eligible for or receive such benefits, the definition is then tied to the goals of the program. For example, the Social Security Administration (SSA) uses a narrow definition of disability tied to the total inability to work, which is a *much* narrower definition than one based on activity limitations. Not only is the SSA definition narrower, but becoming a recipient of benefits involves a complex application process that favors people with greater cultural and economic resources. People are more likely to be approved for social security benefits if they have access to a well-qualified personal physician who will attest to their disability, an educational level sufficient to work through many forms and procedures, transportation to attend meetings at the SSA, and the resources to hire a lawyer if needed. As such, if we measure disability by the receipt of SSA benefits, we exclude a wide array of people who live with disability but who have not applied for or been enrolled in SSA programs.

Qualitative Approaches to Measure Disability

Using a very different approach, **qualitative research** foregoes the goals of counting disability and standardizing the measurement of disability across time and place, and instead it offers techniques to dive deeply into examining the meanings and experiences of disability (Mazumdar & Geis, 2001; Taylor et al., 2016). Qualitative researchers ask broad, open-ended questions to delve into the meaning of disability and the meaning-making processes among groups, institutions, and societies. They may ask something as simple as "What does disability mean to you?" or they may ask many in-depth questions to understand the complexity of disability identity and experience.

This approach has many advantages. It corresponds with the common sociological idea that disability is a social construction that varies by time and place (Taylor et al., 2016). For example, work on intellectual disability has shown that the meaning of intellectual disability has changed over time, and as the meaning changed, so too did stereotypes and policies (Carey, 2009; Trent, 1994). Some groups, like the D/deaf community,[1] actively debate the meaning of disability and how and if it applies to their community. Qualitative inquiry enables researchers to explore the varied meaning systems at play, who believes what, why, and to what consequence.

This strategy also encourages sociologists to explore the complex ways that disability may or may not be understood across diverse cultures. For instance, some cultures may have no concept comparable to modern America's idea of "disability." In her work among modern Indian immigrant communities in America, Susan Gabel and her coauthors (2001) found that there was no meaningful translation of the US Census questions on disability for these communities. Hindu ideas of the body, sickness, and disability are rooted in beliefs about karma, mind-body-spirit connection, and spiritual well-being, not biomedical perspectives. Although predetermined quantitative measures seek to generalize and standardize notions about disability, sociologists find that the meaning of disability shifts through time, place, and social context. Therefore, quantitative measures yield a count, but not one that necessarily reflects the varied understandings and experiences of disability. In-depth, inductive, qualitative research better enables this type of "meaning" research.

---

[1] People who are "deaf" with a lowercase "d" consider deafness to be an impairment. People who are "Deaf" with an uppercase "D" consider Deaf people to be a linguistic and cultural minority.

As a key disadvantage, though, qualitative work does not typically yield widely generalizable statistics. Insofar as statistics aid in policy planning, qualitative work may come up short in this regard. Also, in-depth and open-ended questions can also be very time-consuming to analyze, and different researchers may find different patterns.

Table 2.1 summarizes the varied approaches to measuring disability.

TABLE 2.1 Approaches to Measuring Disability

Definition Disability Is	Sample Measurement	Advantages	Disadvantages
The experience of limitations and difficulties	Do you experience difficulty in self-care?	Distinguishes impairment and disability Gathers data on a variety of difficulties Policy relevant Yields high rates	Uses a deficit-approach Might be too broad Requires many questions
The presence of biophysiological conditions	Do you have any of the following conditions?	Gathers prevalence rates for a variety of impairments	Conflates impairment and disability
Self-Identification	Do you have a disability?	Measures self-identification Easy, one question	Many people with impairments and difficulties do not self-identify Yields low rates
The experience of social disadvantage	Have you encountered buildings which were inaccessible?	Connects well to social model Gathers information on the environment Useful for social reform	People only "count" if and when they experience disadvantage Fluid and dynamic Harder to measure person/environment interaction Requires many questions
Eligibility or receipt of disability benefits, services	Are you eligible for disability services at your university?	Policy relevant Relatively easy to measure	Policies are created for specific purposes so the counts are limited based on program
Not predefined (Qualitative)	What does disability mean to you?	Treats disability as a social construction Allows diverse definitions	Harder to "count" disability or determine prevalence rates Challenging to compare "disability" across groups or cultures

Considering Data Literacy

Once you understand these different approaches, you can evaluate the implications of the statistics in research. For example, this chapter opens by using statistics from the American Community Survey (ACS), which measures disability by asking six questions that assess difficulties with key tasks.

What do the data tell us? Because the ACS asks six questions covering different types of difficulties, we learn the prevalence rate of these difficulties. We can then examine if these difficulties correlate with social disadvantages such as unemployment and poverty, which may be very useful for considering policy.

What do the data not tell us? First, the ACS does not ask specific questions about mental, emotional, or learning disabilities, although these are relatively common forms of disability. They may be captured in the question measuring difficulties in remembering, concentrating, and making decisions, but they may not be. Thus, the ACS may lead to a considerable undercount of particular kinds of disability. Furthermore, from these questions, we do not learn about the environmental contexts and barriers. We do not know, for instance, if people have difficulty working because of their biological impairment (the question assumes this reason), because employers will not hire and accommodate people with their impairment, or because of a lack of accessible transportation given their impairment. Without this information, we may struggle to formulate the best policy solutions.

Once we understand the range of measurement approaches and their advantages and disadvantages, we can best assess the quality of the information gathered and the biases and perspectives built into the data.

Ethical Issues in Researching Disability

In many ways, researchers who study disability rely on the same research methodologies and face the same challenges as sociologists who study any other topic. However, disability does present several particular issues for researchers. This section explores several important ethical and methodological challenges of researching disability.

Harm to Research Participants

Any discussion of disability and research must acknowledge the long history of harm imposed on people with disabilities by researchers (Oliver, 1992, 2002; Stone & Priestly, 1996). People with intellectual and mental disabilities, forced into institutions and wielding little power by which to protect themselves, were among the populations especially vulnerable to the abuses of experimentation (Stobee, 2011).

To offer some examples, in 1942 as part of a federally funded research project, doctors injected male patients of a Michigan mental hospital with an experimental flu vaccine and later exposed them to the flu without patient consent. In 1963, researchers injected elderly, ill men at New York's Jewish Chronic Disease Hospital with cancer. From 1963 to 1966, researchers exposed children diagnosed with intellectual disabilities at Staten Island's Willowbrook State hospital to hepatitis (Goode et al., 2013). Most infamously perhaps, in the **Tuskegee experiments** from 1932 to 1966, the US Public Health Service denied treatment to 600 Black men with syphilis in order to track the progression of the disease. The US is not alone in its history of abuse. Nazis in Germany targeted people with disabilities and people in concentration camps for experimentation (Caplan, 1989). Unethical research on people with disabilities continues to be a global problem.

The above examples focus on medical experimentation, but the history of harm is broader. People with disabilities have withstood countless psychological and sociological research studies to study topics like their maturation, deviance and obedience, reactions to various rewards and punishments, and techniques to improve their performance at school and in jobs. This research, however, may not have yielded a significant improvement in the lives of those who endured being a research subject or even for people with disabilities broadly.

In response to various scandals involving research with human subjects, in 1974 the National Research Act established **Institutional Review Boards** (IRBs) to proactively monitor research on human subjects and ensure its adherence to ethical guidelines. Federal guidelines identified **vulnerable populations**—groups who, based on the history of abuse and continued vulnerability, would be protected by IRB protocols. These populations include (not an exhaustive list) children, people with physical and mental disabilities, people with chronic health conditions, prisoners, and people who are economically disadvantaged. Research on vulnerable populations now faces heightened scrutiny, and researchers must justify their reasons for researching these populations, document the process for obtaining informed consent, and justify any potential for harm.

Exclusion from Research and the Silencing of Disabled Voices

While the harm of research with disabled participants is a concern, so too is their exclusion from research. Systematic exclusion from social research silences the voices of people with disabilities and erases their experiences (Mietola et al., 2017; Santinele Martino & Schormans, 2018). This is particularly troubling because people with disabilities have a unique set of experiences and perspectives, and without an understanding of them, our knowledge is shallower.

Research often builds knowledge based on the perspective of White, able-bodied men, but this is inadequate. Indeed, the inclusion of a diversity of people fundamentally shifts one's understanding of the world. Feminist sociologist Dorothy Smith (2005), for example, argued that sociology must try to see the world from the perspective of marginalized populations and to use sociology for the benefit of those populations, serving as a "sociology for people." Taking up this call, feminist sociologists (e.g., Heidi Hartmann, Patricia Hill Collins, Nancy Naples) have examined how women's perspectives lead to the reconceptualization of sociological theories. For example, Marjorie DeVault's (1991) scholarship reconceptualized the study of work. Whereas male scholars typically defined work as paid work, she included the varied forms of unpaid and invisible labor in which women engage. By doing so, she showed how women's invisible labor often undergirds male privilege and patriarchy.

Similarly, the inclusion of people with disabilities in research transforms the way sociologists conceive of the world. To offer an example, including people with disabilities in research has transformed the way researchers understand domestic violence. Measures of domestic violence usually begin with a list of violent activities (e.g., hitting, pushing, kicking) and inquire if people have experienced those forms of violence perpetrated by intimate partners. Through interviewing people with disabilities about the violence they endure, though, researchers identified additional forms of domestic violence more unique to this population, such as the removal of assistive technologies, the denial of basic care, and threats of institutionalization. Without this broader conceptualization of domestic violence, sociologists would overlook these occurrences, even though people with disabilities and older Americans are among the groups most likely to experience domestic violence. Thus, research that does not include the experiences and perspectives of people with disabilities yields an incomplete and skewed picture of the world. In effect, disability serves as an analytic lens, providing new questions to ask, new ways to gather data, and new interpretations in understanding the world.

Although we need to include people with disabilities in social research, they are underrepresented in it. Why? We'll discuss a few important reasons.

Let's start with a consideration of biased sampling. Sampling is the process by which researchers select who will be included in the research study. **Biased sampling** is a type of error that occurs when decisions about sampling lead to an incongruence between the sample and the population, in this case a systematic underrepresentation of people with disabilities. Social research often purposefully excludes people in "institutional settings," including nursing homes, psychiatric hospitals, and even group homes for people with intellectual disabilities. Yet, many people with disabilities reside in these kinds of settings. For example, one-third of people receiving services for intellectual disabilities live in group homes (Parsons et al., 2001). People in institutional settings have very important experiences and opinions, but they rarely have the opportunity to share them.

The process of ethical review through the Institutional Review Board (IRB) may compound this problem. As discussed, the IRB reviews research proposals to ensure compliance with ethical guidelines, and they focus extra attention on populations identified as vulnerable to harm. Although people with disabilities are identified as vulnerable for good reasons, the IRB may be reluctant to approve almost any research involving disabled research subjects in an effort to protect people with disabilities from harm and to protect researchers and universities from controversy and liability (Santinele Martino & Schormans, 2018). Researchers are steered away from people with disabilities and encouraged instead to speak with family members and professionals about disability, as if nondisabled people can fully represent the disability experience. People with disabilities are effectively silenced.

Furthermore, people with disabilities are more likely to live in settings with **research gatekeepers**—people whose approval is necessary for people with disabilities to participate in research. For example, to access people who live in nursing homes, group homes or other agency-run facilities, researchers must get agency approval. Agencies, though, may deny access to their participants for a wide variety of reasons. They may see research as inconvenient, an invasion of privacy, or a liability issue. For example, Steve Taylor and Robert Bogdan (1998) argued that state institutions denied researchers access to residents in an effort to hide poor conditions and silence resident complaints. Parents and legal guardians also act as gatekeepers, adding an additional layer of complexity to access (Matysiak, 2001). If people have been legally adjudicated incompetent, guardians must consent to research participation; however, there is no easy way for a researcher to know who is under guardianship or who is not. Not all people in institutional settings or group homes are under guardianship, and not all people who live in the community are legally competent. To be "safe" (to protect respondents from harm and researchers from liability), the IRB and researchers may decide to treat all people with disabilities as if they are incompetent. This assumption of incompetence, though, unfairly stereotypes and excludes people with disabilities, especially people with intellectual and mental disabilities (Santinele Martino, 2018).

Even if people with disabilities are included in the overall sample, they are still less likely to participate in research due to *inaccessible data collection techniques*—techniques to gather data that fail to offer a range of ways for a diversity of people to participate. For example, national surveys often utilize telephone surveys, but this method undercounts people who are economically disadvantaged, homeless, deaf, or have communication disabilities (as a note, people with disabilities are also disproportionately among those who are economically disadvantaged and homeless). Internet surveys face many similar disadvantages. Interviewers usually have no training in ASL or communication technologies and often do not make materials available in accessible formats like large print, Braille, or electronic formats.

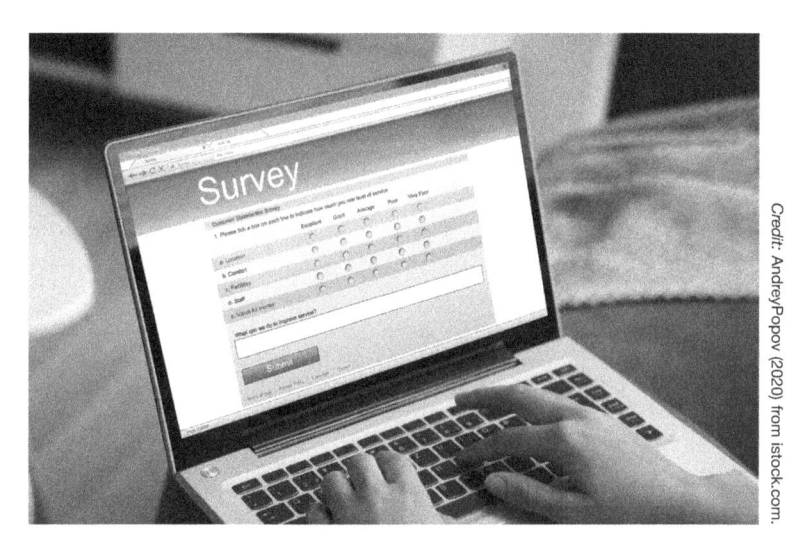

PHOTO 2.3 Internet surveys are increasingly common and not always accessible.

Few researchers have even tried to best capture the lived experiences and perspectives of nonverbal people with significant disabilities (Mietola et al., 2017). Instead of interviewing people with disabilities, researchers will sometimes rely on **proxy respondents**—people who participate in research on behalf of another person. Proxy respondents are asked to answer the questions as closely as possible to the imagined answers that would have been given by the person with a disability. Research, though, has shown that proxies do not reliably answer in the same way as the person with a disability and that the use of proxy respondents is likely more common than necessary. Too often, proxies are used for the researcher's ease and to lower research costs rather than because people with disabilities are unable to communicate for themselves (Parsons et al., 2001).

Power and the Research Process

Including people as research respondents is an important step in knowledge production, but it is only a step. Researchers set the research agenda, including the goals and outcomes of any given study. However, very few researchers are people with disabilities. The underrepresentation of researchers with disabilities is related to many factors, such as the accumulated disadvantages in education which hinder the attainment of advanced degrees, employment discrimination, and ableism in higher education. The expectations and the lack of accommodations in the research process—such as the expectation to conduct research in inaccessible homes and communities, to communicate in standardized ways, and work long hours on tight deadlines—also may present barriers (Burke & Byrne, 2020). Therefore, people with disabilities have little opportunity to shape the research agenda, and instead the priorities of disability research are established primarily by people without disabilities.

Some activists and scholars argue that disability research can only truly be useful to the disability community to the extent that people with disabilities participate in and *exercise control over the research process*. Research methodologies such as Feminist Methodology, Participatory Action Research and Emancipatory Research take up this call. Before we explain these methods, let's take a step back and look at the broader debate in Sociology regarding power and the research process.

Since Sociology's formation as a science, sociologists have debated the reasons and the methods for doing research (Guba & Lincoln, 2005; Taylor et al., 2016). Durkheim ([1938] 2013), for instance, promoted **positivism**—the view that there is an objective world to be discovered through scientific methods conducted by unbiased researchers. In this view, it does not matter who conducts the research as long as they are well-trained, objective, and unbiased. In order to remain unbiased, the researcher must not be committed to any particular finding or political action; science and politics must be kept separate. Many contemporary sociologists, including some who do disability research, adhere to this belief.

Other scholars, like Karl Marx ([1888] 1978), however, argued that the claim to objectivity was false. Humans can only understand the world through our subjective, and intersubjective, experience of it. Because meaning is created through social interaction, science cannot be emptied or removed from this process. Indeed, science in any given society often relies on and represents the values, relationships, and social structures of that society. For Marx, elites typically control science, and therefore science too often supports and legitimizes inequality. Michel Foucault (1980) expanded on this idea, arguing that power and knowledge are inseparable; those in power create dominant discourses that then reinforce the power inequities. Rather than a single objective reality, knowledge is produced within a power structure and wielded by those in power. Resisting the power imbalance often embedded in research, some scholars promote critical theory and praxis. **Critical theory** seeks to develop knowledge that reveals and challenges unjust power structures, while **praxis** is the use of theory and research to achieve social justice. Who wields science and for what purposes, then, is a central issue in the ethics of research.

Taking up the call for a science committed to social justice, feminist scholars created a range of methodological strategies to guide feminist methodology (Harding, 1987; Reinharz, 1992; Smith, 2005). Some key principles of **feminist methodology** (Davis & Craven, 2016; Leavy & Harris, 2019) include:

- The production of knowledge that prioritizes the voices and experiences of women;
- A commitment to reveal and challenge power differentials, focusing on gender analysis and an intersectional view of women's realities (i.e., taking into account race, class, sexuality, ability, etc);
- A rejection of the positivist orientation to instead embrace subjectivity and reflexivity, acknowledging the researchers' values, social position, and impact on a given community;
- A rejection of the traditional researcher-subject hierarchy and the creation instead of processes that empower everyday women to act as experts of their own lives and contribute to knowledge production;
- A commitment to serving as an active ally in the feminist movement and producing knowledge useful for the improvement of women's lives.

Patricia Leavy and Anne Harris (2019, p. vi) state that feminist methodology is "about doing research that is embedded in and accountable to 'real life' and making real life better—not just for women, but for all—and to realize that these are not separate projects but interconnected ones."

As disability activism grew and the social model took hold in the academy, disability scholars also demanded a change in methodology. Some disability scholars, such as Jenny Morris (1993), Linda Blum (2015), and Laura Mauldin (2017), draw on feminist methodologies to inform their work, highlighting the intersection of disability and gender oppression and/or utilizing methods that prioritize the voices and expertise of women in relation to their disability experience.

Other scholars articulate a model of "emancipatory research" specific to disability research (Barnes & Mercer, 1997, 2008; Oliver, 1992, 2002). Explicitly tied to the social model of disability which sees disability as an experience of social oppression, **emancipatory research** is a research methodology with "an avowed commitment to the empowerment of disabled people through a process of political and social change while also informing the process of doing disability research" (Barnes, 2008, p. 2). In this approach, researchers actively engage in the political struggle of people with disabilities for justice. Formulations of emancipatory research vary, but they tend to stress the following principles:

- Conducting research that reveals and challenges social inequity and oppression of people with disabilities;
- Empowering people with disabilities and their representative organizations to control the research agenda, process, and product, thereby to transform the researcher-researchee relationship as larger social-political relations of power are also transformed;

- Practicing researcher accountability to the disability community, including the conduct and dissemination of research that is useful and accessible to the community;
- Serving as an ally for the political empowerment of people with disabilities.

Another methodology commonly used by scholars with an orientation toward praxis is participatory action research. **Participatory Action Research** (PAR) addresses issues identified by specific communities, in ways that are useful to the community, with the full and active participation of all relevant stakeholders. Like feminist and emancipatory approaches, PAR challenges traditional power inequalities in research, engages with communities, and includes community members as coresearchers. However, this method is broader in some ways than feminist or emancipatory methods, because it encourages active engagement with any community to meet any pressing research needs. Thus, the goal is not necessarily social justice. A community might want, for example, to evaluate a particular type of assistive technology or address a problem in Medicaid policy—issues that are relevant and useful but may not lead to political emancipation. Another distinction is the level of commitment to the community. PAR researchers do not necessarily sustain a long-term political commitment to the same community. They may conduct a single research project with a community, and then move on to assist another community.

These methodologies—feminist, emancipatory, and PAR—encourage researchers to take on the role of **scholar-activist**, using research to advance social justice. Scholar-activism is not without critics of course. Criticisms include, for instance, that a commitment to only transformative methodologies may diminish the quality and variety of knowledge produced (Danieli & Woodhams, 2005). Furthermore, the demand to disclose disability and unite with the disability community potentially may burden scholars with disabilities (Rinaldi, 2013). Yet, despite criticisms, many scholars remain deeply committed to transformative research.

Research methods in the study of disability continue to evolve. For example, contemporary researchers continue to explore best practices in the inclusion of people with disabilities as research partners (Hollinrake et al., 2019; Tregaskis & Goodley, 2005). Mietola and colleagues (2017), for instance, developed strategies to explore the experiences of people who are nonverbal and have significant intellectual disabilities, a population often excluded from research. Current scholars conducting intersectional scholarship also continue to challenge the control of scholarship by White scholars with and without disabilities. For example, Leroy Moore Jr. and his collaborators (2016) wrote a provocative piece criticizing the privilege of White disability scholars who exercise greater control over the research agenda and disproportionately reap the rewards that flow from research, such as recognition as experts and the receipt of grant funding, while doing little to support the expertise, activism, and scholarship rooted in communities of color. Thus, disability research continues to struggle to be broadly inclusive and to empower the range of people with disabilities in the processes and benefits of research.

Conclusion

Disability offers a window into many of the challenges and debates within sociological research, such as how to best define "disability," if and how researchers should strive to create research opportunities accessible to all, and the role of the researcher in challenging oppression. If you conduct research on disability, you might consider issues like:

- How should I define disability and how does this choice shape my findings?
- Are my method and research materials—the consent form, the survey, the method of administration—accessible to people with a variety of disabilities?
- Will the research process and the research products benefit the community I am studying or do they primarily advance my own interests?
- What are my ethical obligations to the people and community being studied?
- How might I best create and disseminate knowledge that is useful to a community?
- How might people with disabilities be included in the research process and/or in the processes of dissemination and policy-making based on the research?

And even if you do not conduct your own research, hopefully now you will be better able to assess the meaning behind the statistics related to disability and the quality of the research.

KEY TERMS

Biased sampling 36
Critical theory 38
Emancipatory research 39
Feminist methodology 39
International Classification of Functioning, Disability and Health (ICF) 27
Institutional Review Boards (IRBs) 35
Operationalized 26
Participatory Action Research (PAR) 40
Positivism 38
Praxis 38
Proxy respondents 37
Qualitative research 32
Quantitative research 26
Research gatekeepers 36
Scholar-activist 41
Tuskegee experiments 34
Vulnerable populations 35

RESOURCES

Suggested Reading

Barnes, Colin. 2008. "An ethical agenda in disability research: Rhetoric or reality?" In *The handbook of social research ethics*, ed. Donna M. Martens and Pauline E. Ginsberg, 458–473. London: SAGE. Explains emancipatory research and assesses its potential.

Burke, Ciaran, and Bronagh Byrne, eds. 2020. *Social research and disability: Developing inclusive research spaces for disabled researchers*. Routledge. A collection focusing on barriers to inclusion in research and strategies for inclusion.

Houtenville, Andrew, and Marisa Rafal. 2020. *Annual report on people with disabilities in*

America: 2020. Durham, NH: University of New Hampshire, Institute on Disability. https://disabilitycompendium.org/annualreport. A nicely formatted research report compiling disability statistics that can be used both for the statistics alone as well as to assess the information garnered from particular measures of disability.

Mietola, Reeta, Sonja Miettinen, and Simo Vehmas. 2017. "Voiceless subjects?: Research ethics and persons with profound intellectual disabilities." *International Journal of Social Research Methodology* 20(3): 263–274. An example of recent methodological innovations to develop inclusive research methods.

Videos and Film

"The Grounded Academic: Disability, Poverty, and Health Care – Action Research in Rural Guatemala." https://www.youtube.com/watch?v=5CYhKFmlvSk. A short discussion by Dr. Shaun Grech about action research in poor, rural areas in Guatemala (7 minutes).

"Participatory Data Collection for Disability-Inclusive City: Solo City." https://www.youtube.com/watch?v=FUkvQ_NwNSk. A short video documenting participatory data collection in Solo City, Indonesia (5 minutes).

ACTIVITIES

1. **Measuring Disability**
   Imagine that your university wants to conduct a survey to assess the degree to which students feel a sense of belonging and community at your university. The university wants to measure this sense of belonging among several different groups of students, including students with disabilities. Considering the various measures of disability discussed in this chapter, lay out (a) three approaches you could use to measure disability, (b) develop specific question(s) to measure disability at your university using each of the three approaches, and (c) discuss advantages and disadvantages for each approach. Finally, select an approach and question(s) and explain why it is the most advantageous for the university to use.

2. **Examining and Evaluating Data**
   Click on the link to Houtenville, Andrew, and Marisa Rafal. 2020. *Annual report on people with disabilities in America: 2020*. Durham, NH: University of New Hampshire, Institute on Disability. https://disabilitycompendium.org/annualreport. What kind of measure is used for disability in this report? What are the advantages and disadvantages of this measure? What are some of the report's most interesting findings? What does this report tell us about disability in modern America? What doesn't it tell us that you wish you knew?

3. **Including Underrepresented Populations**
   Read *Voiceless Subject?* by Mietola, Miettinen, and Vehmas (listed above). Consider why people with significant disabilities are often excluded from social research and why/if it matters. What strategies did the authors develop to include this population? How effective were the strategies? What information could they gather? What information could they not gather? How broadly applicable is this technique for, say, the Census? Would you say this is emancipatory research?

4. **Considering the role of the IRB and accessibility**
   Review your university's IRB submission forms and suggested consent letter.

Consider how/if the IRB protects people with disabilities. Also consider how/if the IRB allows inaccessibility and/or if it demands acccessibility. In particular, review the IRB sample consent letter and consider its accessibility for diverse populations.

5. **Debate the researcher's role in fostering social justice**
Should scholars be a neutral party or should they be scholar-activists in the fight for social justice? What are the advantages and disadvantages of either role?

CHAPTER 3

Social Constructions of Disability Through Time and Place
A BRIEF HISTORY

Learning Outcomes

3.1 Define historical comparative analysis.

3.2 Examine the role of religion in shaping disability in ancient civilizations.

3.3 Compare and contrast the role of religion, economy, and government in medieval Europe and China in shaping disability.

3.4 Compare and contrast disability in early America and colonial Caribbean, especially the role of colonization and slavery.

3.5 Identify the social structures shifting American and Indian views of disability in 1850–1950.

3.6 Evaluate the progress and limitations of disability activism in modern societies.

Chapter Synopsis

This chapter provides brief historical overviews of disability in various places and time. Rather than trying to provide a comprehensive history, the vignettes strive to showcase a diversity of ideas about disability and the role of social structures—such as the economy, religion, and government—in creating, shaping the meaning of, and responding to disability.

Historical Comparative Analysis

Did you know that the Greek god Hephaestus was portrayed as disabled, as well as powerful, skilled, and married to the goddess of beauty? Did you know that the royal courts and wealthy households of medieval Europe housed people with intellectual disabilities and dwarves who served as entertainment and sometimes as counselors? Or that between 1907 and 1960, the United States sterilized more than 60,000 disabled people without their consent in a political quest to rid the nation of disability? Disability history reveals a fascinating diversity of beliefs about and responses to disability.

One of the primary methodologies used by sociologists is **historical comparative analysis**—the examination of a social phenomenon as it occurs across time and place in order to assess causal relationships. This technique provides a window into social construction, revealing that the ideas and norms one may take for granted are really products of time and place. Furthermore, it enables an analysis of potential causal factors as they play out through history. Sociologists might compare, for instance, different economic systems, religious systems, etc., as they exist and intertwine with other systems and influence disability.

The historical vignettes provided in this chapter are relatively brief, and they highlight the following points:

1. Disability is socially constructed, and as such the definitions, explanations, and treatment of disability vary considerably.

2. History does not reveal a simple linear "progression" from negative to positive treatment of disability. Each time and place involves complex and contradictory beliefs and responses.

3. Ideas about disability are rooted in the social environment, including (among other factors) the economic, political, and religious structures of the day (DePoy & Gilson, 2011). Ideas about disability change as social structures change.

Early Civilizations in the Ancient World: Egypt, Greece, and Rome

Ancient Egypt

Our knowledge about disability in Ancient Egypt is sparse. Because people endured hard labor, lacked basic nutrients, and had little opportunity for medical care, physical impairments were common. Ancient Egyptian art and texts depict a range of physical variations, including leg and back deformities, back humps, and dwarfism. Egyptians likely saw these differences as commonplace and treated them using religious and early medical practices. Ideas about the supernatural dominated their understanding of the world, and Egyptian physicians were also religious leaders who specialized in treating ailments believed to be associated with particular gods (Weiss & Lonnquist, 2017).

Evidence indicates that people with varied bodies were generally well-accepted and included in everyday life (Mahran & Kamal, 2001). In Egypt's **polytheistic religion**—a religion with a belief in multiple gods—several gods had physical atypicalities, including the god Bes, who was depicted as a dwarf and believed to protect women and childbirth (David, 2016). Moral writings of the day portrayed some physical traits now associated with disability as divine attributes bestowed by the gods. They also taught respect and care for people who might be vulnerable due to such variations.

People with different bodies seem to have been included in work as well. The family-based, agricultural economy provided opportunities for people with diverse bodies to work as they were able with family support. Tomb artwork, dating back to 4500 BCE, showed people with varied bodies engaging in a range of work alongside others in their communities. People with impairments could hold high social positions in the Egyptian court and receive burial in costly tombs. Dwarfism, in particular, carried a positive connotation and elicited respect (David, 2016). Table 3.1 offers highlights of how structure influenced "disability"[1]:

TABLE 3.1 Social Structure in Ancient Egypt

Social Structure	
Economy	Physical labor caused impairment, but small communities and agricultural production encouraged the integration of most people.
Religion	Religious polytheism included diverse bodies; religious beliefs influenced medical treatment.
Medicine	Early medical practices and specializations were usually understood in the context of devotion to particular gods.

Ancient Greece and Rome

As in ancient Egypt, physical differences and limitations were common. Laes (2018) estimates that 30%–35% of children born did not reach their first birthday. Blindness and deafness resulted from sickness and aging. Ancient Greek and Roman texts discuss incapacities of intellect and reason.

In explaining disability, ancient civilizations often looked to supernatural reasons, believing that disability was a punishment for breaking religious and social norms. Deafness, for example, was described in ancient Greek writings almost solely as a curse (Edwards, 1997). Positive views of disability also existed. In their polytheistic religion, some deities, like the Egyptian deities, experienced disability. The Roman god of fire and forge, Vulcan, and his Greek counterpart, Hephaestus, were disabled yet powerful, skilled, and married to the goddess of beauty.

PHOTO 3.1
Roman God of fire and forge, Vulcan, With Crippled Foot

---

[1]DePoy & Gilson's (2011) analysis of the social construction of disability also examines the role of social structure, focusing on similar key social structures.

As Christianity grew in popularity, religion and disability remained linked but in different ways. In the *Bible*, the Christian god used disability to punish humans for sin, test their faith, and provide them with an opportunity to engage in charity (Yong, 2007). In this **monotheistic religion**—religions with a belief in one god—Christians viewed their sole god as perfect, not disabled. Although humans experienced disability, salvation was often presented as a heaven free from physical and spiritual impairment (Yong, 2007). Thus, as Christianity rose to prominence, disability was set apart from the divine.

Alongside religious interpretations, empirically based medicine was developing. **Hippocrates**, known as the "Father of Medicine" (460–377 BC), argued that diseases were physical manifestations with physical causes. In the humoral theory, Hippocrates proposed that illnesses occurred due to an imbalance of four bodily fluids—black bile, yellow bile, blood, and phlegm—and treatments, therefore, needed to restore the physical balance of these fluids. Other explanations focused on psychology or mind-body interaction, such as the belief that if a pregnant woman gazed upon a deformed person, her shock might lead to her own child's deformity. Considering the complex blend of religious, magical, superstitious, and medical explanations and healers, Weiss and Lonnquist describe ancient Rome as an "open medical marketplace" (p. 17).

Responses to disability varied considerably. Some responses were quite harsh. The **Twelve Tables**, the first legal code of the Roman Republic (451 & 450 BC), allowed the patriarch of the family to kill, abandon, mutilate, and sell his children, and disability was considered a legitimate reason to do so (Laes, 2018). Greek philosopher Aristotle extolled intelligence as both a divine gift and as a prerequisite to citizenry. He supported laws barring those without sufficient intelligence or mental reasoning from political participation and allowing the killing or abandonment of deformed infants. He included people born deaf or without spoken communication as among those unfit for the responsibilities of citizenship, a view that restricted opportunities for these populations for centuries thereafter.

Despite these harsh responses, recent scholarship has discovered great complexity in the ancient response to disability (Penrose, 2015; Rose, 2003). Laes argues, "On the one hand, disabled people in antiquity were more strongly integrated into society; on the other hand, they were subjected to a wide variety of mechanisms of exclusion" (p. 22). As in ancient Egypt, there was no systematic attempt by the government or professionals to identify and segregate people with disabilities. People largely worked alongside and contributed to their families and communities as they were able. Evidence suggests that many families raised children with disabilities. Some differences were valued. Romans considered blindness as a possible path to divine insight. Some wealthy households purchased or hired disabled people, especially those with intellectual disabilities ("natural fools") and with "exotic" disabilities, to serve as entertainment. While this situation hardly seems positive, some entertainers received respect, care, and support. Men wounded in battle often received honor and possibly state-funded pensions (Winzer, 1997). See Table 3.2 for a summary of social structure and disability in Ancient Rome and Greece.

TABLE 3.2   **Social Structure in Ancient Rome and Greece**

Economy	As an agricultural economy with family farming, families had some flexibility to work alongside each other and accommodate difference.
Religion	Religious views were mixed. The Greek pantheon of gods included disability, whereas Christianity distinguished disability and the divine.
Government	As civilizations grew, responses to disability shifted slowly out of family to governmental responses via policy and law. The rise of democracy in Greece increased concerns about and stigma of disabilities associated with intelligence and reason.
Family	Agricultural societies tended to bestow considerable power in the hands of the patriarch to decide if and how he wished to incorporate disabled members into the household.
Medicine	Alongside spiritual treatments, medicine grew more scientific.

Medieval Era—5th Century to 1400

Medieval Europe

The fall of the Roman Empire ushered in the Middle Ages in Europe. Spanning from the 5th to 15th century, the Middle Ages that dominate our cultural images—a time of feudalism, knights, the Crusades, a powerful Catholic Church, and the Black Death—is primarily from 1100 to 1400.

As with ancient civilizations, in the Middle Ages impairment was common. Agricultural labor caused spinal and limb injuries, and malnutrition led to disease, stunted growth, and deformity. Acute diseases rampaged the population, most notably the Plague which killed approximately one-third of the European population (1347–1350). Leprosy, a disease known for causing skin lesions, swept through Europe and caused chronic disability.

To consider how Europeans thought about disability in the Middle Ages, let's start with the Catholic Church. The Catholic Church was the most powerful institution in Europe during the Middle Ages, and it offered mixed messages regarding disability. Disability was often believed to be caused by either the *absence* of the divine or the *presence* of direct divine intervention (Wood, 2017a). Either way, the task of the impaired person was to strengthen their faith in the hopes of attaining cure. Nondisabled Christians were expected to serve as conduits of god's love by treating the unfortunate disabled person charitably and even channeling miracles of faith healing (Kuuliala, 2016). Thus, on the one hand, the Catholic Church stigmatized people with disabilities by associating disability with sin. On the other hand, disability presented a valuable opportunity to participate in suffering akin to Christ's suffering and to publicly display one's charity (Tovey, 2016).

The control of the Catholic Church extended to medicine and systems of care (Metzler, 2013). Medicine was dominated by religious leaders. Monasteries offered care to travelers, the vulnerable, poor, sick, and impaired. Almshouses (houses of charity) provided temporary housing for a range of the poor and dependents. Hospitals based in religious establishments cropped up throughout Europe, some of which specialized in particular ailments including leprosariums and the first mental hospitals.

PHOTO 3.2
13th Century Fresco of Jesus Healing Lepers

The medieval economy largely relied on feudal agriculture, but began shifting toward mercantilism, including the increased use of paid labor, trade, and urbanization. In **feudalism**, a small number of lords controlled the land, and serfs lived and worked the lord's land with their families. Life was difficult and deprivation common; however, peasant families usually had sufficient flexibility in their work to accommodate bodily variations, and they benefited from including all family members to the maximum degree possible in accomplishing their work. In contrast, merchants had little incentive to hire people with disabilities. Under mercantilism, the economic marginalization of people with disabilities grew, and disability became associated with poverty and charity (Metzler, 2013).

Religious ideologies blended with economic exclusion to encourage the sorting of those deserving of charity from the undeserving. Charity, which was once offered to those in need relatively indiscriminately, now relied on the moral categorization of people. People with disabilities were increasingly seen as unable to work and occupied a position as *legitimate* recipients of charity. For example, Louis IX founded an early residential hospice for the blind and granted its residents license to beg at the doors of Parisian churches (Wheatley, 2002). The exclusive "privilege" of receiving charity encouraged others to fake disability, though, and suspicion of and hostility toward beggars and people with disabilities grew (Wheatley, 2010). While charity helped some people to survive, tying disability to charity sparked the long historical trajectory toward treating people with disabilities as objects of pity, segregation, and exclusion (Metzler, 2013).

This trajectory toward increasing economic exclusion and suspicion, though, was only in its earliest stages. Most people with disabilities continued to live and work alongside their families and in their communities. The concept of original sin common in Catholicism marked all people as sinful, and people with disabilities were not unique in needing to strengthen their faith. Disability did not disqualify elites from their social rank; rank was mostly determined by birth. King Richard III of England had a curvature of his spine, and King John of Bohemia was blind. Royal courts and wealthy households kept "fools" (both "natural" and professional) for entertainment (Metzler, 2016). Henri-Jacques Stiker (1999, p. 65) summarizes the treatment of disability in the Middle Ages by saying that the time period offered "an acceptance at times awkward, at times brutal, at times compassionate, a kind of indifferent, fatalistic integration." Table 3.3 summarizes the role of social structure in this era.

TABLE 3.3 Social Structure in Medieval Europe

Economy	Most peasants were illiterate, in poor health, and worked alongside their families. The emergence of mercantilism increased economic exclusion. Entrenched inequality gave elites rights to their social position regardless of ability/disability.
Religion	The Catholic Church dominated views of disability. Increased formalization of charity encouraged discernment between the deserving and undeserving poor.
Government	Disability was not a primary concern of government policy. Frequent wars produced disability.
Family	Family was a key social unit, providing care and work.
Medicine	Medicine was practiced largely within the confines of the Catholic Church.

China

To move elsewhere in the globe, China offers an interesting case in this same time period. The material in this section draws heavily on Emma Stone's (1998) scholarship. Whereas scholarship traditionally depicts the Middle Ages in Europe as a dark time with few cultural developments, China enjoyed artistic and technological growth, such as innovations in paper production, the use of paper money, and the development of an advanced imperial government with a sprawling, efficient bureaucracy staffed by educated personnel. In contrast to Europe's imposition of Christianity, China allowed religious pluralism, with Confucianism, Taoism, and Buddhism as the major religions. Of these, Confucianism most clearly pervaded state activities. The Chinese government, influenced by Confucian ideologies, played a significant role in defining disability (Stone, 1998).

Confucianism is a philosophy founded by Confucius that proposed a series of teachings and social guidelines to attain social order and harmony. Order represented an ideal state of being, achieved through following clear rules, attaining balance, and abiding by the social hierarchy. In contrast, disorder (of the person, family, society) was seen as threatening the entire social fabric. Illness and impairment represented one potential source of disorder (other sources include, for example, disobeying one's elders or breaking the law) and therefore could be undesirable.

Confucian beliefs mingled with beliefs from other religious systems. The Buddhist idea of karma could suggest that disability was punishment for deviance (one's own or one's ancestors). Popular beliefs in demons, fairies, and a range of supernatural and magical beings often linked disability to evil. In 556 AD, a Ming Dynasty medical text stated, "Illnesses have many causes, yet they are all related to evil" (Xu Chunfu, cited in Stone, p. 67).

Responses to disease and disability varied widely. To the extent that disability threatened order, interventions attempted to restore order. These included a vast array of healing options, such as folk remedies to expel demons, acupuncture, herbal remedies, surgery, and specialized medical treatment (fields such as ophthalmology, pediatrics, and gynecology were already established). Although highly varied, each option was likely infused with a Confucian worldview prioritizing the values of social order and harmony. If one could maintain order—one could work, participate in religious practices, and uphold family obligations—then one achieved success regardless of one's body. If one could not, one was impaired regardless of one's body.

China had a well-developed administrative government. During the Tang Dynasty (618–907), the government developed a categorical system ranking the severity of disability. For instance, the category of partial disability included blindness in one eye, deafness in both ears, the lack of two fingers or a thumb on one hand, the lack of three toes or a big toe from a foot, or the lack of hair. The category of total disability included complete insanity, the lack of two or more limbs, and blindness in both eyes. This system informed public policies such as exemptions from the military, access to reduced taxation, allowances in criminal proceedings, and the reduction of one's land allocation (Richardson et al., 2019). Primarily though, care and order were attained through the family. Table 3.4 summarizes the role of social structure in China in this era.

TABLE 3.4   Social Structure in Medieval China

Economy	The agricultural economy provided family flexibility for integration.
Religion	Pluralism with a Confucianist focus on order and harmony positioned disability as a threat if it disrupted order.
Government	An expansive bureaucratic state institutionalized disability policy.
Family	The family played a central role in providing care and maintaining order.
Medicine	Developing specializations operated within religious and moral frameworks.

Early Modern Period to 1850

Early Modern Europe

Ideas about disability greatly transformed during the Renaissance and Enlightenment. The dominance of religion waned, and science flourished. While in some ways a time of progress, these shifts also led to increased identification and exclusion of people with disabilities (Franzese, 2009).

The **Protestant Reformation** challenged the hold of the Catholic Church and advocated a personal relationship between man and god without mediation by priests, an ideal facilitated by growing literacy rates and Gutenburg's printing press which made *the Bible* more widely available. A personal relationship with god was premised on intellect and active participation in one's faith. In other words, to attain salvation, the faithful had to read scripture and actively *choose* Jesus as one's savior. The emphasis on active participation and literacy, rather than God's will, led reformers like Martin Luther and John Calvin to argue that people with mental and cognitive disabilities (which in their view included deafness and communication disabilities) could not attain salvation if they were seen as unable to learn the *Bible* and communicate their commitment to god (Franzese, 2009).

Traditional and newer beliefs mixed in complex ways (Bearden, 2019). Traditional beliefs in the role of Satan and witchcraft still proliferated, and disability was often thought to be an omen, usually negative but sometimes positive. Royal courts continued to keep "natural fools," serving as entertainment and sometimes in a more powerful role as truth-teller to those in power (Bingham & Green, 2016; Secmezsoy-urquhart, 2016). Dwarfs and people of short stature were commonly associated with magic and fairies, and their presence in the court was thought to provide a "sense of opulence" and wonder (Secmezsoy-urquhart, 2016).

These religious beliefs blended with Enlightenment philosophies, which held reason and science to be the hallmarks of humanity and the path to perfection. The philosophy of **Humanism**, for example, argued that, through reason and empirical observation, humans and societies could progress toward excellence (Braddock & Parish, 2001). Enlightenment political philosophy (e.g., Locke, Hobbes) stressed the right of the rational citizen to participate in political activities. Man could (and must) reason and actively intervene in the world to create both personal and social perfection. The ideal of the rational citizen, though, excluded many populations considered to be irrational, including children, women, slaves, colonized peoples, people perceived as intellectually and mentally deficient, and nonproperty owners (Carlson, 2009; Hirschmann, 2013).

Culturally, as rationality became a central value, people sought to display their rationality by showing heightened self-control. The litany of etiquette grew, fashion became more restraining, and displays of emotional and physical "messiness" (e.g., toileting, lovemaking, crying, sickness) were remanded to private spaces. Disabilities involving a lack of physical or emotional control grew more stigmatized. In the Age of Reason, one had to control one's mind and thoughts, and the unstable mind became the enemy (Foucault, 1965).

Humans were now seen as uniquely active and transformable. John Locke's concept of **tabula rasa** posited that humans were born a blank slate and accumulated knowledge through sensory experience. Education therefore was the key to attaining human excellence. The mission of transformation via education potentially included people with disabilities. Beginning in the 1500s in Spain, systematic efforts began to develop and teach sign language, and by the 18th century schools for the deaf had emerged throughout Europe, radically transforming the idea of deaf people from unintelligent lost souls to potentially redeemable citizens (Davis, 1997b). Education for blind students followed suit.

The promise of education as a transformational tool eventually extended to intellectual disability, although not as successfully. In 1846 with the publication of *The Moral Treatment, Hygiene, and Education of Idiots and Other*

Backward Children, Eduoard Sequin (1812–1880) became the first scholar to systematically lay out a method of educating children with intellectual disabilities (Winzer, 1993). Children with intellectual disabilities, though, did not as easily transform into productive citizens, and schools were quickly replaced with large-scale custodial institutions.

Progress for people with mental illness was uneven. Religious explanations (e.g., witchcraft, demon possession) subsided. Explanations and treatments increasingly turned toward the natural, although treatments were often misinformed and brutal, such as submersion in ice and whippings (Franzese, 2009). The use of confinement increased. "Madhouses" housed a wide diversity of people seen as immoral or unreasonable, including those seen as mentally ill, wives rejected by their husbands, social dissidents, beggars, heretics, and addicts (Foucault, 1965).

Mercantilism continued to grow, and international trade, exploration, and empire-building became central activities of European states. By 1800, European countries controlled approximately 35% of the globe (by 1914, they would control approximately 84%). Colonialism produced disability internationally via global warfare, slavery, and the disempowerment of local colonized populations. Economic inequality grew, and European governments became increasingly involved in regulating poverty, which often included provisions related to disability. For example, the 1601 English Poor Laws gave local communities responsibility for their poor, dependent and disabled. Table 3.5 summarizes the role of social structures in Early Modern Europe.

PHOTO 3.3
William Norris Confined in Bethlem Hospital for 12 Years

Early America

In *A Disability History of the United States,* historian Kim Nielsen (2012) begins by explaining the views of indigenous people. While very diverse, indigenous peoples commonly believed people could and should contribute to the interdependence of the community. "The spirit chooses the body" summarizes the belief that the spirits provided everyone with a purpose and the body necessary to fulfill that purpose (Nielsen, 2012, p. 1). Physical atypicality

TABLE 3.5 Social Structure in Early Modern—1850 Europe

Economy	Family-centered agricultural economies provided family flexibility for integration. Growing mercantilism increased the exclusion of people with disabilities from work and the regulation of poverty. Colonial rule disabled indigenous populations and increased their poverty.
Religion/Philosophy	Declining role of religion. Protestantism emphasized active participation in salvation and positioned some as beyond salvation. Humanist philosophies suggested the perfectibility of people; education offered transformation for some, but confinement was seen as necessary for others.
Politics/Law	Democratic government required an active citizenry, leading to increasing concerns about intellectual and mental disability. States developed a broader array of formal policies related to disability.
Family	Families were still expected to provide primary care for disabled family members.
Medicine	Scientific knowledge grew, but confinement was largely nonmedical and often abusive.

was not completely free from stigma; impairments sometimes were believed to be an outward manifestation of a deeper problem (e.g., disfavor by the ancestors, punishment for deviant behavior). As such, healing ceremonies and remedies addressed holistic issues of body, mind, and spirit within the community, not physicality alone. Life held many challenges for people with specific impairments. Nomadic tribes moved over difficult terrain, food was at times scarce, and work intense. These conditions posed distinct challenges for people with frail or vulnerable bodies, but there was no effort to systematically identify or segregate people based on physical/mental disability.

Colonization—the process of establishing settlements and control over an area and the people in that area while retaining strong ties to the settler's country of origin—violently undercut the capacity of indigenous people to integrate people with diverse bodies/minds into their communities (Nielsen, 2012). Disease, warfare, the loss of land, deforestation, and forced dislocation disrupted long-held methods of community survival.

Colonists came to America for many different reasons, such as seeking fortune, the opportunity to own land, and/or freedom from religious persecution. Colonial communities made do as best they could. They had little reason or means by which to segregate people with disabilities. Impairment was common, and, if someone could work, they did. Agricultural work centered on family farms, offering families the flexibility to best incorporate the range of skills available.

If one could not work, the family held primary responsibility for care, and the community often provided assistance if the family could not. Almshouses and workhouses served a wide assortment of the poor and dependent, including orphans, widows, the elderly, disabled, ill, addicted, and poor. These sites were places of last resort due to their awful conditions and the stigma of dependence.

Sharp variations existed by class and by family. Wealthy families, for instance, might hire servants to support family members with disabilities, or they might hide relatives with intellectual or mental disabilities if they chose.

Enlightenment philosophies heavily influenced American revolutionaries, like Ben Franklin, Thomas Jefferson, and James Madison. The Enlightenment ideals of reason and democracy focused attention on the "problems" of intellectual and mental disabilities, and some states restricted the rights to contract, marry, and vote (Carey, 2009; Wickham, 2001).

The shift in Europe toward the identification, treatment, and education of people with disabilities spread to America. The first American hospital—founded in 1752 in Philadelphia—included a wing for people with mental illness, and hospitals and wards specifically for mentally ill patients cropped up in several states. In 1817, Thomas Gallaudet cofounded the American School for the Deaf in Connecticut, and in 1829 Samuel Howe established the first American school for the blind. As in Europe, people with blindness and deafness came to be seen as educable and therefore as possible citizens, whereas those with mental and intellectual disabilities were seen as less amenable to transformation and therefore as burdens.

Despite the Enlightenment ideal of reason, many colonists were strongly religious. Puritan leaders Increase Mather and his son Cotton Mather preached that disability was the work of Satan, and they fostered an environment in which dissident, odd, and mentally ill women faced accusations of witchcraft (Hinshaw, 2007). As in Europe, people with intellectual and mental disabilities were widely seen by Protestants as incapable of attaining salvation (Yong, 2007).

PHOTO 3.4 Women who were aging, disabled, and perceived as deviant were especially vulnerable during the Salem witch trials

Despite dramatic rhetoric linking disability to sinfulness, disability in everyday life usually carried little stigma (Trent, 1994). For example, historian Penny Richards (2004) documents that in the mid-19th century, despite his intellectual disability, Thomas Cameron held a job, carried out household responsibilities, attended social events, and voted. Similarly, despite his 1885 adjudication as incompetent, William Littlepage served in the Confederate army, married, fathered children, and worked on his farm although he did not manage the finances of it (Carey, 2009).

Thomas Cameron and William Littlepage benefited, though, from their race and class; both were White men with families that owned land and provided support. For others, disability led more directly to exclusion (Baynton, 2001). The science of the day declared women to be intellectually inferior, even suggesting that higher education impaired their mental and reproductive capacities. This association with inferior mental and intellectual functioning (i.e., disability) was used to deny women the rights to vote and own property (Baynton, 2001; Nielsen, 2012).

Racist ideologies presented Africans as uniquely without reason, intellect, or morality (Barclay, 2021; Field, 2017). Slavery was portrayed by its proponents as a benevolent management system which offered savages opportunities to be productive and avoid the trappings of their own evil inclinations. Slave resistance was interpreted by White slave owners as mental illness. American physician Samuel Cartwright famously created the diagnosis of **drapetomania** to diagnose the rebellious act of slave escape as mental illness, and freedom was said to lead to mental illness for African Americans. Of course, slaves understood disability very differently. They recognized that disability resulted from the brutality of slavery—such as the violence of capture, the voyage, forced labor, harsh punishments, mental trauma, and rape (Barclay, 2014). Table 3.6 summarizes the role of social structure in early America.

TABLE 3.6 Social Structure in Early America

Economy	Largely agricultural with slave labor, leading to very different disability experiences by race.
Religion/Philosophy	Many communities were highly religious. Protestantism fostered alarm regarding intellectual and mental disabilities but also charity and care; The Enlightenment focused attention on reason and the lack of it.
Politics/Law	The early stages of democracy led to disability laws related to voting, policy and pensions, and used disability to justify the exclusion of women, African Americans, and others from democracy.
Family	The family continued to play a central role in providing care.
Medicine	Medical knowledge grew, but treatments remained largely ineffective.

Colonial Caribbean

After Columbus's voyage to America in 1492, Spain began claiming territories in the Caribbean, as well as South and Central America. Covetous of Spain's financial and military advantage, the Dutch, British, and French competed for territory. To focus on British colonies in the Caribbean, Britain colonized Bermuda (1612), St. Kitts (1623), Barbados (1627), and Jamaica (1655). Colonization brought disease and war, decimating much of the islands' indigenous populations. The English seized the islands to establish extensive sugar plantations, and they shipped in millions of slaves to work the plantations. As seen in America, racist ideologies depicted Africans as intellectually and mentally deficient. Black skin and disability were said to constitute unnatural signs of an offense against the Christian god (Kennedy & Newton, 2016). Whereas early America had a diverse economy which included slavery, the economy of British Caribbean colonies relied almost exclusively on slave labor. Hence, the centrality of inequality and exploitation, and their relationship to disability, was even starker in the Caribbean.

The Caribbean economy was an agricultural slave economy that operated as an industrial economy, a "synthesis of field and factory" (Mintz, 1985, p. 46) driven by production and profit. Agricultural production was not rooted in family economy, did not provide local subsistence or family flexibility in terms of work, and eradicated families' capacity to integrate people with disabilities. Production revolved around profit; owners reaped the profit, while slaves earned no wages and received no access to the product (sugar) (Mintz, 1985). Without wages or political freedom, enslaved people could not care adequately for their own family members, and local populations could not invest in local businesses, diversify the economy, or build a political system that provided care and benefits to its population. Not only were slaves deprived of money, but British ownership meant that most money left the country. As such, almost no investment was made in Caribbean infrastructure or economic development beyond what was needed for the plantation economy.

Disability was part and parcel of the plantation system, and disablement and health care were each calculated in terms of cost and benefits for plantation owners (Daen, 2017; Kennedy & Newton, 2016). Jamaican plantation owners, for example, kept slave rosters which included three categories of ability/disability—able, under cure, and disabled (Daen, 2017). Many of the slaves "under cure" required care due to beatings, revealing the complex calculation by masters who balanced the loss of profit from slave disablement against the profit gained by fostering a culture of fear (Daen, 2017). Treatment was provided based on the profit motive of the owner, not as a human right or for the slave's well-being.

Public care for disability was meager and controlled by colonial administrators. Care specifically for mental illness in Jamaica began in 1819, with the addition of 12 cells for "maniacal patients" to the public hospital at Kingston. Almost immediately, reports indicated overcrowded and filthy conditions, abusive treatment, the rampant spread of disease, and a high patient mortality rate (Jemmott, 2013; Jones, 2008). Disability studies scholar Shaun Grech argues that this history of colonization, racism, and disablement continues to impact the Caribbean to the present day, explaining the high percentage of people with disabilities living in the poorest countries of the global South in abject poverty (Grech, 2012). Table 3.7 summarizes the role of social structure in the colonial Caribbean.

TABLE 3.7 Social Structure in Colonial Caribbean

Economy	Agricultural industrial production using slave labor caused disability, defined slaves as biologically inferior, and undermined care.
Religion	White Christian religion was used to legitimize slavery
Politics/Law	Colonial rule offered slaves no rights, and local populations received little public provision.
Family	Slavery undercut the ability of families to provide care to each other.
Medicine	Medicine was controlled by the British and given based on cost-benefit analysis.

1850–1950

The United States

At the conclusion of the American Civil War (1861–1865), America was still a primarily agricultural nation, but that changed quickly. Railways, cars, and highways opened opportunities for transporting goods, new inventions spurred demand, and factories produced goods cheaply and efficiently. Simultaneously, America's population grew rapidly (23 million people in 1850, 76 million in 1900 and 151 million by 1950) and urbanized (the urban population equaled 15% of the population in 1850, 40% by 1900, and 64% by 1950) to radically reshape the everyday life of Americans.

Rather than family economies rooted in tight-knit communities, increasingly Americans lived in cities, worked for and alongside strangers, and encountered a new level of racial, national, and religious diversity. Adding to this social turbulence, traditional inequalities were being challenged. The Civil War emancipated slaves, but new forms of discrimination took hold. Women gained suffrage in 1920, and the car, birth control, access to higher education, and the culture of the roaring twenties ushered in a new era of opportunity and sexual liberation for women.

Also signaling a major change, the medical profession gained greater prestige (Abbott, 1988; Freidson, 1970). Advances in medical knowledge, such as germ theory, the discovery of vaccinations, and knowledge about sanitation, dramatically improved success rates. In 1847, physicians formed the American Medical Association (AMA), and over the next several decades the AMA gained control of medical accreditation and secured the ideological dominance of Western medicine. **Western medicine** treated the body like a machine with independent parts and trained doctors to specialize in specific parts, rather than offering a holistic view of body, mind, and spirit. It celebrated medical intervention via drugs and surgery, creating a "magic bullet" approach to health. By 1950, physicians were among the highest paid and most respected of the professions.

The massive social changes of the era intertwined with medicalization to transform the understanding and treatment of disability (Rothman, 1971; Trent, 1994). We see this effect in many of the most significant social trends of the era, including eugenics, institutionalization, rehabilitation, and education.

Francis Galton coined the term **eugenics** to refer to the science of population improvement through selective breeding. Eugenicists sought to identify hereditary traits and use this knowledge to encourage breeding of the fit and prevent breeding by the unfit (Garland-Thomson, 2015; Snyder & Mitchell, 2006). Eugenicists argued that the wealthy White Anglo class had proven its inherent biological "fitness" and should be encouraged to breed. In contrast, they argued that the unfit bred recklessly, inundated the nation via unchecked immigration, and threatened to overwhelm the nation with "defectives" (Kline, 2005). Their argument blamed widespread social problems, such as growing poverty, crime, and social conflict, on the "unfit." Laid out by Harry Laughlin (1922, p. 521), the unfit included:

(1) feeble-minded; (2) insane (including the psychopathic); (3) criminalistic (including the delinquent and the wayward); (4) epileptic; (5) inebriate (including drug habitués); (6) diseased (including the tuberculous, the syphilitic, the leperous, and others with chronic, infectious and legally segregable diseases); (7) blind (including those with seriously impaired vision); (8) deaf (including those with seriously impaired hearing); (9) deformed (including the crippled); and (10) dependent (including orphans, ne're-do-wells, the homeless, tramps and paupers).

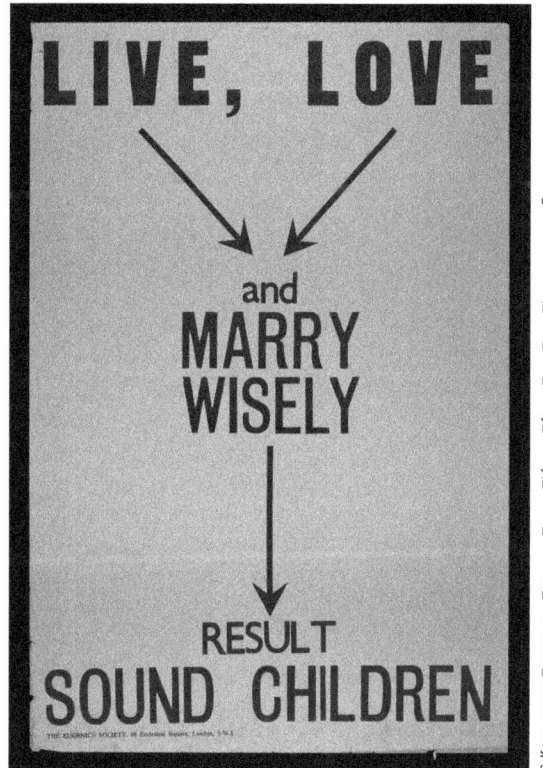

PHOTO 3.5
A Eugenics Society Poster (1930s)

These categories were deeply gendered and racialized. Racial and ethnic minorities were far more likely to be labeled as insane, feebleminded, or criminal. Women's sexual deviance, such as sex out of wedlock or sexual relations across the races, was used as proof of their feeblemindedness and mental illness (Rembis, 2011; Stern, 2016).

In response to the perceived threat of the unfit, eugenicists advocated institutionalization and sterilization. They presented these policies of social control as medical "treatments." Institutional populations grew at an astounding rate. For mental hospitals, from 1890 to 1910 the institutional population grew from approximately 74,000 to 187,000 residents (Braddock & Parish, 2001). For people with intellectual disabilities, from 1904 to 1910, the institutionalized population grew 44.5% and from 1910 to 1923, it increased another 107.2% (Carey, 2009). Institutions, though, typically failed to cure their patients or successfully transition them to self-supporting lives. Increasingly, they offered primarily long-term custodial care, warehousing those considered undesirable and dependent (Ladd-Taylor, 2017; Trent, 1994). In institutions, overcrowding swelled, conditions worsened, treatment and education declined, and abuse and neglect became rampant (Burghardt, 2018; Reaume, 2009; Rossiter & Rinaldi, 2018).

Compulsory sterilization served as another social control mechanism. Between 1907 and 1930, over 60,000 people were sterilized without their consent (Reilly, 1991). Eugenicists praised sterilization as a means by which to prevent the intergenerational spread of disability while also lessening the potential burden of parenthood on people with disabilities. In reality, most disability was not genetic, and decisions about sterilization typically had far more to do with the community's fear of economic dependence and sexual deviance (Ladd-Taylor, 2017). While institutionalization and sterilization were said to halt the internal spread of disability, eugenicists also supported immigration restrictions for non-Western Europeans, to prevent entry to a wide range of people perceived as mentally or physically unfit or likely to become a "public charge" (Dolmage, 2018; Molina, 2006).

Institutionalization, sterilization, and immigration restrictions fit within the broader agenda of the Progressive Era. During the progressive era, Americans embraced the idea that the state could implement social reforms to improve society (Trent, 2013). Education, in particular, seemed to offer a path to improve individuals and society. In this context, special education for children with disabilities rapidly grew, but from the outset it had sharply conflicting goals. On the one hand, special education sought to educate those who could become productive members of society. Education for deaf and blind children increased, and Gallaudet University became the first university for deaf students. On the other hand, special education became a mechanism by which to identify "defective" children and divert them into poorly resourced classes/schools or exclude them from public education altogether, creating a massive system of educational segregation. As explained by the director of child guidance for the Board of Education in Newark in 1928, "The public schools are training for citizenship, and a child who, because of very poor learning ability, will never be self-supporting or able to participate in civic life is an institutional, and not a public school, problem" (Robinson, 1928, pp. 367–368). Poor and minority children were more likely to have their diagnosis used to justify their exclusion.

Resources were also channeled into medical rehabilitation, encouraged by the pressing needs of disabled veterans returning home from World Wars I and II. In contrast to institutionalization, rehabilitation offered many people effective treatments in the community and enabled their return to work and other valued roles. It also had its downsides. Rehabilitation focused on those people most likely to become employable, especially White men with mild physical disabilities. Furthermore, it relied on a medical model of disability that overlooked issues of discrimination. People with disabilities, organizing into the League of the Physically Handicapped (established 1935) and the American Federation of the Physically Handicapped (1940), explained that the high rates of unemployment of people with disabilities were caused by discrimination and inaccessibility (Jennings, 2016). Despite their activism, the state consistently saw disability as a *medical* problem needing cure and treatment. Those who did not attain sufficient cure were marked as "unemployable" and channeled into the expanding system of state benefits provided through Social Security.

In popular culture, disability increasingly became associated with danger and deviance, manifesting in the ugly laws, the freak show, and, ironically, charitable campaigns. In 1867, San Francisco passed its **"ugly law,"** banning people with visible deformities from public spaces, and other cities followed suit (Schweik, 2009). Whereas the ugly laws tried to hide disability, freak shows put it on display. **Freak shows** presented a wide assortment of people—including people with unique physical features (conjoined twins, dwarfs), people of varied nationalities and ethnicities (often portrayed as savages or exotically tribal), and people with gender-bending personas (e.g., bearded women, intersex people)—as exhibits for entertainment. Both the ugly laws and the freak shows reinforced the social categories of "normal" and "abnormal," placing people with disabilities squarely in the abnormal category (Bogdan, 1990; Garland-Thomson, 1996).

Charity relied on another stereotypical response—pity for the deserving poor. **Poster child campaigns** spread, depicting cute, helpless children who, with the gift of charity, could access medical treatment and thereby cure (Longmore, 2016). These fundraising efforts encouraged research and opened access to rehabilitation, treatment, and services. However, they also portrayed disabled life as pitiable, left people with disabilities dependent on the whims of others, and fueled a charity industry in which profits flowed largely to people without disabilities rather than empowering people with disabilities (Longmore, 2016). Furthermore, charity divided people with disabilities between deserving and undeserving, channeling money to cute, White, middle-class children with physical and later intellectual disabilities while overlooking adults with disabilities, people with mental disabilities, and minorities with disabilities.

World War II was a turning point for America in many ways. World War II led to more veterans returning home with disabilities than any war previously. Fighting against the Nazis—who targeted the Jewish community, people with disabilities, people deemed sexual deviants, Romani, and others for extermination and medical experimental—exposed the injustice of America's own eugenic policies. The fight for freedom and democracy overseas emboldened marginalized populations to fight against oppression at home. The post-war economy also boomed, and the size, budget, and programs of the government grew. Americans, including Americans with disabilities and their family members, began organizing in greater numbers than ever before to fight for rights and resources. Table 3.8 summarizes the role of social structure in America during 1850–1950.

PHOTO 3.6
Conjoined twins Daisy and Violet Hilton (1927)

India

Liberated from colonial rule in 1776, the United States developed a vibrant economy and emerged as a world leader. In contrast, India experienced a later period of British colonization. Direct British rule began in 1858 and lasted until

TABLE 3.8 Social Structure in America, 1850–1950

Economy	Industrial assembly lines led to industrial accidents and excluded atypical bodies/minds. Employment based on profit motive decreased integration.
Religion/Philosophy	Science, and pseudoscience like eugenics, came to dominate ideas about disability. Eugenics blamed people with disabilities, the poor, and other marginalized groups for social ills.
Medicine	Physicians gained prestige and developed increasingly effective treatments, but the medicalization of disability also enabled social control and segregation.
Politics/Law	State disability infrastructure grew, including disability benefits, special education, rehabilitation, and systems of social control (e.g., ugly laws, exclusion from public school, public institutions, sterilization). Early disability rights groups began organizing.
Family	In industrial societies, families held less control over work, education, and integration. Few community supports existed to help families, and they began to organize for change.

1947 when India was partitioned into two nations—a Hindu-majority India and Muslim-majority Pakistan. Colonial rule stunted India's economic development in this era and altered its views of and responses to disability.

Hinduism offered mixed understandings of and responses to disability. It teaches the ethics of compassion, charity, and respect for elders (Narayan, 2004). Alternatively, the idea of karma could be used to assert that disability is a punishment for previous wrongdoings, and Hinduism's focus on social order may present disability as a potential threat (Anand, 2013). In traditional Indian society, the values of family, community, harmony, and charity meant that many people with disabilities were often integrated and supported in their families and communities, but exclusion and harm were also very possible. The lines between inclusion and exclusion, though, can be hard for those looking through a Western lens to discern (Anand, 2013). Begging, for instance, is a long-standing tradition in Indian culture rooted in the value of charity, and people with physical differences were seen as legitimate beggars. This practice of charity offered financial support and potentially acknowledged the beggar's humanity, although Westerners tend to view begging as a form of humiliation and exclusion.

Many cultures do not share a concept of disability similar to the Western view, and this is true for India in this time period. Shilpaa Anand's (2015) research offers a compelling example of the challenge of researching "disability" in non-Western contexts. While under colonial rule, smallpox was endemic in parts of India, leading to high rates of blindness and disfigurement, Western medicine considers smallpox a disabling disease. In contrast, some Indian communities associated the same event with the goddess **Sitala**, the goddess of sores, pustules, and diseases who, according to believers, would visit the village and bring either wrath or auspicious tidings. Her arrival could be due to different reasons, and interpretations of events led to different rituals. Blindness resulting from Sitala could be understood as a punishment or a blessing, depending on the local interpretation. She might cause blindness, cure it, or both. This dynamic local interpretation differs significantly both from Western medical views of viral disease and from typical Western religious views of disability as demon possession, witchcraft, or a challenge from god (Anand, 2015).

Regardless of the views of Indians, British colonizers imposed their own view of disability. For the British, Indians were inherently disabled, seen as biologically and mentally inferior (Kalyanpur, 2015). Moreover, the British blamed Indian "backwardness" (e.g., superstitious religious beliefs and poor parenting) for the high rate of disabilities (Nair, 2017). Colonial administrators and missionaries imposed Western views of disabilities, building residential schools for Indian children with disabilities and asylums for people with intellectual and mental disabilities, cutting Indians with disabilities off from their traditional systems of community support, and creating new forms of stigma (Kalyanpur, 2015; Miles, 2015). Colonizers also discouraged begging, which was the economic livelihood of many disabled people and their families (Nair, 2017).

Meanwhile, colonization stunted India's economic growth, and vast poverty led to and exacerbated disablement. The British used India for agricultural production, shipping raw materials back to England for industrial production, selling manufactured goods back to India, and retaining the profits. Through the time of British rule in India, Indian workers saw no increase in per capita income (McQuade, 2017). Most telling perhaps, from 1872 to 1921, Indian life expectancy dropped by 20% (McQuade, 2017). Meanwhile, the British economy industrialized, and its workers saw gains in income and life expectancy.

India today has a very complex economy but still has areas of extreme poverty. Many of India's disabled people struggle for basic survival. According to India's 2011 Census, 27% of disabled children ages 5–19 never attended school. Among the total disabled population, 45% were illiterate. Only 36% of the disabled population was employed. Girls were 14 percentage points less likely to have any schooling compared to boys, and women were 24 percentage points less likely to be employed than men (Disabled Persons in India, 2016). The high levels of poverty and disablement today are rooted in their colonial history. Table 3.9 summarizes the role of social structure in colonial India.

TABLE 3.9 Social Structure in Colonial India

Economy	Colonial agriculture for export and limiting investment in infrastructure led to underdevelopment and poverty, increasing disability and decreasing services.
Religion/Philosophy	Hinduism is a prominent influence; British Christianity was used to support a belief in the superiority of White Europeans.
Politics/Law	Colonial rule conferred minimal health care or infrastructural support, while disempowering Indians.
Families	Family life was highly valued, but poverty and disempowerment undercut the ability of families to provide care.
Medicine	Colonial rulers imposed Western views of disease and institutionalization regardless of traditional Indian practices.

1950 to the Present Day

The United States

By 1950, American disability policy focused on rehabilitation and/or segregation (Pelka, 2012). Institutionalization for people with mental illness in psychiatric hospitals peaked around 1955, with approximately 558,000 residents of public psychiatric hospitals. For people with intellectual disabilities, institutionalization peaked in 1969 with 190,000 residents of public institutions. In the mid-1960s, at least one million children with disabilities were denied public education due to disabilities. Stigma remained intense and few community services existed, leaving families to provide care or abandon their family members to institutions.

Disability activism blossomed in the latter half of the twentieth century (Fleischer & Zames, 2011). Motivated by post–World War II optimism and the successes of other activist movements of the 1960s, and deeply frustrated by wretched institutional conditions and the vast amounts of money wasted on ineffective institutional care, activists with disabilities and parents worked to challenge the institutional system. They demanded rights and community services, including public education, supported residences and worksites, and access to the public services and opportunities enjoyed by nondisabled citizens (Stroman, 2003).

The courts proved to be a particularly effective strategy for activists. In the landmark case, the 1971 Pennsylvania Association for Retarded Children (PARC) vs. Pennsylvania, the court required the state of Pennsylvania to provide public education to all children with disabilities. A series of similar lawsuits quickly led Congress to pass The Education for All Handicapped Children Act of 1975 (now the Individuals with Disabilities Education Act (IDEA)), guaranteeing all disabled children the right to a free and appropriate public education. This success was followed closely by lawsuits seeking institutional reform and/or closure. These cases encouraged the movement toward deinstitutionalization and the creation of community services (Carey, 2009).

Early success emboldened activists. Historically, disability activism was organized according to distinct impairment groups, such as the National Association of the Deaf (formed 1880), the National Federation of the Blind (1940), and the Paralyzed Veterans of America (1946). Increasingly though, people with disabilities recognized common concerns and banded together in groups like Disabled in Action (1970) and ADAPT (1983) (Nielsen, 2012; Scotch, 1998; Switzer, 2003). Disabled leaders formed the American Coalition of Citizens with Disabilities (1974) to function as a voice of people with disabilities in Washington DC's policy making. New organizations also arose for populations that previously had not had a political voice. In the 1970s, psychiatric survivors organized groups like the Insane Liberation Front and the Mental Patients' Liberation Project. In 1990, activists with intellectual disability formed the national organization Self-Advocates Becoming Empowered, and in 2006 autistic activists established the Autistic Self Advocacy Network.

People with disabilities demanded rights and access, instead of charity and treatment. Using the social model, they argued that their poverty and exclusion resulted from discrimination—not their biology—and that society needed to change. They demanded empowerment, or, in other words, control over the decisions, policies, funding, and services that affected them, summed up in the mantra "Nothing About Us Without Us" (Charlton, 2000; Pelka, 2012). These themes resonate through the major activism of the era, such as the Independent Living Movement, the Section 504 sit-ins, and activism to secure the passage of the ADA.

The Independent Living Movement is a social movement focused on ensuring the rights, supports, and access for people with disabilities to control their own lives. It began in 1960s Berkeley, California when a group of disabled college students and other adults organized a system of collaborative peer support for independent living, such as assistance finding accessible housing, accessible transportation, and wheelchair repair. In 1972 the Berkeley Center for Independent Living (CIL) opened, operating on the "then radical notion" that people with disabilities should exercise control over their own lives and that such control required the provision of support, advocacy, and information (Pelka, 2012, p. 198). The CIL ensured that its leadership remained in the hands of people with disabilities (OToole, 2015; Pelka, 2012). There are now over 400 CILs nationwide.

In Washington DC, Congressional staffers working on the federal 1973 Vocational Rehabilitation Act included an antidiscrimination statement—called **Section 504**—with wording similar to the 1964 Civil Rights Act: "No otherwise qualified handicapped individual in the United States... shall, solely by reason of his handicap, be excluded from participation in, be denied the benefits of, or be subjected to discrimination under any program or activity receiving federal assistance." Activists like Frank Bowe of the American Coalition of Citizens with Disabilities (ACCD) believed that this new law could dramatically alter the civil rights of people with disabilities (Pelka, 2012; Scotch, 1984). However, the law had no formal regulations to guide its implementation, rendering it ineffective.

Five years later, regulations still had not been passed. Activists organized the **504 sit-ins** to protest. Hundreds of people with disabilities descended and occupied the 10 regional offices of the Department of Health, Education and Welfare (HEW). Most left after only a single night, but demonstrators in San Francisco stayed for 25 days and nights. When the Carter administration finally signed the regulations, the activists left in victory. The 504 sit-ins fundamentally changed the national perception of people with disabilities, from charity recipients to formidable activists. The sit-ins transformed the identities of participants as well (Fleischer & Zames, 2011; OToole, 2015). Many of the demonstrators had never engaged in protest, and this act of communal defiance strengthened their sense of empowerment and their bonds to each other. Activist Kitty Cone describes, "it was the public birth of the disability civil rights movement. People's image of themselves changed, and people felt so proud of themselves" (quoted in Pelka, 2012, p. 282).

Although decentralized, fragmented, and largely unknown to the American public, the disability rights movement achieved many political successes (Switzer, 2003), described in greater length in Chapter 7. The pinnacle achievement was **The Americans with Disabilities Act of 1990** (ADA), which prohibits discrimination against people with disabilities in employment, public services, public transportation, and telecommunications. In just a few decades, activists had radically transformed the legal and policy framework for disability (Davis, 2015). Although many changes occurred slowly, the numbers of people in institutions declined, access to education increased, ramps and other access features were added, and people with disabilities became a more visible part of American society. These changes had psychological effects as well, fostering the belief that people with disabilities were rightful citizens and participants in society, deserving of respect and inclusion.

Despite the many positive changes, vast challenges continue to exist for people with disabilities. Unemployment and poverty continue unabated; indeed, since the passage of the ADA there has been no consistent decrease in the employment gap between people with and without disabilities (Maroto & Pettinicchio, 2015). Without sufficient income, many people cannot afford personal assistance, services, or accessible equipment. Many people with disabilities fall through the cracks of the American health care system, especially people with mental illness and minorities. While many institutions have closed, many people with disabilities still are placed in large-scale, segregated residential and service settings. Smaller service settings like group homes too often have an institutional structure, in which professionals clearly retain power, people with disabilities exercise little power, and cost-efficiency reigns. Educational systems have been slow to embrace inclusion. The rates of imprisonment for people with disabilities is also shockingly high; more people with mental health diagnosis are imprisoned today than institutionalized in psychiatric hospitals at their peak (Rembis, 2014). The rights which seemed to have been already secured by laws are constantly threatened, especially from politicians seeking to reduce public expenditures on social welfare.

Meanwhile, the rate of disability remains high in America. Facing rising expectations and hypercompetitive environments, children are diagnosed with learning and mental disabilities at higher rates than ever before. Across the lifespan, the rate of mental health diagnoses and use of prescription medicine have skyrocketed. Modern warfare continues to produce disability, especially amputations, traumatic brain injuries, and mental health disabilities. Ironically, the success of medicine itself creates disability as people who would not have survived in the past (e.g., premature babies, people with serious injuries, people aging with multiple illnesses) now live longer but with disabilities.

Inequality continues to shape the disability experience in America. For example, Native Americans and African Americans experience disproportionately high rates of disability, less access to services and civil rights, and lower survival rates. Women with disabilities earn less than men with disabilities, marry less often, and have lower rates of life satisfaction. Table 3.10 summarizes the social structure in the United States 1950 to the present day.

TABLE 3.10 Social Structure in the United States 1950 to the Present Day

Economy	Capitalism, driven by profit, often excludes those deemed less productive.
Religion/Philosophy	Dominant values of materialism, intellect, beauty, and youth present challenges for people with disabilities. Disabled activists introduced the social model and demanded rights.
Politics/Law	Widespread activism led to the passage of many disability rights laws, but, due to limited enforcement and funding, rights are always under threat.
Family	Families still are the primary source of care and support, but they now have little power over education, work, service system, or community infrastructure.
Medicine	The medical model continues to dominate disability policy, but it has been challenged by the social model. Diagnosis and medical intervention continue to be very common, leading to positive and negative effects.

Brazil

As a final comparison, we will look at Brazil 1950 to the present. Through this case, we can see the effects of globalization on Brazil's disability policy, as well as the influence of Brazil's unique local culture and politics.

To offer a very brief political history, Brazil was colonized by Portugal in the 15th century and gained independence in 1822. Once self-governing, Brazil shifted between democratic and authoritarian regimes. The most recent dictatorship, the Pinochet regime, lasted from 1964 to 1985. Through the 1980s, Brazil slowly re-democratized, holding open democratic elections in 1985 and ratifying a new Constitution focused on civil and human rights in 1988. With the election of Jair Bolsanaro in January 2019, some fear a return to authoritarian rule.

Turning to disability, Brazil's approach to disability was heavily influenced by increasing **globalization**—the influence of individuals, companies, and governments across national and cultural borders. Brazilians imported many diagnoses, treatments, and approaches from the United States and Europe, including eugenics, institutionalization, and segregated special education (Block & Fátima, 2014). In Brazil, stigma and the social isolation of people with disabilities discouraged disability activism, and political repression made activism a dangerous endeavor. Still, though, people found ways to resist. Psychiatrist Nise de Silveira, for example, challenged the brutality of institutionalization, advocated for community-based services, and founded a clinic for former institutional patients where they could engage in healing through positive activities like art therapy. Parents, especially mothers, began organizing to increase services for children with intellectual disabilities and autism. These mothers tended to be politically connected (e.g., wives of generals), were seen as politically nonthreatening, and could operate within the confines of authoritarianism (Block & Fátima, 2014; Bregain, 2013).

In the 1970s and 1980s, health and disability activism blossomed, influenced by global disability rights movements but also by Brazil's unique culture and context. One of Brazil's significant activist organizations, Fraternidade Cristã de Doentes e Deficientes (Christian Fraternity of the Sick and Disabled), drew on the Catholic tradition of liberation theology to fight for the liberation, inclusion, and full participation in society of the sick and disabled (Bregain, 2013). Brazil is 65% Catholic, and it has the world's largest Catholic population. Other organizations flourished as well, as people with disabilities fought for greater access to education and rehabilitation opportunities. In the 1980s, as the government worked to enact a new Constitution, activists lobbied the Constitutional Assembly and then participated in writing portions of the Constitution which specifically addressed the rights of people with disabilities. The new Constitution was ratified in 1988, the same year that the first Center for Independent Living was established in Brazil.

Over the next decades, Brazilian activists achieved remarkable legislative success, and Brazil is in some ways a legislative model for disability rights (Carvalho et al., 2014; Sátyro & Cunha, 2014). Its constitution explicitly details the civil and human rights of Brazilians with disabilities. Additional laws prohibit discrimination against people with disabilities and mandate accessibility. Brazil signed on to the **2008 United Nations Convention on the Rights of Persons with Disabilities**, an international treaty in which countries agree to uphold a broad range of human rights for people with disabilities. One hundred seventy-seven countries have signed onto this convention, but the United States has refused to participate. Brazil's 2015 Inclusion of People with Disabilities Act established legal quotas to promote inclusion, such as mandating that at least 3% of public housing be made available to people with disabilities, 2%–5% of hiring by large companies (with 50+ employees) be people with disabilities, and at least 10% of hotel rooms be accessible.

Despite these legislative victories, the situation for people with disabilities remains dire. The laws lack funding, mechanisms for implementation, and enforcement measures (Kirakosyan, 2016). Persistent poverty, inequality, and insufficient infrastructure (e.g., lack of clean water, basic health care, and safe housing) block integration and participation for most people with disabilities, except those in the upper classes. Rosangela Berman Bieler, former president of Rio's CIL, explains:

The country suffers from misery and malnutrition, as well as the lack of prevention, education, and sanitation, among other problems. In this country, where social injustice is represented by unfair distribution of income, one percent of the population is richer than all of the poor and 60% of the inhabitants earn only US $40 a week. This is why the majority of the 15 million people with disabilities in Brazil are in pitiful condition. Lacking resources and information, with survival as their main battle, they are forgotten by their families, the community and competent authorities. They are outcasts deprived of social life, dignity, and citizenship (quoted in Charlton, 2000).

In 2015, the United Nations Committee on the Rights of Persons with Disabilities recognized the significant advances made in Brazil since ratifying the Convention, but it noted with grave concern the persistent high rates of institutionalization, lack of community services, educational segregation, broad use of guardianship, and vulnerability of women and indigenous people with disabilities (United Nations, 2015). In 2018, the Human Rights Watch reported on the terrible conditions in Brazil's institutions, many of which are privately run and left unmonitored by the government (Human Rights Watch, 2018). Table 3.11 summarizes the social structure of Brazil 1950 to the present.

TABLE 3.11 Social Structure in Brazil 1950 to the Present

Economy	Its developing economy results in great economic inequality, leaving many people with disabilities without the basic necessities.
Religion/Philosophy	Catholicism is the dominant religion, influencing views of disability and activism.
Politics/Law	Political repression suppressed activism, but re-democratization and the passage of a new constitution encouraged it. Activism in Brazil has been shaped by Western disability rights activism and the United Nations.
Families	Inequality and poverty make the provision of care within families difficult.
Medicine	Imported Western ideas (e.g., diagnosis, institutionalization) shaped many responses to disability.

Conclusion

Sociologist Max Weber argued that sociologists must examine social phenomena in their historical time and place. Because humans create meaning, the meaning of any phenomenon changes due to unique interactions across social structures. Thus, sociologists do not strive simply to articulate how disability is understood in a given time and place; they also seek to determine what social structures shape that understanding. The histories in this chapter provide a window, albeit very incomplete, into understanding how structures like economy, religion/philosophy, politics and law, family, and medicine, shape understandings of and responses to disability.

KEY TERMS

504 sit-ins 65
Colonization 54
Confucianism 50
Drapetomania 56
Eugenics 59
Feudalism 49
Freak shows 61
Globalization 67
Hippocrates 47
Historical comparative analysis 44
Humanism 52
Independent Living Movement 65
Monotheistic religion 47
Polytheistic religion 45
Poster child campaigns 61
Protestant Reformation 51
Section 504 65
Sitala 62
Tabula rasa 52
The Americans with Disabilities Act of 1990 65
Twelve Tables 47
Ugly law 60
United Nations Convention on the Rights of Persons with Disabilities 67
Western medicine 58

RESOURCES

Suggested Readings

Barclay, Jennifer. 2021. *The mark of slavery: Disability, race, and gender in antebellum America*. Champaign, IL: University of Illinois Press. An examination of intersectional oppression and American slavery.

Burch, Susan, and Michael Rembis, eds. 2014. *Disability histories*. Champaign, IL: Illinois Press. An upper-level anthology of disability history.

Davis, Lennard, ed. 2018. *Beginning with disability: A primer*. New York, NY: Routledge. A reader with three short, accessible chapters on disability history, including "Disability History" by Susan Burch and Kim Nielsen, a 5-page discussion of the challenges and contributions of disability history.

Kim E. Nielsen. 2012. *A disability history of the United States*. Boston, MA: Beacon Press. A very accessible book examining American disability history.

Henri-Jacques Stiker. 1999. *A history of disability*. Ann Arbor, MI: University of Michigan. A historical analysis from ancient to modern times.

Online Resources

Disability History Museum. Available at https://www.disabilitymuseum.org/dhm/index.html. Hosts a range of online exhibits and documents, focusing on US disability history including Helen Keller, institutionalization, and sign language.

Online Timeline. *Parallels in time: A history of developmental disabilities*. Minnesota Council on Developmental Disabilities. Available at http://mn.gov/mnddc/parallels/.

Videos and Films

"*Crip Camp: A Disability Revolution.*" 2020. A documentary film directed, written and co-produced by Nicole Newnham and James LeBrecht, recounting a liberating summer camp for teens with disabilities and the dawning of the Disability Rights Movement (1 hour 48 minutes).

"*Lives Worth Living.*" 2011. A documentary on the disability rights movement in the United States, focusing on activism leading to the Americans with Disabilities Act (60 minutes).

"*Suffer the Little Children.*" 1968. A news expose on Pennhurst State School and Hospital in Pennsylvania. Aired in 1968, it played a key role in building momentum for deinstitutionalization (50 minutes).

ACTIVITIES

1. **Disability in time and place**
   Individually or in groups, students select a country and era, preferably one not discussed in the chapter. Write and/or present on understandings of disability and an analysis of what social factors shaped that understanding.

2. **Considering social structure**
   As a briefer class exercise, divide students into groups and assign each group a social structure or two (e.g., economy, religion/philosophy). Students should review the chapter and consider how their selected social structure varies by time and place. Then, consider how the variations in one's social structure correlate with changing understandings of and/or response to disability.

The Complex Experience of Disability

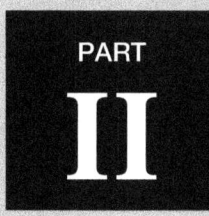

PART II

CHAPTER 4

Inequality and Ableism

Learning Outcomes

4.1 Explain how disability and inequality may manifest differently in caste and class societies.

4.2 Define the minority model as applied to people with disabilities.

4.3 Describe ableism and its intersections with other systems of oppression.

4.4 Examine ableism as it manifests through prejudice, discrimination, and institutional ableism.

4.5 Evaluate the role of inaccessibility in maintaining inequality.

4.6 Identify the connections between ableism, segregation, invisibility, and violence.

Chapter Synopsis

In sociology, a minority group is one that experiences profound and long-term disadvantage in relation to a majority group who exercises greater power and holds more resources. The minority model of disability asserts that people with disabilities are a minority group who experience social disadvantage, enforced via prejudice, discrimination, and structural inequalities. This chapter documents stratification and inequality, defines ableism, and begins to explore the ways that ableism leads to and perpetuates inequality through prejudice, individual discrimination, and institutional discrimination.

Stratification Systems: Caste Versus Class

When thinking about inequality, students often think about prejudice and discrimination as they occur on an individual level. We want to begin, though, by thinking about inequality on a macro, societal level. Every society has a range of resources, including those that are necessary for survival (e.g., food, housing, and health care) and those that are more broadly valued in the culture (e.g., art, technology, access to particular rituals, access to particular clothing and food). Every society also creates a **stratification system**—the ways in which a society groups and ranks people within a social hierarchy, so that groups have systematically different access to resources. Associated with the stratification system, belief systems then serve to justify inequality.

Stratification systems are characteristics of societies, not individuals. Two of the most common types of stratification are caste and class systems. The differentiation between caste and class focuses on two factors: (a) whether one's status is ascribed (one is born into it) or achieved (one earns it) and (b) the degree of social mobility. Each system has different ways of manifesting inequality, and disability potentially operates differently in each system.

A **caste system** is a stratification system in which one's social position is assigned at birth (an ascribed status) and there is very little social mobility. The status one is born into remains the same through life—e.g., if one is born into a farming family, one dies in a farming family. India's historical caste system offers an example. In this system, people were born into one of following castes: Brahmin (the highest caste, religious leaders), Kshatriyas (political elites and warriors), Vaishyas (artisans, tradespeople, and farmers), Shudras (servants), and those who were born outside of the caste system (the lowest status) as an "untouchable." Other societies also have castes or partial caste systems. Societies with royalty, landed aristocracy, and peasants/serfs, such as feudal Europe and feudal Japan, as well as slave societies and highly racialized societies, have strong caste characteristics (Wilkerson, 2020).

In caste systems, disability may have less influence on one's life chances than in class societies. Since one's position in the stratification system is determined by one's family's social position at birth, disability may hinder or encourage success in a particular caste, but it probably does not determine one's placement in a particular caste. As noted in Chapter 3, some royalty and nobility had impairments (e.g., blindness, madness, scoliosis) but were not deprived of the status accorded to them by birth.

In fact, to the extent that birth in a high caste ensured the privilege of living off the work of others (e.g., peasants or serfs), physical ability may have irrelevant in some ways. What one might see as disablement today might have been understood as a status symbol among elites to highlight their freedom from labor. For example, the Chinese practice of foot-binding—a painful practice meant to produce tiny, delicate feet for women which also hindered their mobility—began in Chinese royal courts. Elite women were prized for their beauty, and being carried rather than walking reinforced their prestige. The corset, which cinches the waist, restricts activity, and misshapes the ribs, similarly became fashionable in European royal courts among women of leisure. Thus, disabling fashion prominently displayed one's wealth, status, and freedom from labor.

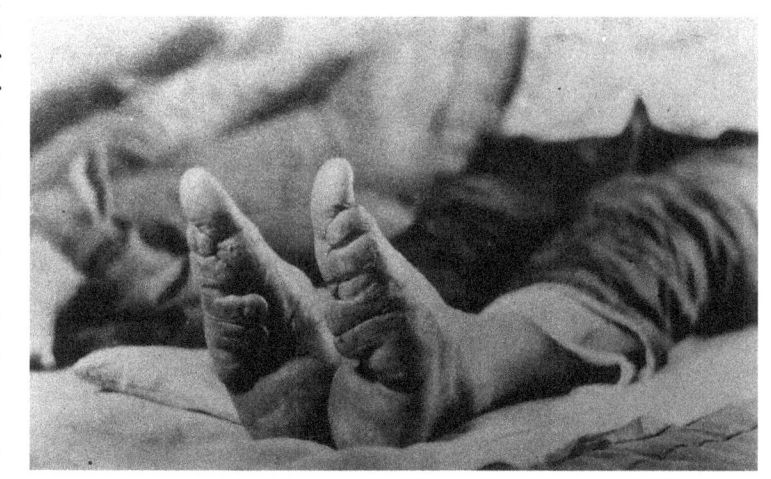

For those in the lower castes, disability was common and hardly warranted attention. The inability to work due to disability might have devastating consequences for peasants, but families worked together to provide as best they could

PHOTO 4.1
Effects of Foot Binding

Credit: "Feet of a Chinese woman in an isolation hospital in Mauritius" by For. Arfo. (between 1900–1999). Obtained from Wellcome Collection. https://wellcome-collection.org/works/zhvjpvnk

manage. In contrast with the privileged castes, for those in the lower castes particular forms of disablement may have been imposed on them by elites to reinforce their lower caste standing and ensure their work. For example, foot-binding among poor Chinese women served, not to demonstrate their leisurely lives, but to ensure their subjugation and long hours toiling at seated work such as weaving and sewing (Bossen & Gates, 2017). Slave owners purposefully disabled slaves in ways that reduced the risk of their escape and hindered their intellectual development, while retaining the slave's labor potential (Daen, 2017). Thus, similar physical conditions occurred for different reasons and meant different things for different castes, shaped by the status conferred at birth.

A **class system**, in contrast to a caste system, is a stratification system that allows social mobility across economic positions (i.e., people may gain or lose jobs, income, and wealth) and confers status based on achievement. In a class system, one must compete and earn one's social position through talent, skill, or luck. Class systems are ideologically connected to **meritocracy**, an ideology that suggests that one's social position should be based on one's earned achievements. In a pure class system, one only has access to rewards achieved through one's own work.

For some in a class system, their talents may bring success regardless of disability. For example, physicist Stephen Hawking, author of *A Brief History of Time*, achieved international praise for his intellectual prowess. The automated voice of his augmented speech device, which he began using after losing his voice due to Lou Gehrig's disease, became a popular symbol of his brilliance. Ray Charles and Stevie Wonder, iconic African American, blind musicians, each rose to fame and fortune due to their musical talents. Others may rise to prominence by bringing their disability to the fore. Dancer Alice Sheppard and artist Riva Lehrer, for example, have been pioneers in the creation of disability culture, and their success in their respective fields is tied to their innovations in incorporating diverse bodies into dance and art. Their celebration of disability is central to their success.

PHOTO 4.2
Musician Ray Charles

Credit: "Photo of Ray Charles in one of his classic poses at the piano." By Maurice Seymour (1969). Obtained from Wikimedia Commons. https://commons.wikimedia.org/wiki/File:Ray_Charles_classic_piano_pose.jpg

Disability, though, may greatly disadvantage one in a class system. First, impairments may hinder one's abilities to compete in particular ways, and class systems are often fiercely competitive. For example, intellectual or learning disabilities may hinder one's educational success, especially in societies with narrow definitions of educational success and a focus on standardization, which then leads to jobs with lower incomes; physical and sensory disabilities may limit participation in certain manual occupations, especially in the absence of accommodations. Second, ideologies of individualism and meritocracy common in class systems may justify ignoring, or even creating, inaccessible environments that reduce access to opportunities. If everyone competes for their own resources, there is little individual incentive to ensure equal access. Rather, competition may encourage attempts to block or undercut access for others. Therefore, class societies may not prioritize creating accessible schools and workplaces. Third, although theoretically class systems *should* be based on meritocracy, no system is pure. Instead, discrimination based on disability and other intersecting marginalized identities influences one's social position and reduces access to opportunities regardless of one's actual skills and merit.

Although modern America has some characteristics of a class system, aspects of caste also remain. The economic status one is born into, as well as one's gender and race, matter. Children with disabilities are more likely to live in poor households than children without disabilities (Hogan, 2012). Poor children are more likely to acquire a disability due to factors such as poor nutrition, overcrowded and unsafe conditions, and lack of health care. In addition to one's family, increasing evidence shows the significant impact of one's neighborhood, which affects access to education, resources, and opportunities (Kohen et al., 2008). Children from high SES families and wealthy neighborhoods have access to better education, accrue more cultural capital, experience better health, and develop a disposition toward leadership and problem-solving, all of which serve them well in competing for America's job market. Similarly, children with disabilities born to wealthier families and in wealthy neighborhoods enjoy better access to health care and therapies; their schools are more likely to provide accommodations and to support children in their educational development; and their families have greater resources by which to create accessibility and foster development. In contrast, children who grow up in low-income families and in neighborhoods with concentrated poverty are more likely to become disabled, and they have less access to high-quality health care and therapies. Schools in low-income neighborhoods too often ration special educational services, offer special educational services that become "dead-end" tracks with little promise for social mobility, and rely more heavily on punishing children despite disability diagnoses (Holt et al., 2019; Voulgarides, 2018). Thus, children with disabilities in poverty may face far greater obstacles than children with disabilities who grow up in wealthy families who can tap into a wide array of resources. Although there is social mobility, class position is often reproduced through the advantages and disadvantages associated with one's birth and childhood.

People With Disabilities as a Minority Group

In a class system, everyone is supposed to be judged based on their merits. But we know that isn't always the case. In sociology, a **minority group** is a group that experiences profound and long-term disadvantage in relation to a majority group who exercises greater power and holds more resources. The **minority model of disability** asserts that disability is a product of systemic disadvantage and views people with disabilities as a group with inferior access to power and resources (Asch & Fine, 1998; Barnartt & Seelman, 1988; Barnes, 2019; Hahn, 1985; Scotch, 2000).

By many measures, people with disabilities as a group are disadvantaged in America. We can return to statistics from the 2018–2019 American Community Survey (Houtenville & Rafal, 2020, first presented in Chapter 2). Only 38.9% of people with disabilities are employed, as compared to 78.6% of people without disabilities. Twenty-six percent of people with disabilities are in poverty, compared to 11.4% of people without disabilities.

Not only are people with disabilities far less likely to be employed and more likely to be in poverty, but they experience higher levels of material hardship. **Material hardship** measures the inability to meet one's needs. It considers not only income but also necessary costs. Forms of material hardship include food hardship (hunger or insufficient food), bill-paying hardship (difficulties paying for utilities, rent, or mortgage), health hardship (unmet medical and dental care needs), and housing hardship (living in substandard housing). A study by Julia Drew (2015) found that focusing on poverty alone underestimates the hardship experienced by people with disabilities because they tend to have higher expenses. Across all groups of people with disabilities, even full-time workers and college graduates, between 40% and 70% of people with disabilities experienced at least one form of material hardship.

Activists and policy makers designed the Americans with Disabilities Act of 1990 (ADA) and the ADA Amendments Act of 2008 (ADAAA) to address economic inequality by removing barriers and prohibiting discrimination in the workplace. Despite optimism after their passage, evidence is clear that the gap between people with and people without disabilities in employment rates, earnings, and poverty have not decreased over time (Maroto & Pettinicchio, 2015). In fact, the gap has widened. Figure 4.1 shows the persistent (and slightly increasing gap) in average earnings among people with disabilities and people without disabilities who are employed. Figure 4.2 shows the widening gap in employment of people with and without disabilities from 1988 to 2014.

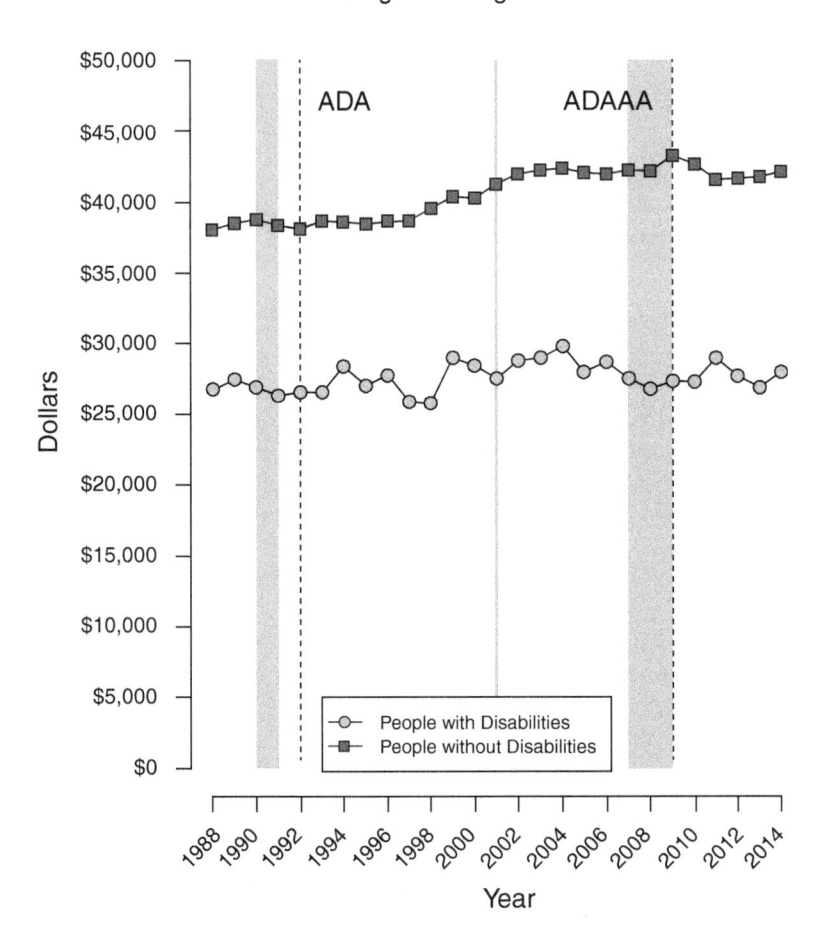

FIGURE 4.1 **Average (Mean) Earnings 1988–2014 for Working-Age People Using Current Population Survey Data**

Source: Reproduced from Maroto & Pettenicchio, 2015.

FIGURE 4.2 Average Percentage Employed 1988–2014 for Working-Age People Using Current Population Survey Data

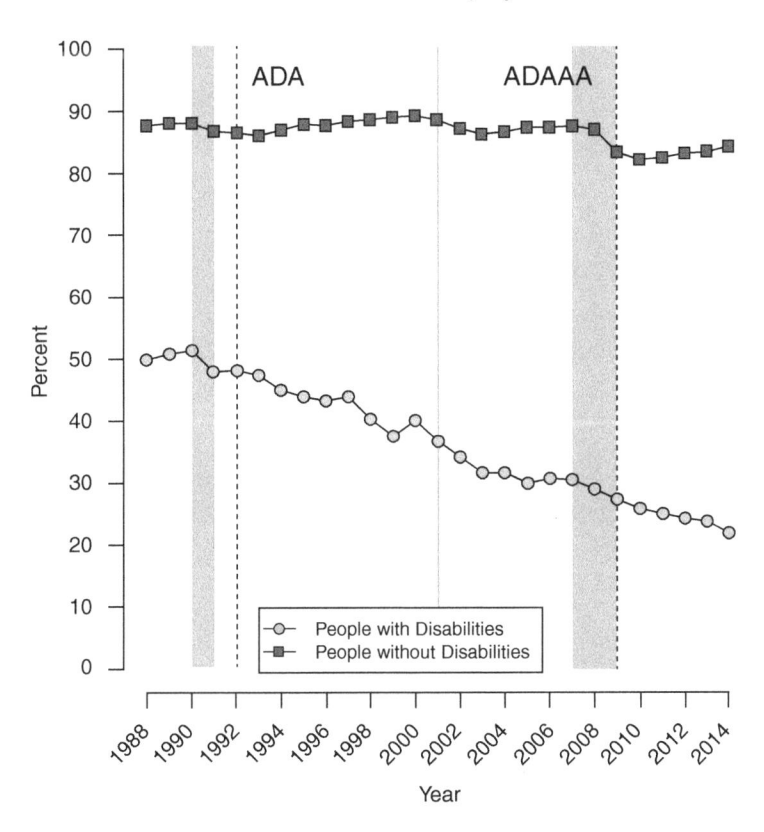

Source: Reproduced from Maroto & Pettenicchio, 2015.

Why do we see chronic inequality between people with and without disabilities, despite legislative efforts like the ADA? Explaining the inequality of people with disabilities is multifaceted and will be addressed through the remainder of this book as we explore a host of social structures such as family, economy, politics, health care, education. In this chapter, we set the groundwork by exploring the concept of ableism, including prejudice, discrimination, and institutional ableism.

Ableism

Most people are acquainted with the ideas of racism and sexism; however, many have not heard of the parallel idea for disability—ableism. **Ableism** is a worldview that assumes the superiority of able bodies and minds and the inferiority of those who do not fit in within the normative expectations. In an ableist worldview, the disabled body is viewed as "less than," and people with disabilities are expected either to strive toward cure/rehabilitation or accept relegation to an inferior status (Campbell, 2009; Chouinard, 1997).

Ableist attitudes manifest in everyday interactions in many ways. One might:

- Overgeneralize the implications of a trait, such as assuming that people who are deaf lack intelligence or can't enjoy music;
- Demand a particular way to do something without considering or offering flexible ways to accomplish a goal, such as underestimating a student's knowledge because they underperform on a single testing strategy like multiple choice exams;
- Assume that people with disabilities have a tragic life, such as believing people who use a wheelchair would be better off dead or feeling pity for them;
- Exclude people with disabilities, such as refusing to hire a qualified person with disabilities due to stereotypes of unreliability.

Ableism is extremely common in American society. In fact, due to the dominance of medical perspectives regarding disability, people are taught to associate disability with tragedy, to believe that people with disabilities should want to be "fixed," and to approach people with disabilities as objects of pity (Clare, 2017; Oliver, 1990). Pity is not always a negative sentiment, but it can be denigrating to people with disabilities when their lives are automatically assumed to be pitiable and defined by suffering. Also, pity too often ignores that social factors like discrimination and inaccessibility really undergird the challenges people with disabilities face in life.

Ableism is deeply intertwined with racism, sexism, and other forms of oppression. Talila Lewis (2020) argues that ableism is "a system that places value on people's bodies and minds based on societally constructed ideas of normalcy, intelligence, excellence and productivity. These constructed ideas are deeply rooted in anti-Blackness, eugenics, colonialism and capitalism. This form of systemic oppression leads to people and society determining who is valuable and worthy based on a person's appearance and/or their ability to satisfactorily [re]produce, excel and 'behave'."

Lewis and other scholars argue that racism *relies on* ableism to define people of color as biologically unfit and to deny rights and access on the basis of that presumed biological unfitness (Kres-Nash, 2016; Lewis, 2020). Sexism and heterosexism similarly define particular bodies as inadequate and deny rights on this basis. Indeed, historian Doug Baynton (2001) shows that the concepts of ability/disability have been central to movements both to deny and to gain civil rights, as those who seek to deny particular populations rights portray them as biologically and mentally unfit/inferior to exercise rights and those seeking rights present themselves as "able" (e.g., competent, rational, and productive). Through all of these debates lies an underlying assumption that it is acceptable to deny rights due to disability and an evaluation of biological inferiority. Ableism also relies on racism, sexism, and heterosexism as definitions of what is normative depend on who wields the power to position themselves as the norm.

Ableism plays out on many levels, including prejudice (belief), discrimination (behavior), and institutional ableism (structure). Let's consider each in relation to disability.

Prejudice

Attitudes often shape behavior, sometimes without even knowing it. **Prejudice** is a set of preconceived negative attitudes and beliefs about a social group. Prejudice is intimately tied to **stereotypes**—generalizations which are often false, simplified, and/or negative, about a group, which may be used to judge individual people.

Stereotypes about disability are both impairment-specific and cross-disability (Nario-Redmond, 2020). *Impairment-specific stereotypes* assign traits or judgments to people with a specific disability. For examples, people who are blind are stereotyped as helpless and/or gifted with mystical wisdom (Longmore, 2003a; Manning, 2009); people with autism are often described as being in a world of their own and/or as brilliant savants (Biklen, 2005); and people with psychiatric disabilities have been increasingly portrayed in the media as violent, although they are more likely to be a victim of violence than to perpetuate it (Metzl, 2018; Phelan et al., 2000). Each of these stereotypes (even "positive" stereotypes) simplifies the impairment and the person, leads to a narrow set of expectations, and ultimately discounts the humanity of people with disabilities.

In contrast with impairment-specific stereotypes, *cross-disability stereotypes* are applied to the broad range of people with disabilities. In other words, people with diverse disabilities are often seen as more similar to each other than different. Some of the most common stereotypes of people with disabilities include that they are dependent, tragic, and (the flip side of tragedy) heroic. A 2010 study by Michelle Nario-Redmond examined stereotypes by disability and gender. She asked respondents to list traits considered by society to be stereotypical of each group. The most common stereotype for disability was dependence, which was mentioned by 91% of respondents. Seven of the top 10 stereotypes for disabled men and disabled women were the same: dependent, incompetent, asexual, unattractive, weak, passive, and heroic. Nondisabled men and women, in contrast, shared fewer stereotypes. Only three of the top ten traits for nondisabled men and women overlapped: ambitious, independent, and domineering. None of these three traits were among those shared by disabled men and women. Thus, men and women with disabilities were depicted as far more alike than men and women without disabilities.

Moreover, Nario-Redmond analyzed the stereotypes that most exclusively defined each group (in other words, stereotypes that were common for one group and rarely used for the others). Nondisabled men were described as *employed* and nondisabled women as *nurturing*, results which reflect expected gender stereotypes in the United States. However, disabled men were described as *angry* and disabled women as *vulnerable*, results which reveal the perceived consequences of not meeting gender expectations in society.

People with disabilities tend to experience a mix of positive and negative stereotypes. They are seen as heroic and innocent (positive stereotypes), as well as dependent, tragic, and incompetent (negative stereotypes). Keep in mind that even positive stereotypes can be harmful. The view of people with disabilities as heroic is often rooted in the belief that disability is a tragedy. If society believes that disability is a fate worse than death, then just surviving can be portrayed as heroic; if society expects nothing from you, then any typical accomplishment (e.g., high school graduation, marriage, getting a job) can be heralded as heroic. In her 2014 TedTalk, Stella Young, a woman with a physical disability, vividly describes her experiences with people congratulating her for the most basic tasks, like getting out of the house and attending school. She argues that assumptions about her heroism and her incompetence were connected to each other, both reflecting the ways in which society underestimates and pities people with disabilities.

This blend of positive and negative stereotypes falls in line with predictions from the Stereotype Content Model (Fiske et al., 2002; Glick & Fiske, 2001). The **Stereotype Content Model** predicts that two types of traits—warmth and competence—are particularly important in determining the content and outcomes of stereotypes. *Warmth* refers to perceptions of a group's motives and moral qualities, such as likability, honesty, and friendliness. *Competence* refers to perceptions of a group's ability and resources to carry out its agenda, such as their intelligence and power. People with disabilities, like children and the elderly, tend to be perceived as high warmth and low competence (Glick & Fiske, 2001). In other words, they are generally considered friendly and compliant (warm), as well as dependent and incapable (incompetent). As such, they are generally seen as unthreatening.

According to the Stereotype Content Model, each combination of stereotypes leads to certain responses. The combination of warmth and incompetence common for people with disabilities leads to paternalism (treating people like children) and pity, because it is believed that this group is not threatening and needs to be taken care of. In contrast, for groups that are seen as warm and competent, one might show deference. For groups that are seen as cold and incompetent, one might objectify, segregate, and denigrate them. While paternalism and pity are negative responses, they may be less harmful than these other potential responses. Table 4.1 further explains the model.

Although pity is a common response to disability, it is important to note that people with disabilities have certainly been subjected to objectification and segregation. At different times in history and for a variety of reasons, people with disabilities have been seen as cold and incompetent and therefore threatening, leading to harsh reactions. For example, when eugenics was at its height in the early twentieth century, eugenicists blamed people with disabilities for crime, poverty, and social dysfunction (Snyder & Mitchell, 2006; Trent,

TABLE 4.1 Stereotype Content Model

	Competence/Status Low (Incompetent)	Competence/Status High (Competent)
Cooperative High (Warm)	Stereotype: Warm & incompetent Who: Disabled, elders Feel: Pity, sympathy Behavior: Protect, subordinate "Legitimate dependents"	Stereotype: Warm & competent Who: Allies, students Feel: Pride, admiration Behavior: Deference, respect "Reference ingroups"
Cooperative Low (Cold)	Stereotype: Cold & incompetent Who: Poor, immigrants Feel: Disgust, contempt Behavior: Objectify, segregate "Illegitimate dependents"	Stereotype: Cold & competent Who: Rich, jews Feel: Envy, resentment Behavior: Scapegoat, harass "Aspirational groups"

Source: Reproduced from Nario-Redmond (2020), p. 181, with modifications.

1994). They portrayed people with disabilities as immoral and degenerate, not innocent and compliant. This led to mass institutionalization and compulsory sterilization in the United States and campaigns of extermination in Nazi Germany. In modern America, people with mental illness face accusations of being violent and dangerous, leading to high incarceration rates (Metzl, 2018). People with disabilities increasingly face accusations of receiving "extra" privileges and of sucking resources from society, also leading to harsh reactions (Dorfman, 2020).

In fact, research suggests that implicit biases regarding disability may be much more negative than explicit reporting suggests. Social pressure to be positive about people with disabilities likely skews self-reported attitudes. **Implicit Bias** refers to the unconscious attitudes and stereotypes that shape our behaviors. Tests for implicit bias ask people to make very quick associations, thereby minimizing one's ability to think about the socially acceptable answer. Disability Implicit Association tests (Pruett & Chan, 2006) examine the strength of association between disability status and positive and negative evaluations. These tests reveal a very pervasive negative bias against people with disabilities (Rohmer & Louvet, 2018). Seventy-six percent of respondents showed a stronger preference for people without disabilities than for people with disabilities, one of the strongest effects across social groups including gender, race, sexuality, and political orientation (Nosek et al., 2007).

Studies of social distance also indicate that people feel social pressure to express a positive regard for people with disabilities, but often hold an implicit negative bias against them. A classic 1980 study by Melvin Snyder and his colleagues offers a vivid example (Snyder et al., 1980). Undergraduates were asked to watch a movie in a dorm common room setting. In the first scenario, there were two seating areas, one with a wheelchair user present and one with a nondisabled person present. The same film was being shown in both seating areas. In the second scenario, there were again two seating areas, one with a wheelchair user present and one with a nondisabled person present, but the areas were showing different films. For both scenarios, Snyder recorded with whom the undergraduate sat. When there was no choice of movie, 58% of subjects sat with the person with the disability. When there was a choice of movies, only 17% of subjects sat with the person with the disability. Given the random assignment of movies, it seems that, when subjects could justify avoiding the disabled person by claiming to prefer a different movie, they tended to do so. When they had no justification (they couldn't say they preferred a particular movie), a majority sat with the person with a disability to avoid being *seen as* biased. This suggests that efforts to include people with disabilities are heavily dependent upon societal pressure. This may further help explain why segregation and isolation can so quickly lead to violence against and neglect of people with disabilities. Without direct social pressure to be kind, people may act on negative biases.

Discrimination

Beliefs, and even our implicit biases, often shape behavior. Strong negative beliefs about disability, particularly beliefs regarding the incompetence, dependence, and tragic nature of people with disabilities, lead to discrimination in many areas of life. **Discrimination** is the unequal treatment of people based on a group membership such as gender, race, or disability.

Health care and treatment. *Labeling theory* argues that a label can become a master status, so that people respond to one's label rather than to one's actual behavior. In the classic 1973 study of labeling, "Sane in Insane Places," David Rosenhan sent eight people, including himself, to mental hospitals (Rosenhan, 1973). They were instructed to each say that they briefly heard voices (words such as "empty" and "hollow"), and then they were instructed to act as they normally would. All were admitted, received diagnoses of schizophrenia, and stayed in the hospital for between seven and 52 days. While in the hospital, the label of schizophrenic shaped staff perceptions of the patients' behavior. For example, when patients paced up and down the halls due to boredom, nurses interpreted this behavior as a symptom of mental illness; when they took notes for the study, nurses labeled the notetaking as a compulsive behavior. Moreover, doctors interpreted the patients' past in light of their label—a phenomenon known as retrospective labeling. The doctors identified signs of family trauma and abuse in the patients' past, which they believed led to mental illness. They also engaged in anticipatory labeling, assuming that the patients' futures would be shaped by their schizophrenia. In other words, once the label of schizophrenia was applied, the actual behavior of the patient no longer mattered; their pasts and futures were seen in light of the label. The patients reported feeling dehumanized, objectified, and ignored. All but one were released with the label "schizophrenic in remission." To gain release, they all had to agree that they were mentally ill and would take antipsychotic medication. Thus, the negative consequences for seeking help for a relatively minor (and, in this instance, fake) symptom were substantial.

In today's world, we continue to see negative stereotyping of people with disabilities in health care (Iezzoni et al., 2021; Robey et al., 2006). Health care providers have been socialized into a culture of curing and fixing (Cassell, 2005). As such, they tend to have negative attitudes toward living with a chronic disability. Indeed, doctors' attitudes about the quality of life of people with disabilities tend to be just as negative, or more negative, than the public's (Pendo, 2008), and far more negative than the opinion of people with disabilities themselves (Gill, 2000). A recent study found that 80% of US physicians believed people with significant disabilities had worse quality of life than nondisabled people, only 57% strongly agreed that they welcomed patients with disabilities into their practices, and only 41% expressed confidence in their ability to provide the same quality of care to patients with disabilities as provided to other patients (Iezzoni et al., 2021).

Negative stereotypes impact access to and the quality of medical care. For example, the stereotype of asexuality hinders access to gynecological and reproductive care. Doctors too often assume or even assert that women with disabilities should not need access to contraceptives, family planning, and testing for sexually transmitted diseases (STDs) (Dillaway & Lysack, 2015; NCD, 2009). Women with disabilities wait longer for a diagnosis and receive less care for STDs. As will be discussed in the chapter on family, medical professionals are far more likely to identify new mothers with disabilities as "high risk" and call in social services than new mothers without disabilities, although problems like challenges with breastfeeding may be common for both sets of women (Frederick, 2017). In a vicious cycle, internalized stigma related to disability leads to poorer physical health, lower physical functioning, and greater pain, yet health care can be harder for people with disabilities to attain (Brown & Batty, 2020).

Education. Students with disabilities have lower rates of high school and college graduation than students without disabilities, and studies show part of the educational achievement gap is due to ableism, including stereotypes and low expectations. In a phenomenon called the **self-fulfilling prophecy**, expectations can lead to the very outcome they expect. Sociologist Dara Shifrer (2013) used a national dataset of 10th graders to examine the extent to which the educational achievement gap between disabled and nondisabled students was due to the disability itself (e.g. reported difficulty reading, IQ), factors like socioeconomic background and educational motivation, or the negative impact of the disability label. Due to the large dataset, Shifrer was able to compare students who were alike in terms of many factors (e.g. grades, motivation level in school, behavioral record, socioeconomic status) but differed on whether or not they had a label of learning disability (LD) or not. Among *otherwise similar students*, teachers were 82% less likely to expect students with LD labels to receive a bachelor's degree (BA) or higher compared to students without the LD label. Parents were 48% less likely to expect their children with LD labels to achieve a BA or higher than parents of children without a label. Thus, *controlling for their background and academic record*, teachers had much lower expectations of students with LD diagnoses than students without.

Elissa Molloy and Michelle Nario-Redmond (2007) found that college faculty similarly held lower expectations of students with learning disabilities. Faculty believed that students with disabilities were more likely to drop out and might perform better in less rigorous majors. They held lower expectations *even when told that the students with disabilities had high grades*. Low expectations held by teachers may have a grave impact on the opportunities and careers that students are channeled toward and the way students come to see their own potential.

The negative impact of labels may be especially harmful to students of color and students from low socioeconomic backgrounds, for whom disability labels are less likely to lead to helpful resources and more likely to lead to segregation and low expectations. Research by Shifrer and her colleagues (2011) shows that the disproportionate labeling of minorities as disabled could be explained largely by SES. In other words, poor children (a disproportionate number of poor children are children of color) were disproportionately labeled as learning disabled, creating the illusion that their poor performance was due to their own individual biology/deficits rather than systemic inequities in educational treatment and access. Research by Colin Ong-Dean (2009) and Beth Ferri and David Connor (2005) further argue that race and class inequalities in diagnosis are part of a long history of naturalizing inequality for racial minorities and using disability as a means to justify their segregation.

The workplace. As noted earlier in this chapter, dependence and incompetence are two of the primary stereotypes associated with disability, and these stereotypes hinder success in employment. Employer attitudes specifically contribute to the low rate of employment among people with disabilities. A review of scholarship on employer attitudes and disability conducted by Robert Gould and his colleagues (2015) reported that "Stigmatized perceptions of disability impact a variety of employment decisions, including hiring, advancement, and providing reasonable accommodations." Employers express concerns about lower productivity, higher costs (e.g., accommodations, absenteeism) and the fear of litigation (Gould et al., 2015; Kaye et al., 2011). Interestingly, employers with experience hiring people with disabilities are more likely to hire someone with a disability again. Thus, the actual experience of employing someone with a disability dispels many of the negative stereotypes (Hernandez et al., 2004).

Employees with disabilities, in comparison to employees without disabilities, report lower pay, less job security, and more negative treatment by their employers (Schur et al., 2017). Studies show that people with disabilities who perceive high levels of stigma are less likely to disclose their disability in the workplace (Goldberg et al., 2005). Anticipating negative stereotypes, employees with disabilities may decide not to request workplace accommodations (Engel & Munger, 2003). Therefore, although the ADA is supposed to ensure access to accommodations, many people do not feel comfortable asking for them. Moreover, in a phenomenon called **Stereotype threat**, the anxiety produced by negative stereotypes itself might lead to poor performance. For example, Arielle Silverman and Geoffrey Cohen (2014) found that among blind adults, higher levels of perceived stereotype threat in the workplace were associated with lower well-being and higher unemployment.

Institutional Ableism

Institutional discrimination, and more specifically for our purposes, **institutional ableism** occurs when broad institutional patterns such as policies, procedures, and funding systems disproportionately disadvantage or harm people with disabilities. These effects may be intentional or not, but regardless of intent, they create and maintain systemic inequality. This inequality is not reliant on prejudiced individuals; in fact, individuals may express positive attitudes regarding people with disabilities, yet the systems in place ensure the perpetuation of inequality. The following chapters will explore many instances of institutional ableism. In this chapter, we will highlight two examples that document how institutional ableism works to perpetuate inequality.

The Institutional Bias. In the sociology of disability, the term "institutional" may take on different meanings. One meaning refers to the patterns found in society's social structures (e.g., education, health care). For instance, the idea of "institutional discrimination" calls attention to the patterns of inequality embedded in and manifest through policies and laws. A second meaning of "institutional" refers to the disempowerment of people with disabilities by placing them in segregated, often large-scale, settings called institutions. For instance, institutional care is provided in segregated settings where one exercises little control over one's life. The **institutional bias** refers to both—the ways in which the channeling of people with disabilities into large-scale, segregated settings ("institutions"), rather than community settings, is encouraged by and embedded in our national laws and policies ("institutionalized").

Care in institutional settings is deeply problematic because it deprives people of liberty and individual choice. As Erving Goffman discussed in his 1963 book *Asylums*, **institutions** are settings which operate around a centralized authority, enforce standardized rules, demand conformity, and erase individual difference. In institutional settings, people have limited choices; they do not choose their roommates, staff, daily activities, daily schedules, or even when or if to take a shower. They cannot come and go based on their own preferences. Their lives are *administered*, shaped by institutional needs like staffing schedule and cost efficiencies. Because citizens have a constitutional right to freedom, long-term institutional care should be avoided except in the most dire circumstances, when essential for the safety of the person with a disability or others. Most services administered in institutional settings can be provided, often more effectively and at a lower cost, in community settings while retaining individual liberty.

The legal rights to liberty and access to the community have been inscribed in law in the Americans with Disabilities Act and in Supreme Court decisions (e.g., Olmstead vs. L.C., 1999). However, America still heavily relies on institutional care. For example, a 2011 court case determined that North Carolina "fails to provide services to individuals with mental illness in the most integrated setting appropriate to their needs in violation of the ADA. The State plans, structures, and administers its mental health service system to deliver services to thousands of persons with mental illness in large, segregated adult care homes, and to allocate funding to service individuals in adult care homes rather than in integrated settings" (Smith, 2012). There is a similar reliance on segregation in the provision of housing, day programs, and vocational opportunities for people with developmental disabilities. Also, many older Americans who would prefer to live in their homes with in-home assistance are forced into nursing homes.

Why does the US still rely so heavily on institutional care despite the ADA's community mandate? The federal policies that fund long-term care favor institutional settings. In 1965, legislation mandated that Medicaid and Medicare financially support long-term care in nursing homes and institutional settings for people who met the financial and medical eligibility requirements. The law did not similarly mandate federal financial support of community services or individualized personal assistance. A Robert Wood Johnson report stated, "Nursing home care in the United States is an entitlement—any person who is eligible for nursing home services cannot be denied that service if there is a nursing home bed available… Personal assistance services delivered in the community does not have such an entitlement status" (Quoted in Center for an Accessible Society, n.d.). This means that individuals who need long-term care and support can more easily access public funding if they are placed in an institutional setting rather than if they stay at home with individualized services. Policies created in the 1960s continue to channel people with disabilities into institutional settings, depriving them of liberty. Thus, the *institutional bias* perpetuates segregation, even if individual attitudes seem accepting of the inclusion of people with disabilities in the community.

Employment Disincentives and Occupational Structures. Economic inequality has also been persistent. The Americans with Disabilities Act (ADA) was intended to increase the employment of people with disabilities by prohibiting discrimination. Why hasn't the economic situation improved despite its passage? We have already discussed the role of attitudes; employers continue to hold negative attitudes about employing people with disabilities. In addition, sociologists Michelle Maroto and David Pettinicchio (2015) argue that the **occupational structure**—the patterns of the distribution of work, earnings, and employment inequality—must also be taken into account to explain the lack of positive change over time.

These occupational structures include the concentration of people with disabilities in low-wage and part-time jobs (Maroto & Pettinicchio, 2015), the reliance on entrepreneurship (Schur, 2003), and work/benefits policy. People with disabilities who work are highly concentrated in low-wage, service sector jobs. According to Schur et al. (2013), 58% of the employed people with disabilities work in occupations with low or very low wages. Because of the wage scale common in the United States, people making minimum wage, even if they are working full-time, often live in poverty. Moreover, because the "standard" work environment demands 35+ hours of work a week and offers little time off or flexibility, many people with disabilities are channeled into part-time work and entrepreneurship. Entrepreneurship may provide more flexibility but may yield little pay or benefits for people with disabilities. Furthermore, because employment can threaten one's eligibility for public benefits including access to Medicaid/Medicare, people with disabilities may be discouraged from working unless they can maintain full-time employment that will confer pay and benefits comparable to or better than Social Security payments and Medicaid (Longmore, 2003b). Therefore, even if employers' attitudes change, the structure of work and the distribution of pay and benefits for work remain in place and disadvantage people with disabilities in the workplace.

Ableism and Inaccessibility

In addition to prejudice, discrimination, and institutional discrimination, an understanding of the perpetuation of disability inequality requires a consideration of issues such as inaccessibility, segregation, invisibility, and violence.

Ableism and inaccessibility are deeply intertwined. **Access** refers to the power and opportunity to enter, use, participate in, and have a sense of belonging or control over a social space or interaction (Titchkosky, 2011; Williamson, 2015). Access may be physical, shaped by factors such as landscape, architecture, and technology. More broadly, access is social and relational, shaped by factors such as interpersonal relationships, money, communication systems, and policy (Kafer, 2013). Disability activist and scholar Jacobus tenBroek argued that people with disabilities must have the "right to be in the world" and to be from unnecessary confinement (1966), situating access as a cornerstone of disability rights. Access enables (and inaccessibility disables) the practice of basic civil rights, such as the rights to assemble, to vote, to move freely through the nation, to enjoy public spaces and services, and ultimately to freedom and the pursuit of happiness. Ableism is an ideological underpinning of inaccessibility, because it encourages the idea that people with disabilities don't need or shouldn't have access.

Inaccessibility potentially hinders people with disabilities in all areas of life, such as housing, work, religion, leisure, education, technology, and health. To develop a few examples, health care is shockingly inaccessible. One study found that 65% of alcohol and drug abuse treatment programs that were approached by a person with a significant physical disability denied the disabled person services based on inaccessibility (West et al., 2009). Sociologists Heather Dillaway and Catherine Lysack (2015) found inaccessibility to be a major barrier for women with physical disabilities seeking gynecological health care. The inaccessibility of doctor's equipment, like their examination tables, makes it impossible for some people to get a proper exam. Doctors also lack knowledge to safely assist people in transferring from wheelchairs to tables and to conduct safe exams, with one participant describing most physicians as "amateurs" when it comes to assisting and examining women with physical disabilities. Thus, even though people with disabilities on average need more medical care, they have difficulty accessing it.

For housing, few homes and only 1% of the rental housing market are accessible (cited in Stevens, 2020). Moreover, accessible housing tends to cost more. In his study of minority men with spinal cord injury, Noam Ostrander (2008) found that, after rehabilitation, most of these men returned to inaccessible housing and communities. They relied on family and friends to assist them, at times carry them, in and out of inaccessible homes/ apartment buildings. Inaccessibility limited their movement, threatened their safety (e.g., they could not safely leave their homes in case of emergency), and damaged their self-esteem.

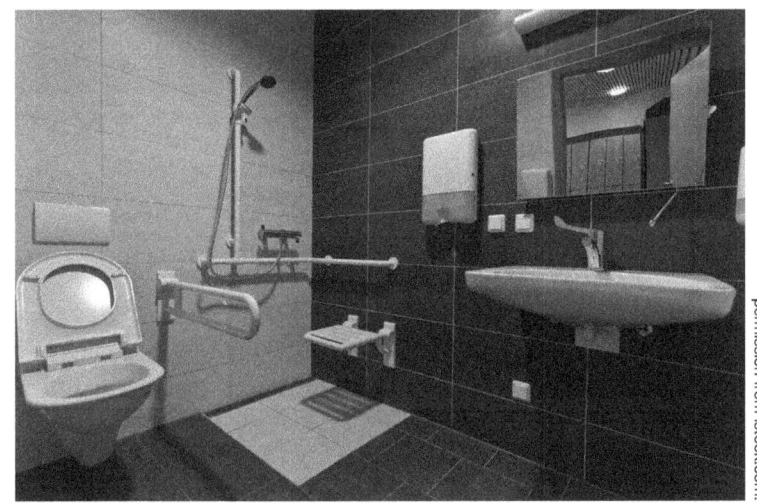

PHOTO 4.3 Accessible bathrooms enable disabled people to move comfortably and safely, but most homes lack these features

Even the places where people worship are often inaccessible. Because religious organizations are exempt from the Americans with Disabilities Act, the access issues are often grave: steps leading into buildings, pews with no room for people in wheelchairs, cavernous rooms without adequate systems for people with hearing impairments or ASL, liturgical rituals that expect specific forms of participation (e.g., silence, kneeling, repeating prayers), and paternalistic attitudes that portray people with disabilities only as objects of charity. Thus, although people with disabilities believe in religion at the same rate as those without disabilities, they are less likely to participate in religious services (Kessler Foundation & NOD, 2010).

Inaccessibility is not just a product of happenstance or ignorance. Sociologists argue that the organization of social spaces, and the distribution of people and goods through these spaces, are processes shaped by power (Löw, 2016). Accessibility and inaccessibility emerge from decisions about who should be included. Sociologist Tanya Titchkosky's (2011) study of higher education offers a useful example of the social processes underlying accessibility and inaccessibility. University students face a host of access issues, such as buildings without elevators or ramps, electronic systems that don't work with screen readings, lack of ASL interpretation, expansive campuses with little transportation and 10 minutes between classes, and classroom materials that are not in accessible formats. University buildings, curricula, and policies were largely constructed "as if they never imagined the incredible variety of bodies, minds, senses, emotions, and lives that are 'us'" (p. 26). The presumed absence of disabled people from higher education was so well established that it went largely unquestioned. As people with disabilities now demand access to higher education, past inequities are revealed. However, too often administrators justify past and present exclusions with statements like *these buildings were built long ago* (as if exclusion made sense in the past), *we don't have the money* (as if cost legitimizes unequal education), *we are working on it* (as if slow progress over decades should still satisfy demands for equality), and *we didn't realize* (as if ignorance of disability is a legitimate excuse). Instead of committing to equitable access, administrators often respond with long-held justifications and half-measures to satisfy legal requirements while still regarding students with disabilities as a **justifiably excluded type**—a set of people for whom exclusion is largely accepted. Titchkosky's work points out that the exclusion of people with disabilities is often assumed to be acceptable and even necessary for the best interests of people with disabilities and/or of society. Once exclusion is seen as justified, this leads to segregation, invisibility, and violence.

PHOTO 4.4
Hanging out with other college students is sometimes difficult due to inaccessibility

Ableism and Segregation, Invisibility and Violence

The segregation of people with disabilities is widespread and often unquestioned. Historian Nicki Pombier Berger first realized the extent of segregation when her son was unexpectedly born with Down syndrome. She remembered, "I never had a meaningful encounter with a person with intellectual disability until I gave birth to one. As I began to process this fact in those early days, I saw that this was by design: the world, written by and for an idea of 'normal', has kept us apart" (Quoted in Carey et al., 2020).

Commonly, people believe the myth that segregation is the best solution to meet the needs of people with disabilities. Drawing on lessons from the civil rights movement, disability rights activists have challenged this myth, declared that separate is not equal, and demanded the rights to inclusion and empowerment. Demanding inclusion does not mean that there are never instances in which people with disabilities may benefit from specialized services or enjoy participating in groups specifically for people with disabilities. It does mean that the imposition of segregated environments on people with disabilities, especially over long periods of time and/or across multiple systems, systematically denies the "right to be in the world."

Although segregation is often explained as in the best interest of people with disabilities, it is usually upheld for very different reasons, such as cost efficiency, bureaucratic ease, and the preservation of the routines, practices, and power differentials expected by people without disabilities. For example, despite evidence of the positive impacts of inclusive educational practices, school districts continue to defend their reliance on segregated education based on costs, insufficient professional training, inaccessible buildings, and the negative impact of program disruptions.

Al Herzog's (2017) work on religious ministry offers an illuminating discussion of segregation versus inclusion. To meet the religious needs of people with disabilities, many congregations have, with good intentions, created "special" religious programs and services for people with disabilities. The problem with services for people with disabilities, however, is that they position people with disabilities as marginal to the religious community. Special services imagine that the needs of people with disabilities cannot be met in environments with people without disabilities. In contrast, Herzog encourages the creation of *inclusive* services open to all. Inclusive services do not ignore disability. Rather, they ensure accessible environments, minimize complicated language, and provide flexibility in practice and movement (e.g., people can move about and stim, people who use aug-mented communication de-vices can sing in the choir). Inclusion imagines many ways for diverse people to participate. Not all people would love this service; there could be services delivered in other styles too. But many people— disabled and nondisabled— might love it, including parents with small children, young adults looking for more active and flexible ways to participate, and older people who might benefit from the accessibility features.

PHOTO 4.5
Inclusive children's church choir.

Segregation, although historically heralded by medical experts and policy makers as optimal for people with disabilities, reenforces the devaluation of people with disabilities, denies liberty, and makes people with disabilities largely invisible. Out of sight, out of mind. Disempowered and invisible, people with disabilities become highly vulnerable to neglect and violence. The rates of violence against people with disabilities are shocking. According to the Bureau of Justice Statistics, between 2009 and 2015, individuals with disabilities were at least twice as likely to be victims of violence as individuals without disabilities, and people with mental and intellectual disabilities were at the highest risk (Office of Victims of Crime, 2018). Both men and women with disabilities had higher rates of sexual violence than men and women without disabilities (Basile et al., 2016). The World Health Organization (Hughes et al., 2012) reported that globally children with disabilities are almost four times as likely to experience violence than children without disabilities. The majority of disabled victims of violence know their perpetrators, and 20% believe that they were targeted because of their disability. Sociologist Mark Sherry (2016) argues that hate crimes against people with disabilities are far more common than recognized. Despite the high rate of victimization, only a small percentage of people with disabilities receive victim services (Office of Victims of Crime, 2018). Violence is often wielded against those who are vulnerable to it due to their invisibility, powerlessness, lack of social connections, inability to report violence or lack of credibility.

Segregation fosters all of these conditions, whereas inclusion fosters a strong network of relationships with people in the community and serves to protect people from abuse (Condeluci, 2009).

In addition to interpersonal violence, people with disabilities have also experienced mass, systemic violence committed by the state and professionals. Large-scale institutional hospitals for people with disabilities quickly became warehouses with little treatment and mass dehumanization, neglect, and abuse. Under compulsory sterilization laws, more than 60,000 people labeled as disabled were sterilized without their consent (see Chapter 3). People with disabilities have been the victims of medical experimentation (see Chapter 2) and violent medical "treatments," including electric shocks, social isolation, and confinement to cages. Through war, colonization, mass incarceration, and forced displacement, the state also creates disability. Indeed, although we often imagine disability as a product of nature, state violence is strongly related to the creation of disability. Chapter 9 will explore violence committed as part of transnational capitalism.

Conclusion

Ableism is common. In fact, it's widely accepted to view people with disabilities as tragic, to assume that they suffer, and to treat them as objects of pity. Many Americans believe that the poverty of people with disabilities is a natural result of biological limitations, with little consideration of the impact of discrimination and policy. Yet, ableism and the varied ways it manifests—prejudice, discrimination, institutional ableism, inaccessibility, segregation, and violence—are central to creating and perpetuating the inequality of people with disabilities.

KEY TERMS

Ableism 77
Access 86
Caste system 73
Class system 74
Discrimination 81
Implicit Bias 81
Institutions 84

Institutional ableism 84
Institutional bias 84
Justifiably excluded type 88
Material hardship 75
Meritocracy 74
Minority group 75
Occupational structure 85

Prejudice 79
Self-fulfilling prophecy 83
Stereotype 79
Stereotype Content Model 80
Stereotype threat 84
Stratification system 72

RESOURCES

Disability Memoirs Related to Ableism

Brown, Keah. 2019. *The pretty one*. New York, NY: Atria.

Heumann, Judith. 2020. *Being Heumann: An unrepentant memoir of a disability rights activist*. New York, NY: Penguin Random House.

Lehrer, Riva. 2020. *Golem girl: A memoir*. New York, NY: Random House.

Rousso, Harilyn. 2013. *Don't call me inspirational: A disabled feminist talks back*. Philadelphia, PA: Temple University Press.

Academic Books

Campbell, Fiona K. 2009. *Contours of ableism: The production of disability and abledness*. London: Palgrave Macmillan.

Nario-Redmond, Michelle R. 2020. *Ableism: The causes and consequences of disability prejudice*. Hoboken, NJ: Wiley.

Titchkosky, Tanya. 2011. *The question of access: Disability, space, meaning*. Toronto: University of Toronto Press.

Academic Articles

Banks, Joy. 2018. "Invisible Man: Examining the Intersectionality of Disability, Race, and Gender in an Urban Community." *Disability and Society* 33, no. 6: 894–908.

Maroto, Michelle, and David Pettinicchio. 2015. "Twenty-Five Years After the ADA: Situating Disability in America's System of Stratification." *Disability Studies Quarterly* 35: 3, https://dsq-sds.org/article/view/4927/4024.

Nario-Redmond, Michelle R. 2010. "Cultural Stereotypes of Disabled and Non-Disabled Men and Women: Consensus for Global Category Representations and Diagnostic Domains." *British Journal of Social Psychology* 49, no. 3: 471–88.

Collected Essays

Brown, Lydia X. Z., E. Ashkenazy, and Morénike Giwa Onaiwu, eds. *All the weight of our dreams: On living radicalized autism*. DragonBee Press.

Catapano, Peter, and Rosemarie Garland-Thomson, eds. 2019. *About us: Essays from the disability series of the New York Times*. Leveright.

Wood, Caitlin, ed. 2014. *Criptiques*. Word Press.

Blogs

Disability Visibility Project. Guest blog posts (many discuss ableism). https://disabilityvisibilityproject.com/category/guest-blog-posts/.

Invisible Disability Project. 2017. "Flip the Script by Calling Out Disability First," https://www.invisibledisabilityproject.org/call-out-ableism.

Talia A. Lewis. 2019, March 5. "Longmore Lecture: Context, Clarity, and Grounding," https://www.talilalewis.com/blog (discusses ableism and racism as mutually inclusive).

Cara Liebowitz. 2015, March 3. "Every Day Ableism and How We Can Avoid It." In *The body is not an apology* (website). https://thebodyisnotanapology.com/magazine/everyday-ableism-and-how-we-can-avoid-it/.

Videos

Patty Berne and Stacey Milbern. 2017. "Ableism is the Bane of My Motherfuckin' Existence." https://www.youtube.com/watch?v=IelmZUxBIq0 (5 minutes).

Frank Stephens. 2018. "I am a Man with Down Syndrome and My Life is Worth Living..." https://www.youtube.com/watch?v=1d8ocuPrlT8 (10 minutes).

Stella Young. 2014. "I'm Not Your Inspiration, Thank You Very Much," *Ted Talk*. https://www.youtube.com/watch?v=8K9Gg164Bsw (9 minutes).

ACTIVITIES

1. Take the disability implicit bias test and reflect on how and you (or others) develop disability bias. https://implicit.harvard.edu/implicit/takeatest.html

2. Take the "20-Question Quiz to Determine Your Disability Literacy," by the Paul K. Longmore Institute on Disability, and reflect on the questions and your results. https://longmoreinstitute.sfsu.edu/20-question-quiz-determine-your-disability-literacy

3. Watch the video clips above and consider the common and unique themes relevant to ableism discussed by each person.

4. Identify instances of individual and institutional ableism that occur in your university setting (Perhaps reading a chapter from Tanya Titchkosky's book *A Question of Access*). Consider the impacts of individual and institutional ableism on students with disabilities.

CHAPTER 5

Culture and Disability

Chapter Synopsis

In disability scholarship, culture often takes center stage, as sociologists bring to light the contested meanings of disability, the consequences of those meanings, and the strategies used to disseminate and institutionalize meanings (Green & Loseke, 2020). This chapter discusses the elements of culture to showcase the construction of culture and disability. We then discuss the intersection of culture and power. Much of American culture is deeply ableist; however, activists and artists with disabilities are redefining disability and American culture in ways that embrace diversity and demand access.

Culture and the Elements of Culture

Although many people treat disability as a biological fact, the history of disability reveals that societies think about disability very differently. This variation speaks, at least in part, to the role of culture, one of the most fundamental ideas for sociologists. **Culture** may be defined as a people's "way of life," encompassing their symbols, values, customs, artifacts, and rituals. It is the mechanism by which a group's social environment is made meaningful (Geertz, 1973). For cultural sociologists, culture is not a set of objects or ideas to be explained. Rather, it is the dynamic processes of meaning-making that underlie all social

Learning Outcomes

5.1 Analyze the elements of culture as they pertain to disability.

5.2 Theorize how cultural processes create and sustain inequality, including discourse, representations, and habitus.

5.3 Debate the degree to which disability culture acts as a subculture or counterculture (or neither).

phenomena (Spillman, 2002). Cultural sociologist Jeffrey Alexander (2003, p. 12) argues that every action "is embedded to some extent in a horizon of affect and meaning."

To consider how culture shapes disability, we start with the six basic elements of culture identified by Michael Kimmel and Amy Aronson (2009): values, symbols, language, rituals, norms, and material culture. We will consider each of these elements.

American Values and Disability

Values provide collective ideals about right and wrong and identify what is important in a given society. In 1970, sociologist Robin Williams Jr. identified 12 "core" American values (Williams, 1970):

1. *Achievement and Success.* Americans measure personal worth in terms of wealth, power, occupational prestige. Life is a competition to be won.
2. *Individualism.* Individual-level wants and needs typically take precedence over communal ones, and success/failure is framed in terms of individual initiative.
3. *Activity and Work.* Americans identify strongly with their occupations and value being busy. A hectic schedule is a sign of success.
4. *Efficiency and practicality.* Task completion should be performed in the most efficient manner, prioritizing time and convenience.
5. *Science and technology.* Science and technology are understood to signal American superiority in areas from military to health care.
6. *Progress.* Americans strive for continual growth, improvement, and change.
7. *Material comfort.* Material wealth largely defines success and should be used for one's comfort. Successful people deserve to enjoy the rewards of their success.
8. *Humanitarianism.* Americans believe in individual-level kindness and charity.
9. *Freedom.* Individuals should be free to pursue their interests with minimal collective or government constraint.
10. *Democracy.* Democratic government is seen as the superior form of government.
11. *Equality of rights.* Although there is inequality, Americans profess the importance of equal rights.
12. *Racism and group superiority.* Even in the context of equal rights, Americans often believe that "their" group is superior to others in particular ways.

Sociologists often make several general points when they discuss values. Value sets may contain internal inconsistencies, such as the tensions between individualism and humanitarianism. Values are only "loosely coupled" with action (Swindler, 1986). For example, professing the value of freedom does not mean that one will act to protect freedom. Moreover, values change over time. Would the above list still be the same if we interviewed Americans today? While all of these points are true, we want to highlight four different points as we consider the relationship between values and disability.

First, American values are often expressed in ways that are ableist and contribute to the marginalization of people with disabilities. Let's consider the first two values listed: achievement and individualism. The value of achievement is often defined by the accumulation of wealth, occupational prestige, and "winning," which creates a challenging environment for people with disabilities. As soon as children are born and throughout their youth, their progress is carefully measured, compared to others, and experienced as a competition. In our hypercompetitive environment, each success/failure serves to herald future glories or predict later doom. In this context, we can perhaps understand Heather Kirn Lanier's (2015) frustration when she was told by her doctor that her daughter Fiona was "way behind." She wrote:

> *Way, way behind, he said. I saw a race. Numbers on the backs and fronts of runners, all children. The able-bodied kids charging ahead, the whites of their brains all fatty and luxurious with myelin, sending and receiving impulses with standard issue speed. I saw them racing toward a finish line. I saw a ribbon fall when their chests touched it, and I saw arms raised in victory... The metaphor makes a competition of human development, one in which my daughter is ultimately dismissed because, let's face it, in this competition, she will never "catch up."... There is no winning when this kind of language is applied to my daughter or anyone like her.*

Lanier is not underestimating her daughter's abilities. Rather, she is criticizing a culture that only values people who can attain a particular version of success and relegates others to the junk pile, discarded in segregated environments with few opportunities and little respect. Typical achievements—such as one's first teenage job around the neighborhood, high school graduation, getting a driver's license, building a career, and starting a family—may elude people with disabilities because of their specific limitations and/or because of the social isolation and discrimination they experience. The attainment of wealth and occupational prestige presents an even greater problem given that people with disabilities are disproportionately unemployed, underemployed, and in poverty. Thus, people with disabilities may struggle to feel respected given the narrow definition of achievement commonly extolled in America.

The second value—individualism/independence—also poses considerable problems for people with disabilities. Many Americans praise individualism while simultaneously relying on their parents, friends, and communities for support. In contrast, when people with disabilities rely on others, they risk accusations of dependence and subsequent infantilization and/or invalidation (Charlton, 2000; Zola, 1982). The perceived dependence of people with disabilities has been used to justify their placement in institutions and the loss of their civil rights. Some states allow children to be removed from their parents' custody due to parental disability, even with no proof of neglect or abuse. This unequal treatment is based on stereotypes that people who need care cannot also provide care.

The risks associated with dependence are so great that people with disabilities feel compelled to achieve and display their independence constantly. Robert McRuer (2006) refers to this as **compulsory able-bodiedness**—the demand that people with disabilities perform as able-bodied people or risk exclusion. Disabled sociologist Irving Zola (1982, p. 226) discussed this pressure in his life, saying, "if I could do it, there was a moral imperative *to* do it, no matter how tired I was or what risk it demanded."

The other values could also be analyzed as to how they incorporate ableism. For example, the value of efficiency demands things be done in the quickest, easiest way. In an inaccessible society though, hiring or even including people with disabilities is often perceived as inefficient, leading to and justifying their marginalization.

Values are often defined in opposition to disability, such that the value itself implies ability and its absence equals disability. This is a subtler point than the first one. For example, the first point suggests that independence as typically defined might be hard for a person with a disability to achieve in an ableist society. The second point argues that independence is actually defined in relation to disability so that independence and disability are constituted as opposites. Throughout American history, disability has often been defined *as dependence*, as the inability to work and attain self-sufficiency. Still today, the Social Security Administration defines disability as the total inability to work. Thus, disability is seen, not as the presence of a particular impairment, but as the inability to live independently without assistance due to an impairment. This view prevents people with disabilities from showcasing their abilities because the very label of disability has been defined in terms of dependence.

We could again proceed through the list of values, examining the constructed binary relationship between disability and each value. For humanitarianism, for example, it's not just that people with disabilities struggle to take on the role of humanitarian due to high rates of poverty. Rather, via religion and government benefit systems, disability has been defined as a category of those in need of charity. The relationship to the value is predefined. If one is in a position to give charity, by definition one must not be disabled. This makes accepting a label of disability a risky proposition because it fundamentally alters one's social position; people now assume one's status as a charity-recipient rather than charity-giver (Galvin, 2004).

Third, America is a richly multicultural and diverse nation, and therefore the values most directly impacting someone's life may vary. Asian American women with disabilities, for example, may be embedded in communities with dominant American values and/or with common Asian values such as respect for elders and the value of harmony. Thus, Asian American women might have a different experience of disability than other women. Stereotypes of Asian women as passive and of people with disabilities as childlike may diminish the respect they receive in relation to either set of values (Tsao, 2016).

Fourth, values are not set in stone, and disability activists have set out to redefine and transform the landscape of American values. Ed Roberts (1939–1995), for example, helped build the Independent Living Movement, an early strand of the Disability Rights Movement. Roberts became a quadriplegic at the age of 14 due to polio. He used personal assistance and technology including a wheelchair, an iron lung (a large machine that compresses one's lungs to facilitate breathing), and a portable oxygen machine. Due to his extensive needs, some people thought he should spend his entire life in a nursing home, but Roberts had other ideas. He wanted to live in the community and exercise control over his own life. Roberts redefined independence, not as the absence of needing assistance, but as exercising control over decision-making (Fleischer & Zames, 2011; Pelka, 2012).

Disability activists also reformulated the idea of humanitarianism, summed up in the slogan "Piss on Pity." People with disabilities may require assistance and support, but activists like Vic Fickelstein and Liz Crow argue that people with disabilities should receive support as a *right*, not as charity. A modern humanitarian society, they argue, provides the basic support citizens need as human and civil rights.

Global Focus

Different groups and nations hold different values which shape ideas about and response to disability. To offer a comparison to the United States, Nigeria is one of the most powerful nations in Africa. Dominant values in Nigeria include:

- Religion—Religious beliefs are diverse, including Islam, Christianity, and indigenous religions. Nigerians tend to see a world in interaction with supernatural forces;
- Family—The extended family is the primary organizational unit, and the ethos of cooperative labor and care within extended family is strong;
- National pride—Expressing pride in Nigeria's power, a favorite saying is "When Nigeria sneezes, the rest of the African nations catch cold";
- Communal harmony—The longstanding practices that sustain community social order are paramount. This includes the values of patience, tolerance, and harmony;
- Hard work—The Nigerian economy is largely agricultural. Strength, perseverance, and hard work are all valued, as are the wealth to which they hopefully lead.

For people with disabilities, these values may be supportive in some fashion. Some disabled people are seen as blessed, and they are given positions of importance in shrines for the god Obatala (Nyangweso, 2018). Families display a strong commitment to caring for family members after disablement and as they age (Bassey et al., 2019). On the other hand, Nigerian values (like American values) are infused with ableism. Religious beliefs often present people with disabilities as ghosts, defiled gods, or products of witchcraft or divine punishment. This dehumanizes people with disabilities and justifies ritual cleansing and even killing to protect communities. The emphasis on family, while partially protective, is also hierarchical and patriarchal, which means that the eldest males in the family hold the power to abandon disabled family members, command disabled family members to beg, or impose female genital mutilation (Dwojuxigbe et al., 2017). Some disabilities take on particular meaning in the Nigerian context. For example, albinism is a condition in which people's hair, eyes, and skin have little color. Indigenous religions associate albinism with defiled gods and ghosts. Some people believe that potions made with the body parts of people with albinism lead to long life and wealth, while others believe that sex with an albino girl/woman cures HIV/AIDS. As such, people with albinism live in fear of mutilation, rape, and death (Etieylbo & Omiegbe, 2016).

Symbols and Language

A **symbol** is anything that carries meaning, serving as a marker for some thing or idea. For example, a flag may symbolize a nation, a ring may symbolize marital commitment, and a piece of paper may symbolize the worth of $5, $10, or $20. Symbols are a building block of communication and culture. Through interaction, we create and share symbols, building a common relationship to the world around us (Berger & Luckmann, 1966; Mead, 1934). **Language** is perhaps the most important symbol set, the way in which humans create and communicate complex systems of meaning.

According to the **Sapir-Whorf thesis**, in addition to reflecting reality, language shapes our understanding and experience of the world. To apply this to disability, we can consider how words both reflect and create different ideas about disability. For example, words change through time related to intellectual disability, such as fool, simpleton, idiot, moron, mental defective, mentally retarded, and intellectually disabled. These words *shape* how one thinks about intelligence, who and how many people are identified with each term, and how to respond. As we've discussed (Chapter 3), in Medieval Europe, "fools" carried little stigma and could hold coveted positions in the royal court with the ear of the king. In contrast, the "feebleminded"—a medical term coined in the era of eugenics—assumed that people with disabilities posed a grave threat to society. The term "mental retardation" became popular in the 1950s. Rather than seeing intellectual disability as a threat, it suggested that child development was simply slower for this population. Thus, although each term refers to intellectual disability, they each embed the philosophies and values of the era.

Terms and Phrases Now Considered Inappropriate

Handicapped

Vegetable

Defective

Freak

Retarded

Wheelchair-bound

Suffers from

Victim of

Because language shapes our perceptions and relationships, debates about disability language rage. Many older terms and phrases are now considered inappropriate because they reflect pity, a focus on abnormality, or other outdated assumptions. Many professionals now use **person-first language**, a convention which places the person before the disability. For example, instead of "the epileptic girl," person-first language suggests "the girl with epilepsy." Instead of "the disabled" or "the disabled person," person-first language suggests "people with disabilities." This convention avoids reducing a person to their disability and focuses on the person as a holistic being who has a disability among other traits (Snow, 2001).

Many disability activists, though, prefer **identity-first language**, a language convention which places the disability in the forefront (e.g., disabled person, autistic activist, Deaf dancer). This choice of language signifies disability pride, the idea that disability is a valued trait central to one's identity. Of this choice, Cara Liebowitz (2015) states:

Though person-first language is designed to promote respect, the concept is based on the idea that disability is something negative, something that you shouldn't want to see. After all, no one tells me that I should call myself a person with femaleness or a person with Jewishness. I'm a Jewish woman. No one questions that. Yet when I dare to call myself a disabled person, it seems the whole world turns upside down. That's because gender and religion are seen as neutral, if not positive, characteristics. The idea of separating the disability from the person stems from the idea that disability is something you should want to have separated from you, like a rotten tooth that needs to be pulled out. Disability is only negative because society makes it so.

Some people with disabilities have reclaimed derogatory words, such as "crip" or "gimp." **Reclamation** of a word is to take a derogatory term and instill it with group pride. Author Nancy Mairs, for example, chooses to identify as "a cripple" because she finds the word descriptive, accurate, and boldly unapologetic (Mairs, 1986). "Mad" activists powerfully wield the double entendre of the term "mad"—they have been labeled and persecuted as "mad" (insane) and they are "mad" (angry) about their subjugation. Women, minorities, and the LGBT+ community have similarly reclaimed the use of derogatory words as an act of empowerment, particularly expressed in-group communication.

Although the complexity of disability language can be frustrating, sociologists recognize that language carries meanings, and these meanings vary by groups, contexts, and power dynamics. A term used in-group may not carry the same meaning if said by someone outside of that group. Furthermore, the diversity of perspectives on disability (e.g., medical model, social model, disability as personal tragedy, etc...) leads to conflicts regarding language. People who rely on the medical model will likely use different words than those who use the social model, for example. The marginality of people with disabilities further amplifies the politics associated with language, because people with disabilities rarely control the words used about them. Empowerment includes respecting the right of people to self-identify, even if it makes life a little confusing. As feminists have long said, politics is personal and the personal is political.

Let's consider symbols other than language. Disability is symbolized in many ways, and like words, these symbols reflect and shape meaning. One of the most common disability symbols is the international symbol of access (Ben-Moshe & Powell, 2007). Below (see Figure 5.1) are three accessibility symbols. In the first image (on the left), the person is static and singular in its

FIGURE 5.1 Accessibility Symbols

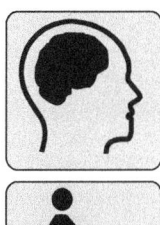

Source: www.istock.com essentials #903065442 (seated), #875669898 (wheelchair on the go), and #1073019390 (variations logo).

depiction; the middle image shows a wheelchair user "on the go." The image to the right juxtaposes four pictures. How might these different images lead people to think differently about disability and access?

Disability itself is often used as a symbol—or a metaphor—for other things, typically for social ills (Mitchell & Snyder, 2000). Common phrases like "blind justice" and "the blind leading the blind" do not refer to actual blind people; rather, blindness serves as a metaphor for objectivity in the first example and incompetence in the second (Dorfman, 2016). Not surprisingly, people who are blind may take offense at these uses of blindness, and the metaphors may contribute to stereotypes which hinder blind people. In political rhetoric, national enemies and terrorists are often portrayed as "mad" fanatics (Patel, 2014). In a court of law, few terrorists would be allowed to use the insanity plea to reduce their responsibility. Rather, the use of "madness" is metaphorical, serving to dehumanize the enemy and delegitimize their political position. American eugenicists and German Nazis described undesirable populations as "diseased," portraying them as direct threats to national "fitness." Thus, the use of disability language in the popular media often has little to do with the actual lived experience of people with disabilities. Instead, it serves as a metaphor for a variety of social ills.

Finally, let us briefly consider issues of language access. Language is the primary mode by which people communicate complex meanings. What happens when someone does not use the dominant language? In ancient Greece, people without spoken language, including many deaf people, were considered unintelligent. Still today, D/deaf people struggle to be treated as capable and intelligent. Signed languages offer the opportunity to engage in a vibrant culture, but, because they are not the language of the majority, users of signed languages often experience marginalization. Similarly, people who use technology to communicate, people who are blind and break communication norms (e.g., they may not look at people when they speak), and people who are nonverbal all risk social exclusion and devaluation if they fail to adhere to expected patterns of communication.

Language around the Globe

As discussed in Chapter 2, many cultures do not have a word for "disability," because specific impairments like blindness and schizophrenia are not seen as sharing something in common (Gabel et al., 2001). Moreover, the words used to describe specific impairments may carry different interpretations than in the United States. For example, hallucinations may be interpreted as religious experiences and labeled as such. In James Charlton's (2000) work on international disability activism, he discusses the ways in which languages around the world reinforce negative stereotypes of people with disabilities. In Zimbabwe the Shona word closest to disability, *chirema,* means totally useless, and the word for blindness, *bofu,* means someone without freedom. In Latin America, *miasvalides* (less valid) and *discapitados* (less capable) are commonly used. Latin American activist, Maria Paula Teperino stated, "Lots of work needs to be done with language. People usually call us *aliejado*, which means cripple. I believe inaccessibility has a lot to do with this because people see us being carried into buildings and they think we are sick" (Charlton, 2000, p. 67).

Norms and Rituals

Norms set forth expected behavior, and **rituals** provide opportunities to engage in routinized behavior in order to reinforce meaning systems and unify people within a culture. Depending on the significance of the norm, the consequences for norm-breaking range from mild to severe.

Life with a disability may sometimes feel like one big norm-breaking experiment. Indeed, while some disabilities are readily apparent, others become visible primarily through norm-breaking. For example, Sharon is a student with visual impairments, but, because she has partial vision and well-developed blind skills, most of her peers do not know she has low vision. When she uses a computer, however, she uses a 24-point font size, sits very closely to the computer, and/or finds a quiet spot to use text to speech software. Sharon hears students remark or joke about what they considered to be her odd or even rude behavior. Other behaviors rooted in disability may be considered more deviant, such as making unexpected noises, rocking back and forth, or drooling, and may elicit more serious consequences.

Rituals provide routinized opportunities for collective expressions of meaning and unity. Because they are highly routinized and collectively meaningful, failure to participate as expected can lead to social exclusion. Religious services, for example, may be highly ritualized, and congregations may discourage attendance by those who do not act in expected ways. The movie theater has clear rules and rituals, and behavior deemed deviant can quickly lead to comments or even expulsion.

Zach Richter's (2016) work analyzes the ritual of the family dinner. The values underlying the family dinner include family communication and intimacy; however, for people with autism, the dinner table may become a site of rehabilitation to teach norms such as exercising bodily self-control (not stimming, rocking), maintaining eye contact, and engaging in conversational turn-taking. The family dinner becomes a site of **normalization**—the process by which people with disabilities are socialized into expected behaviors with the goal of participating in and taking on valued roles in society. Normalization may have merits; however, when the *performance of the ritual* of the family dinner (the outward expression of normalcy) takes priority over the values of intimacy and family communication, the person with autism may experience the family dinner as exhausting and isolating. Proponents of normalization promise that adherence to normative behavior will facilitate inclusion. Autistic activists and scholars, on the other hand, challenge this view of inclusion, asking: inclusion on whose terms? And at what cost? If people cannot be autistic in their own homes with their own family, where can they relax and express themselves?

The link between disability and norm-breaking is so strong that sociology's initial exploration into disability was through the study of deviance. Indeed, people with mental illness are often punished rather than supported. Today, more people with mental health diagnoses reside in America's prisons and jails than resided in mental hospitals at their peak (Ben-Moshe et al., 2014; Rembis, 2014). Boys from minority communities are particularly likely to be diagnosed with emotional and behavioral disabilities, placed in segregated special educational tracks, offered few educational resources, and punished for any deviance via the criminal justice system (Erevelles, 2014; Ware et al., 2014). Thus, the consequences of norm-breaking by people with disabilities continue to be severe, especially for those already stereotyped as deviant.

Material Culture

Material Culture includes the tangible products made in a culture and the tools and processes of producing those items. Material culture plays a critical role in creating, identifying, and responding to disability.

Let's consider clothing. Before mass production, families would sew their own clothes. Clothing could be easily personalized to fit diverse bodies, and therefore, different bodies did not require different styles of clothing. Mass production of clothing, on the other hand, relies on and demands standardized bodies (e.g. two arms of equal length, two legs of equal length, a straight back...). Mass produced clothing, therefore, excludes people with diverse bodies from participating in fashion. Fashion prioritizes aesthetic value. In other words, how something looks is as important, or more important, than its function. People express themselves through fashion and enjoy connecting to various communities through their fashion choices. Instead of popular and fun fashions, though, people with disabilities often must rely on items that are blandly functional and even ugly in their appearance. Prosthetics, wheelchairs, hearing aids, and adaptive clothing often evoke the image of a patient rather than someone who is popular and fun.

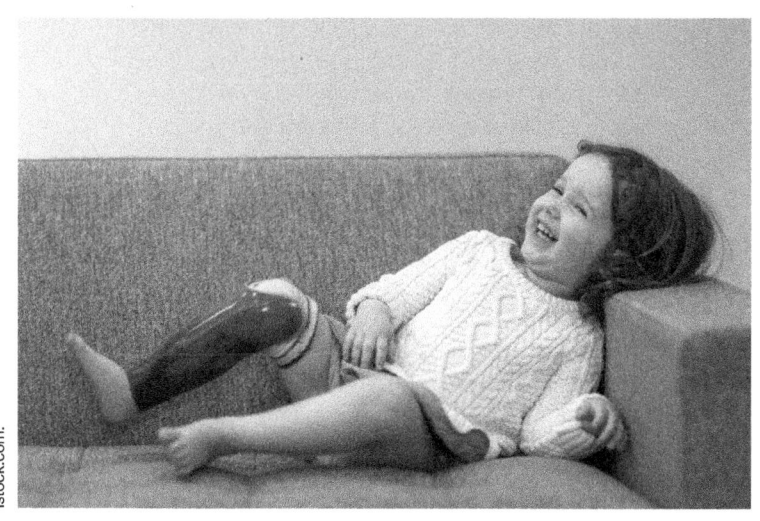

PHOTO 5.1
Fun choices like this pink and blue prosthetic help people express their personality

There is no reason these products must be ugly; rather, society has deprioritized access to beauty for people with disabilities and thereby marked people with disabilities as less worthy. Vice versa, the creation of beautiful and fashionable items for people with disabilities signifies their worth and facilitates inclusion (Depoy & Gilson, 2018). As examples, Tommy Hilfiger's innovative adaptive fashion line offers its popular style paired with adaptive features to facilitate dressing, like magnetic buttons, Velcro pockets, adjustable hems, and easy to open necklines. Whimsical prosthetic covers and sporty wheelchairs encourage people to celebrate their diverse bodies.

Cultural Oppression and Inequality

How does culture relate to systems of power? Karl Marx and Friedrich Engels ([1845] 1978) argued that culture is rooted in the means and relations of production. Those who control the means of production (e.g., the capitalists) have the power to produce **ideology**, a belief system constructed by the ruling class to legitimate and support the means and relations of production. Why might capitalists create ideology relative to disability? According to scholars such as Andrew Scull (2015) and Michel Foucault (1965), disability presents a threat to capitalists insofar as people with disabilities slow or disrupt the pace and structure of standardized, profit-driven work. Furthermore, as family members must provide care to disabled loved ones, disability may divert able-bodied people out of the workplace. Therefore, it is in capitalists' interests to (1) demean disability to compel all those able to work to do so, (2) regulate the categories of disabled/able to ensure that no workers are allowed to fake disability to avoid work, and (3) provide low-cost care or benefits to both effectively remove people with disabilities from the workplace and enable their family members to work. Cultural values such as independence, achievement, and work ethic serve capitalists by encouraging people to believe that they *want* to labor, while simultaneously producing intense shame should they fail to do so (Charlton, 2000).

Indeed, these ideas are so pervasive that they are hegemonic. **Hegemony** (Gramsci, [1889] 1971) refers to a set of beliefs promoted by the ruling class that have become so dominant throughout society that they are widely accepted as true, natural, and inevitable. Promoted via schools, churches, government, labor market, and the media, the value of a "fit" body—and the corresponding "tragedy" of a disabled one—becomes so pervasive that people no longer see the capitalist interests behind this belief and instead accept it as fact (Charlton, 2000).

Narratives and Discourses

Intertwined with, but not necessarily reducible to, economic interests, are broad cultural narratives and discourses that shape views of disability. **Narratives** are the stories that people create and tell as a way to construct meaning (Green & Loseke, 2020). **Discourses** organize meanings in ways that constitute knowledge and inform our behavior; they provide the parameters of acceptable narratives, shaping and constraining the ways we think. For example, in the Middle Ages, the Catholic Church in Europe largely controlled the discourse on disability. One might see disability as punishment for sin, a test of faith, a result of witchcraft, or a gift from God (four different narratives), but each adheres to and exists within the range of acceptable answers that associate disability with the divine (discourse).

In modern America, discourses regarding disability are less focused on religion, but discourses still legitimize inequality. We will look at three, often interrelated, discourses: Social Darwinism/eugenics, meritocracy, and the medical model.

Social Darwinism embraces the maxim of the survival of the fittest. This maxim suggests that the human race and society both evolve toward perfection when society allows open, unhindered competition such that the strong rise to the top and the weak fall to the bottom. The strong will be more likely to marry and breed, passing their superior traits to the next generation, whereas the weak will face destitution, have few children, die earlier, and therefore their genetic lines will end. Social Darwinists argue that social welfare policies that help the poor and disabled undercut the positive influence of natural selection. Therefore, they argue against state welfare programs, such as state-subsidized health programs, Social Security, and even public education. Eugenicists take this sentiment further, suggesting that the creation of a better population should not just be left to nature. Rather, the state should improve population quality through policies which encourage selective breeding and protect society from public health threats including disease, disability, and degeneracy (Snyder & Mitchell, 2005). These ideologies led to mass institutionalization and sterilization in the United States and programs of medical extermination, sterilization, and extermination in Nazi Germany.

Social Darwinism and eugenics still influence thinking about disability today. People with disabilities face stereotypes that they cannot and should not parent. Fetuses identified with birth "defects" are aborted at high rates; about two-thirds of fetuses identified with Down syndrome are aborted (Schrad, 2015). People often assume that the world would be better if disability, and people with disabilities, were eradicated (Estreich, 2019). Challenging these beliefs in relation to people with Down syndrome, self-advocate Frank Stephens (2018) advised, "See me as a human being, not a birth defect, not a syndrome. I don't need to be eradicated."

A second, closely related, narrative that justifies the inequality of people with disabilities is Meritocracy. **Meritocracy** asserts that one's social position should be based on one's earned accomplishments. Meritocracy is connected to a belief in individualism. People who believe that America is a meritocracy and embrace individualism show less support for social welfare programs and antidiscrimination efforts (Eppard et al., 2020). Ideals of meritocracy are used to justify the denial of social support and even accessibility, since each person is expected to compete for their own success (much like in Social Darwinism). Moreover, meritocracy glosses over the structural inequalities that shape outcomes, presenting the wealthy as if they earned their position, and the poor as if they failed to work hard enough.

As noted in Chapter 1, medical discourse is the dominant discourse of disability today. Although presented as objective science, the medical model is itself a belief system, promoted by an industry and its professionals that create winners and losers. The veneer of science and objectivity, though, enables medical practitioners to claim the status of truth, which confers a significant form of power (Estreich, 2019; Foucault, 1965). According to **medical discourse**, disability and illness are biological problems which should be defeated through medical cure. Success means attaining the normative, or even ideal, healthy body. Because health is a hegemonic ideal, the idea that health is superior to illness or disability seems natural and right.

Disability scholars, though, illuminate the dangers, even violence, associated with the devotion to health and cure. As discussed in Zach Richter's (2016) work, rehabilitation to attain normalcy may be prioritized over leisure, intimacy, and disability pride, as people with disabilities are endlessly forced to work toward rehabilitation goals. Many group homes use a model of *active treatment* where every moment is considered to be a teaching moment. Preparing dinner, eating dinner, postdinner conversation, an evening game of cards, and watching the television all become fodder to train people with intellectual and mental disabilities to perform everyday skills as normally as possible. Imagine your life if, during every moment, a professional watched, assessed, and prompted your progress toward goals established by professionals. What might your evenings look like? What might the professionals disapprove of or deny you?

The metaphor of war is common in medical lingo (Cassell, 2005; Wilson, 2004). In this value system, the sick must battle disease and disability. Disability is the enemy. Accepting a life of disability is considered cowardly and is deemed a failure. The value of cure surpasses consideration of other risks or costs (Clare, 2017; Kim, 2017). Treatments may be used even when they offer little benefit. Joan Cassell's study of hospital intensive care units (ICUs) reveals instances of "cruel, useless, and unnecessary" treatments given to dying patients in order to preserve the illusion of fighting, even when death is certain (2005, p. 156).

And what of disabilities that have no cure? In *War on Autism*, Anne McGuire (2016) shows how the medical discourse of disease and cure permeates autism narratives. Rather than encouraging parents to accept and support their child, some autism media campaigns tell parents that autism has stolen their child and that their child must be saved. This rhetoric leads some desperate parents to try experimental and dangerous treatments like administering chemicals to strip toxins out of their child's system (Willingham, 2013). Eunjung Kim (2017) uses the term **curative violence** to describe violence committed in the attempt to cure, hide, and/or ultimately eradicate people with incurable disabilities. Alison Kafer (2013, p. 28) states that in America's culture of cure, "the only appropriate disabled mind/body is one cured or moving towards cure."

Part of the power of these discourses is that they perpetuate inequality, without appearing to be antidisability. Eduardo Bonilla-Silva's book *Racism without Racists* (2003) argues that ideologies rooted in liberalism and meritocracy prevent interventions to achieve equality, overlook institutional disadvantages, and uphold the status quo. These ideologies perpetuate racial inequality, even in an era when fewer White people espouse explicitly racist views. White people do not need to be openly racist to benefit from race privilege; they need to only ensure the status quo with institutionalized inequality, which they can do through embracing individualism and meritocracy. Similarly, with longstanding systems of segregation and marginalization already in place, ideologies of individualism, meritocracy, and the ideal body preserve ableism even as people's attitudes toward disability seem to grow more accepting.

Representation

In addition to discourses, representations also serve to perpetuate inequality. **Representations** are symbolic imagery which create and reflect the meaning of a social phenomenon, in this case disability. In his classic theories of racial oppression, W. E. B. Du Bois ([1903] 1994) pointed out the ways that Whiteness was represented as a cultural ideal, whereas Blackness became associated with ignorance, evil, and depravity. Similarly (and often in intersection with racial and gendered representations), able bodies and minds are positioned as the norm, and all else is treated as an unexpected and undesirable deviation, at best a "special" circumstance that requires "special" accommodations, at worst a threatening deviation requiring eradication (Davis, 1997a; Garland-Thomson, 1997).

A key part of establishing ableism as the cultural norm and ideal is to erase disability representations in history and the media, in effect making disability invisible (Brown, 2019). Disability is erased from history, except as objects of medical progress (Burch & Nielsen, 2015). Beethoven became deaf, Albert Einstein had a learning disability, Vincent Van Gogh experienced depression, Harriet Tubman had seizures, Frida Kahlo was disabled after polio and a trolley accident, and Stephen Hawking had a motor neuron disease—yet in history texts, disability receives little attention, with almost no consideration for how disability shapes experience or how people with disabilities shape society.

In popular culture, few main characters have disabilities, and, of those, most are White males. A 2016 report by Stacy Smith and her colleagues analyzing the

100 top grossing movies of 2015 documents that only 2.4% of the characters who spoke or had names were characters with disabilities (Smith et al., 2016). Eighty-one percent of these were male, 71.7% were White, and 0% were LGBTQ+. This can be compared to national statistics—18% of Americans have a disability, women and poor people are disproportionately likely to report disability, and African Americans and Native Americans report the highest levels of disability. Reflecting on the lack of representations of Black women with disabilities in romantic comedies, author Keah Brown (2016) asks, "How are we, black girls with disabilities, supposed to see ourselves as worthy of romantic love, worthy of the chance to feel at home in our bodies and personalities, if the only representation we receive is that of a plot device or a joke?"

When disability is portrayed, it is largely inaccurate. For example, Nan Johnson's (2017) study of deafness in the media argues that, since deafness is an invisible disability, the media relies on physical and behavioral stereotypes to mark the character as deaf for the audience. Myths such as the perfect deaf lip-reader and/or the perfect deaf speaker are common and used to advance the plot and ensure the comfort of a hearing audience.

Indeed, the perspectives and experiences of people with disabilities often are deprioritized, and instead disability is used as a dramatic technique to inspire drama or provoke pity or fear (Mitchell & Snyder, 2000). Some stereotypes about disability are especially common, including disabled characters as a villain, a poster child, a joke, or an inspiration (Berger, 2013; Brown, 2003; Longmore, 2003a).

PHOTO 5.2
Boris Karloff in Frankenstein

The disabled villain is one of the most common media representations, playing off common stereotypes of disabled people as angry and bitter (Berger, 2013). For example, Disney's Maleficent turns evil once her wings are cut off, and Frankenstein's monster turns villainous due to the rejection he receives based on his deformity. When viewers see Captain Hook, Scar (Lion King), Freddy Kruger, or Darth Vader, they do not usually think about these characters as disabled, yet each has prominent physical features associated with disability (in fact Captain Hook and Scar are defined by their physical features). In the 2019 horror movie *Us*, Lupita Nyong'o styled her "creepy" voice specifically based on a disability called spasmodic dysphonia which causes spasms of the larynx. Why? Disability is used to make a villain scarier and to physically mark evil. By making evil physically identifiable, viewers confront their social anxieties while also distancing from them. They know when to run. Moving off the screen, entertainment companies have created "haunted" houses and virtual reality horror "attractions" based on mental hospitals and institutions, flippantly drawing on the traumatic history of segregation and abuse for other people's amusement (Solomon, 2019).

Another common representation of people with disabilities relies on pity. People with disabilities are displayed to evoke sympathy. For example, in *Breaking Bad*, Walter White's cancer and his son's cerebral palsy offer the moral justification for his transformation into a drug dealer; he needs to take care of those around him. In *A Christmas Carol*, Ebeneezer Scrooge's positive moral transformation is marked by his embrace of Tiny Tim, who is disabled and ill. Poster child campaigns are designed to tug at one's heartstrings so that the audience will donate money. While a more sympathetic depiction than the villain, these depictions use disability primarily to evoke pity, as a vehicle to create drama, and as a foil by which to explain the moral actions of nondisabled characters.

A third common media representation relies on disability for laughs. From the classic adventures of *Mr. Magoo* (an older man with limited vision who experiences all manner of mishaps) to Jim Carrey and Jeff Daniels in *Dumb and Dumber* to Dori's memory loss in *Finding Nemo*, audiences are socialized to laugh at the mistakes and norm-breaking associated with disability. While some comedians with disabilities use humor to skillfully raise awareness of the experiences of people with disabilities and even to challenge ableism (Bingham & Green, 2016; Haller & Becker 2014), other comedies use disability more directly as the butt of jokes.

PHOTO 5.3 Tiny Tim and Ebeneezer Scrooge, A Christmas Carol

A fourth common media representation is the overcoming story, centered on a "supercrip" who overcomes their disability and achieves either normalcy or even superhero status. *People Magazine*, for example, regularly publishes stories of people who have overcome sickness and disability in order to offer heartwarming and inspiring content to their audiences. The presentation of deaf-blind author and activist Helen Keller, one of the only figures with a disability discussed in the K-12 classroom, typifies this narrative. Her story is usually presented as a journey from darkness to triumph when, with the help of her teacher Anne Sullivan, she learns to communicate. The story ends there. The story isn't primarily about Helen Keller's life. Although she goes on to lead a full life as an activist who often criticized capitalism, patriarchy, and ableism, students hear almost nothing about that. Instead, the story presents Keller as a brave hero and is meant to inspire children to overcome their own obstacles (Souza, 2020).

Supercrip stories can be very positive, but they are also problematic. Often they are used to motivate nondisabled people to overcome their challenges, rather than to understand the disability experience and perspective. Stella Young (see resource section at end) famously referred to this as **inspiration porn**—the objectification of disabled people for the motivation and inspiration of nondisabled people. It's okay to be inspired by the amazing things that people achieve. However, when teachers only present that Keller learned to communicate and not what she *said*, then are students really inspired by Helen Keller, or is she being used as a motivational tool to encourage children to overcome their challenges? The supercrip narrative individualizes success, diverts attention away from the

PHOTO 5.4
Public intellectual Helen Keller

sociopolitical changes people with disabilities need to participate in society, and implicitly denigrates and blames people with disabilities who cannot or choose not to overcome disability.

To gauge the quality of disability representations, we can consider several factors.

- Control. People with disabilities rarely control the way disability is represented, which leads to many misrepresentations. Ensuring greater control of representations by people with disabilities helps to promote more realistic and relevant representations. Control might include, for example, authorship, direction/production, and the inclusion of actors/actresses with disabilities.

- Perspective. Stories are too often told from the perspective of nondisabled story-tellers and assume a nondisabled audience. In contrast, representations that center the perspective of people with disabilities enable the audience to experience the world through the lens of people with disabilities.

- Accuracy and realism. Disability representations are too often inaccurate. In contrast, representations that dive deeply in the lived experience of people with disabilities raise awareness and provide new, interesting, and relevant insights.

- Diversity. Disability representations are too often a single character and too often White and male. In reality, busy streets are not free of people with disabilities, and schools don't have only one child with a disability. Disability representations that include multiple, diverse characters with disabilities, who vary by gender, race, religion, sexuality, disability, and body type, better reflect reality.

- Complexity. Disabled characters tend to be unidimensional, intended to inspire or to provoke pity, fear, or a laugh. In contrast, people with disability are multidimensional, with varied roles, beliefs, and abilities/disabilities, and should be represented as such.

- Challenging Ableism. Disability representations often reinforce ableism, teaching the audience that disability is a personal tragedy best overcome through personal motivation or medical cure. In contrast, people with disabilities confront an inaccessible society with high levels of prejudice. Representations that challenge ableism serve to support social change.

Habitus and the Reproduction of Inequality

Inequality is not simply imposed from above; it is instilled through socialization in the context of systemic inequality. We will discuss socialization at greater length in the following chapter. Here we pay specific attention to the ideas of cultural capital and habitus in the reproduction of inequality.

Capital is a resource which can be used to accrue more resources. Money is the most discussed form of capital. In capitalism, money can yield more money; your $10 investment can become $20 or more dollars. Culture can also serve as capital. **Cultural capital** is the set of knowledge, behaviors, and skills that indicate a particular lifestyle (usually associated with prestige) and that helps one attain social mobility. The accrual of cultural capital begins early, as children are exposed to particular books and scheduled activities, taught to sit attentively, and encouraged to engage "appropriately" in-group events. Later in life, cultural capital may include knowledge of the fine arts, travel, politics, etiquette, and fashion. Cultural capital may be challenging, though, for people with disabilities to accrue. Low expectations and tracking in schools place many children with disabilities in nonacademic and segregated classes. Social isolation limits exposure to socially valued knowledge and practices. High rates of poverty and inaccessibility exclude people with disabilities from the fine arts, travel, and fashion.

A lack of social capital further exacerbates the problem. **Social capital** refers to the ways in which relationships may serve as resources, such as helping one find a job, identifying appropriate health care, gaining entry to a desirable social club, and introducing one to potential romantic partners (Granovetter, 1974; Putnam, 2000). Social isolation is one of the greatest problems faced by people with disabilities. A survey by the Kessler Foundation and National Organization on Disability (2010) found that people with disabilities are significantly less likely to engage in social activities than people without disabilities (see Table 5.1). Interestingly, the largest gap is in access to the internet, an increasingly vital form of cultural and social capital these days.

TABLE 5.1 Involvement in Social Activities for People With and Without Disabilities, 2010

	People With Disabilities	People Without Disabilities	Gap in Percentage Points
Socializes with close friends, relatives, or neighbors at least twice a month	79	90	11
Goes to a restaurant at least twice a month	48	75	27
Goes to church, synagogue, or any other place of worship at least once a month	50	57	7
Uses a computer/electronic device to access the Internet	85	54	31
Very satisfied with life	34	61	31

Data Source: Kessler Foundation/NOD Survey of Americans with Disabilities, 2010.

Specific populations, such as people with intellectual disabilities, experience more dramatic disparities. For example, they are far less likely to report friends and support systems beyond family and paid service providers (Friedman & Rizzolo, 2018).

One's economic, cultural, and social capital influences one's everyday interactions and activities, which in turn shapes one's dispositions—or, in other words, one's sense of how society works and one's place in it (Bourdieu, 1984). As people accrue experiences and develop dispositions over time, they create their **habitus**—"the deeply ingrained habits, skills, and dispositions that we possess due to our life experiences." They become comfortable in some settings and with some tasks, come to see their skill set in a particular way, and develop a sense of identity tied to their habitus. When confronted with choices about actions to make (or not), they draw on our cultural toolkit (Swindler, 1986)—the range of symbolic skills and perspectives developed over time. One's toolkit reflects past experiences across areas of life.

These ideas suggest that, insofar as people have access to different experiences and opportunities, they develop certain skills and responses and fail to develop other skills and responses, which in effect reproduces inequality. Thus, if two people are in the same situation requiring action, they may act differently because they have built a different repertoire of meanings, skills, and habits (or have been denied opportunities to build particular meanings, skills, and habits) that shape their response. This may look like personal preference or individual choice, but really reflects the accumulated knowledge, skills, and experiences built over years rooted in opportunity structure.

To offer a specific example, consider how these processes may occur in schools. To the degree that children with disabilities receive education in segregated classrooms, they may lack exposure to "cool kid" culture. They may not learn how to "hang out," invite people over, talk about popular films, behave at dances, or interact across the genders. Youth with disabilities in high school are less likely to have first jobs or date. Rebellion against parents—a common teen milestone—is harder to accomplish if one is dependent on one's parents for care and transportation (Berger, 2013).

Over time, the child who is tracked in disability-specific classes and settings may not learn to participate comfortably in mainstream youth culture and may instead learn habits and skills useful for the world of segregated disability services. As the child matures into a teen, they and their parents may be hesitant to look for a job in an integrated setting because the teen lacks mainstream skills and may be more accustomed to disability-specific settings. Thus, the inequality in opportunity and skills now becomes reflected in choices by people with disabilities and their family members. If the teen does look for a job in an integrated setting, their lack of social skills may also be used by employers to justify denying them the job. Exclusion from an integrated workplace further deprives them of opportunities to build cultural and social capital. Thus, segregated settings tend to create a vicious cycle. Rather than preparing people for integration, they usually channel people with disabilities into additional segregated settings.

Cultural Resistance and Disability Culture

Paul Longmore (2003) famously referred to disability culture as the "second phase" of the disability rights movement. In the first phase, disabled activists use political and legal strategies to secure equal rights and demand access. In the second phase, **Disability Culture,** people with disabilities express their perspectives and create a way of life that embraces and centers disability. They create a range of cultural products (e.g., art, dance, books, film) that illuminate and prioritize the lived experiences of people with disabilities and celebrate their value in society (Brown, 2002).

Disability Culture is often characterized by the following elements:

- Forging a collective identity among people with disabilities;
- Embracing disability pride—the evaluation of one's disability as value-added, having pride not *despite* disability, but *because of* disability;
- Centering the disability experience and communicating a worldview from the perspective of people with disabilities;
- Exploring and incorporating unique bodily movements, rhythms, expressions;
- Incorporating technology, prosthetics, and devices into one's identity, lifestyle, and art;
- Promoting access via the use of diverse modalities and methods of participation;
- Recognizing and rejecting injustice and ableism, across the myriad identities that people with disabilities hold; and
- Demanding control of the representation of disability by people with disabilities.

Disability culture has grown tremendously in the past 30 years, and there are now many dancers, poets and writers, actors, comedians, artists, filmmakers, academics, and others who contribute to its diversity and vibrancy. The resource section contains several links to examples of disability culture.

Not every idea or piece of art produced by a person with a disability is part of disability culture. Indeed, many people with disabilities share values and perspectives similar to the mainstream culture, including shame associated with disability and/or a desire to attain what is presented as normal. In contrast, Disability Culture typically resists and challenges the mainstream. In this way, it is explicitly political. Its stance as outside the mainstream culture leads to the question of whether disability culture is a subculture, counterculture, or both.

A **subculture** is a group united by shared beliefs and practices, distinguished from the mainstream but not in opposition to it. Anime fans, ballroom dancers, extreme sport enthusiasts, and civil war reenactors offer examples of subcultures. They are cohesive collectivities with shared beliefs and practices that are not shared by most in the mainstream, but they also are not seen as a threat to it. Insofar as disability culture communicates unique ideas central to a cohesive group of people with disabilities without threatening the mainstream, they form a subculture. For example, disability culture is a subculture if it seeks to include people with disabilities into mainstream American culture without threatening it, such as seeing people with disabilities as beautiful while still valuing beauty and demanding people with disabilities receive opportunities for success while still valuing meritocracy and achievement.

A **counterculture** actively challenges the dominant culture and seeks to usurp it. It is revolutionary. Hippies, the Black Panther Party, NeoNazis, and Occupy Wall Street activists are examples of countercultures. How revolutionary are the ideals and goals of disability culture? In some ways, disability culture is quite revolutionary. Disability culture rejects many key American values. It emphasizes interdependence rather than independence, values all people regardless of success, rejects the culture of shame and cure placed on disability, and advocates extensive social welfare programs to meet everyone's basic needs rather than meritocracy. Disability justice activists, for example, demand a fundamental reorganization of the American system. **Disability justice** is a strand of disability activism that is committed to ending intertwining systems of oppression (e.g., ableism, racism, sexism, heterosexism) and empowering and addressing the needs and interests of those most impacted by the violence of oppression (Berne, 2015). Disability justice activists criticize capitalism for its valuation of people based solely in terms of their production and profit value. They call for a system that ensures collective access to the resources of society, liberates all people, and leaves no one behind in poverty or in segregation (Sins Invalid, 2015). By calling for a fundamental redistribution of resources, revaluation of people, eradication of systems of oppression, and a change in the global system of inequality, disability justice activism expresses countercultural demands.

As with many social movements and diverse populations, it may be that disability culture is subculture, counterculture, and part of the dominant culture, as different activists and artists take varied approaches to achieving better lives for people with disabilities. These strands may work together, or they may be in tension as some people embrace America's values and others reject them.

Conclusion

Culture operates on the macro and micro levels, constraining members of society and/or offering them the tools of resistance. For people with disabilities, culture can feel very oppressive. Medical narratives pushing cure, and America's obsessions with beauty, wealth, and competitiveness can feel coercive, demanding people remake themselves to better fit American ideals. Yet, people with disabilities also embrace the tools of culture to express their identities, offer counter-narratives, and build a strong sense of community. Thanks to pioneers in disability activism and culture, people have greater choice in whether to accept or resist mainstream American ideals and conceptions of disability.

KEY TERMS

Capital 109
Compulsory able-bodiedness 96
Counterculture 112
Cultural capital 109
Culture 93
Curative violence 105
Disability culture 111
Disability justice 112
Hegemony 103
Identity first language 98
Ideology 102
Inspiration porn 107
Language 98
Material Culture 102
Medical discourse 104
Narratives 103
Normalization 101
Norms 101
Person-first language 98
Reclamation 99
Representations 105
Rituals 101
Sapir-Whorf thesis 98
Social capital 109
Social Darwinism 103
Subculture 111
Symbol 98
Values 94

RESOURCES

Academic Books and Articles on Disability and Culture

Bingham, Shawn C., and Sara E. Green. 2016. *Seriously funny: Disability and the paradox of humor.* Boulder, CO: Lynne Rienner. An academic book examining the use of humor historically and in the lives and politics of comedians with disabilities.

Brown, Steven E. 2002. "What Is Disability Culture?" *Disability Studies Quarterly* 22, no. 2: 34–50.

Green, Sara E., and Donileen R. Loseke. 2020. "New Narratives of Disability: Constructions, Clashes, and Controversies," *Research in social science and disability* (vol. 11). Bingley: Emerald. A collection of academic papers focusing on narratives of disability.

Mitchell, David T., and Sharon L. Snyder. 2000. *Narrative prosthesis: Disability and the dependencies of discourse.* Ann Arbor, MI: University of Michigan Press. A challenging book that is foundational in the study of disability and culture.

Moore, Leroy F. Jr. 2017. *Black disabled art history 101.* Xóchitl Justice Press. A short primer in the art and activism of Black and Brown disabled artists.

Piepzna-Samarasinha, Leah Lakshmi. 2018. *Care work: Dreaming disability justice.* Vancouver, BC: Arsenal Pulp Press.

Memoir and Collections Related to Disability Culture

Breath and Shadow: A Journal of Disability Culture and Literature. www.abilitymaine.org/breath/.

Lehrer, Riva. 2020. *Golem girl: A memoir.* New York, NY: One World.

Harilyn Rousso's *Don't call me inspirational.* Philadelphia, PA: Temple University Press. A memoir of an activist and artist with disability.

Wong, Alice, ed. 2020. *Disability visibility: First-person stories from the 21st century.* New York, NY: Vintage Books.

Wood, Caitlin, ed. 2014. *Criptiques.* Word Press. https://criptiques.files.wordpress.com/2014/05/crip-final-2.pdf.

Wordgathering: A Journal of Disability Poetry and Literature: wordgathering.com/index.html.

Websites

Disability Visibility Project. https://disabilityvisibilityproject.com/about/. An online community dedicated to creating, sharing, and amplifying disability media and culture.

Institute on Disability Culture. http://www.instituteondisabilityculture.org/links.html. An online resource center to promote disability culture.

Videos of Disability Culture

"Alice Sheppard on Disability Dance and Access." A talk by dancer Alice Sheppard, blending clips of her dance (8 minutes). https://www.youtube.com/watch?v=c-qfZA1V7Yo.

Axis Dance Troupe, "To Color Me Different." Disabled and nondisabled dancers perform in productions that expand ideas about dance and disability (5 minutes). https://www.youtube.com/watch?v=qi7KNDtpXJA&list=PL846D244CD9104171&index=4.

Ayisha Knight, "Until." Features Deaf spoken word artist Ayisha Knight (2 minutes). https://www.youtube.com/watch?v=q3ufVYN3t8M&index=2&list=PL846D244CD9104171.

Crip Culture Montage. A brief collection of dance, poetry, and other expressions of disability culture (4 minutes). https://vimeo.com/10023901.

Deaf West Theatre, "Big River Montage." Brief clip of a production of Big River, performed in ASL and spoken English (1 minute). https://www.youtube.com/watch?v=OnTHClb-6NY.

"Disability Culture Rap" Part 1 (11 minutes) and Part 2 (12 minutes). 2000. Featuring poet and performer Cheryl Marie Wade, offers a look into the disability community as a cultural and political minority. https://www.youtube.com/watch?v=j75aRfLsH2Y&list=PLFSN8Gq2aKY_I7LepLe6didCt_i-6z3aI https://www.youtube.com/watch?v=WTO2vn0dkaU&list=PLFSN8Gq2aKY_I7LepLe6didCt_i-6z3aI&index=2.

Krip Hop Nation, "I'm the First, Please!" Performer Leroy Moore challenges the idea that disability culture and disability hip hop is new. (4 minutes, 30 seconds). https://www.youtube.com/watch?v=gcHkVTb_JM.

"Vital Signs: Crip Culture Talks Back". 1995. Directed by David Mitchell and Sharon Snyder. Fanlight Productions. Documentary featuring disabled performers and cultural workers.

ACTIVITIES

1. Using the history chapter, consider how values differ by time/place and how these values affect views of disability and people with disabilities.

2. Watch several of the videos in the Resource section on Disability Culture. Explain how they show the elements of disability culture. Discuss your reaction to these clips. Using these examples, discuss whether disability culture is an expression of mainstream American culture, a subculture, or a counterculture.

3. Have each student select a different popular television show or movie that includes a character with a disability. Consider the points developed in the chapter related to gauging the quality of disability representations. For each point, how does your representation fair (e.g., do people with disabilities control the representation, who's perspective is assumed…). Have students compare their findings.

4. Watch Stella Young's "I'm Not Your Inspiration, Thank You Very Much" at https://www.ted.com/talks/stella_young_i_m_not_your_inspiration_thank_you_very_much/transcript?language=en. Why does Young find it problematic when people with disabilities are presented as inspirational?

CHAPTER 6

Disability Identity and Socialization

Chapter Synopsis

This chapter draws on sociological theories of the self and socialization to explore issues of disability identity. Because disability is often culturally stigmatized, individuals with disabilities potentially take on that stigma when/if they identify as disabled, and therefore many people avoid incorporating disability into their identity. Younger generations, and especially those born with disabilities, though, are increasingly likely to display disability pride. More complex than simply stigma or pride, disability identity is multifaceted and fluid, and people choose to claim or deny disability, conceal or display it, for many reasons.

Learning Outcomes

6.1 Apply the Looking Glass Self to reflect upon disability identity.

6.2 Analyze the complexity of statuses and orientations that shape disability identity.

6.3 Use Mead's theory of socialization to discuss disability socialization.

6.4 Describe the varied strategies and reasons for disability impression management, including passing and displaying disability.

6.5 Explain how the concept of fluidity shapes ideas about disability.

6.6 Reflect on the implications of technology on the experience of disability.

Disability Identity and the Self

Identity is often seen as a matter of psychology, as a sense of self that emanates from within a person. Sociologists, however, view identity as a social *product* and *process*. According to Julia Miele Rodas (2015, p. 103), **identity** is "the idea of self understood within and against the social context." Through identity, one is positioned within society, seen as a part of or apart from the variety of groups that exist in society. **Disability identity** is the part of identity that relates to disability, that interprets the meaning of disability for oneself and in relation to society (Darling, 2013).

According to symbolic interactionists, we come to understand our social world through social interaction and the shared production and exchange of meaning. Our "self" is one of the many phenomena given meaning through interaction. According to Charles H. Cooley ([1902] 1983) in his theory of the **Looking Glass Self,** a person defines one's self through the feedback received from society. To elaborate, in this theory, a person:

1. Imagines how they appears to others (e.g., I think others see me as funny because they laugh at my jokes);
2. Considers the social judgment tied to this appearance (e.g., I think being funny is usually a good thing because people smile at my jokes, but I worry that sometimes people may be laughing at me); and
3. Based on one's evaluations of others' reactions, develops a sense of self including traits and an evaluation of oneself (e.g., I perceive myself as funny and usually feel positive about it but have a tinge of self-doubt).

According to this theory, disability shapes identity to the extent that it influences the feedback we receive from others. For example, those who are treated as if they do not meet the American ideals of beauty—due to disability or other reasons—may struggle to see themselves as attractive. In her memoir, *Don't Call Me Inspirational,* Harilyn Rousso (2013) explains that her sense of sexuality developed much later in life than for most girls because she was treated—by her parents, boys, and even her friends—as if her cerebral palsy rendered her asexual. On the other hand, her mother and teachers praised her intellect, and she came to see herself as smart and career-driven.

Disability, Status, and Roles

Interactions relevant to developing a self occur within a social structure that includes social statuses, roles, and patterns of opportunity. A **status** is a socially recognized position, and **roles** are the expected behaviors associated with any given status. As a simple example, being a student is a status with the expected roles of studying, attending class, and preparing for a career. Statuses and roles influence our identity in several ways. They provide ritualized opportunities to perform certain behaviors, place us in particular relationships to other people, and shape the evaluations we receive. Thus, being a student may become an important part of your identity because you spend a lot of your time engaging in the associated roles, because your relationships are largely based on being a student, and because much of the feedback and evaluation you receive is in reference to your status as a student.

Not everyone, though, has access to every status. Opportunity structures create patterns of access to particular resources, including statuses. For example, to be a college student, one needs to graduate from high school, gain particular skills through high school, and have access to funding. Not everyone can attain the status of a college student.

Disability may dramatically affect one's statuses, roles, and overall identity. Disability may itself be a status with expected roles. It may also affect access to other statuses, potentially limiting the range of statuses available but also potentially opening opportunities to statuses.

Disability as a Status and the Sick Role

First, let's consider disability as a status itself. Is being a person with a disability a socially recognized position with associated roles? Evidence suggests it may be. Disability influences the reactions received, expectations held, and opportunities provided.

Historically and still today in many ways, disability is associated with the "sick role." Theorized in 1951 by Talcott Parsons, the sick role constitutes the social expectations of people who are sick or disabled. Parsons argued that, because the sick person cannot fulfill their expected duties, they are deviant; however, via the **sick role**, society provides a functional path to address this deviance, mandating that the sick person recognize their illness and comply with medical treatment in order to ensure their quick return to their duties. In exchange for taking on the sick role, the sick person receives certain privileges, including temporary exemption from duties and the avoidance of blame. Because the sick role confers privileges, physicians serve as gatekeepers to this role and ensure that only people with legitimate medical conditions gain access to it. Thus, the sick role, according to Parsons, is functional for both the individual who is encouraged to strive to restore their health and for society which is protected from sickness as well as the threat of people who fake sickness.

People with disabilities are often cast into the sick role. They are expected to seek medical treatment, follow medical guidelines, work toward cure or optimal functioning, and they may be expected to accept "exemption" from valued social roles like working or parenting.

Although Parsons imagined the sick role as a win-win for individuals and society, many people with disabilities resent the ways in which this role is foisted on them, regardless of their wishes. Parsons conceived of the sick role as short-term and beneficial, but people with chronic disabilities may be cast in a permanent state of sick role, and therefore feel *excluded*, rather than temporarily exempted, from valued social statuses (Hahn, 1983; Zola, 1982). For people with mental illness, for example, the sick role led to the use of long-term institutionalization and the loss of rights, often against their will and in the absence of effective treatment. Even when treatment is effective, many people with disabilities challenge the expectation of seeking cure and the reduction of their identity to sickness without regard for the positive aspects of disability identity or all other aspects of identity such as lover, citizen, neighbor, or worker (Clare, 2017).

While some people resent the imposition of the sick role, others want to occupy the sick role but lack access to it. Despite sickness or disability, they are blamed for their condition, lack adequate access to health care, and are compelled to be productive (Welsh, 2018). This is particularly common for people with episodic, invisible, and contested conditions, such as depression, fibromyalgia, and chronic fatigue. In her study of people with invisible disabilities, sociologist Melissa Welsh found lack of access to the sick role to be a common theme. She quotes a respondent:

> *I can no longer do half the things I used to. I lost my boyfriend because he thought I was "crazy" and "psycho."... No one believes the pain or the*

depression. I am told to "suck it up" or "get over it" or "just deal." Even my doctor thinks I am faking. But the pain is real even if no one knows or understands. I feel like a failure every day. I have little to no support system (quoted in Welsh, 2018, p. 141).

Even people with well-documented diseases and disabilities may be denied access to the sick role due to discrimination and lack of resources. In her classic study, *Mama Might Be Better Off Dead*, Laurie Abraham (1993) documented the failures of urban health care which left low-income sick people, who were often people of color, without access to desperately needed health care. Thus, some people are denied the sick role because of the ambiguity of their sickness, while others are denied it due to discrimination and/or the lack of resources.

Scholars have pointed to other statuses commonly imposed on people with disabilities, such as the status of charity recipient or eternal child. Social theorist Georg Simmel (1971) stressed that social positions are relational; they shape interaction across sets of people. People with disabilities are often cast as the dependent one in their relationships, as the object upon which others act. In contrast, people without disabilities are seen as having the power and skills to help or even rescue disabled people, and they are given a position of authority and respect such as caregiver, professional, or philanthropist (Galvin, 2004).

Disability, Stigma, and the Invalidation of Access to Other Statuses

Not only may people with disabilities at times feel confined by their status as a person with disabilities, but the achievement of other statuses may be effectively cut off based on negative social reactions to disability. Erving Goffman (1963, p. 3) defined **stigma** as an attribute that reduces a person "from a whole and usual person to a tainted, discounted one." More than just a negative stereotype, a stigmatized trait (e.g., disability, race) *discredits* a person from claiming valued identities and opportunities. Due to stigma, society often presumes that people with disabilities are not sexual beings, rights-bearing citizens, valued athletes, responsible parents, or worthwhile employees. Without access to other roles, disability may act as a **master status**, a status that dominates the ways in which others think about disabled people, interact with them, and confer or deny opportunities to them (Fine & Asch, 1988; Hughes, 1945).

In its extreme form, stigma can lead to **social death**—the denial of legal and social personhood. Discussing race, former slave and abolitionist Frederick Douglass ([1850] 2009) argued that slavery defined African Americans as property, not persons, and as such they could be denied rights, segregated, and even killed (see also Patterson, 1982). While not a "neat" comparison (the histories of disability and race are very different), people with disabilities have experienced the denial of the status of a person, and this is all the more common when stigmatized traits such as disability and race intersect. For example, contemporary American philosopher and Princeton faculty member Peter Singer argues that personhood requires consciousness, so that people without consciousness (e.g., people in comas, people with very significant intellectual and cognitive disabilities) are not valid persons. As such, he argues, they should hold no legal rights. Eugenics depicted people with disabilities as biologically inferior, and thereby as legitimate targets for institutionalization, sterilization, and deportation. Mental institutions stripped inmates of their previous identities, and their rights—a process Erving Goffman referred to as mortification (1961).

Without social or legal "personhood," the oppression of and perpetuation of violence against people with disabilities becomes shockingly easy (Hughes et al., 2012; Sherry, 2016). Moreover, such violence is often excused. People with disabilities, for instance, suffer high rates of violence and even homicide at the hands of family members (filicide is the term used for killing a family member). Family members who kill family members with disabilities receive notoriously little punishment and, instead, often are given sympathy. These homicides are cast as mercy killings or as "understandable" given the unrelenting stress of caregiving.

Consider a 2019 case in which a grandmother killed her 30-year-old disabled grandson because she worried no one would care for him after she died. The *New York Times* (Taylor, 2019) reported the police captain as saying, "This is a difficult case for detectives… Partly we feel bad for an individual who feels that the only option is to take another human being's life because they're so worried about their care after they've gone." While some people may regard his sympathy as understandable, the Disability Day of Mourning (n.d.), an organization that tracks filicide of people with disabilities, recorded 692 cases in 2018 in the United States alone. When a nation offers pity to those who feel compelled to kill their family members due to lack of care options, yet fails to ensure the provision of adequate care, something has gone awry.

Popular films further legitimate death as the only acceptable option for people with disabilities. Films like *Me Before You* (2016) and *Million Dollar Baby* (2004) promulgate the idea that people with disabilities should want to die and celebrate their heroic acceptance of death. Such movies provoked sharp criticism from the disability community, who advocate instead for the provision of social supports for people with disabilities to live fulfilling lives. After the release of *Me Before You*, disability organization Not Dead Yet created an awareness poster that read "Me Before You is little more than a disability snuff movie, giving audiences the message that if you're a disabled person, you're better off dead," with the hashtags #LiveBoldly? We already do! and #MeBeforeEuthanasia (Pring, 2016).

Global Focus: Stigma

Stigma against people with disabilities is found in many societies. In her memoir *One Little Finger* (2011), Malini Chib describes that, when she was born in India with cerebral palsy, doctors told her mother she would be a vegetable. As a child, adults and other children would ignore her or stare at her. Similarly, in describing his youth as a blind boy in India, Anmol Bhatia (2017) explains that blindness is very stigmatized and is seen as a karmic punishment for misdeeds of a previous life. Blind children are expected to become beggars and have almost no access to services or education.

Given the theory of the Looking Glass Self, one might expect Chib and Bhatia to internalize this stigma, which they did early in their lives.

(Continued)

Global Focus: Stigma *(Continued)*

However, they also had access to other sources of feedback which provided counter-narratives and opportunities. Chib's well-educated family moved to England for her treatment and early education, where she was recognized as highly intelligent. Moreover, her mother learned progressive models of education, and, when they returned to India, she established a school for children with disabilities. Chib credits her family with her intellectual and physical survival. Bhatia's parents sent him to the United States to attend the Arkansas School for the Blind, where he learned Braille, how to use a white cane, and to see himself as deserving of full participation in society. As beneficial as this socialization was, it came at a cost as well. In Arkansas, he struggled to meet the role expectations of being a Hindu, such as maintaining a vegetarian diet and celebrating Hindu holidays.

Chib and Bhatia grew into activists, not simply in reaction to the stigma, but because they had access to alternative discourses about their potential role in society and access to the resources to achieve alternative statuses and roles.

Collective Disability Identity and Disability Pride

Because the cultural influences on identity for people with disabilities have traditionally been negative, people with disabilities have struggled to build positive identities. Recently, however, the emergence of disability culture and activism have created new identity options—new statuses—for people with disabilities. In her memoir, *My Body Politic*, Simi Linton (2006) describes one of her first encounters that suggested to her the possibility of a nonmedical, nontragic identity. After a serious car accident and her transition to using a wheelchair as a young adult, Linton was unsure of her future and uncomfortable with the way many people presumed her fragility and asexuality. She moved to Berkeley California, the epicenter of the burgeoning Disability Rights Movement. Soon after her arrival, she saw an utterly simple yet shocking sight of a man in a wheelchair having fun and flirting with young women. She describes:

> *I stopped short. There on the corner, facing me, was a man sitting tall in a sporty black wheelchair. Wavy blond hair fell down his bare back. He wore only tattered jeans and leather sandals. He was not alone. Three women swirled around him, dancing and skipping. Each woman held a container of yogurt, and each, with gusto, was throwing handfuls of the stuff at him. He answered them. He scooped up the cream from his naked chest and off his sun-burnished shoulders, and lobbed it back. There was yogurt in their hair, running down each and every cheek, dribbling down one woman's thigh, another's forearm.... The California sun was streaming down on them and they were laughing to beat the band...Yes, I thought, if that's disability, I can do that. He made it look fun and sexy. Not woeful and sick-like (2006, pp. 42–43).*

In this moment, Linton encountered an example of disability as ordinary, fun, youthful, and sexy. The man was treated as an equal, not as a patient.

Linton decided to shape an identity for herself that was fun, fiercely proud, and engaged in disability activism.

Disability identity, though, is not simply an individual choice. For people with disabilities to enact an identity as an equal and valued person, they must be understood by others as such, and the social structures must support access (Carey, 2013; Ridolfo & Ward, 2013). In other words, people with disabilities cannot attain an identity of equal citizen simply by ignoring the injustices they face. Criticizing the notion that all disabled people need is a "good attitude," Stella Young (2014) quips, "no amount of smiling at a flight of stairs has ever made it turn into a ramp." Without access and rights, one may not become a student, an employee, a spouse/partner, or an athlete, for example. An identity as an equal citizen necessitates social structures and relationships that recognize a person as such.

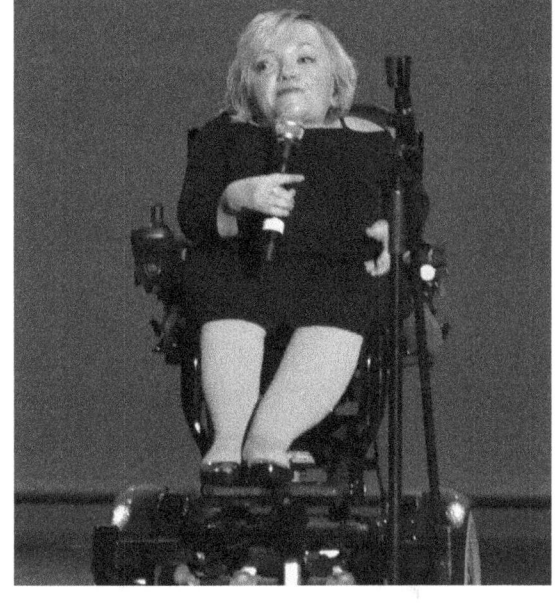

PHOTO 6.1 Journalist, comedian, and activist Stella Young (2013)

Thus, activists forged a **collective political disability identity** which frames disability as a social construct, rejects narratives of disability as individual tragedy, unites people with disabilities on the basis of their shared experience as an oppressed minority, and demands access and rights (Rodas, 2015). Rather than the sick role, some people take on a **disability activist role**—a social status in which people with disabilities are expected to fight for empowerment and social justice. As Simi Linton (1998) states in her classic work *Claiming Disability*, people with disabilities "are bound together.... by the social and political circumstances that have forged us as a 'group.'" This new identity envisions people with disabilities as a minority group, akin to sociological definitions of race that rely on the historical experience of oppression as the basis of racial group identity rather than biology. It also encourages **disability pride**, the evaluation of disability as a positive, valuable aspect of one's identity. Disability pride does not celebrate one's accomplishments *in spite of* disability; rather it celebrates accomplishments *because of, flowing from, and rooted in* one's disability. Rosemarie Garland-Thomson (2019, p. 8) explains, "Becoming disabled means moving from isolation to community, from ignorance to knowledge about who we are, from exclusion to access, and from shame to pride."

This collective political disability identity did not exist in any widespread manner before the 1960s. People saw themselves as blind, deaf, mentally ill, etc... but people who were blind, for example, did not typically act in solidarity with people with mental illness or vice versa. Disability—an umbrella term uniting people with bodies/minds judged to be atypical and/or devalued –emerged as an explicitly political construction. *Political engagement*

PHOTO 6.2 Disability activist outside of the US Capitol Building

fostered disability identity, and disability identity emerged as inherently political.

Identity Politics refers to social/political activism which seeks "to alter the self-conceptions and societal conceptions of their participants" (Anspach, 1979, p. 765). Social movements of the 1960s and after, such as the feminist movement, the civil rights movement, LGBTQ+ activism, and the disability rights movement, pay particular attention to issues of identity and rights. A central feature of these movements is challenging negative stereotypes, building pride, and uniting sufficient numbers of people under a collective identity to fight for equal rights (Siebers, 2008).

Increasingly, educators, psychologists, and physicians believe that it is valuable to nurture the development of a positive disability identification. Psychologist Carol Gill (1997) asserts that a positive disability identification is a crucial component of a disabled person's psychological and social development as a whole and empowered person. Gill's theory of **Disability Identity Development** lays out four types of integration that must be achieved in the process of building positive disability identification:

1. Coming to feel we belong (Integrating into society)—Believing in and developing the confidence to assert one's right to be fully included in society alongside people with and without disabilities;

2. Coming home (Integrating with the disability community)—Overcoming internalized ableism to develop meaningful relationships with others with disabilities with whom one might share experiences, interests, and perspectives;

3. Coming together (Internally integrating our sameness and differentness)—Affirming one's differences based on disability, while also affirming one's ties to mainstream society; in essence, embracing a multicultural experience as both disabled and part of the mainstream.

4. Coming out (Integrating how we feel with how we present ourselves)—Expressing oneself as authentically disabled in public.

According to Gill, by recognizing the value of one's disabled self, integrating it into one's identity and social relationships, and demanding inclusion *as a disabled person*, one comes to feel "whole" as a disabled person.

Disability identity, and identity politics more broadly, though, have been criticized on various fronts. Some say that identity politics essentializes differences. In other words, it demands that people form communities based on their biology, rather than their freely chosen interests. Others argue that people have many identities, but identity politics prioritizes only disability identity. Another criticism is that the political focus on disability pride is misplaced when many people lack basic material resources such as food, shelter, and health care. That said, without the willingness to claim disability and unify on that basis, individuals are left largely unable to collectively advocate for social justice (Siebers, 2008).

Darling's Typology of Disability Orientations

Many people who report limitations or difficulties that might count as disabilities do not *identify* as disabled. Iezzoni and McCarthy (2000) found that 70% of people with a major mobility impairment identified as disabled, and Ridolfo and Ward found 63% of respondents with mobility impairments identified as disabled. A national study by the National Organization on Disability found that 47% of people with significant limitations shared a sense of common identity with other people with disabilities (NOD, 2000). Of those who do not identify as disabled, some see their condition as irrelevant or not very limiting, while others engage in **dis-identification**—the explicit rejection of the label of disability, disability identity, and/or group membership based on disability.

Identifying as disabled varies based on many factors. For example, the *age of disability onset* is an important factor. People who are born disabled or acquire disabilities early in life are more likely to identify as disabled and to develop disability pride than those who acquire disability later in life for whom disability is often experienced as a loss and a threat to established roles and identity (Jemta et al., 2009). Studies of young children with disabilities compared to children without disabilities show no difference in self-esteem (Connors & Stalker, 2007; Sze & Valentin, 2007). As people age, however, people tend to internalize ableist assumptions and see disability as stigmatizing. Thus, people who acquire disabilities late in their life are less likely to identify with the identity of "disabled" or see themselves as connected to a broad, cross-age coalition of "people with disabilities." Rather, they tend to portray impairment as a normal part of aging and align with others who are aging (Priestly, 2001).

The next chapter, Chapter 7, will discuss intersectionality at length, including how gender, sexuality, and race may impact disability identification. Here, we will focus on Rosalyn Darling's (2013) **Typology of Disability Orientations**, which offers a way to theorize disability identity by focusing on four key variables: *acceptance* of the norms and goals of the cultural majority and/or *acceptance* of the disability subculture and *access* to the goals and norms of the cultural majority and/or *access* to disability subculture. Darling argues that one's orientation toward disability varies based on these variables, as seen in Table 6.1.

To explain Table 6.1, let's review each orientation. People with a *Typicality* orientation desire to be part of the cultural majority and have access to it, while rejecting the value of the disability subculture. People within this category tend to have strong ties to and feel included in the dominant culture. They primarily live and work among nondisabled people. They distance themselves from their disability, either feeling shame or treating disability as an irrelevant trait.

TABLE 6.1 Darling's Typology of Disability Orientations

Orientation	Norms/Goals of Cultural Majority - Access	Norms/Goals of Cultural Majority - Acceptance	Norms/Goals of Disability Subculture - Access	Norms/Goals of Disability Subculture - Acceptance
Typicality	Yes	Yes	Yes or No	No
Personal activism	No	Yes	Yes	No
Affirmative activism	Yes or No	No	Yes	Yes
Situational Identification	Yes	Yes	Yes	Yes
Resignation	No	Yes	No	No
Apathy	Yes or No	No	Yes or No	No
Isolated Affirmative activism	No	No	No	Yes

Source: Darling (2013), p. 91.

Personal Activists desire membership in the dominant culture but lack access to it. They may use activism to attain goals associated with the dominant culture, such as medical treatment or integrated education. They often seek these goals as an individual, not as part of the disability community and without identifying with the broader agenda of the disability subculture. Darling offers actor Christopher Reeve as an example. Reeve most famously played Superman in the 1978 film and became paralyzed after an equestrian accident. He used his celebrity status to raise funds for medical research toward cure, but he rarely joined disability activists in the fight for accessibility or antidiscrimination laws.

In contrast, *Affirmative Activists* accept the goals of the disability subculture and have access to it. They tend to use the social model of disability, express disability pride, and work to affirm the value of disability identity. Activists like Ed Roberts who worked to build the infrastructure needed for people with disabilities to enjoy independent living and Simi Linton who fosters positive disability identity through disability culture and art serve as examples of leaders in affirmative disability activism.

Situational Identification is possible for those who have access to both the dominant culture and the disability subculture, accept the value of each, and move between these cultures as they wish. These people may enjoy opportunities alongside nondisabled people in which disability is not especially relevant, while also participating in an active disability community and fighting for disability causes as needed.

For those who wish to be part of the dominant culture but lack access to either the dominant culture or the disability culture, Darling uses the term *Resignation*. This might include, for example, people who, due to poverty or racism, feel barred from the dominant culture yet also have little exposure or access to disability culture.

For those who lack acceptance of both dominant culture and disability culture, Darling uses the term *Apathy*. People in this category do not wish to be a part of either culture.

Finally, *Isolated Affirmative Activism* describes people who accept the goals of the disability subculture but lack access to it. She notes early disability leaders like Ed Roberts who initially had no disability community to join. This category might also include people for who are socially isolated due to disability, discrimination, or inaccessibility, and lack access to others with disabilities.

How does one come to hold a particular disability identity? Although Linton's "yogurt story" depicts a transformational moment, identity development occurs throughout one's life via the processes of socialization. We turn now to consider these processes.

Socialization

Socialization is the process by which one learns the values, beliefs, and practices of culture, including how one fits into it. The psychological theories of Jean Piaget and Erik Erickson conceptualize socialization through the lens of typical development in childhood and through the lifespan. Since these theories accord value to typical development, they cast people with disabilities as deviant. Indeed, child psychologist Erickson institutionalized his disabled child at birth and told his other children that the child had died (Friedman, 1999; Nielsen, 2012). Erikson's biographer posits that his disabled child may have served as a hidden contrast to his conceptualization of healthy childhood development (Friedman, 1999).

In contrast with psychological theories, sociological theories of socialization do not propose universal norms of healthy development. Rather, they consider the processes by which people come to understand and internalize the values of their society/societies. The most famous of these theories is Mead's (1934) theory of role-taking. Through role-taking—the interactional skill of seeing oneself from a given social position (e.g., seeing yourself from a teacher's perspective, seeing yourself from a parent's perspective)—one comes to understand what traits and social positions are available and how one might fit in and among them. **Mead's theory of socialization** lays out three stages through which people develop their role-taking skills—the play stage, the game stage, and the generalized other.

Socialization begins with the play stage, an early stage in which children engage in one-on-one role-taking with significant others. During the play stage, children learn the roles associated with important statuses (e.g. parent, baby, teacher, student), how they are evaluated while in these roles, how to interact with people in other roles, and how to evaluate others. Thus, they begin learning that their behavior and interactions are shaped by their statuses and their relationship to other statuses. As an example, if one is playing cops and robbers, pretending to steal money is responded to very differently if one is playing the cop versus if one is playing the robber. Early on then, children begin learning the expectations associated with varied roles. Although they may not yet have a concept of disability, they are learning that cops, for instance, are expected to run and to communicate orders like "stop" or "put your hands in the air."

In the game stage, children engage in multiple, simultaneous acts of role-taking. To use the game of baseball as an analogy, they learn to interact in a complex environment where lots of people expect different things from them and respond to them differently, and they are expected to interact simultaneously across these different statuses. They do not need to actually play each status; rather, they need to learn what's expected of each status, how the statuses relate to each other, and how/where they fit in and relate to each status. As they interact across multiple statuses, they also make choices about how to fit into the network of statuses, whose feedback they will value, and, in doing so, they develop their sense of self. In this stage children with disabilities begin to develop a sense of whether and where they will be included, on what basis, and how they are perceived by a range of different people like their peers and teachers, laying the foundations for the content of their disability identity. Children without disabilities learn how and if to interact with children with disabilities, if children with disabilities are their peers or somehow "special" or deviant.

In the final stage, called **the generalized other,** people internalize broad social values and expectations, and they learn to evaluate themselves from the standpoint of the general community. At this point, they can self-direct and judge their own behavior. They are well-socialized individuals. As an example, in the United States, this might include understanding the value of financial independence and internalizing society's judgment of people who achieve or fail to achieve it. For many people with disabilities, they must figure out how and if they can be valued, given the dominance of this value. Alice Wong (2019) describes how she initially resisted applying for Medicaid because she thought public benefits were for "those people," and she imagined herself as relatively affluent and self-reliant. Despite her self-image though, she needed Medicaid to survive. She says, "Once I got over myself and realized I had a right to Medicaid, it made a difference" (p. 28). In effect, she discovered a way to resist her internalized stigma regarding Medicaid recipients and instead used her right to Medicaid to validate her identity as a rights-bearer and citizen.

Socialization is dynamic and dependent on one's interactions, culture, feedback, and opportunities. Linton's socialization, for example, might have been very different if she had not moved to Berkeley. **Agents of socialization** are the people, groups, and social institutions that teach a person the culture's way of life and shape how that person comes to see themselves as fitting into that culture. Agents of socialization may include family, peers, school, religion, and mass media, among others. People experience different levels of exposure to various agents (e.g., some people with disabilities are more embedded in religious institutions than others), and the messages delivered by any given type of agent vary widely (e.g., some religions practice faith healing, others preach charity, and others liberation theology). Given the complexity of agents and messages, there is no single outcome of the socialization process for people with disabilities.

That said, we can imagine how disability might variably factor into these stages. To do so, we'll draw on Rod Michalko's (2002) sociological analysis of blindness in America, *The Difference that Disability Makes*. Sociologist Rod Michalko slowly became blind during his childhood. Through his early childhood (in the play and then game stage) as a sighted boy, he learned the roles of an American boy, such as playing sports and acting tough. Less consciously, he learned **"sighted ways,"** the cultural conventions highly reliant on sight, such as the value of looking people in the eye when they speak and taking turns in conversations based on the merest glances. Having learned to act in accordance with these social norms, Michalko felt secure in his masculinity and welcome in his "sighted homeland."

As he progressively lost his vision, though, his place in the game, literally (sports) and metaphorically (society), was threatened. To retain his connection to his male peers and his masculine identity, Michalko switched from baseball to basketball; the larger ball enabled him to continue to play sports, display his masculinity, and retain the respect of his male peers. But as his vision worsened, it threatened his ability to play sports, and therefore his status among his peers. Similarly, his difficulty navigating the classroom increased. He struggled to see the blackboard and to participate in class activities, which also threatened the way his teachers and peers evaluated him and assessed if he was able and worthy to learn alongside his peers. For Michalko's teen self, it seemed that the very survival of his identity and his value depended on passing as sighted. He set out to act as "normally" (i.e., sighted) as possible: "I came to see sightedness as a culture with customs, folkways, and gestures—with its own language. I imitated this culture to perfection" (p. 9).

These "sighted ways" were not functional for Michalko, except to ensure continued acceptance from the people around him. Despite his increasing blindness, he made sure to "look" at people who were talking, to nod in acknowledgment, and to endlessly consider how he appeared to someone sighted. Moreover, he learned to conceal his **"blind work"**—the strategies used by blind people to navigate and enjoy the world around them. For instance, people who are blind may touch things in their environment to gather information. They may rely on sound, vibrations, and smell. However, touching is frowned upon in the sighted world. Think of the sharp social disapproval one might receive for touching another person, touching someone else's possessions, or even just getting fingerprints on the variety of objects in one's social environment. The sighted world also frowns upon actions like overt sniffing, spinning to take in one's sensory environment, and the constant narration of events by a sighted person to a blind person to assist them in understanding events in their environment. Thus, blind people learn to touch covertly, sniff soundlessly, and receive voiced interpretation via earbuds.

Michalko explains that the rehabilitative goal of removing "blindisms" (a form of normalization) prioritizes the sighted world and demands that the blind person constantly imagine what they look like to the sighted. In other words, through formal (e.g., education, rehabilitation) and informal (peers) agents of socialization over a long period of time, *Michalko learned to perform and evaluate himself by the standards of the sighted community. The sighted community served as his generalized other.* By the standards of sightedness, though, he constantly risked failure. Only as an adult, when he gained exposure to the sociological ideas of social construction, met disability rights activists, and became a part of an activist blind community, did he begin to challenge the invalidation of his perspective and embodiment as a blind man and to embrace blindness as a valid personal, social, and political identity.

PHOTO 6.3
Learning blind skills like using Text-to-Speech accessibility features can be important to a positive disability identity

Embodiment, Impression Management, and Performativity

Michalko's story also opens a door to discussing the role of the body in identity. Rooted in Enlightenment thought (see Chapter 3), people in Western cultures often think of the self as rooted in the mind, including one's thoughts, perspectives, personality, and preferences. They often imagine that the body is not central to shaping identity. In contrast, theories of embodiment argue that the body mediates one's experience and understanding of the world. They point to three key ideas that we will explore: (a) our bodies shape our experiences, interactions and opportunities, and therefore who we are; (b) society's distribution of resources and opportunities affect our bodies; and (c) our bodies are a key mechanism by which we express our identities.

To elaborate on the first idea—that our bodies shape who we are—Michalko's story reveals that his experience with the world and therefore his sense of his own identity shift as his sight diminishes. His sense of security, the basis for his peer relationships, and his ideas of justice transform as his changing body repositions him from a member of the majority into a member of a minority. Similarly, Nancy Mairs, in her memoir *Waist High in the World*, explains that her experience as a wheelchair user with multiple sclerosis fundamentally shapes her identity: "This is my perpetual view, from the height of an erect adult's waist. And the difference has consequences" (1996, p. 16). Constant barriers—such as encounters with stairs, curbs, and inaccessible bathrooms—communicate to her that her presence is neither wanted nor needed: "The world as it is currently constructed does not especially want—and plainly does not need—me in it" (p. 87). This experience as an unwanted outsider changes the way she views herself, others, and society.

The second point regarding embodiment and inequality argues that social inequality has a direct impact on our bodies. To offer some examples, the oppression of women in many cultures leads to the impairment of their bodies in order to achieve culturally valued goals, including the practices of foot-binding, genital mutilation, and cosmetic plastic surgery. Oppressed populations are vulnerable to poverty and war, so people in the poorest regions of the world experience disability at greater rates. The bodies of people with disabilities are physically constrained through "therapeutic" regimes like institutionalization and applied behavioral analysis. These examples show a few of the ways in which the body becomes a site where inequality is enacted and made manifest. In a cyclical relationship, oppression breeds disability, and disability raises one's consciousness of oppression as one comes to see society from the perspective of one who is excluded.

Third, bodies are central to how people enact their identities. According to Erving Goffman (1956), all people engage in **impression management**—the use of outward strategies to actively display one's identities and compel desirable feedback. Goffman's argument should not be reduced to the idea that people "fake" their identities. Rather, they act a certain way to cue others as to their identity and to be acknowledged and respected as who they see themselves to be. For example, one might wear a varsity jacket to cue others that being an athlete is an important aspect of one's identity.

The body is a medium of impression management. Like all people, people with disabilities engage in **impression management techniques**, the host of strategies used to present a particular self to the world, receive acceptable feedback, and enable a positive self-identity. Bodies, though, may constrain and/or open new possibilities for these techniques. For example, to assert authority, professors will often stand, move around the room, and speak loudly. It may be more challenging to assert authority if these physical techniques are not available. Professors with disabilities may use alternative strategies, such as displaying their intellect and building strong relationships with students.

Impression management, especially in first encounters, is particularly fraught for people with disabilities because they must deal with the likely effect of stigma. In other words, they enter new situations potentially already discredited and must manage the stereotypes and deftly assert their desired identities. Thus, for people with disabilities, impression management is a pressing and challenging endeavor. In the prior discussion of sighted and blind work, Michalko engaged in impression management by performing sighted work to increase his likelihood of acceptance by the sighted community. Similarly, Tara Fannon's (2016) research with blind women reveals the host of impression management techniques they used to negate stigma and assert competence. For Fannon's respondents, attention to their outward appearance played a crucial role in managing stigma. Women learned to apply make-up, style their hair, and develop their personal fashion style in order to communicate their personality, their validity as women, and their competence more generally. They explained that the failure to exhibit the skills of attractiveness and self-care could be used against them, as evidence of their incompetence.

Impression management techniques vary considerably and might include assimilation (as shown by Michalko's early years and many of Fannon's respondents), self-isolation, humor, confrontation, and activism. Shawn Bingham and Sara Green's (2015, 2016) work on comedians with disabilities offers a compelling example of the ways in which people with disabilities may learn to use humor to diffuse tension, appear likable, educate people without disabilities about the lives of people with disabilities, and/or challenge stereotypes. One of the comedians they interviewed, Maysoon Zayid, is a Palestinian Muslim woman with Cerebral Palsy (CP). In her Ted Talk "I have 99 problems… Palsy is just one," she opens with jokes that put her disability front and center. Because her body shakes, she jokes, "I am not drunk, but the doctor who delivered me was." She goes on to confront stereotypes about the causes of CP including divine punishment and genetics, saying "I didn't get it [CP] because my parents are first cousins… which they are." Through humor, Zayid delves into the taboo subject of disability, welcomes people into her world, and challenges ableism. Many of the comedians interviewed by Bingham and Green began using humor early in their lives to challenge negative stereotypes and while maintaining positive relationships.

Navigating the Concealment or Display of Disability Identity

In impression management, one of the key decisions that people with disabilities make is whether to try to pass as nondisabled or actively display disability. **Passing** involves the concealment of a stigmatizing trait (Darling, 2013; Samuels, 2015). The visibility of some disabilities makes passing impossible, but other disabilities are largely invisible, and they are only made legible in particular contexts (e.g., the special ed classroom, the "short bus") or through markers (e.g., stimming, assistive technology) (Brune & Wilson, 2013).

People may choose to pass as nondisabled for a variety of reasons, including to deal with feelings of internalized shame, to gain opportunities denied to people with disabilities, and/or to refute stereotypes imposed upon them (Brune & Wilson, 2013). Historically, great pressure was placed on people with disabilities to pass. Indeed, passing was imperative to one's welfare at a time when disability might lead to institutionalization, sterilization, job discrimination, and exclusion from public schools. Robert Edgerton's classic 1967 study of recently deinstitutionalized people with a label of mental retardation showed the care they took to conceal their institutional histories and to establish themselves as "normal" members of the community (Edgerton, [1967] 1993). Still today, passing can be a valuable tool. As an example, members of the military and police officers risk losing their jobs if they disclose physical and mental disabilities. *Identities are not simply personal choices; they connect one, or block one, from resources.* Passing, therefore, is more likely when disability is tightly connected to the denial of resources and opportunities (Carey, 2013).

With the emergence of disability activism, however, the distribution of resources shifted, and therefore the calculation for passing also shifted. There are now more reasons to identify as and actively engage in **disability display**—the purposeful public presentation of disability identity and traits. Tobin Siebers (2008) theorized why people with disabilities might choose to publicly display their disability. These reasons include:

1. To achieve political ends, such as the dramatic 1990 "Capitol Crawl" when disabled activists crawled up the steps of the Capitol building in Washington DC to vividly demonstrate the humiliation and exclusion caused by inaccessibility.

2. To communicate valuable information, such as using a white cane to communicate to fellow pedestrians and drivers that one may not move or respond as expected, or the use of a wheelchair by someone who can walk but tires quickly to signal to others that they may move slowly or require assistance.

3. To reject the demand for able-bodiedness, such as when students claim disability and their right to accommodations and in the process challenge the idea that all people should be evaluated based on the same standards.

4. To use the common prejudices regarding disability to their advantage instead, such as revealing one's intellectual disability to be excused from a rule or revealing an amputation to garner desired attention.

5. To reinforce the value of able-bodiedness, such as showing how one "overcame" one's disability and/or to display the tragedy of one's disabled body, such as poster children who display their disability to raise money for medical research for a cure.

6. To fraudulently reap the rewards to disability when one is not disabled. Siebers referred to the display of disability by people without disabilities to reap rewards as "disability drag," such as when able-bodied actors play disabled characters and receive accolades for their great achievement. Indeed, society increasingly worries about disability fraud and the false claiming of disability to receive benefits (Dorfman, 2020). We see this concern, for example, in news coverage regarding upper-class students who falsely claim disability to secure extended time on the SAT and workers who fake disability to receive workers compensation benefits.

Performativity

As discussed above, Goffman argues that people actively manage displays of their identity. Judith Butler's (1990) theory of performativity pushes this thinking further. **Performativity** argues that identity is *nothing more than* a series of enacted performances which exist in relation with some set of cultural expectations regarding particular identities. Writing about gender, Butler posits that gender is the repeated enactment of gendered performances based on some set of cultural expectations, repeated so often that one's "gender" seems a part of one's self. Although one comes to feel a particular gender, gender and identity more broadly are inherently dynamic. One can learn, unlearn, and create how to perform and thereby shift one's gender.

Similarly, sightedness, sanity, and health, for example, are performed. Examining the performance of sanity, Peta Cox (2013) lists several of the rules of a good performance: do not mutter to oneself, do not stare at strangers for too long, and do not rock, move erratically, drool, or twitch. She then asks: if one can consistently perform sanity, is one sane? In other words, if one hears voices, feels desperately sad, or fears social interaction BUT simultaneously can perform in social interaction as "normal," control one's symptoms, and never falter, is this sanity? Is sanity the *absence* of fear, sadness, or irrationality, OR is it *the ability to act in expected ways* despite fear, sadness, or irrationality? Ultimately, whether one is considered sane or insane may rest in the *display* of normality or abnormality. Society tends to accept the experience of sadness, fear, and irrationality, but is less likely to accept the outward display of odd or deviant behavior.

Disability Identity as Fluid

People often think of disability as a static identity category, meaning that one simply would be disabled or not. However, disability is fluid, meaning that the relevance, experience, and display of disability shifts depending on one's changing body, the particular social context, and benefits of and access to various strategies (Barnartt, 2010). To elaborate, bodies themselves change. Disability is a status which one may enter or leave, although not always based on one's choice. Indeed, the term **temporarily able-bodied** calls attention to the fact that most people one day will enter the status of disabled.

More than a single transition, though, people may move in and out of disablement. Someone with cancer may be disabled the day of each chemotherapy session, but not otherwise; someone with multiple sclerosis may have extended bouts of symptoms and then extended periods without symptoms; people with depression may move in and out of emotional cycles. Moreover, disability varies by social context, a point made by the social model. Disability will be more or less relevant in some contexts than others. At an accessible home and workplace, for example, a wheelchair user may perform their roles fully. However, in an urban area where many small shops have one or two steps to get in and the bathrooms are small, the environment creates disablement and prevents wheelchair users from shopping, eating, and toileting.

Relationships and interactions also vary, and disability may be more or less relevant in any given interaction. When interacting in the disability community, disability may be highly salient. When interacting with work colleagues, disability may become salient if one experiences inaccessibility or if disability provides a fresh perspective, for example, but not otherwise. Disability is only one aspect of someone's identity, and therefore the salience of disability identity—the relevance of disability identity in a given situation—may vary. Thus, the ideas of disability as a status or fixed identity may be challenged by the fluidity of disability in interaction with shifting bodies, environments, and relationships.

The Meaning of the Body: Cyborgs, Transhumanism, and Inequality

In the final section of this chapter, we briefly consider the relationship between the body, disability, technology, and identity. Technology is increasingly integrated into our bodies, lives, and relationships, fundamentally transforming the human and social experience (Mauldin, 2016). Technology might be external (e.g. wheelchair, augmented communication device), attached (prosthetics), internal (pace-maker, microchip) or chemical (drugs that affect mood or sharpen attention or memory).

Technology may have many benefits in relation to disability. Adaptive technology may increase functionality and thereby reverse or reduce the social disadvantage of disability. Technologies such as glasses are so common and effective that most people with correctable vision limitations do not identify as disabled at all. Medication alleviates disabling symptoms for many conditions. These technologies may come to feel like a valued extension of one's self as they are incorporated into one's life. Indeed, disability culture embraces the inclusion of equipment in self-expression—such as in disability dance, art, and sexual expression—and explores the unique ways that technology extends and shapes our humanity.

More dramatically, technology offers the potential to transform disability into superhuman abilities. According to Donna Haraway (1991), the **cyborg** melds body, mind, and technology in ways that disrupt traditional dichotomies of ability/disability and natural/unnatural to create limitless possibility. As technology advances, progressing from the wooden prosthetics to bionics, from mind-numbing pills to sophisticated chemical blends that sharpen acumen, technology enhances human ability such that people may come to *desire* bionic limbs, artificially constructed features, internal computer chips that log

CHAPTER 6 Disability Identity and Socialization   133

our information, and drugs that induce mental stability and heighten acumen (Brashear, 2013). What was once seen as disability then becomes a potential path to enhanced abilities.

Transhumanism is a philosophy that advocates the development and use of technology to enhance the human mind and body, encouraging human/machine hybridization. Transhumanists imagine a world in which human/machine hybridization erases disability and expands human potential. Critics of transhumanism, though, fear that access to human enhancement will set off a race toward enhancement, creating new issues of stigma, disability, and inequality. Given the high cost of advanced technology, the wealthy with or without disabilities may purchase enhancements, while disabled poor people may be left without access to simple, reliable technology like wheelchairs. The wealthy might pay for a host of surgical enhancements for function and appearance (think of the fictional residents of the Capitol in the Hunger Games), while the poor continue to die early, unable to afford basic health care. In a situation of grave inequality, the access of the wealthy to purchase enhancements could fuel an ever increasing gap in human capital and ability. Indeed, as more people purchase enhancements, the failure to have enhancements could itself become the social equivalent of disability. For example, as antiaging technologies such as botox, wrinkle reduction therapies, hair dye, and plastic surgery become common, natural aging might increasingly become stigmatized and associated with disability.

PHOTO 6.4
Cyborgs meld body, mind and technology

While enhancements may confer advantages and prestige, the social status of people who blend humanity and machine is by no means consistently positive. Society polices the borders of humanity and often excludes those deemed unnatural. As an example, the Paralympics is an elite sporting event for athletes with disabilities that takes place alongside the Olympics. Athletes with disabilities are segregated into separate games, supposedly to allow for an appropriate level of competition. Using his prosthetic "cheetah legs," however, runner Oscar Pistorius beat the times of nondisabled runners. Rather than celebrating his success and welcoming him into the Olympics, nondisabled athletes accused him of having a technological advantage–his cheetah legs absorbed shock and didn't tire—and the International Association of Athletics Federation (IAAF) attempted to ban him from competing in the 2008 Olympics. They defended this ban by defining his body as unnatural and therefore ineligible for competition against natural athletes.

Other concerns about the natural body infiltrate sports. Trans women competing in women's sports face accusations of benefiting from unfair advantages. The policing of sex/gender in sports has led to the identification of "normal" testosterone levels for men and women. Even women born with unusually high, naturally produced, levels of testosterone now may face exclusion from women's sports. In 2018, the IAAF announced guidelines for allowable testosterone level and required female athletes with higher levels of testosterone to artificially lower their levels. Thus, the meaning and acceptance of natural or modified bodies varies considerably based on what benefits are accessed and by whom.

Conclusion

In conclusion, disability identity is complex and multifaceted. It offers a window to examine many sociological issues of identity such as impression management and the meaning of the body. Lennard Davis (2013) argues that disability is the ultimate "postmodern" identity—socially constructed, rapidly shifting, performed in different ways, and resistant to any sense that identity is fixed or natural.

KEY TERMS

Agents of socialization 126
Blind work 127
Collective political disability identity 121
Cyborg 132
Disability display 130
Disability identity 115
Disability Identity Development 122
Disability pride 121
Dis-identification 123
Generalized Other 126

Identity 115
Identity Politics 122
Impression management 128
Impression management techniques 128
Looking Glass Self 116
Master status 118
Mead's theory of socialization 125
Passing 129
Performativity 131
Roles 116

Sick role 117
Sighted ways 126
Social death 118
Socialization 125
Stigma 118
Status 116
Temporarily able-bodied 131
Transhumanism 133
Typology of Disability Orientations 123

RESOURCES

Disability Memoirs Related to Identity and Socialization

Clare, Eli. 1999. *Exile and pride: Disability, queerness and liberation.* South End Press.

Connolly, Kevin M. 2009. *Double take: A memoir.* New York, NY: Harper Publishers.

Greely, Lucy. 2003. *Autobiography of a face.* Harper Collins.

Johnson, Roland (as told by Karl Williams). 1994. *Lost in a desert world.* Plymouth Meeting, PA: Speaking for Ourselves. Available online at https://www.disabilitymuseum.org/dhm/lib/detail.html?id=1681&page=all

Linton, Simi. 2006. *My body politic: A memoir.* Ann Arbor, MI: University of Michigan Press.

Michalko, Rod. 2002. *The difference that disability makes*. Temple University Press.

Rousso, Harilyn. 2013. *Don't call me inspirational: A disabled feminist talks back*. Philadelphia, PA: Temple University Press.

Academic Readings

Bingham, Shawn C., and Sara E. Green. 2015. "Aesthetic as Analysis: Synthesizing Theories of Humor and Disability Through Stand-Up Comedy." *Humanity and Society* 40, no. 3: 278–305.

Darling, Rosalyn B. 2013. *Disability and identity: Negotiating self in a changing society*. Boulder, CO: Lynne Reinner. Tobin Siebers, Disability Theory.

Goffman, Erving. 1963. *Stigma: Notes on the management of spoiled identity*. New York, NY: Simon and Schuster. New York: First Anchor Books. Films.

Siebers, Tobin. 2008. *Disability theory*. Ann Arbor, MI: University of Michigan.

YouTube Clips of Comedians with Disabilities

Blue, Josh, "Josh Blue Stand-up" https://www.youtube.com/watch?v=LQxBEqqj0Bk.

Nina, Ghiselli, "Adventures of an Outspoken Woman Who Stutters," https://www.youtube.com/watch?v=3DZKO0717Vs.

Zayid, Maysoon, "I've Got 99 Problems... Palsy is Just One," https://www.ted.com/talks/maysoon_zayid_i_got_99_problems_palsy_is_just_one?language=en.

YouTube Clip on Assisted Suicide and Not Dead Yet

Liz Carr Speaks to UK Parliament on assisted suicide legislation, http://notdeadyetuk.org/resources/ (12 minutes).

Films

Audible. 2021. Netflix. Follows football players at a deaf high school as they navigate family, relationships, and football. (38 minutes).

Crip camp: A disability revolution. 2020. Netflix. Tells the story of a group of disabled youth who met at camp and went on to become disability activists (1 hour and 48 minutes).

Fixed: The science/fiction of human enhancement. 2013. Explores questions of disability, ability, and technology (61 minutes).

Invitation to dance. 2014. Documentary about disability in modern American, using Simi Linton's life as the frame of the documentary (1 hour and 26 minutes).

Temple Grandin. 2010. A Hollywood biographical drama about Temple Grandin, an autistic woman whose successes include revolutionizing the cattle industry (2 hours).

ACTIVITIES

1. Read a memoir (see resources) by a disabled author and consider: (a) how the looking glass self affected their disability identity, (b) how the agents and processes of socialization shaped their identity, and (c) the techniques they used to pass, display disability, or otherwise manage their impressions.

2. As if you were a college administrator, what policies, activities or strategies could you develop to foster disability pride? Develop a university plan to do so. Consider the advantages and disadvantages of proactively intervening to support disability pride. Consider Gill's theory of positive disability identification. How might a program

address each aspect of Gill's theory in practice?

3. Read Bingham and Green's article on humor (see resources) and watch the clips of disability comedians (see resources). Explain impression management, and, in light of Bingham and Green's theories, describe how comedians with disabilities use humor for impression management.

CHAPTER 7

Intersectionality: Gender, Sexuality, and Race

Chapter Synopsis

The construction and experience of oppression intertwines across multiple systems of power—an idea referred to as intersectionality (Crenshaw, 1989). Ableism, racism, sexism, classism, and other forms of inequality mutually form and interact, often reinforcing each other (Lewis, 2020; Miles, 2019). This chapter examines the intersections of disability with gender, sexuality, and race to examine the ways in which ableism is gendered, sexualized, and racialized, and the ways in which inequalities by gender, sexuality, and race are shaped and reinforced by ableism.

Gender

Prevalence of Disability by Gender

According to the 2019 American Community Survey, women are slightly more likely to be disabled than men (12.7% vs. 12.4%) (www.disabilitystatistics.org/).[1] This gendered outcome holds across racial groups, except for Native Americans and Alaskan Natives for whom 17.3% of men report disabilities, compared to 16.6% of women.

Learning Outcomes

7.1 Apply a feminist disability studies framework to discuss gendered constructions and outcomes of disability.

7.2 "Crip" sexuality by exploring the barriers to sexuality and imagining how to build a society that values and enables sexuality and pleasure for all people.

7.3 Examine the ways in which race intertwines with the disability experience.

---

[1] Disabilitystatistics.org's data tool provides data on demand. Data from the 2019 American Community Survey were retrieved November 2021.

This pattern varies by age and disability, though. Figure 7.1 draws on the American Community Survey, which defines disability as those who report difficulties in any of the following areas: hearing, ambulation, vision, self-care, cognition, and independent living. It shows that boys (aged 5–17) are more likely to have all types of reported disabilities than girls. The difference is particularly striking for cognitive disabilities, which leads to the higher representation of boys in special education than girls. However, disability shifts with age. In adults ages 18–64, men are more likely to report hearing disabilities and cognitive disabilities, but women are more likely to report disabilities in ambulation, vision, self-care, and independent living. For adults ages 65 and over, women report more of all types of disabilities other than hearing. Thus, as Americans age, women are increasingly likely to report disability.

Figure 7.2 uses data from the 2014 Survey of Income and Program Participation, which asks adults about a different set of disabilities: communication, mental and physical disabilities. Results from this survey indicate that women are more likely than men to report having a disability and having more than one co-occurring disability. They are more likely to report mental and physical disabilities, whereas men are more likely to report communication disabilities.

To understand prevalence rates by gender, we must consider more than just biology. Due to gender roles, boys may be diagnosed with cognitive disabilities more often than girls because they are more rambunctious, whereas girls may be more compliant and socially adept. Even if the disabilities reflect biological reality, biology is shaped by gender inequality. For instance, the disability gap between men and women may grow with age because women earn lower incomes, exercise less control over their lives, and experience more abuse, all of which may contribute to their higher rates of impairment.

FIGURE 7.1 Prevalence of Disability Type by Gender and Age, 2018[2]

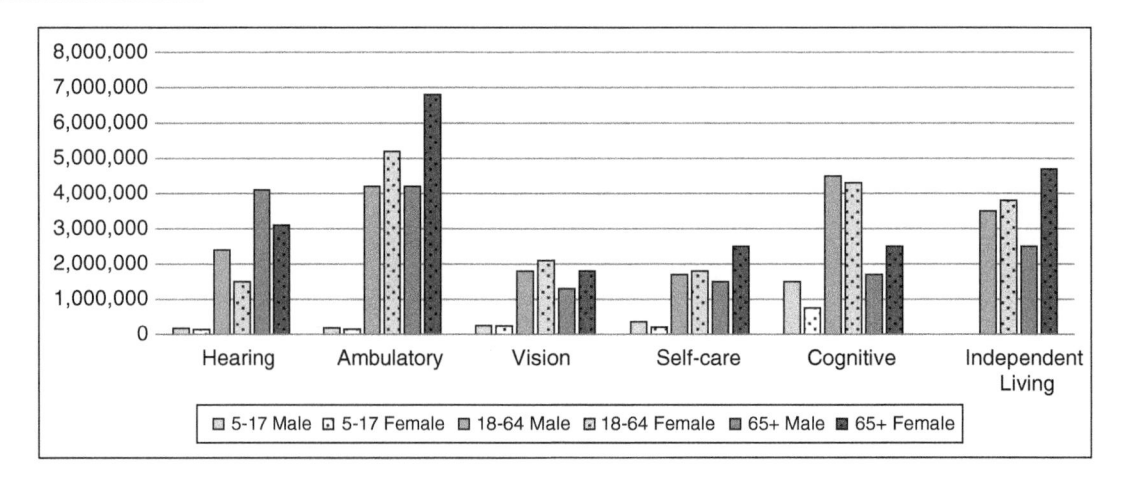

Data Source: US Census Bureau (2020), drawing from the American Community Survey 2018.

---

[2] Data Source: US Census Bureau, 2020, drawing from American Community Survey 2018. Data published at https://www.census.gov/content/dam/Census/library/visualizations/2020/comm/living-with-disabilities.pdf

FIGURE 7.2 Percentage of Adult Disabled Respondents by Disability Type and Gender, 2014[3]

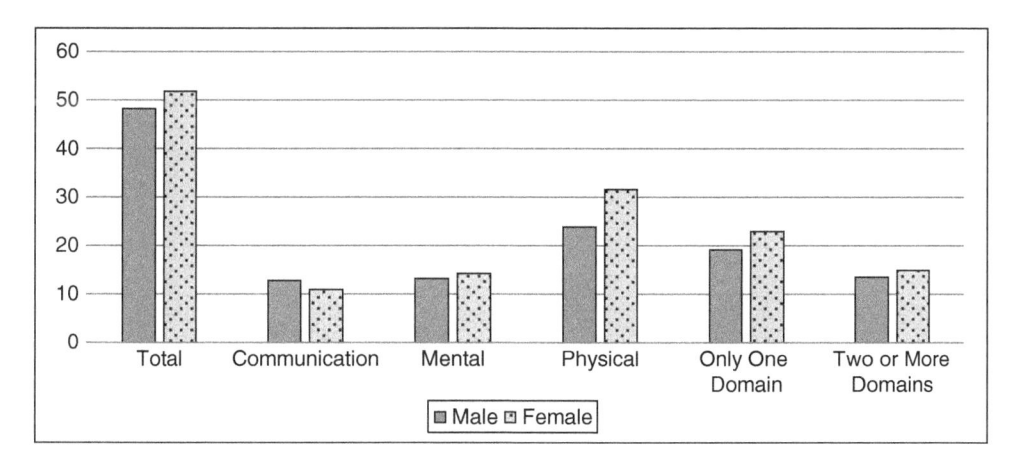

Data Source: US Census Bureau, Social Security Administration Supplement to the 2014 Panel of the Survey of Income and Program Participation, Sept-Nov 2014 (Taylor, 2018).

The differences in disability prevalence by gender are starker on a global scale. In low- and middle-income countries, women constitute up to three-fourths of the disabled population. In these countries, women experience greater risk due to limited education, poor workplace conditions, limited healthcare, and violence (European Women's Lobby, 2011).

Feminist and Intersectional Frameworks

Our brief look at prevalence rates highlights the importance of exploring the relationship between gender and disability. **Feminist disability studies** aim to document and explain the intersecting experiences and inequalities of gender and disability and to pursue social justice for women with disabilities (Asch & Fine, 1988; Blum, 2020; Garland-Thomson, 1997; Hall, 2011; Naples et al., 2019). Feminist disability scholarship is overtly critical of oppression and is political in its orientation, following the feminist mantra that the "personal is political."

Feminist disability studies has been expanded to address additional intersecting systems of inequality. The **Feminist Intersectional Disability Framework** explicitly includes race and class, as well as gender and disability (Miles, 2019). Miles explains the framework's key assumptions:

First, race, class, gender, and other markers of difference, and the associated systems of oppression, collectively contribute to how disability is acquired, experienced, and socially constructed. Second,

---

[3]Data Source: Taylor, Danielle M. 2018. "Americans with Disabilities: 2014," drawing on data from US Census Bureau, Social Security Administration Supplement to the 2014 Panel of the Survey of Income and Program Participation, Sept-Nov 2014 https://www.census.gov/content/dam/Census/library/publications/2018/demo/p70-152.pdf. Author created chart, from published data.

the intersection of race, class, gender, and ability oppression contribute to disabled women of color's differential access to resources, opportunities, and treatment in society. Third, disabled women of color experience marginalization within dominant majority communities (i.e., White, able-bodied, middle-class communities), as well as within their minority communities (i.e., black, disabled, poor communities). Finally, ableism is commonly an unaccounted predictor of structural inequality. Because many social problems examined by researchers exclude disability inquiry and its intersections, the conclusions developed to rectify these problems are often incomplete and inadequate.

Constructions of Disability and Gender

Gender and disability are both *social constructions*. Many sociologists distinguish between sex and gender, such that sex refers to biological/anatomical differences, while gender refers to the norms, roles, and opportunities associated with being male, female, or another gender. Similarly, many sociologists distinguish between *impairment*, referring to biophysiological differences/limitations, and *disability*, which refers to the socially constructed norms, roles, and opportunities associated with being seen or regarded as able or disabled. Thus, neither gender nor disability flows directly from biology. For example, nothing about having a uterus means that one is less able to write software code, yet women have traditionally been seen as less adept at science and technology. Similarly, nothing about the physicality of being blind means that one cannot be a good parent, yet society too often assumes that myth to be true.

To say that gender and disability are social constructions does not deny the importance of *embodiment*—the idea that our bodies shape our experience of the world and that the social conditions of the world shape our bodies. The body—including the lived experience of the body, understandings of the body, valuations of different bodies, strategies of controlling and normalizing the body—is central to understanding the intersection of gender and disability (Hall, 2011; Siebers, 2008). For example, women's bodies may experience pregnancy and breastfeeding, whereas men's bodies do not. In a society where men are situated as the norm, pregnant and breastfeeding bodies are cast as problematic. Women may be denied access to needed support—such as time to pump milk while at work, safe spaces to breastfeed, and prenatal healthcare—thereby creating disablement (Hoffman, 2021). Thus, biological experiences intersect with systems of meaning and values.

An analysis of disability and gender often starts with the idea of **gender roles**—the norms, beliefs, and behaviors associated with masculinity and femininity. Gender roles shape the experience of disability, and disability shapes gender roles.

To look first at women, some gender stereotypes may be reinforced by disability stereotypes. Both women and people with disabilities are stereotyped as weak, incompetent, and dependent. For women with disabilities, then, these stereotypes are intensified (Nario-Redmond, 2010, 2020). While disability and gender stereotypes may reinforce each other, that is not always the case. Instead, disability may bar women from occupying traditionally feminine roles. The primary stereotype of femininity is nurturance, but women with disabilities are often stereotyped as asexual and inept at mothering and caregiving (Frederick, 2017; Walsh, 2011). Beauty is another key expectation of femininity, yet disabled women are often made to feel that their bodies are not acceptable or beautiful (Lehrer, 2014; Liebowitz, 2014). Scholars Adrianne Asch and Michelle Fine (1988) describe disabled women as occupying a state of "rolelessness" because they may be denied the traditional female role of nurturer *as well as* the traditional male role of worker/provider.

Gender roles, though, vary by race, class, and other demographic categories. Whereas White women have often been seen as dependent and weak, Black women have been expected to work, fueling the stereotype of the "strong black woman." This stereotype (and many other factors) leads Black disabled women to have a different experience of disability than that of White women. As shown in Angel Miles's (2019) scholarship, the stereotype of the strong, Black woman may have positive features, celebrating resilience, sacrifice, and empowerment. Yet, it also compels Black disabled women to feel like they must achieve more with fewer resources, a sentiment which stigmatizes their need for care and supports. For example, one Black, disabled, female participant in Miles's study expressed her preference to give care and support rather than receive it, saying, "I like helping other people physically, spiritually, and financially. And so, you know, I like being able to pay people to do things for me. You know? I'm not a person that always has to have something done for me." Although disabled Black women earn less and face greater obstacles than disabled White women, they are expected to work harder with fewer supports.

Women with disabilities vary in their response to gender roles. Some women embrace femininity and demand the right to occupy feminine roles, such as sexual partner, fashion icon, and mother. For example, Keah Brown (2019) created the hashtag #DisabledandCute where women could post pictures showcasing their beauty. Karen Hitselberger (2020) created the website ClaimingCrip.com, where she states, "Reclaiming and redefining what it means to be beautiful in a body that falls outside of society's standards of beauty is powerful and it is political." Other women with disabilities such as Aimee Mullins, Aaron Philip, and Kennedy Garcia are pioneers in the world of high-fashion modeling.

Many women feel pressure to perform their gender roles and worry about the negative consequences of failure. In Tara Fannon's (2016) study of women with visual impairments, some participants felt that poor appearance might be used against them, as an indicator of broader faults like incompetence. One woman stated, "I suppose I put pressure

PHOTO 7.1
Disabled women often feel pressure to perform expected gender roles

Credit: OneClearVision (2013). Reproduced with permission from istock.com.

PHOTO 7.2
Displays of femininity may help disabled women be accepted and decrease stigma

on myself to look a certain way firstly to make a good impression, and also… because of my vision impairment… I feel that if I don't look a certain way people may think that I am not able to do it." Another interviewee stated, "you have to look healthy," because people are quick to assume that blind people are sick or incompetent.

Whereas the roles of disability and femininity tend to reinforce the inferiority of disabled women, disability conflicts with the power typically accorded to men (Gerschick, 2000; Gerschick & Miller, 1995; Hahn, 1989). Masculinity in America is defined through strength and entitlement. Men are presented as providers, independent, rational, aggressive, and powerful (Kimmel, 1996). Disability, though, suggests dependence and incompetence, and, therefore, it can have an emasculating effect. In her study of disability among people of Cape Verdean descent in America, Dawna Thomas (2017) found that her participants described disability as worse for men than women, despite the fact that disabled women experienced greater poverty and violence. Whereas nondisabled men enjoyed the status of "kings" (Thomas, p. 452), disabled men lost their status, especially if they could not provide for their families. Thus, the difference in power between nondisabled and disabled men was far greater than for nondisabled and disabled women.

The loss of male privilege, exacerbated by high unemployment rates, fuels the stereotype of disabled men as angry (Nario-Redmond, 2010). Indeed, in the American narrative of disability, disabled men are expected to be angry. In *Fighting Polio Like a Man*, historian Daniel Wilson (2004) documents that men with polio were encouraged to frame their experience of polio in terms of war: polio was the enemy, disabled men were soldiers fighting a war, and achieving normal physical functioning was the victory. Treating polio as a war effectively motivated men to engage in rehabilitation and regain as much physical functionality as possible, but also left them angry and desolate about lifelong disabilities. Through the process of rehabilitation, their bodies had become their enemy.

Because masculinity is a privileged status and disability is not, many disabled men will strongly identify with masculinity and minimize their disability. To do so, they may strive to perform masculine roles and/or reformulate these roles to better suit their bodies and abilities (Gerschick & Miller, 1995). For instance, disability sports may provide a space for the expression of masculine traits (Berger, 2009). The 2005 film *Murderball*, which focuses on Paralympic wheelchair rugby players, documents the hypermasculinity of many of the athletes. Access to elite disability sports, though, is not available to all disabled men. It requires resources, a community of disabled athletes, the ability to travel, and certain physical abilities, and sports may yield fewer rewards as men age. Rather than embracing or reformulating hegemonic masculinity, some men might reject hegemonic masculinity altogether (Gerschick & Miller, 1995).

The intersection of masculinity and disability may yield different outcomes depending on class, race, age, and sexuality (Shuttleworth et al., 2012). Noam Ostrander (2008) studied urban men of color with violently acquired spinal cord injury, and he documented the barriers they faced in performing masculinity. The men often lived in inaccessible apartment buildings, which increased their dependence on others. Racism and ableism blocked employment opportunities and caused poverty. Racism fueled the stereotype that their disabilities resulted from illegal activities, and they were denied the honor given to White disabled men who are assumed to be disabled due to accidents or military service. They also felt vulnerable to violence and unable to protect themselves or their loved ones. One participant stated "[Before the injury] I walked where I wanted to walk, I drove where I wanted to drive, I hung where I wanted to hang. People know I'm lame now. They know my weakness" (p. 593). To reinforce their masculinity, participants engaged in a variety of strategies, such as wearing an army jacket to resist the stereotype of gang violence and carrying a weapon to ensure they could protect themselves.

PHOTO 7.3 Athletics is one way that disabled men may display their masculinity

We have discussed the construction of male and female gender roles, but the **gender binary**—the cultural construction of gender as only two genders, male and female, which are presented as mutually exclusive types—itself can also be challenged (Egner, 2019; Gerschick & Miller, 1995). Ironically perhaps, exclusion from gender roles may provide people with disabilities opportunities to explore alternatives to traditional gender roles, including transgender and **gender queer identities**—identities that blur or reject the gender binary. **The Neuroqueer movement**, for instance, is a movement that rejects conformity, affirms people's right to be visibly autistic or neurodivergent, and embraces the fluidity of identity in gender, sexuality, and ability, and thereby simultaneously challenges traditional gender roles and compulsory ablemindedness (Egner, 2019; Walker, 2015). Autistic activist Shane Bentley offers an example. Bentley (2017, p. 299) remembers feeling both too visible and invisible in their life as "an undiagnosed autistic and unacknowledged biracial agender person, as if a silencing invisibility cloak concealed my reality even from my own sight." Over time, Bentley challenged the layers of expectations declaring, "I don't have to keep trying to meet societal expectations and pass as "normal," because there is nothing wrong with how I am" (p. 305).

Liberation from societal expectations, though, is not easily attained. People who make nonnormative choices regarding their gender identity may be pathologized. In other words, their choices may be interpreted as a *symptom* of mental or intellectual disability. They may even be placed in counseling or subjected to behavioral modification regimes to correct their gender expressions. Trans men and women routinely must accept the label of a mental health disorder—gender confusion or gender dysphoria—in order to access the medical services they desire (Paur, 2017). No such label of mental illness is required for gender-conforming men and women to alter their bodies to enhance their gendered appearance. When people with disabilities attempt to make nonnormative gender choices, they may be portrayed as too incompetent to understand their own gender identity (Santinele Martino, 2020). Moreover, because people with disabilities are often in social contexts in which they exercise less control over their own lives, those who wish to defy gender expectations may be denied the opportunities and resources to express themselves, such as access to particular clothing, make-up, social networks, and settings.

Gender, Disability, and Unequal Outcomes

Disability leads to differential outcomes by gender. Many of these outcomes disadvantage women, especially women of color, although disabled men face challenges as well. We could look at many outcomes, but we will focus on economics, relationships, and sexual violence.

To look at economics first, studies have consistently found that women fare worse economically than men. Across race and at every level of education, men make more money than women (Gould & Kroeger, 2017; United States Bureau of Labor Statistics, 2020b). The rate of women in poverty has been growing, especially among single women with children, a trend referred to as feminization of poverty. Disability further exacerbates this trend. Women with disabilities have higher poverty rates, lower household incomes, and lower employment rates than men with disabilities (Figure 7.3). Even among those receiving public disability benefits, disabled women receive less money in disability benefits than disabled men. Social Security Disability Insurance (SSDI) benefits are based on one's work history and prior income. Since men are more likely to have a work history and to have higher lifetime earnings than women, they tend to receive more money through the disability benefits system.

Adding in race and education, Michelle Maroto and her colleagues (2019) document **hierarchies of disadvantage**—patterns of stratification in which multiply marginalized populations experience greater disadvantage—in which disabled women of color with less education earn the least and have the highest poverty rates. Interestingly, though, more advantaged groups, such as White well-educated men, may experience the greatest negative impact of disability on earnings because they have the most to lose. In other words, because White, well-educated, nondisabled men make the most money, the income gap between disabled and nondisabled is the greatest.

FIGURE 7.3 **Rates of Poverty and Employment by Disability and Gender, 2020 (Ages 25-54)[4]**

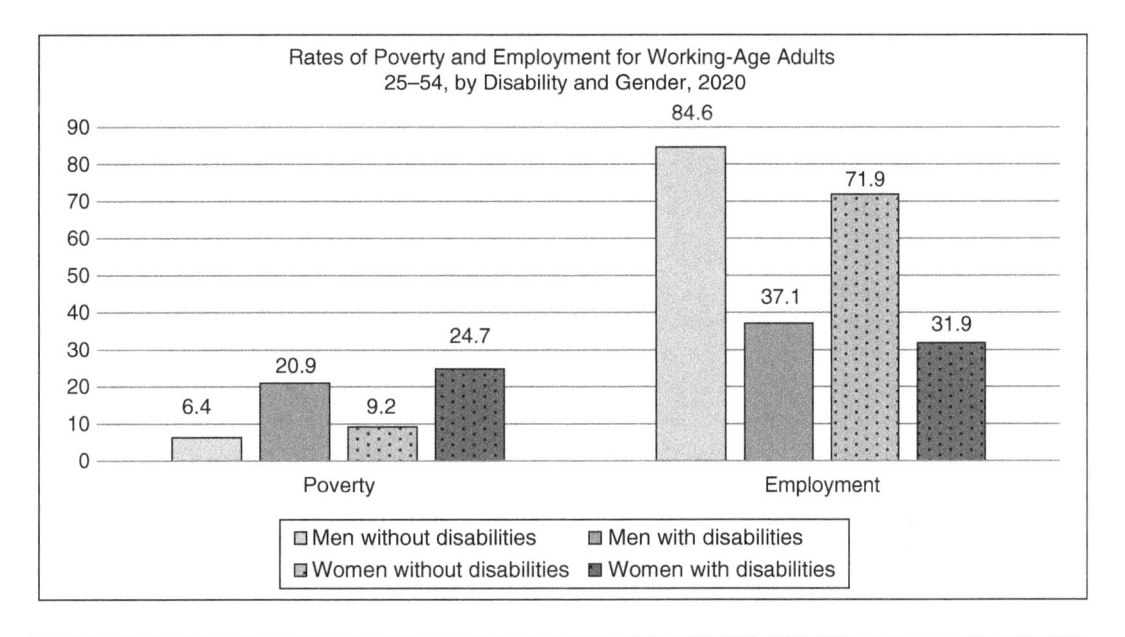

Rates of Poverty and Employment for Working-Age Adults 25–54, by Disability and Gender, 2020

Category	Men without disabilities	Men with disabilities	Women without disabilities	Women with disabilities
Poverty	6.4	20.9	9.2	24.7
Employment	84.6	37.1	71.9	31.9

Data Source: Data from the Current Population Survey Integrated Public Use Microdata Series (IPUMS), 2020 Annual Social and Economic Supplement, as reported by McLaren et al., 2021.

Not only do women with disabilities earn less, but they also experience a greater negative emotional toll due to unequal working conditions. Robyn Brown and Mairead Moloney (2019) studied the impact of working conditions on depression. They found that women with disabilities earned less, experienced more stress, and had less creative and autonomous jobs than women without disabilities, men with disabilities, and men without disabilities. These factors decreased psychological satisfaction with work and increased depressive symptoms. Thus, limited job opportunities for women with disabilities did not just lead to lower pay; they harmed disabled women's psychological well-being.

Another area of inequality is tied to relationships, including dating, marriage, pregnancy, and caregiving. The chapter on family (Chapter Eight) discusses some of these issues, so here we raise them briefly. Because the stigma of disability discredits women from claiming valued feminine traits like beauty, sexuality, and caregiving, it can be very challenging for women with disabilities to find romantic partners (Berger, 2009, 2013). Women with disabilities face discrimination in childbearing and parenting (Blum, 2020; Fritsch, 2017; Lewiecki-Wilson & Cellio, 2011). Disabled activist and parent Corbett OToole (2015) lays out the many barriers disabled parents face, including inaccessible housing, poverty, and lack of transportation; the presumption that people with disabilities are unfit parents; the lack of services and supports to assist with parenting; and the lack of reproductive healthcare. She states, "When disabled people do become parents, they often experience extreme prejudice. If the

---

[4] American Community Survey, 2003–2007; author created chart using data from online data feature at disabilitystatistics.org/reports.

disabled parent has a non-disabled partner, it is usually presented by non-disabled people that the non-disabled partner is 'the real parent'" (p. 255).

Violence is a third area of gendered outcomes. According to the Bureau of Justice Statistics, between 2009 and 2015 individuals with disabilities were at least twice as likely to be victims of violence as individuals without disabilities, with people with mental and intellectual disabilities at the highest risk.[5] Monika Mitra and her colleagues (2016) examined the likelihood of being a victim of sexual violence in the past year and in one's lifetime and found both gender and disability increased risk. Figure 7.4 displays their findings. Looking at lifetime sexual violence victimization, 25.6% of women with disabilities reported victimization, compared to 14.7% of women without disabilities, 8.8% of men with disabilities, and 6% of men without disabilities. Looking at sexual violence victimization in the past year, 5.3% of women with disabilities reported victimization, compared to 2.7% of women without disabilities, 3.5% of men with disabilities, and 2.5% of men without disabilities.

For both measures (lifetime victimization and victimization last year), women with disabilities reported the highest rates of victimization, and men without disabilities reported the lowest. However, it is also important to note that men with disabilities had higher rates of victimization than men without disabilities. For sexual victimization in the past year, men with disabilities had a higher rate of victimization than women without disabilities. Abuse against disabled men, though, often goes unacknowledged, and male victims rarely receive adequate services.

FIGURE 7.4 Percentage of Sexual Violence Victimization in One's Lifetime and in the Past Year by Gender and Disability, 2005–2007

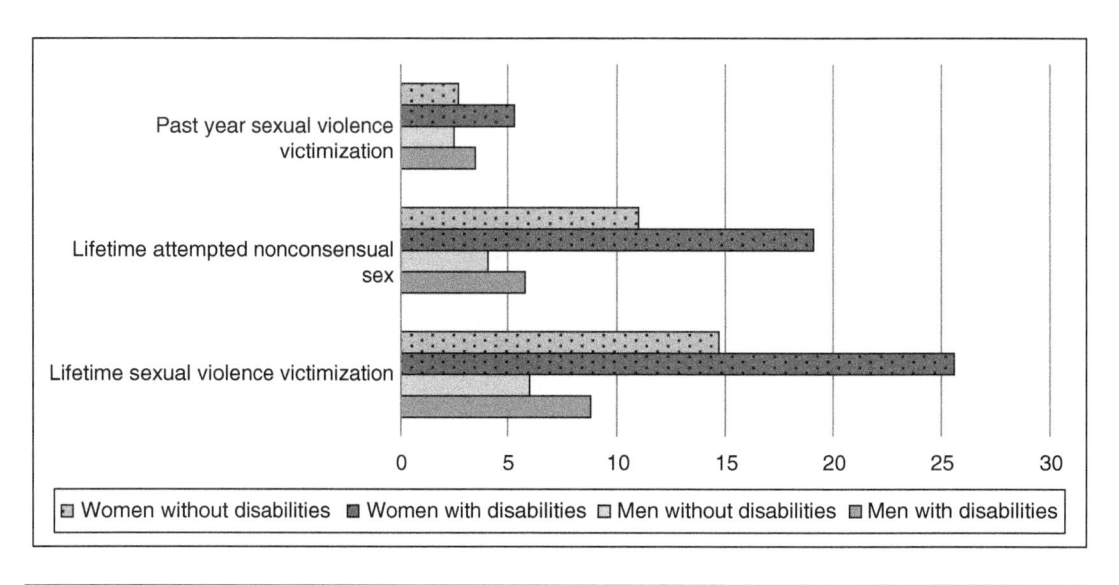

Data Source: Monika Mitra et al. (2016), drawing on 2005–2007 data from the Behavioral Risk Factor Surveillance System.

---

[5]Office of Victims of Crime, *Crimes Against People with Disabilities* (2018), available at https://ovc.ncjrs.gov/ncvrw2018/info_flyers/fact_sheets/2018NCVRW_VictimsWithDisabilities_508_QC.pdf.

Disability and the Feminist Movement

The feminist movement strives to achieve social equity for women. Despite the increased vulnerability of disabled women to poverty, isolation, and violence, the feminist movement has been slow to prioritize disability issues. Similarly, disability activism historically focused little attention on gender issues. Over time though, disabled women worked to bring attention to women's issues (Rousso, 2013). For example, in 1974 Deborah Kaplan and Susan Sygall created the Disabled Women's Coalition to foster consciousness-raising and activism among women. Barbara Faye Waxman was among the pioneers fighting for the sexual and reproductive rights of people with disabilities. Corbett OToole established the Disabled Women's Alliance in 1989 and organized international conferences focusing on gender inequality, parenting, and women's health. These women, and many more, laid the foundation for continuing efforts toward equality.

Sexuality

Sexuality closely intertwines with, but is distinct from, gender. **Sexuality** encompasses one's sexual identity, orientation, behavior, and relationships. While there is debate about the biological and social roots of sexuality, society's expectations regarding sexuality and the privileging of **heteronormativity**—society's construction of heterosexual orientation, behaviors, and relationships as the norm and as valued above other sexualities—are social constructions.

People with disabilities are often denied opportunities to explore, express, and enact sexuality. Disabled author Anne Finger states (1992, p. 9), "Sexuality is often the source of our deepest oppression; it is also often the source of our deepest pain. It's easier for us to talk about—and formulate strategies for changing—discrimination in employment, education, and housing than to talk about our exclusion from sexuality and reproduction." Sexuality—including the denial of it, the constrained parameters placed on it, and the violence of sexual abuse—has been central to the oppression of people with disabilities. In response, the demand for sexual self-determination and pleasure has become central to disability politics.

Sexuality is not only socially constructed; it is political. It involves power on the micro and macro levels. In *The History of Sexuality,* Michel Foucault ([1978] 1990) argues that, during the 18th and 19th century, sexuality increasingly came under state and professional control, especially by a new cadre of "experts" in the medical and psychological fields. These experts identified some people, bodies, and acts as "normal" and others as "abnormal." Those designated "abnormal" required intervention via punishment (e.g., the incarceration of prostitutes and pedophiles), normalization (e.g., medical therapies to "cure" queer sexuality), and/or surveillance (e.g., the watchful eye of parents to ensure girl's purity). Ideas of ability/disability undergirded this system, with a growing number of feelings and behaviors identified as sexual disorders, such as homosexuality, gender dysphoria, and sex addiction. Homosexuality[6], for example, was listed as a mental disability in the Diagnostic Statistical Manual until its removal in 1973.

Sexual control and shame are tools of political oppression. Abby Wilkerson (2011) explains that those with the greatest social privilege are granted the

---

[6]Homosexuality is an outdated term, only used here because it was a medical diagnosis. To shed medical pathology in relation to sexual orientation, sociologists today typically do not use this term.

veneer of respectability and given the greatest latitude in their sexual expressions. Marginalized populations, on the other hand, are often framed as sexual deviants. Shame and surveillance are used against them to undercut their agency. For instance, White Southerners portrayed Black men as sexual threats to legitimize surveillance, segregation, incarceration, and even lynching. Historians Susan Burch and Hannah Joyner (2007) tell the story of Junius Wilson (1908–2001), a deaf Black man in Jim Crow south, who was charged with rape. Although he was never convicted, he was institutionalized in a state mental hospital for 76 years. Deafness, blackness, and the suggested threat of sexual perversion were sufficient to deny him his liberty for almost his entire life.

A brief dive into history reveals several key points regarding sexuality and disability. First, in the 18th and 19th century as capitalism and medicalization expanded, both sexuality and disability came under increasing medicalization and social control. Second, control of disability and sexuality intertwined. People with disabilities were defined as sexually dangerous. Eugenicists, for example, advocated compulsory sterilization and prophylactic institutionalization (institutionalization during childbearing years to prevent reproduction) to ensure people with disabilities did not reproduce and spread their "defects." Vice versa, those labeled with disordered sexuality were marked as disabled and in need of correction.

Third, the integration of people with disabilities into society was and often continues to be dependent on forfeiting the right to sexuality (McRuer, 2015). For example, during eugenics, one path to freedom from institutionalization was to agree to sterilization. As another example, as parents in the 1950s and 1960s fought to establish community services for people with intellectual and developmental disabilities, they portrayed people with disabilities as eternal children. Eternal children, parents argued, deserved education and services. While the image of the eternal child was useful in advocating for services, it erased adulthood and sexual maturation. In exchange for the provision of services, the state in effect treated people with developmental disabilities as asexual (Carey, 2009). Today, many people still must give up their rights to sexuality to receive residential services such as group homes and nursing homes.

Barriers to Sexuality

Michael Gill (2015, p. 3) uses the term **sexual ableism** to describe the "system of imbuing sexuality with determinations of qualifications to be sexual based on criteria of ability, intellect, morality, physicality, appearance, age, race, social acceptability, and gender conformity." In other words, in a system guided by sexual ableism, only some people are seen as deserving pleasure and sexuality. The barriers to self-determined exploration, expression, and enactment of sexuality for people with disabilities are numerous (Stevens, 2011). The list below is not all encompassing but offers some of the key barriers.

Negative Attitudes. People with disabilities face many, and often contradictory, stereotypes about their sexuality. These stereotypes include portraying people with disabilities as overly sexualized and unimpeded by moral convention. This stereotype encouraged the institutionalization of Junius Wilson (Burch & Joyner, 2007). Another common stereotype is that people with disabilities are dangerous in their sexuality, especially in relation to reproduction. People with disabilities are portrayed as potentially spreading disability to the next generation genetically and/or via poor parenting

(Frederick, 2017). A third stereotype is people with disabilities as asexual, such as the portrayal of people with developmental disabilities as eternal children and people with autism as preferring isolation (Kafer, 2013; Santinele Martino, 2020). Discussing the range of negative attitudes that lead to the "erasure of queer autistic people," Alyssa Hillary (2014, p. 130) states, "Unfortunately for us, these fundamental cultural beliefs are ones which erase our sexualities, especially our Queer sexualities."

Lack of Education and Knowledge. Many children with disabilities do not receive sex education, and the sex education programs that are offered rarely address disability. Programs created specifically for people with disabilities tend to focus on risk, preventing abuse, and heterosexual relationships (Gill, 2015). Social isolation and stigma hinder learning about sexuality from peers, while the lack of privacy and dependence on caregivers reduces opportunities for sexual exploration (Santinele Martino, 2019). In a groundbreaking study of the sexual politics of disability by Tom Shakespeare and his colleagues (1996, p. 15), one of their participants explained, "Information is power, and disabled people still don't have enough of it."

Policies that Hinder Sexuality. Many residential services, such as nursing homes and group homes, formally and informally discourage sexual relationships. This may be, for example, through denying privacy (e.g., no locked doors) or denying and regulating guests (e.g., no overnight guests, no guests allowed to shower with a resident). The *lack of policies* may also be problematic. Without clear policies that affirm sexual rights, staff may be hesitant to support sexuality or they may see supporting sexuality as outside of their job description (Achey, 2020). On a more macro level, the SSI marriage penalty (discussed in Chapter 8) penalizes marriage among disabled people by reducing public disability benefits.

PHOTO 7.4
Marriage Equality Activist

Relational Inequality. Too often people with disabilities have little power over their lives, and instead they live in settings and relationships where others exercise tremendous control (Hillary, 2011). For example, while some parents are supportive of their offspring's sexuality, others may not allow them to date, have sex, or express nonheteronormative identities. Unlike other young adults, disabled adults may not have the same opportunities to leave their parent's home. For people with paid staff, staff may cater to the wishes of parents. Without explicit policies that affirm sexual rights, staff are often guided by their own moral codes (Gill, 2015; Santinele Martino, 2019).

Inaccessibility and segregation. People with disabilities experience barriers to engaging in a fulfilling social life. Many social clubs, bars, and events are physically inaccessible. Think of college social life. How much of the "party scene" occurs in fully accessible venues? Disability scholar and sexologist Bethany Stevens (2015) recalls her frustration when inaccessibility excluded her from seeing the Vagina Monologues, a play that grapples with sexuality from women's perspectives. Disabled sex educator Drew Gurza (2017) describes the inaccessibility of Greenwich Village in New York City—a neighborhood known for its vibrant LBBTQ+ community: "I know I can't get my wheelchair inside these sacred spaces where my community comes (pun intended)." Educational segregation separates and stigmatizes youth with disabilities, while inaccessibility in employment increases poverty and makes dating, independent living, and privacy more difficult to attain (Shakespeare et al., 1996).

Lack of Useful Healthcare and Medicalized Pathology. Doctors too often ignore the sexuality of disabled patients. They fail to provide information on birth control and overlook signs of sexually transmitted diseases. Not only can it be difficult to find useful sexual and reproductive healthcare, but healthcare explicitly pathologizes disability and sexuality, especially nonheterosexual sexuality. As with gender noncomformity, healthcare professionals still may diagnose nonheterosexual identities *as* indications of mental illness. For example, one young woman recalled seeking mental health services for depression, eating disorders, and drug use. Her therapist saw her queer identification as intertwined with these problems and recommended, as part of her therapy, conformity to heterosexuality. She explained, "the premise from which most talking treatments are delivered is a heterosexual, able-bodied, WASP perspective. And I just don't fit that mold" (Shakespeare et al., 1996, p. 86).

Violence, Exploitation and Vulnerability. As noted in the section on gender, the rate of sexual violence and abuse against people with disabilities is high. Vulnerability is increased due to factors such as social isolation, social stigma, the lack of adequate sexual education, the paucity of opportunities to gain experience, as well as the impairments themselves which may impact the ability of people to understand, communicate or protect themselves from sexual violence. Fear of violence and sexual exploitation then drive professionals and parents toward protection and surveillance, rather than building education, skills, and opportunities. Rates of violence are particularly high for people in LGBTQ+ communities, and the intersection of disability and LGBTQ+ can pose grave risks (Wilkerson, 2011).

Disability as an Opportunity for Sexual Exploration

Even in the midst of constraints, people with disabilities engage in sexuality. Studies by Alan Santinele Martino (2019) and Michael Gill (2015) document that staff and parents are often apprehensive about assisting or even allowing sexuality, but people with disabilities often resist this paternalism and find ways to engage in sexuality. In fact, rather than protecting people with intellectual disabilities, restrictive environments may push them into high risk situations, such as masturbating in work bathrooms or having sex outdoors.

Whereas barriers to sexuality are common, some disabled people enjoy supportive environments and relationships. For example, although many parents avoid dealing with the sexuality of their disabled offspring, others enable it. Les Gallo-Silver and colleagues (2017) share the story of a young man they refer to as Boyd, who came out as gay to his parents at the age of 14 and became disabled at 17. His father served as his primary caregiver, and, at first, Boyd had very little privacy. One day his father walked in on him masturbating, and Boyd expressed his desire to have a sexual life and his frustration at his lack of privacy. Through open communication, he and his father established a supportive relationship in which his dad provided Boyd with privacy or with assistance as needed. Gallo-Silver and her colleagues (p. 204) explain, "Paradoxically, the privacy Boyd required—privacy which would be considered an unquestioned human right in most other situations—could only be achieved through interdependence.... Boyd spoke out and took control of his sexual life by directing his own care."

When sexuality is self-determined and supported, disability can reveal new perspectives, approaches, and opportunities. Robert McRuer (2015, p. 170) describes sex as both a site of oppression and "a profoundly productive site for invention, experimentation, and transformation." The typical view of sex is largely bound to the performance of penis–vaginal intercourse, yet by recognizing and validating different bodies, abilities, and movements, ideas about pleasure may expand. Earlobes, toes, soft strokes, sex talk, and more can provoke intense pleasure. Bethany Stevens states, "Opening our minds about the confines of sex is the tool to understanding how we all can engage in pleasure giving and receiving" (quoted in "Access Points," 2017). Disability may also enhance intimacy through greater thoughtfulness and communication. Although many people feel uncomfortable discussing their sexual desires, disability may encourage open discussions about how to give and receive pleasure.

Disability may also challenge norms around body image and sexuality. "Crip" and "queer" perspectives share a rejection of the value placed on ideals like "normal" and "healthy" (Shildrick, 2015). For example, poet, musician, and artist Leroy Moore rejects society's desexualization of his disabled body and instead celebrates his desirability. In his poem "Droolilicious," Moore (2014, p. 25) embraces his attributes, including drooling, slowed speech, and a unique stride, as integral to his sex appeal, as what might make others drool in desire for him.

Contested Sexual Politics

The politics of sex are highly contested. In *Intimate Citizenship*, Ken Plummer (2003) argues that the modern world creates new opportunities and challenges regarding the most intimate decisions about our bodies, feelings and relationships. New technologies allow and encourage new forms of sexuality (e.g. cybersex, sex chat rooms, revenge porn). Media, technologies, and law have opened a new era of choice around gender identity, sexual identity, and physical bodies (e.g., blurred gender boundaries, surgeries and medications to transform the body and identity, the blending of technology and humanity into cyborgs). But these seemingly private decisions are made within a web of capitalist enterprises, political regulation, and bureaucratic decision-making. Plummer's idea of **intimate citizenship** recognizes that there are increasing public discourses and policies contextualizing people's most private decisions. We see this clearly in the politics of disability and sexuality.

To explore the issue of intimate citizenship, we will discuss two political topics related to sexuality and disability: representation within the adult sex industry and access to paid assistance with sexuality.

Although the adult sex industry generates billions of dollars each year, it largely ignores people with disabilities in its representations and products (Stevens, 2011). Sex toys are often inaccessible, and pornography rarely includes people with disabilities. Some fight for greater visibility and accessibility in this industry. Others, though, charge that pornography is dehumanizing and that the inclusion of people with disabilities fuels exploitation and victimization.

In 1987, Ellen Stohl became the first White physically disabled woman featured in *Playboy Magazine.* The nude photos, though, obscured her disability. In 2020, Marsha Elle, a Black actress/model who uses prosthetics, became the April playmate, and her photoshoot more boldly depicted her as disabled and sensual. She explained her decision to represent the Black disability community in *Playboy*: "I look at my prosthetic as an aid. It helped me to get into the water. It helps me to stand and stand proudly and to be a whole person. I don't look at it as a negative, and to see *Playboy* showing there's beauty in me as a whole and my prosthetic is part of me and doesn't make me weird, it's important. It's good that we can show our legs, or our disability, whatever it may be, and make it normal. It transcends further than just me being sexy, it's me being normal. It's me being a human. I have a sensual side" (Uwumarogie, 2020). Whether or how disability representations in pornography challenge sexual ableism or feed exploitation continues to be debated.

Another contentious issue is paid sexual assistance. One form of sexual assistance involves paying personal assistants to facilitate sexual behavior, such as assisting with undressing, positioning, providing necessary equipment, and/or cleaning after a sexual act. Most personal assistants receive no training in the respectful facilitation of sexuality. As noted above, some assistants may be very supportive, and others may be very uncomfortable, refuse to assist, or will only support particular behaviors.

More controversial forms of assistance involve sex surrogacy and paid sex workers. Sex surrogates work, often in conjunction with a sex therapist, to help a client address concerns related to their body, intimacy, and sexuality. Discussions of sex surrogacy entered public realm via the film *The Sessions.* Based on Mark O'Brien's true story, *The Sessions* tells the story of a paralyzed 38-year-old virgin who decides to use a sex surrogate to explore his sexuality. For some people with disabilities sex may be shrouded in mystery. They may have to work through body shame, the possibility of pain or injury, the lack of sexual partners, and the role of equipment. A sex surrogate offers a path to safely build sexual skills. Surrogacy, however, is often stigmatized, unavailable, and expensive. Some people with disabilities dislike its medicalized, clinical approach. Others may use paid sex workers, an option that makes partners available even when stigma and social isolation limit other avenues. However, paid sex work is illegal in most states and is also stigmatized. While some disability activists fight for policies that expand access to surrogacy and/or sex workers, others feel that these approaches medicalize or commercialize the sexuality of disabled people while failing to address many of the barriers to nonpaid, intimate connection.

Activism, Sexual Rights, and the Politics of Pleasure

For a long-time, disability movement leaders focused on "public" issues like accessibility and employment and avoided discussing sexuality. The early disability rights movement did little to embrace HIV/AIDS activism or trans activism, although AIDS is a disabling disease which often provokes tremendous discrimination and people who are trans are forced to accept medicalized labels to access care and services (Mog & Swar, 2008; OToole, 2015). At the San Francisco Independent Living Center in the 1970s, Corbett OToole (2015, p. 211) remembers that gay activists were "expected to keep their silence" so as not to distract from the issues of access and rights.

These days, disability activist communities are increasingly acknowledging the importance of sexuality and **sexual rights**—rights which confer control over one's body and freedom to engage in private, intimate acts (Fegan et al., 1993). Some activists frame sexuality activism as broader than rights. For example, the politics of pleasure fights to ensure the context, access, and supports one need to experience pleasure. In her book, *The Politics of Pleasure,* Adrienne Maree Brown (2019) argues that power often entails access to and the validation of pleasure. For example, wealthy people have far greater freedom to do drugs for fun, whereas drug use by the poor leads to incarceration. Heterosexuals can engage in visible displays of affection, whereas those in the LGBTQ+ community often cannot. Brown states, "pleasure is a measure of freedom." From this perspective, freedom requires that all people have access to pleasure and that the social structures support equitable access to pleasure. Bringing disability into the discussion of pleasure, Bethany Stevens (2011) argues "politicizing sexual pleasure and oppression of disabled people through enacting cripsex is a powerful way to affirm our humanity."

Race

Race is a social construction in which people thought to share perceived biological traits—often tied to skin color—are grouped together and believed to share socially significant characteristics. Racism confers advantages and disadvantages based on race. People often believe that racism only involves individual-level beliefs about inferiority and superiority based on race, but **institutional racism** (also known as systemic racism) refers to when processes leading to differential racial outcomes are embedded in social structures and policies, even if there is no explicit distinction by race in the policies (Bonilla-Silva, 2003; Ray, 2019; Rolnick, 2019). For example, public schools produce differential outcomes by race, even though there is no law mandating separate racial treatment. These outcomes are shaped by complex factors like patterns of residential segregation, funding mechanisms for schools, and differential access to resources in neighborhoods, as well as biases that teachers hold that they may or may not recognize. Historically, America shifted from explicit and legally enforced racism (e.g., slavery, Jim Crow laws) toward color-blind racism (Bonilla-Silva, 2003). **Color-blind racism** means that people use subtle ideologies, such as cultural differences and meritocracy, to distinguish among people in ways that mask yet also perpetuate racial stratification.

Challenging racism therefore requires redesigning social systems in ways that ensure racial equity.

Racial inequality is deeply intertwined with disability. Due to racism—including differential access to power, prestige, freedom, income and wealth, neighborhood resources, and quality healthcare—African Americans and Native Americans have higher rates of disease, disability, and premature death than Whites (Morris & Asante-Muhammed, 2017; Phelan & Link, 2015). Racial and class inequalities become *embodied* as people physically and mentally experience the advantages and disadvantages that flow from one's race (Krieger, 2005).

Prevalence of Disability by Race and Outcomes

Let's begin by discussing the prevalence of disability by race. Being a racial minority alone does not increase the likelihood of disability; some minority groups have higher rates than others. As shown in Figure 7.5, Native Americans have the highest rate of disability (17.2%), and Asian Americans report the lowest rates (7.2%) (US Census Bureau, 2019).[7] Racial disparities increase with age. For adults ages 18–20 years old, 6% of Whites and 7% of African Americans report disabilities, but, for adults ages 61–65, 20% of Whites and 30% of African Americans report disabilities. Younger Hispanics have lower disability rates than Whites, but for adults ages 60 and over, Hispanics have higher rates (Goodman et al., 2017).

Sharp differences exist in the impact of disability by race. As outlined in a report by the National Disability Institute (Goodman et al., 2017) (see

FIGURE 7.5   Prevalence of Disability by Race, 2019[8]

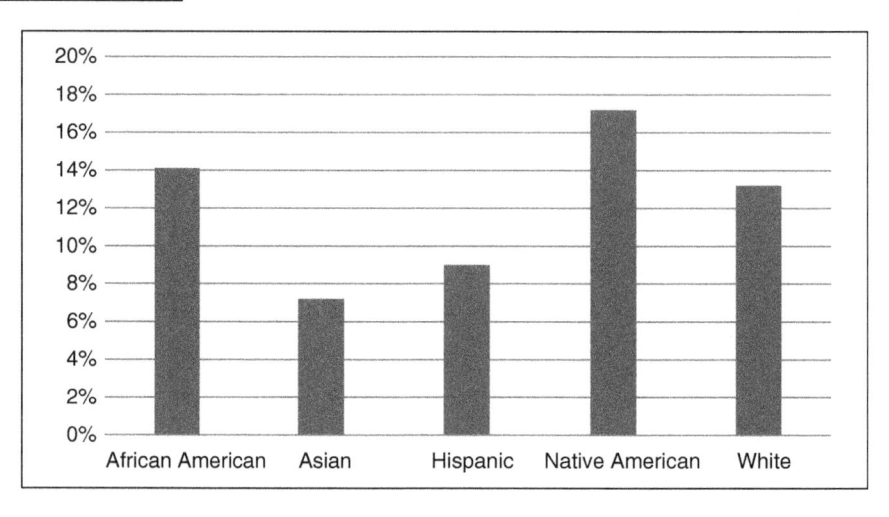

Data Source: American Community Survey 2019, US Census.

---

[7]To note, Latino is defined by the Census Bureau as an ethnicity, not a race, but because they experience systemic disadvantage, sociologists often include Latinos in analyses of race.
[8]Data Source: American Community Survey 2019, US Census, Disability Characteristics Table ID S1810 https://data.census.gov/cedsci/table?q=disability&tid=ACSST1Y2019.S1810&hidePreview=false. Author created chart.

FIGURE 7.6 Percentage in Poverty by Race and Disability Status, 2015[9]

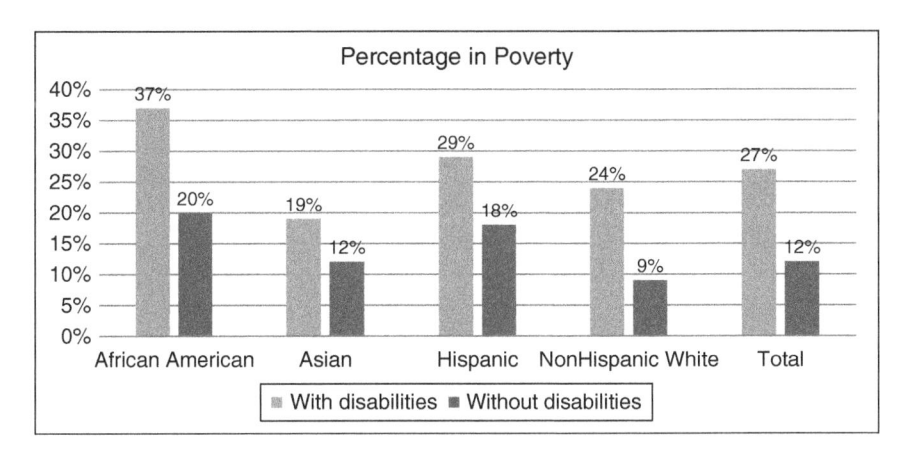

Percentage in Poverty

Race	With disabilities	Without disabilities
African American	37%	20%
Asian	19%	12%
Hispanic	29%	18%
NonHispanic White	24%	9%
Total	27%	12%

Data Source: American Community Survey, 2015, as reported in Goodman et al. (2017).

Figure 7.6), African Americans with disabilities have almost double the rate of poverty (37%) than Whites with disabilities (24%) or Asians with disabilities (19%). African Americans with disabilities also have a distinctly lower employment rate (25% vs. 35% for Whites, 35% for Hispanics, and 39% of Asians) (Figure 7.7). Hispanics and African Americans with disabilities have lower rates of achieving a bachelor's degree (9% for both groups), compared to Whites with disabilities (15%) and Asians with disabilities (26%) (Figure 7.8). Through these data, a clear pattern of racial and disability disadvantage emerges.

As noted earlier in the chapter, disabled women of color with less education earn the least and have the highest poverty rates (Maroto et al., 2019). We see this trend in the rates of attaining a bachelor's degree as well (Figure 7.8). African Americans and Hispanics are less likely to attain a bachelor's degree than Whites and Asians. However, if we look at the difference between those with and without disabilities within each race, Asians have the largest gap (26 percentage points), followed by Whites (20 percentage points). Thus, disability considerably undercuts the advantages enjoyed by Whites and Asians, while it exacerbates the disadvantages experienced by African Americans and Latinos.

Racialization of Diagnosis

Statistics focusing on the overall prevalence rates mask the **racialization of diagnosis**—the infusion of values and stereotypes into patterns of diagnosis, leading to differential diagnosis by race. Medical labels have often been used against racial minorities to provide a seemingly objective veneer to political claims of biological and moral inferiority. Below are several examples of the racialization of diagnosis.

---

[9]Data from the 2015 American Community Survey, as reported in Goodman, Morris, & Boston, 2017 https://www.nationaldisabilityinstitute.org/wp-content/uploads/2019/02/disability-race-poverty-in-america.pdf. Tables have been re-created.

FIGURE 7.7 Employment Rates by Disability & Race

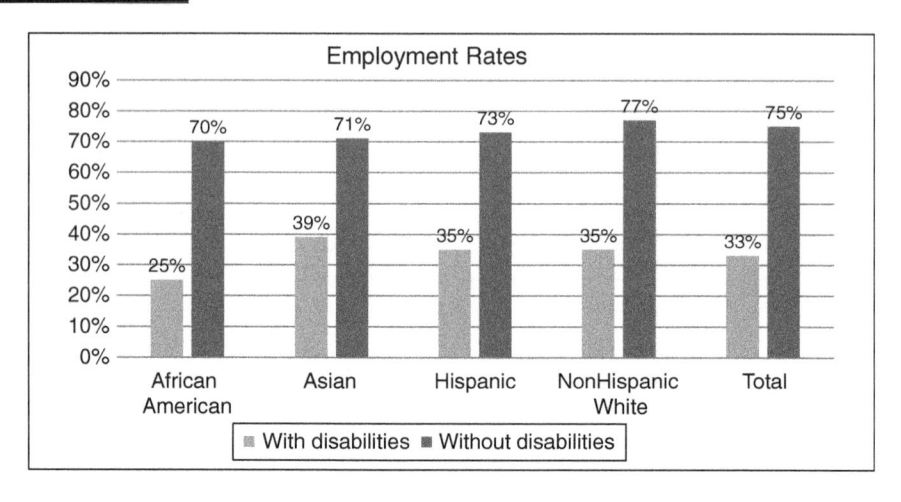

Employment Rates

Race	With disabilities	Without disabilities
African American	25%	70%
Asian	39%	71%
Hispanic	35%	73%
NonHispanic White	35%	77%
Total	33%	75%

Data Source: American Community Survey, 2015, as reported in Goodman et al. (2017).

FIGURE 7.8 Education Rates by Disability & Race

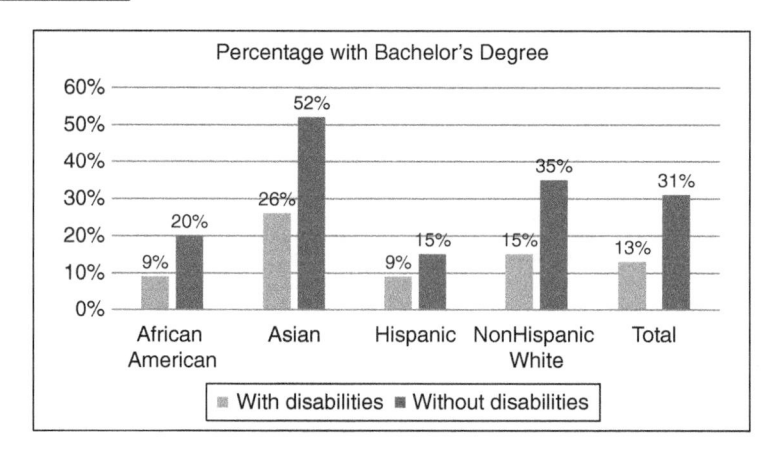

Percentage with Bachelor's Degree

Race	With disabilities	Without disabilities
African American	9%	20%
Asian	26%	52%
Hispanic	9%	15%
NonHispanic White	15%	35%
Total	13%	31%

Data Source: American Community Survey, 2015, as reported in Goodman et al. (2017).

- To support slavery, medical professionals claimed that African Americans were unable to withstand the rigors of freedom and that mental illness was more common among free African Americans than those enslaved (Nielsen, 2012). Physician Samuel Cartwright created the diagnosis *drapetomania* to diagnose rebellious slaves as mentally ill (see Chapter 3).
- In the 1960s, psychiatrists rethought schizophrenia, changing the target population from unhappy White women to African American men deemed dangerous due to their resistance to oppression (Metzl, 2009). The label of schizophrenic enabled the White medical community to institutionalize dissidents.

- Today, African American and Native American children are two to three times more likely to be labeled intellectually and emotionally disabled as White children. In contrast, children of color are less likely to be diagnosed with autism, and they receive diagnosis later than White children (Gardiner, 2017; Silberman, 2016).

The racial differences in diagnosis are not simply a matter of racist labels, though. Living one's life embedded in systems of racial oppression harms the bodies and minds of people of color. In other words, children of color may have higher rates of intellectual and emotional disability due to greater exposure to poverty, stress, violence, and neighborhood disadvantage (Morgan et al., 2019). Thus, it may be that disability in marginalized communities may be *overdiagnosed* in some instances and *underdiagnosed* in others.

Disability and Racial Stereotypes

Disability labels have been used historically to reinforce negative racial stereotypes and ensure racial segregation and exclusion (Baynton, 2001). One of the most damaging has been the stereotype of African Americans as intellectually and mentally inferior/disabled (Stone, 2017). Slavery relied on the dehumanization of African Americans, accomplished in part by ideologies that depicted African Americans as biologically, psychologically, intellectually and morally inferior to Whites (Nielsen, 2012). Proponents of slavery argued that African Americans were in effect too disabled to exercise rights or freedom and benefited from the oversight of slavery. This stereotype continues to impact children of color who are labeled as disabled without acknowledging the environmental disadvantages related to disability. Students of color experience considerable *stereotype threat*—the anxiety that poor academic performance will be used to confirm negative racial stereotypes, which often itself produces poor performance (Wasserberg, 2014).

Another harmful stereotype portrays Black men as dangerous. Black men with physical disabilities face stereotypes that their impairments must be due to gang violence, undercutting the sympathy that is often extended to people with disabilities (Banks, 2018). Corey, a Black college student with cerebral palsy (a disability that usually occurs before or at birth) describes the stereotypes he faces: "If someone [in my neighborhood] was to assume what my disability is, the natural assumption is that I have been shot. So that comes with its own stereotype. It's always assumed before it's asked. [People in my neighborhood] are also shocked when they found out that I've been this way my whole life" (p. 900). The stereotype of the dangerous Black male becomes life-threatening when, for instance, disabled Black men and police interact. Behaving erratically or failing to comply with police orders may quickly result in police violence (Jarman, 2011; Moore et al., 2016; Whitesel, 2017). With self-defense and stand-your-ground laws, even among civilians cross-race interactions may quickly turn violent, and stereotypes of African Americans are then used to justify White violence as within the boundaries of reasonable fear and self-defense (Rolnick, 2019).

The stereotype of laziness also complicates diagnosis, especially for invisible disabilities like depression. Whereas doctors are quick to interpret the sadness and fatigue of White women as depression (some say far too quick), African Americans are less likely to be diagnosed. Almost 18% of Whites report depression in their lifetime, whereas only 10% of African Americans do (Sohail et al., 2014). Doctors resist legitimizing what they imagine to be Black laziness or acknowledging the impacts of racism on the mental health of their patients.

While many stereotypes could be discussed, we'll cover one more—the idea that African Americans do not need, want, or comply with medical assistance. In *The Cancer Journals,* Black feminist Audre Lorde ([1980] 2020) argues that this dehumanizing stereotype leads to unequal diagnosis and treatment. Studies have found that doctors offer White patients more aggressive and beneficial care than Black patients, in part due to stereotypes that African Americans cannot afford, do not want, or will not comply with such treatments (Ro, 2019).

In addition to stereotypes, minorities with disabilities experience invisibility, particularly in the media and in history books. In 2018–2019, only 2.1% of televised series regulars had disabilities, and the representation of minorities with disability was even less common (GLAAD, 2020; Lee, 2019). Keah Brown (2019, pp. 81–82) explains "Black people with disabilities are all but invisible. We simply don't exist. The first and only time I can remember seeing a Black physically disabled woman in a movie was Kerry Washington in *Fantastic Four* as Alicia Masters. This was the first portrayal of disability that I saw where the character didn't struggle with it, didn't treat it like it was ruining her life. This portrayal, while important, comes with its own set of issues. The biggest issue is that Kerry Washington is not actually physically disabled." Thus, even when disability in the Black community was portrayed, African Americans with disabilities did not control the representation.

Disability, Race, and Identity

The association of disability, negative stereotypes, and invisibility complicates disability identity for racially marginalized populations. For instance, because racial minorities have to fight to be recognized as intelligent and rational, recognizing disability entails great risk. Consequently, the disabilities of African American heroes like Harriet Tubman (who had seizures due to a beating at the age of 15 from her slave owner) and Mohammed Ali (who had dyslexia and later Parkinson's disease) have often been ignored (Thompson, 2018). Barbara Jordan was a civil rights and LGBT activist and the first African American woman in the Texas state senate. Despite her proud identification by race and sexuality, she downplayed her multiple sclerosis throughout her career. When plans were announced to erect a statue in her honor that depicted her in a wheelchair, community members complained that the depiction overshadowed her achievements. The statue was redesigned, and the completed statue portrays her standing (Frederick & Shifrer, 2019). Mia Mingus (2017, p. 138) explains, "It can be very dangerous to identify as disabled when your survival depends on you denying it."

Disability is therefore less openly discussed in some minority communities. Discussing the lower likelihood that African Americans identify as mentally ill and seek help for it, Christina Bolden (2016) states, "Black people tend to feel as though their suffering is a normal and expected outcome given our history from slavery to present." Similarly, Black disability activist Johnnie Lacy explains that African American "didn't really identify with disability as a disability, but just as one other kind of inequity that black people had to deal with" (quoted in Lukin, 2013, p. 309). For minorities, disability is one of many concerns, and not necessarily the most pressing one. To the degree that disability is seen as an outcome of racism, racism may be the more salient identity and political focus.

The stigma of disability may also be deeply enmeshed with diverse racial and ethnic cultural belief systems. Explaining the widespread silence about disability in Asian American communities, Grace Tsao (2016) states, "In my culture, however, being diagnosed with muscular dystrophy at age seven meant being seen by some as a form of chastisement or bad karma inflicted on my family for moral wrongs my family may have done in the past or present. In fact, any disability would fall under this category of 'punishment,' whether from birth or as a result from an accident."

Not only are their numerous barriers to building a positive disability identity for racialized minorities, but the benefits of identification may be fewer than for Whites. Special education in America is highly unequal; Black children in special education are more likely to be segregated, to have poorer educational outcomes, and to be subjected to exclusionary punishments (e.g., school suspension) (Voulgarides, 2018). If disability labels in school help White children more than African American children, it makes sense that African American parents would resist these labels. Similarly, Whites tend to live in neighborhoods with greater resources, including disability resources. In contrast, African Americans and Hispanics are more likely to live in economically disadvantaged neighborhoods with fewer high-quality services available. They are more likely to rely on informal networks of care and support (Piepzna-Samarasinha, 2018). Therefore, disability labels do not serve as a conduit to high-quality services in the same way in minority communities.

The political impact of disability identification may also vary by race. White leaders in disability activism typically reject the medical model and instead seek to reform society. This rejection of the medical model, though, is built upon the privilege of access to necessary medical care. They are not rejecting medical care altogether; rather, they are rejecting the imposition of medical labels and cures. Racial minorities, though, too often do not have access to even basic healthcare. In a nation where the Black infant mortality rate is twice the White infant mortality rate, the need for healthcare is fundamental to achieving equality and prosperity (CDC, 2019c). Therefore, access to healthcare has been a crucial aspect of activism for racial justice, whereas the rejection of the medical model seems to ignore their most basic needs (Mollow, 2006; Nelson, 2011).

Disability identity is also complicated by the causes of disability. Many well-known White disability activists celebrate disability pride and embrace the diversity of all bodies. This celebration, though, erases the oppression, exploitation, and violence that cause much of disability in minority communities (Erevelles & Minear, 2013; Paur, 2017). It may be difficult for minorities to embrace disability

PHOTO 7.5
In BIPOC communities, activism related to racial justice may feel more salient in addressing pressing needs

when it results from poverty, violence, and racism. It is also difficult to embrace disability as diversity when one lacks basic resources for healthcare, accessibility, and personal assistance. Rather than celebrating disability, some Black activists vocally disparage their disabled bodies as a way to call attention to the harm caused by racial oppression and the lack of healthcare (Ralph, 2018).

African American Civil Rights Activism and Disability Activism

BIPOC (Black, indigenous, and people of color) communities engage in activism, but their needs and voices have not always been recognized or welcomed by disability rights organizations, which are often led by White people. Akemi Nishida's (2016a) study found that people of color did not necessarily feel a sense of community in most disability groups. One activist stated:

It's not like I've never affiliated with disability movements. However, those people had such a narrow political analysis and centralized disability without looking at other forms of oppression. Also, everyone there was White. I'm very much developing my political identity around race, gender, queerness, and struggling to see what it means to be disabled in the context.... I didn't feel like it was home for me, the disability movements and community (Claudia).

Another activist exposed explicit racism in disability communities, saying, "One day I was sitting in front of [a local disability resource center], and saw two disabled men enter the center. One was Black and the other was White. Shortly after, the Black man left the center, though the White man stayed in and was getting all the information.... Ra-cism is everywhere (Jimmy)."

The fruits of disability activism also have been disproportionately enjoyed by Whites. The Disability Rights Movement has largely been led by White activists who created an agenda focusing on accessibility, personal assistance, and civil rights (Erkulwater, 2018; OToole, 2015). This agenda, though, overlooked the many barriers faced by multiply marginalized groups. For example, disabled activists worked to develop the system of paid personal assistance to ensure control over their services, but Leah Lakshmi Piepzna-Samarasinha (2018, p. 40) explains the limitations of this system for those who experience intersecting oppressions: "Some of us fear that letting anyone in to care for us will mean we are declared incompetent and lose our civil rights... Some of us know that accepting care means accepting queerphobia, transphobia, fatphobia, or sexphobia from our care attendants... Some of us are not citizens. Some of us make twenty bucks too much..." Disabled activists fought for the Americans with Disabilities Act (ADA) which prohibits discrimination on the basis of disability, but it has similarly been criticized for conferring greater benefits to White, educated, and wealthier people with disabilities. The ADA protects "equally qualified" job applicants from disability discrimination, but White applicants are more likely to attain required educational credentials than minority applicants. White and middle-class people with disabilities are more likely to have the resources to hire a lawyer, which is necessary to fight for ADA rights. When activists of color try to address racial disparities within disability activism, White leaders too often call for unity, as if discussions of race will splinter the movement (Erkulwater, 2018).

Disabled activists of color are of course diverse in their goals and strategies. Some people work to bring visibility to their communities, such as Alice Wong's Disability Visibility project and Donna Walton's Divas with Disabilities (Walton, 2011; Wong, 2020). Kerima Cevik focuses on grassroots organizing, which builds on the local community's strengths to protect people with disabilities from systemic racism and ableism and to ensure local needs are met. Care collectives in minority communities create networks of mutual aid that are nonhierarchical, nonexpert, and nonpaid. They serve to foster access to care in ways that are not threatening and build community and political solidarity (Nishida, 2016b; Piepzna-Samarasinha, 2018). Some activists like Leroy Moore and Patty Berne use art and music to communicate the BIPOC disability experience (Moore, 2014). And, still others like Chris Bell challenged the racial hierarchies in disability studies (Bell, 2011). Some use a framework of disability justice, rather than disability rights, which centers the needs and perspectives of the multiply marginalized and employs an intersectional approach to social justice (Sins Invalid, 2015; see Chapter 12).

Because activism relies heavily on social acceptance and resources, it can be especially challenging for activists in marginalized communities to achieve their goals. In a study of parent activism, Amber Angell and Olga Solomon (2017) found that Latino activist parents who fought for resources for their children with autism received very different reactions from school administrators than White activist parents did. School administrators were more likely to treat White parents as savvy negotiators and to accommodate their requests. In contrast, Latino parents faced fierce resistance, as administrators blocked access to prevent what they perceived would be a flood of requests. Catherine Voulgarides (2018) similarly found that schools in majority White areas offered more disability accommodations than schools in minority districts. The schools in minority districts tended to focus on saving money and meeting only the minimum legal standards. Thus, even when BIPOC activists learn the laws, deploy resources, and engage in activism to fight for justice, they face more resistance and discouragement than White activists.

Conclusion

In conclusion, the experience and outcomes of disability vary based on identities and social contexts. While there are political and social justifications for focusing on "people with disabilities" as a whole group, one must remain aware of the significant differences and inequalities that may be overlooked when doing so and the need to address the needs of unique populations as well. Overcoming ableism cannot be achieved by addressing disability alone. Because race, gender, sexuality, disability, and other axes of inequality intertwine with ableism, social justice for one group requires justice for all groups.

KEY TERMS

Color-blind racism 153
Feminist disability studies 139
Feminist Intersectional Disability Framework 139
Gender binary 143
Gender roles 140
Gender queer identities 143
Heteronormativity 147
Hierarchies of disadvantage 144
Institutional racism 153
Intersectionality 137
Intimate citizenship 151
The Neuroqueer movement 143
Racialization of diagnosis 154
Sexual ableism 148
Sexual rights 153
Sexuality 147

RESOURCES

Academic Writings

Blum, Linda M. 2020. "Gender and Disability Studies." In *Companion to women's and gender studies*, ed. Nancy A. Naples, 175–94. Wiley.

Erevelles, Nirmala. 2015. "Race." In *Keywords for disability studies*, ed. Rachel Adams, Benjamin Reiss, and David Serlin, 145–7. New York City: New York University Press.

Fannon, Tara A. 2016. "Out of Sight, Still in Mind: Visually Impaired Women's Embodied Accounts of Ideal Femininity." *Disability Studies Quarterly* 36, no. 1 (online).

Gender and Society Special Issue. 2019. Vol. 33, Number 1, Guest editors Nancy A. Naples, Heather Dillaway, and Laura Mauldin. Contains several articles on disability and gender, some of which also discuss race and sexuality.

Hillary, Alyssa. 2011. "Erasure of Queer Autistic People." In *Criptiques*, ed. Caitlin Wood, 121–46. Word Press. https://criptiques.files.wordpress.com/2014/05/crip-final-2.pdf.

McRuer, Robert. 2006. *Crip theory: Cultural signs of queerness and disability.* New York University Press.

Miles, Angel Love. 2019. "'Strong Black Women': African American Women with Disabilities, Intersecting Identities, and Inequality." *Gender and Society* 33, no. 1: 41–63.

Piepzna-Samarasinha, Leah Lakshmi. 2018. *Care work: Dreaming disability justice.* Vancouver, BC: Arsenal Pulp Press.

Santinele Martino, Alan. 2019. "Power struggles over the sexualities of individuals with intellectual disabilities." In *Dis/consent: Perspectives on sexual consent and sexual violence*, ed. Kelley Anne Malinen, 98–107. Fernwood Publishers.

Memoirs Attentive to Intersectionality

Brown, Keah. 2019. *The pretty one: On life, pop culture, disability, and other reasons to fall in love with me.* New York, NY: Atria. For something shorter, see also Brown, Keah. 2016. "Love, Disability, and Movies," Catapult (website), April 27, 2016. https://catapult.co/stories/love-disability-and-movies, and #disabledandcute.

Brown, Lydia X. Z., E. Ashkenazy, and Morénike Onaiwu, eds. 2017. *All the weight of our dreams: On living racialized autism.* Lincoln, NE: DragonBee Press. Edited collection of first-person narratives related to the experience of autism for people of color.

Clare, Eli. ([1999] 2015). *Exile and pride: Disability, queerness, and liberation.* Durham, NC: Duke University Press. A classic memoir exploring disability, sexuality, class, race, and environmental justice.

O'Toole, Corbett J. 2015. *Fading scars: My queer disability history.* Fort Worth, TX: Autonomous Press.

Wong, Alice, ed. 2020. *Disability visibility: First-person stories from the 21st century.* New York, NY: Vintage Books. See also https://disabilityvisibilityproject.com/, which has interviews, blogs, and a podcast.

Wood, Caitlin, ed. 2014. *Criptiques*. Word Press. Available at https://criptiques.files.wordpress.com/2014/05/crip-final-2.pdf. Lots of short first person narratives about disability, many of which are intersectional.

Films, Television and Videos

#Next20: Disability and Race. A discussion with 3 "change-makers" about race and disability. https://www.youtube.com/watch?v=LstihpPN_5k (56 minutes).

#Raceand: Kay Ulanday Barrett. A discussion of intersectionality of race, gender, sexuality, and class with activist Kay Uldanday Barrett (4 minutes).

Murderball. 2005. Documentary about the US Quad Rugby team (1 hr, 28 min).

Special. 2019. Semi-autobiographical television series about a gay young man with cerebral palsy building an independent life. Episodes 7 and 8 (each 15 minutes long) explore sexuality.

The Sessions. 2012. A Hollywood re-telling, based on Mark O'Brien's life, of a disabled man who uses a sex surrogate to explore his sexuality.

Websites and Blogs

Bethany Steven's blog, Crip Confessions, at https://cripconfessions.com/. Blog focusing on sexuality and disability.

Harriet Tubman Collective. https://harriettubmancollective.tumblr.com/. A collective of black disability scholars and activists with a resource section.

Lewis, Talila. https://www.talilalewis.com/, lawyer and "social justice engineer", with a blog and resources, including on disability, race, and incarceration.

See Wong above.

Women's Disability Activism. http://whitneylewjames.com/disability-activism/. Offers a historical timeline for women's disability activism.

ACTIVITIES

1. Examine the ways in which stereotypes, identities and group culture, differential access to resources, and policies lead to different experiences of disability for varied groups (e.g., men and women, people of different races, and ethnicities).

2. Identify the blog or video of three disabled activists/authors discussing the intersection of disability and at least one other form of inequality. List the key points for each blog/video. Reflect on what experiences are shared and what experiences are unique. Explain/discuss why it is important to consider intersectionality.

3. The Disability Rights Movement has focused on achieving accessibility, rights, and personal assistance and other supports for independent living. Consider how the intersections of other identities and inequalities may shape the key issues, goals, and strategies of disabled activists.

Macro Social Structures and Disability

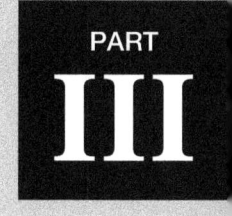

PART III

CHAPTER 8

Family Through the Life Course

Learning Outcomes

8.1 Describe the demographics of disability in the family.

8.2 Analyze what factors shape initial reactions of parents to disability.

8.3 Compare and contrast the experiences of mothers, fathers, children with disabilities, and siblings in the family.

8.4 Explain the factors which may hinder family development (e.g., marriage and parenthood) for adults with disabilities.

8.5 Articulate the differences between aging with a disability and becoming disabled later in life.

Chapter Synopsis

Disability is relational, experienced in and through one's relationships with others. Family relationships are often among the most important. This chapter examines disability and family through the life course, focusing on pregnancy and birth, families with children with disabilities, families with adults with disabilities, and families with aging members with disabilities.

For children, the family is one of the most influential social contexts, providing socialization, the transferal of resources, and the building of connections to society. As they grow older, American youth tend to seek independence from their birth family and later establish families as adults through marriage, cohabitation, and/or childbirth. Some of these families persist through their lifetimes, while others dissolve or reconfigure through separation, divorce, or widowhood. As they move into their elder years, renewed interdependence is common. Aging parents rely on their adult children for support, and adult children, often with their own children, turn to retired parents for assistance. Disability affects all of these stages of the family. In this chapter, first we provide demographic information on disability and the family, and then we consider each of these stages.

Disability, the Family, and Demographics

Disability is a common part of family life. According to the 2000 Census (Wang, 2005), almost 21 million American families (28.9%) have at least one family member with a disability. Adult disability is more common than childhood disability. 18% of families contain at least one adult with a disability, 3.9% of families contain at least one child with a disability, and 5.5% of families report both an adult and a child with a disability. Looking at families with children, Dennis Hogan (2012) estimates that 1/8 (12.5%) of American families with children has a child with a disability.

Census data indicate patterns across American families. Looking at the prevalence of different kinds of disability (Table 8.1), adults were most likely to report employment-related disabilities (13.5%) and physical impairments (9.9%). Children were most likely to have disabilities in "learning, remembering, and concentrating" (2.9%). These disabilities in part reflect the expected tasks of adults and children.

Disability is not distributed evenly across families, and there are differences by race and family form (Wang, 2005). The highest rates of disability are among families of American Indian or Alaskan Native descent (38.5%), followed by families of mixed race (35.9%), Black families (35.7%), Hispanic of any race (33.2%), Native Hawaiian (31.6%), White (27.1%), and Asian (26.5%). Disability is more commonly found in single-headed households. 34.8% of single female-headed households and 31.6% of single male-headed households include a family member with a disability, as compared to 27.3% of married households.

Disability and socioeconomic status (SES) clearly impact each other. Families with disabled members report lower incomes, higher poverty rates, and lower rates of home ownership. As seen in Table 8.2, families with disabled members had a lower median income by $15,360 as compared to families without disabled members. Interestingly, the negative correlation of disability with income occurs both when the disabled family member is an adult (a difference of $10,387) and when the disabled family member is a child (a difference of $11,766).

Families of different races have very different income levels. Looking at rates of poverty (Table 8.3), White families with disabled family members have higher rates of poverty (12.2%) than White families without disabled family members (8.3%). 30.3% of Black families with a disabled family member are in poverty, compared to 25% of Black families without a disabled family member. Thus, disability is negatively correlated with the financial wellbeing of both

PHOTO 8.1
12.5% of American families with children have a child with a disability

TABLE 8.1 Type of Disability in American Families, 2000

Type of Disability	Families With Members With a Disability — Number	Percent	Families With an Adult With a Disability — Number	Percent	Families With Children With a Disability — Number	Percent
Sensory	5,759,550	8.0	3,323,365	4.6	482,630	0.7
Physical	12,004,065	16.6	7,161,740	9.9	500,470	0.7
Mental	7,360,965	10.2	2,850,060	3.9	2,031,865	2.8
Self-care	4,090,905	5.7	1,780,165	2.5	411,975	0.6
Going outside home	9,613,760	13.3	5,696,545	7.9	382,295	0.6
Employment	12,319,470	17.0	9,728,385	13.5	(X)	(X)
With any of five disabilities, excluding employment disability	20,874,130	28.9	12,993,520	18.0	2,840,735	3.9

Data Source: Census 2000, in Wang (2005).

TABLE 8.2 Median Income by for Families With and Without Disabled Members, 2000

Family Characteristics	Median Income (Dollars)
All families	**50,046**
Families without members with a disability	54,515
Families with members with any disability	39,155
All families with a householder who worked year-round full-time in 1999	**61,537**
Families with a householder without disability	62,301
Families with a householder with any disability	51,914
All families raising children	**48,936**
Families raising children without a disability	50,098
Families raising children with any disability	38,332

Data Source: Census 2000, in Wang (2005).

White and Black families, but Black families with and without disability hold a more financially disadvantaged position as compared to White families with and without disability. American Indian and Alaskan Native families have the highest rate of poverty and the highest gap between families with and without

TABLE 8.3   Family Characteristics and Poverty, 2000

Family Characteristics	Families Without Disability Percent in Poverty	Families With Disability Percent in Poverty	Difference in Percentage Points
Race and Hispanic Origin			
White, not Hispanic	4.4	8.3	3.9
Black	19.8	25.0	5.3
American Indian and Alaska Native	19.5	25.5	6.0
Asian	8.7	12.4	3.7
Native Hawaiian and Pacific Islander	13.7	16.7	3.0
Some other race	20.5	25.4	4.9
Two or more races	14.5	19.9	5.4
Hispanic (of any race)	18.5	23.0	4.6
Family Type			
Married-couple family	3.8	7.8	4.0
Family with single female adult	25.3	28.8	3.5
Family with single male adult	12.2	16.8	4.6

Data Source: Census 2000, in Wang (2005).

disability. When looking at family form, 25.3% of single female-headed households are in poverty, and this rate increases to 28.8% for single female-headed households with disabled family members.

Life with a disability costs more, due to expenses such as medical bills, caregiving, accessibility features, and assistive technology. Thus, families with disability earn less on average, yet they must cover more expenses, many of which are necessary for basic survival. As such, they face extraordinary challenges in fostering a healthy and fulfilling environment.

Disability, Family, and the Life Course

In the following sections, we use a life course approach to delve more deeply into the experience of families. We begin by discussing pregnancy and the birth of a disabled child, then families with children with disabilities, families with adults with disabilities, and finally families with older members with disabilities.

Pregnancy and Birth

The birth of an infant with a disability elicits varied and complex responses, such as grief, denial, anger, self-blame, acceptance, and love. Many parents describe the initial discovery of disability as deeply painful. Of her experience with the birth of her daughter with Down syndrome, Jennifer Beitz (2006,

p. 18) writes, "Disappointment. That was my overriding emotion the moment I saw my newborn daughter for the very first time. I felt like I had received a gift that I didn't ask for... My grief was overwhelming as I realized my daughter would never be the child I had been expecting." Michelle Portman (2006, pp. 57–59) writes, "Rage. That is what I felt when my daughter was born with half her head deformed, including the entire right hemisphere of her brain." She also writes, though, of resiliency: "But now I see how Ella's condition has brought me to view our family as a stronger, often better unit whose members will always support one another."

These reactions are connected to the stigma of disability in American society. From the outset, new mothers of children with disabilities feel like they are treated differently. Medical professionals are often insensitive and unsupportive (Carey, 2014; Green, 2003). Friends may feel awkward and disappear. New mothers may not receive many congratulations or encouragement to share their birth stories (Green, 2003). Parent and historian Nicki Pombier (2018) reflected on her own sadness when her son was born with Down syndrome: "Well, why [am I] sad and what does that say about what we expect and what we think of as normal and why is it? Why is it true that I've never had a meaningful encounter with anyone with intellectual disabilities until I've given birth to one? I went to public school, you know I grew up, I've lived many places. Where are they?" Pombier's reflections point out that reactions like grief and fear are fostered by societal decisions to segregate and stigmatize, rather than being natural reactions.

Disability history (see Chapter 3) shows that trends such as medicalization and industrialization in the mid-1800s heightened stigma against people with disabilities. Families no longer worked alongside each other on family farms; they had to leave the house to work, and the provision of family care became more difficult. Capitalist employers demanded profits and shut many people with disabilities out of the workplace. Doctors increasingly played a role in identifying disability, channeling some people into systems of treatment while institutionalizing others. The institutionalization of people with disabilities increased, peaking in the 1950s for people with mental disabilities and the late 1960s for people with intellectual disabilities. Without community services or educational options for their child, parents had to either stay at home to provide care, purchase care, or institutionalize their child. These were difficult decisions, to say the least.

Times have changed, and the parental experience has also shifted in both positive and negative ways.

- *Community services.* Due to many factors, including parent activism, families now benefit from a wide array of community services, making it more feasible for parents to access the expertise and support they need to keep their child at home. Community services, though, are still limited and insufficient. Parents by no means feel assured that they will have the services needed for their child and family to thrive (Anderson et al., 2018; Green et al., 2016; Leiter, 2012).
- *The economy.* The relationship between disability and poverty remains strong. Medical care and accessible childcare are expensive, and parents often need to decrease their work hours to provide care (Hogan, 2012). Moreover, the economic prospects of people with

disabilities are still limited. Thus, parents still fear for their own economic well-being and for their child's long-term economic success.

- *The law.* An array of laws now protects the rights of children and adults with disabilities, such as the Individuals with Disabilities Education Act (IDEA) and the Americans with Disabilities Act (ADA). These laws help assure parents of basic opportunities for their children.

- *Technology.* Due to technological advances, many disabled infants who would have died in the past, such as premature babies, now live. However, technology becomes infused in complex ways throughout the lives of people with disabilities, and parents must make complicated decisions regarding the identification and use of these technologies, often before children are able to form their own opinions (Mauldin, 2016). Pre-natal screening enables parents to abort a fetus (Saxton, 1987), an option that is quite common for certain disabilities like Down syndrome.

- *Cultural expectations and investment.* The birth rate in America declined significantly, from a birth rate of 24 per 1,000 people in 1950 to 12 in 2019. Simultaneously, the amount of time and money parents spend on each child increased (Hays, 1996; Ishizuka, 2019). Parental willingness to invest in infants with disabilities may decline under these conditions (Landsman, 2009).

- *Racial inequality.* Native Americans, African Americans, and Latinos continue to face economic and social marginalization in America. They have less access to contemporary technology, health care, and employment opportunities. Ironically, although disability may pose a greater economic risk for minority families, some minority groups are more accepting of a wide range of differences.

In summary, there have been vast improvements in social conditions, yet the risks associated with disability—stigma, poverty, social isolation—are still very real. Thus, initial parental reactions to disability are tied to these very real social conditions.

Parenting a Child With a Disability

Families who decide to raise their disabled child begin the long process of parenting. Before delving into parenting a child with disabilities specifically, let's review several broad trends related to parenting in America.

First, women have greatly increased their participation in the workforce, but retain primary responsibility for childcare. Almost 55% of mothers with a child from 0 to 12 months are employed, and 75% of mothers with school-age children are employed. Arlie Hochschild (1989) coined the term **the second shift** to describe the dual responsibilities of women who work and hold responsibility for childcare and housework. In fact, as women's labor participation increased, so did their time and energy devoted to parenthood (Bianchi et al., 2006). In a trend called **Intensive Motherhood**, mothers are increasingly expected to provide intensive engagement with their child (Hays, 1996; Wall, 2010).

PHOTO 8.2 Mothers are expected to ensure the educational success and wellbeing of their children

"Supermoms," employed or not, assist with school, chauffeur kids to activities, read and play with their children, and generally ensure concerted cultivation—the provision of the attention and activities required for their children's success in life (Lareau, 2003). The modern demands on mothers are intense, and they face considerable blame when things go awry (Blum, 2007; Ladd-Taylor & Umansky, 1998).

Disability is one of the many things that may be seen as things going "awry." Mothers report feeling **mother blame**, blame placed on mothers for disability specifically and any negative outcomes more generally; and **courtesy stigma**, stigma caused by one's association with stigmatized individuals (Neely-Barnes et al., 2011; Van Wyck & Leech, 2016). Mothers are expected to fulfill the needs of their children and ensure their future success, which are daunting tasks that become even more challenging when disability is added into the equation. Mothers of children with disabilities may need to learn in-home skills, such as particular ways to dress and bathe their child, the administration of medicine and therapies, and new ways to structure rewards and punishments. They must learn to navigate multiple complex bureaucracies (e.g., medical systems, education, social services), to fight for services in these systems and to foster opportunities for their children in a society that often excludes them (Blum, 2015). They are expected to ensure *normalization* (assisting their child to become as close to "normal" as possible and engage in expected roles and rituals), maximization (ensuring their child attains their maximum human potential), and enablement (modifying and creating physical, social, and familial environments to be most conducive to their child's success) (Hogan, 2012). Mothers of children with disabilities often describe themselves, not just as supermoms, but as warriors, fighting to ensure their child's health, rights, and sense of belonging (Blum, 2007; Sousa, 2011).

The role of mothers, and parents more broadly though, has not always been as champions of disability rights (Carey et al., 2020). The pressures toward normalization and maximization may lead parents to focus on cure and erasing disability, rather than embracing disability as a valued form of diversity (Ballou et al., 2021). Parents' own values and interests may conflict with the rights of their children, leading to institutionalizing or sterilizing their disabled children, subjecting them to dangerous treatments, denying them treatment, or denying their sexuality (Burghardt, 2018; Castles, 2004). Although their options are constrained by society, parents wield considerable authority over the lives of their children, sometimes for the better and sometimes for the worse (Reich, 2016).

The family exists in a complex relationship with many other systems which influence the family and shape their response to disability. We will discuss two of these systems, medicine and education.

Navigating Medical Systems and Treatment

Although some disabilities are revealed prenatally or at birth, most disabilities are diagnosed or acquired after birth. Diagnosis and treatment choices involve social processes of decision-making which are heavily influenced by culture, parental beliefs, and access to resources. In American society, treatment decisions are considered largely private—the purview of parents to make in consultation with their doctors—which puts considerable pressure on parents (Mauldin, 2016).

Parents must decide whether, or to what extent, to pursue diagnosis and treatment. Diagnoses such as ADHD, depression, anxiety, and autism, for example, involve a wide range of symptoms, severity, and challenges, and parents weigh the advantages and disadvantages of diagnosis and treatment (Blum, 2015). Diagnosis may offer many advantages. It provides a clearer path to treatment, services, and funding. It offers a *narrative* of the child's behavior that may be preferable to other narratives like deviance. Furthermore, it enables the use of disability laws to protect rights. As an example, without a diagnosis, a child with violent outbursts in school might be labeled a troublemaker and expelled. In contrast, with a diagnosis, the same child might secure an individualized educational plan with strategies to respond to the outbursts and due process rights under IDEA. Thus, diagnosis can be an important tool by which parents resist negative stereotypes and claim rights (Ong-Dean 2009; Prussing et al., 2005).

On the other hand, diagnosis and treatment are not without disadvantages. Disability carries stigma. Children with disability labels face lower expectations in school (Shifrer, 2013), may be channeled into disability-specific settings, and may experience bullying. A disability label, much like a deviance label, can become its own self-fulfilling prophecy. Treatment may also pose risks. For example, medication may benefit particular children, but there are indications of overuse (Zuvekas & Vitiello, 2012). Treatment may also feel oppressive, especially when designed to erase fundamental aspects of children's identities and embodied experience (Ballou et al., 2021; Clare, 2017; Kim, 2017).

Cultural expectations typically pressure parents to comply with medical expertise. Referred to as **scientific motherhood,** mothers are expected to use medical and scientific information to maximize the health and potential of their child (Apple, 2006; Pitts-Taylor, 2010; Singh, 2013). Parents, though, often describe medical professionals as brusque, poorly informed about disability, and focused on fixing disabled children rather than fostering their overall well-being (Carey, 2014; Green et al., 2016). Rather than operating in complete compliance with the medical establishment or rejecting it, parents experience **ambivalent medicalization**—they recognize that the medical model might empower or constrain them, and they therefore have conflicting feelings and practices regarding the use of the medical model (Blum, 2011; Mauldin, 2016).

Education

Education presents many similar challenges for parents. IDEA secured the right to education for children with disabilities in 1975. Despite IDEA, parents often describe their interactions with schools as a struggle (Rogers, 2011). Like medical diagnosis, educational identification of disability has advantages and disadvantages, and, as we will see in Chapter 11 which focuses on education, these vary considerably by school, socioeconomic status, and race. Access to high-quality special educational services often depends on parents' economic, social, and cultural capital (Ong-Dean, 2009). For White and for middle- and upper-income families, diagnosis is more likely to lead to beneficial educational supports and accommodations. In contrast, for children in minority and low-income households, diagnosis and special education are more likely to reinforce low expectations and lead to segregated programming (Ferri & Connor, 2005; Losen & Orfield, 2002). Parents worry that disability labels will be used to deny opportunities rather than provide services, yet they also worry about rejecting professional advice and special educational services (Blum, 2011).

Parent Advocacy

Throughout history, mothers have engaged in **maternal activism**—activism conducted as part of the maternal role to ensure the safety and well-being of their families. Moms have fought, for example, to secure legislation against drunk driving, to expand access to health care, and to restrict child labor. For mothers of children with disabilities, activism is almost a necessary part of the maternal role because many services are only attained through advocacy. Sociologist Rosalyn Darling (1988, p. 141) discusses parental activism as a form of **moral entrepreneurship**—the creative and time-consuming work performed by parents as they seek and create "novel solutions to special problems." Parent Tricia Black (2017) offers a telling example. Tricia's son has a neurological disorder. After he tried three different Boy Scouts troops and found each inhospitable, she decided to start her own "special needs" troop. As her son grew older and his interests shifted to sports, Tricia explained, "there weren't any sports for Michael's age group [age 17]. So I got this great idea to start my own league" (p. 79). Tricia's experiences show the extra effort many parents of children with disabilities must exert just to ensure basic opportunities for their children. In addition to individual-level activism, parents have established state and national organizations to improve the life opportunities of their children.

Impact on Parents

Most parents know little about disability before becoming a parent of a disabled child. Andrew Solomon (2013, p. 15) compares the experience to "having a child who spoke a different language they'd never thought of studying." Indeed, prior to parenthood, many parents hold the same ableist views as the rest of society and wish for healthy children who will achieve in conventional ways.

The stress of stigma, exclusion, care provision, and financial expenses, in a society with minimal supports, can be challenging. Dennis Hogan (2012, p. 55) reports that "nearly one-quarter of mothers of a child with a disability report thinking that their child is usually or always more difficult than other children, in contrast to only 4% of mothers of children without disabilities. More than one-half of mothers raising children with disabilities say that they sacrifice more for their child than most parents, compared to one-quarter of mothers raising a child without a disability." As the severity of disability increases, so do maternal reports of anxiety (Hogan, 2012). Mothers who are marginalized by other factors, such as racism and heterosexism, face additional pressure to defend their parenting choices and prove the worth of their disabled child (Gibson, 2014).

Mothers' employment and income are often negatively affected. Mothers of children with disabilities are less likely to return to the workforce within two years of birth, although most return eventually (Hogan, 2012). Interestingly, maternal employment is highly related to educational level. Among mothers without a college degree, those with disabled children are less likely to work compared to those with non-disabled children. But among mothers with a college degree, those with disabled children are actually more likely to work than those with non-disabled children. Presumably, mothers with a college education are able to secure jobs with sufficient income to purchase in-home care and services and still contribute to the household income. Mothers without a college education find that the costs associated with working often outweigh their pay.

Although much of the research on parenting focuses on mothers, fathers are by no means inconsequential. When faced with increasing financial and care pressures, families tend to resort to more traditional gender roles, with men increasing their hours of work and women decreasing theirs to provide care (Hogan, 2012; Scott, 2010). In his 2003 study of families with children with autism, Gray (2003) found fathers largely experienced the effects of disability indirectly, through the impact of disability on their wives. Newer research, though, has begun to explore the deep emotional impact of disability on fathers who provide care, leading them to re-assess and adjust their roles and worldviews (Jackson, 2021).

The financial and emotional stress of disability, stigma, and exclusion often takes a toll on marriages. "By age ten, just over one-half of parents who were together at the time a child with a disability was born remain together, compared to three-quarters of parents raising a child without a disability" (Hogan, 2012). Divorce rates increase as the severity of disability increases. As a result, mothers of children with disabilities are more likely to become single mothers, further exacerbating financial worries and care demands.

Studies, though, also show positive impacts on the family. Sara Green et al. (2016) show that parents now, as compared in the 1960s and 1970s, are more likely to report positive impacts of disability such as strengthening family bonds, expanding parental skill sets, and broadening parental worldviews. Families often learn to reframe their experiences in positive ways, redefine the idea of normality, and grow more resilient (King et al., 2006).

The Perspective of Children With Disabilities

There are few major sociological studies that examine the experience of family from the perspective of children with disabilities. What we do know paints a complicated portrait.

Children tend to express more positive views of their disability than do their parents. Studies from several countries have found that youth with disabilities to be relatively positive about their lives. Clare Connors and Kirsten Stalker (2007) interviewed 26 children ages 7–15 and found that they described their lives in very ordinary ways. Most reported being happy most of the time, could name people who were important to them, and reported achievements they had made. Whereas youth tended to see their disability as part of their normal existence, parents focused more heavily on the challenges of disability.

Other studies reinforce these limited findings. An Icelandic study of 80 children with and without physical disabilities and their parents measured perceived quality of life, including psychological well-being, autonomy and parent relationships, social support and peers, and school environment (Ólafsdóttier et al., 2019). Children with disabilities were quite positive about their lives and reported the same levels of quality of life as children without disabilities. The only measure that was significantly lower for children with physical disabilities was physical well-being. These researchers found different evaluations from parents though. Children offered a higher assessment of their quality of life on almost all measures than did their parents. Indeed, the negative outlook of parents can itself be a barrier for children with disabilities in attaining disability pride and fully expressing their embodied perspectives and identities (Ballou et al., 2021).

The positive outlook of youth with disabilities is welcome news that challenges the association of disability with tragedy. However, parents' concerns are not totally without merit, since outcome data for youth with disabilities show troubling signs. Compared to youth without disabilities, youth with disabilities are less likely to graduate from high school. They are more likely to experience bullying and violence (NCD, 2000), to have intercourse before the age of 16, to have intercourse without romantic attachment, and to run away (Hogan, 2012). Thus, children tend to be happy with their lives in general, yet the social disadvantages they face are not insignificant.

Siblings

Eighty percent of children with disabilities have a sibling without a disability (Burke, 2004). Historically, sociological research focused on the negative outcomes for non-disabled siblings of children with disabilities, such as internalized shame, jealousy, resentment, and pressure. Over time, however, the picture has become richer and more complex. Connor and Stalker (2003, p. 43) found that children with disabilities experienced "robust [sibling] relationships with fun and conflict in equal measure." Siblings with disabilities both provided and received help, and they did not perceive their sibling relationships as defined by or negatively influenced by their disability. Siblings without disabilities often described their sibling experiences in positive terms and reported benefits including increased empathy, patience, and preparation for helping professionals (Sanchez, 2016).

When siblings experience negative effects, these were at times caused by structural and cultural barriers rather than disability (Sanchez, 2016). For example, unequal gender roles lead female siblings to face greater expectations for the provision of care. Financial constraints limit the resources available to non-disabled siblings. Institutionalization of a disabled child provokes feelings of fear, guilt, and loss among non-disabled siblings (Burghardt, 2018). One of the most significant factors in shaping sibling relationships seems to be parents' attitudes. Parents who display inclusivity and balance the needs of their children are more likely to foster positive sibling relationships than families that are isolated, rigid, and lack coping skills (Sanchez, 2016).

Transition to Adulthood

In America, independence is valued, and Americans often expect grown children to leave their family home and establish their own independent households and families. Embracing this ideal, the *Independent Living Movement* strives to create the social structures and policies needed to enable people with disabilities to gain independence. This ideal, though, masks our **interdependence**—collaboration among people for mutual benefit.

The transition to adulthood poses challenges for youth, disabled or not, as they take on responsibility and autonomy. For youth with disabilities, it is too often a time of peril. The **Disability Cliff** refers to the loss of services upon high school graduation, when young adults with disabilities lose access to a host of services guaranteed by IDEA and enter adulthood facing a far more precarious, unsupportive, and fragmented service environment (Bérubé, 2018; Leiter, 2012). The end of public education poses several problems including:

- Potential loss of daily activity—Whereas education is a right, employment is not. In fact, in 2015 only 35% of young (ages 25–34) adults with disabilities were employed, compared to 78% of young adults without disabilities (NCES, 2016). Many adults lose access to daily activities and social opportunities.

- Potential loss of social services—Whereas a public education is guaranteed, one is only *eligible* for adult disability services (Leiter, 2012). Attaining adult services requires extensive research and planning to investigate, apply for, and secure social services. This complicated process privileges families with extensive capital (Grossman & Mullin, 2020; Leiter, 2012). Moreover, there are long waitlists for services. In Illinois, as an example, the average time on the waitlist for developmental disability services is seven years (Anderson et al., 2018; Fazio, 2019).

- Potential loss of accessibility and accommodations—Educational professionals in K-12 are charged with providing accommodations to ensure an appropriate education. In contrast, colleges and employers rely on young adults to *self-advocate* to obtain services. Young adults, though, may be poorly prepared to do so (Leiter, 2012). Moreover, inaccessible housing and communities present an enormous challenge for attaining independence.

Thus, the challenges to transitioning toward independence are tremendous. For many young adults, these challenges lead to their continued reliance on parents. Young adults with disabilities (ages 25–34) are twice as likely to live with their parents as young adults without disabilities. For some young adults, this extended relationship is positive. Sociologist J. Dalton Stevens (2020) uses the term **Rooting** to describe young adults with disabilities who *choose* to live in their parents' home because it provides a desirable level of accessibility and supports for an independent life. In other words, for these young adults living with parents supports the attainment of adulthood rather than hinders it. Others, though, feel **Stuck in Transition**—young adults who want to establish independent lives but must stay or return home for a variety of reasons, including inaccessibility, financial instability, lack of services, and health needs. Rather than feeling supported in attaining adulthood, they feel blocked from it.

The parent role is often confusing once disabled offspring enter adulthood. Parents who advocated throughout their child's youth find themselves disempowered in systems like higher education and employment, which require young adults to self-advocate. Parents may lose access to their adult offspring's health records and input in their services. Yet, despite their lesser authority, parents are still expected to provide care as needed. Parents who created recreational and worship opportunities for their young children are now called upon to create employment opportunities and support independent living (Caldwell et al., 2020). Indeed, a number of parents have established small businesses expressly to hire their own child and others with disabilities.

For some young adults and their families, disability is a new experience, and the onset of disability in young adulthood has its own challenges. Young adults become disabled in many ways, such as accidents, violence, illness, and the onset of mental health conditions. Young adults, though, may have already established independent lives. They may live in areas geographically distant from their families and have their own physicians, finances, and families. The need for support may cause considerable **role disruption**, the upending of established relational patterns and expectations. For the young adult, disability may threaten the life they have established. Moreover, unlike people who grew up with disability, young adults with acquired disabilities do not have extensive experience living comfortably in their body, adapting to their environment, and practicing self-advocacy skills. Similarly, their parents did not undergo socialization into advocacy and disability management like parents of young disabled children did.

To offer an example, the average age of onset for clinical depression, bipolar disorder, and schizophrenia falls in the mid-20s. These conditions are stigmatized and fluid in their manifestation. The symptoms themselves (e.g., fatigue, loss of self-worth, antisocial withdrawal) may make it difficult for young adults to reach out for help, and family members may not recognize the symptoms. Many college students report their parents initially resist recognition of their mental health concerns, hoping that the student will just "deal with it." For parents who do want to help, young adults may not be covered by parental insurance, and health providers block access to health records except with explicit permission. Parents may see their adult offspring struggling with depression, delusions, or addiction, but have little power to intervene (Engelman, 2018).

Forming (and Dissolving) New Families

Most American adults marry in their lifetime, although marriage is less common now than it has been in the past. Married people enjoy better health, financial security, and social integration. Thus, it is important to consider if people with disabilities have equal access to marriage.

Interestingly, for the first time 2017 data from the American Community Survey revealed no difference in likelihood of being "never married" for people with and without disabilities (Houtenville & Boege, 2019). This seems like good news! This statistic, though, does not account for the timing of disability onset. If people are marrying and then becoming disabled as they age, the overall rate of marriage among people with disabilities might increase, even if single people with disabilities continue to be disadvantaged in the marriage market.

Indeed, data suggest that people with disabilities are still disadvantaged in marriage (MacInnes, 2011; Tumin, 2016). Maryhelen MacInnes (2011) compared the likelihood of marriage for adults with and without disabilities *before* marriage and found that young adults with disabilities have a lower rate of marriage. Rates vary, though, by type of disability. By ages 24–32, nearly half of respondents without disabilities were married, compared to 53% of people with physical disabilities, 43% of people with learning disabilities, 37% of people with mental disabilities, and 21% of people with multiple disabilities. Thus, young adults with physical disabilities were slightly more likely to marry, while people with other types of disabilities, especially people with multiple disabilities, were less likely.

PHOTO 8.3 Romantic unions among people with developmental disabilities are more common now, but many barriers still exist

Rates vary by other factors as well. Whites with disabilities marry at higher rates than African Americans with disabilities (Cohen, 2014). People with disabilities who are employed and have more education marry at higher rates than people with disabilities who are unemployed and/or have less education (Tumin, 2016). People who identify as LGBTQ+ are more likely to have disabilities, to incur disabilities at a younger age, and to marry less often (Fredriksen-Goldsen et al., 2012), although research has yet to parse out how and if disability affects the likelihood of same-sex marriage. It seems likely that barriers faced by LGBTQ+ adults with disabilities, including lack of sexual education, reliance on parents, systems that discourage non-heteronormative sexuality, a lack of media representation, inaccessible dating environments, and discrimination, would negatively impact marriage rates (OToole, 2002).

While disability before marriage decreases the likelihood of getting married, the onset of disability during marriage increases the risk of divorce, especially for younger men with more education and serious disability (Li & Singleton, 2016). Many reasons are offered for the lower marriage rates and higher divorce rates experienced by people with disabilities. For example, ableism brands people with disabilities as asexual and unsuitable romantic partners, and social isolation and inaccessibility limit opportunities for intimate relationships.

Some of the strongest empirical evidence points to the impact of disability on the perceived value of marriage. When asked about the most important reasons to marry, Americans most commonly cite love (88%), lifelong commitment (81%), and companionship (76%). Only 28% suggest financial stability, and 23% say legal rights and benefits (Geiger & Livingston, 2018). Although people say finances are not an important reason to marry, it clearly affects marriage. The theory of **marital value** suggests that marriage is often a rational choice made when the perceived benefits of marriage outweigh the benefits of being single. Disability affects marital value in two ways that we will discuss here: the disability marriage penalty and anticipated economic value.

First, the **disability marriage penalty** refers to the fact that the government uses a married couple's combined income/assets to determine eligibility for public benefits (rather than the disabled individual's income/assets), which can result in the loss of public benefits upon marriage. Many people with disabilities rely on public benefits which are "means-tested." In other words, the benefits are only provided to people with limited financial means. Supplemental Security Income (SSI), Medicaid, Food Stamps and Section 8 housing benefits are all means-tested programs. Using *combined* marital income, therefore, may push one's income or assets above the limit for program eligibility. Even if one qualifies for public benefits, one's benefit amounts may be reduced (see Table 8.4).

Given that living with a disability is expensive, the loss of benefits, income, and/or assets may threaten one's very survival. Self-advocate B.J. Stasio (2010) states, "People with disabilities want to get married. We fall in love and want to make a commitment to the person that we love and become a family. For many it is a religious choice to get married. Yet, too many people with disabilities must choose between getting married and continuing to receive the benefits they need to live from federal programs such as Supplemental Security Income (SSI) and Medicaid."

People with disabilities may choose to cohabitate instead of marry, but even this choice may be restricted. The government may interpret cohabitation as a form of fraud if one benefits from joint income without declaring it. Thus, people with disabilities are pushed to live separately or hide their relationships. For some people, though, sex outside marriage is not an acceptable option. Leila Ahmouda explains, "As a Muslim woman, I cannot live with a man unless I am legally married to him" (quoted in Stern, 2019). State policy, in effect, imposes celibacy on her. This penalty both discourages marriage and encourages divorce for those who become disabled while married.

Second, the onset of disability while married may alter the **anticipated value of marriage** in terms of earnings and costs. This aspect of the marital value theory argues that the risk of divorce increases when disability causes an unanticipated and sharp decline in the economic value of partnership. If the theory of marital value is correct, one would expect disability to have the greatest negative impact when it causes a significant change in anticipated earnings before and after the onset of disability. Hence, divorce would be more likely for those who become disabled early in their working career who

TABLE 8.4 The Disability Marriage Penalty

Limit for two *individuals* on SSI to receive SSI benefits	$4,000 in assets	$1,542 in monthly income
Limit for *a married couple* on SSI to receive SSI benefits	$3,000 in assets	$1,157 in monthly income
Marriage Penalty	$1,000 in assets	$ 385 in monthly income

experience more years of income loss, for those who are well-educated who would have been expected to yield a high salary without disability, for men who typically earn a higher wage than women, and for those who acquire serious disabilities. Perry Singleton (2012) shows that, as expected, in the first two years after disability onset, young, well-educated men with the onset of serious disability experience the greatest increase in divorce. In contrast, disability is less likely to lead to divorce for people who are older, retired, women, and people who were unemployed or were low-income earners prior to disability—those for whom the economic *change* incurred by disability is less dramatic.

Parenting Among People With Disabilities

According to data from the National Health Interview Survey, 4.1 million parents who live with children under the age of 18 have disabilities (6.2%) (Li et al., 2017). Rajan Sonik et al. (2018) place the estimate a little higher, at approximately 10% of parents who live with their children (40% with non-severe disabilities and 60% severe). Thus, it is hardly rare for disabled people to parent. Yet, they face significant obstacles to parenting such as ableism, social/economic marginality, and policy barriers. In light of these barriers, it may not be surprising that women with disabilities are just as likely to want and intend to become mothers as women without disabilities, but they are more likely to report uncertainty about their intentions given the numerous barriers they faced (Shandra et al., 2014).

Ableism and Discrimination

The ideology of *intensive motherhood* demands a selfless, active mother who ensures the success of her children. Disabled women, though, are often judged to be unable to attain these standards, as violating the gendered expectations of motherhood (Blum, 2020; Malacrida, 2009). They are treated as **"risky mothers,"** destined to pass on their own incapacity (Boardman, 2011; Daniels, 2019; Frederick, 2017; Malacrida, 2009) via hereditary passage of "defective" traits (ala eugenics), poor parenting, and/or the social and economic disadvantages common among people with disabilities (Ladd-Taylor, 2017). Their need for care is used to invalidate their ability to give care, despite studies that document that they spend similar amounts of time performing childcare as parents without disabilities (Olkin, 2000; Shandra & Penner, 2017).

These beliefs, and the associated stigma, are embedded in institutional contexts, such as hospitals, social services, the legal system, and schools. For example, hospital culture assumes the incapacity of mothers with disabilities, surveils them, and denies them the same rights and opportunities enjoyed by mothers without disabilities. Angela Frederick (2015) interviewed blind and physically disabled mothers about their birthing experiences and found that doctors frequently assumed that disabled mothers could not be adequate caregivers. For instance, although medical professionals routinely offered support to new mothers experiencing difficulty with breastfeeding, in the case of blind mothers doctors used such difficulties as evidence of the women's inability to provide care and to legitimize calling in social services.

Simultaneously, hospitals offered little support to disabled parents. Describing her interactions with medical professionals while pregnant,

Elizabeth Campbell (2017) explained that doctors instructed her to discontinue taking the medicines necessary for her chronic illness but offered her no alternatives. Several doctors even refused to treat her due to the potential health complications and their lack of experience. Samantha Walsh (2011), a sociologist with a chronic disability, mused that it would be easier to find a physician who would assist her in dying than to assist her with fertility and pregnancy.

Economic Marginality

Disabled parents are portrayed as unable to adequately provide for their children. This stigma is heightened due to the economic disadvantages associated with disability. Comparing parents with and without disabilities, parents with disabilities are more likely to live in households below the poverty line, with food insecurity, and with unmet essential expenses (see Table 8.5) (Sonik et al., 2018). The economic disadvantages occur for people with mild disability, are even more likely for those with severe disabilities, and persist even when people use public benefits (e.g., SSI, SSDI).

Policy

Usually American policy aims to promote and protect the family. This goal, though, has not been extended to include parents with disabilities (Olsen & Clarke, 2003). There are many examples of the ways in which policy subverts parenting by people with disabilities. For most parents, children can only be removed based on proof of neglect or abuse, but 37 states allow the termination of parenting rights based on parental disability (Lightfoot et al., 2010). Parents with disabilities are three times more likely to have their parental rights terminated than parents without disabilities (NCD, 2012a). Furthermore, foster care and adoption agencies use criteria including the physical health of the caregiver, financial stability, and capacity to provide care, which may be used to deny worthy disabled applicants a chance to parent (NCD, 2012a). LGBTQ+ identities likely further hinder parenting as queer adults are delegitimized as potential parents and blocked from parenting services (Tabatabai, 2020). In addition to subverting parenting rights, policies make parenting difficult. For example, Medicaid pays for home-based personal assistance for everyday activities like self-care and cooking but will not pay for assistance with parenting tasks.

TABLE 8.5 Economic Marginality of Parents With and Without Disabilities, 2008

	Parents Without Disabilities	Parents With Non-severe Disabilities	Parents With Severe Disabilities
Household—Mean Income	$73,264	$64,394	$46,3000
Household—Employed	80.8%	74.9	35.1%
Food Insecurity	11.3%	23.0	29.3
Unmet Essential Expenses	18.6%	34.0	43.4%

Data Source: Survey of Income and Program Participation Policy, 2008 (Sonik et al., 2018).

Parenting Outcomes and Practices

Research shows that disability may have positive and negative effects on parenting. Some positive outcomes include that disabled parents may teach their children resilience, diversity, and innovation. Negative effects may include the increased risk of childhood disability, poverty, and stigma, yet many of these outcomes are rooted in social disadvantage, not the disability. For example, Susan Neely-Barnes et al. (2014) studied the impact of parent mental health on child outcomes. Initially, it appeared that parents with mental health conditions were more likely to have children with mental health conditions. However, once environmental factors were taken into account—such as lower education, lower income, residence in rental housing, and single-parenthood—the impact of parent mental health on child mental health was quite small. Thus, as one might expect from the social model of disability, disability presented less of a problem than the social disadvantages associated with disability, such as poverty, discrimination, and the lack of support.

Policy, therefore, affects parenting. In a neoliberal policy context in which people with disabilities are often poor and lack basic supports, their families will also experience these hardships. For example, Whitney Jones-Garcia (2011) describes that her mother had delusions, would run away, and neglect her own personal care and the care of her children. Rather than simply blame her mother or her disability, though, Jones-Garcia looked to the broader lack of social supports/services: "…in a context of a public healthcare system that is woefully inadequate in meeting the needs of people with severe mental illness …, the responsibility for caring rests increasingly with family members, whether we are up for the task or not" (p. 217). People with mental illness have very limited access to individualized, home-based assistance, although these services are more commonly available for people with physical and developmental disabilities. Had her mother had access to such support, Jones-Garcia's family life may have been far more stable.

Parenting is not solely determined by policy, though. Parenting is an embodied practice, influenced by people's bodies and minds (Lindgren, 2011). Some bodies enable or limit specific interactions and tasks (e.g., playing baseball with their child or spending hours at a park on a hot day). Mothers face intense pressure to actively engage in typical ways with their children, and mothers who cannot do so may experience guilt and grief. Many parents with disabilities accept the dominant ideology of *intensive motherhood* and work hard to exemplify this ideal, sometimes at risk to their own health and safety (Cassiman, 2011; Malacrida, 2009).

Other parents resist dominant parenting ideologies and *crip* their parenting style—i.e., develop innovative ways to parent that embrace their unique bodies and minds (Frederick, 2015; Jacob et al., 2017; Lindgren, 2011; Powell et al., 2018). Blind parents may use wearable baby carriers and strollers that can be pulled behind them so that they can safely use white canes and guide dogs. Deaf mothers may use vibrating monitors that detect crying. Mothers who use wheelchairs may buy cribs with doors that swing open. Parents with limited movement may focus on snuggling and singing. Parents may introduce their children to the vibrant disability community and the world of activism. Medical professionals are often ignorant of these creative adaptations, so disabled parents turn to one another for peer support and advice via sites like DisabledParenting.com, Thru the Looking Glass, and the Disabled Parents toolkit.

Global Focus—Sweden, Disability Policy, and the Family

Global comparisons readily show the role of policy in disability outcomes. Sweden has an extensive welfare state. Its government provides subsidized childcare for children from a few months old to the age of 14. Therefore 80% of women work and the rate of poverty for women, including single mothers, is far lower than in the United States. Through National Social Insurance, all parents receive a child allowance and paid sick leave when they or their children are sick. Government programs also help pay for care for disabled children and for in-home personal assistance for adults with disabilities and older citizens. In Sweden, people with disabilities still experience some social disadvantage. They are less likely to marry, and they have higher divorce rates. They also have a lower income and higher poverty than people without disabilities (Swedish Disability Federation, 2007).

A comparison with the United States, though, is shocking. Comparing the poverty rates of people with disabilities across 29 industrialized nations (Schur et al., 2013), the United States has the highest rate of poverty (approximately 47% of people with disabilities are in poverty), and Sweden has the lowest rate (approximately 15%). Only 40% of working-aged adults with disabilities are employed in the United States, compared to 62% in Sweden. People with disabilities are less likely to be on disability-specific benefits in Sweden as compared to the United States because in Sweden all families receive government support. Thus, Sweden has a much stronger infrastructure of support for raising disabled children and for disabled adults to build independent lives, marry, and raise their own children.

Aging and the Family

The **Graying of America**, and the industrialized world more broadly, refers to the increasing proportion of the population that is 65 years of age or older. Due to a combination of longer life expectancy and lower birth rates, the percentage of Americans who are aged 65 and over has more than tripled since 1900, from 4.1% to 15.2%. Just in the past decade, the numbers of people 65+ have increased by 33%, from 37.2 million in 2006 to 49.2 million in 2016 (ACL, 2018). The percentage of those aged 85 and over is also increasing.

As age increases, so does disability. Among those 65 and over, 95% reported at least one area of difficulty on the Census (e.g., 66.5% had difficulties in ambulation, 48% with independent living tasks, 40% with hearing); 14.7% reported more than one area of difficulty. Of those aged 85+, 41.5% reported three or more areas of difficulty (Kahana & Kahana, 2017). Not only does older age lead to disability, but people with early onset disability are now living longer (Molton & Yorkston, 2017). For example, life expectancy among people with intellectual disabilities, cerebral palsy, and spina bifida has substantially increased (Heller, 2010).

The experience of aging with a disability is very different if one has lived with disability versus become disabled in old age. For those with long-term disabilities, they have often accrued disability-skills and strategies to assist with independent living (Heller & Harris, 2012; Kahana & Kahana, 2017). They may have a positive disability identity, strong connections to a disability community, and a host of services in place. As they age, they seek to retain choice and control over their lives, maintain their social connections, and avoid additional disabilities which may complicate their way of life (Molton & Yorkston, 2017). Thus, they have a view of successful aging which incorporates disability and the need for assistance.

Despite these advantages, aging with a long-term disability may still be very precarious. Additional disabling conditions may hinder the adaptive strategies people used. As people with disabilities age, so too may their caregivers. For example, approximately 60% of people with intellectual and developmental disabilities rely on a family caregiver, including 716,000 who rely on a caregiver aged 60+ (Rizzolo et al., 2009). As caregivers age, they may become less able to provide care and/or they may transition care to siblings or professional settings (Coyle et al., 2014). People with disabilities may or may not have influence over these changes and the decisions being made about their care. Yet, it is also very challenging to plan for the future because services are not available on demand and waitlists prevent transition.

PHOTO 8.4 Some people age with their disabilities and others acquire disabilities as they age

In contrast with those who mature with their disability, those who become disabled in older age may have a very different experience. Disability may occur slowly and incrementally, and those with resources can often adapt their environments accordingly. Older Americans who gradually experience limitations are less likely to identify as disabled and instead see themselves as "just getting old" (Priestly, 2003). Those who are married, have living children, and/or who report a satisfactory social life are far less likely to identify as disabled even when they have limitations (Heller & Harris, 2012). The ideology of Successful Aging exacerbates the stigma of disability. The ideology of **Successful Aging** presents the ideal aging process as one where the aging person retains maximal function free from disease and disability (Rowe & Kahn, 1997). By positioning disability as a failure, this ideology hinders identification with disability and involvement in disability activism (Teems, 2016).

For others, the onset of disability later in life may be dramatic and disruptive. Impairments may occur at a time in life when gaining new adaptive skills like American Sign Language (ASL) may be more challenging. Whereas youth with disabilities may benefit from years of training and supports, older people may only be offered a few weeks of rehabilitation before facing an assessment of their likely success at independent living. The lack of community services means that disability can quickly lead to institutionalization in a nursing home and the loss of liberty and rights.

Despite the growing nursing home industry, older Americans tend to prefer remaining in the community as they age and relying on family and informal caregivers. Care may enacted in relationships of beneficial interdependence among family members with different skills, contributions, and needs. For many families, though, increasing care demands related to aging can be daunting. Referred to as the **Sandwich Generation,** one of every seven middle-aged American provides financial support for both children and an aging parent (Miller, 1981; Parker & Patten, 2013). Family members often feel unsupported in care responsibilities for aging parents, and paid elder care can be extremely expensive. The decision to place a family member in a nursing home can be extremely difficult, and many family members feel a complex blend of guilt and relief after placement (Ryan & Scullion, 2000). This dilemma of care—often experienced as a deeply personal trouble—reflects long-standing failures in disability care, including a reliance on institutional care, a paucity of services available in the community, the expectation that families alone can provide sufficient care, and the denial of liberty and rights to people with disabilities.

Conclusion

The family is a complex system, impacted by disability while also shaping the experience of disability. The family has undergone tremendous changes in the last century, but it remains one of the most essential social systems for the provision of love, a sense of identity, socialization, resources, and care.

KEY TERMS

Ambivalent medicalization 173
Anticipated value of marriage 180
Courtesy stigma 172
Disability cliff 177
Disability marriage penalty 180

Graying of America 184
Intensive motherhood 171
Marital value 179
Maternal activism 174
Moral entrepreneurship 174
Mother blame 172
Risky mothers 181
Role disruption 178

Rooting 177
The second shift 171
Sandwich Generation 186
Scientific motherhood 173
Successful Aging 185
Stuck in Transition 177

RESOURCES

Academic articles

Blum, Linda. 2011. "'Not This Big, Huge, Racial-Type Thing, but...': Mothering Children of Color With Invisible Disabilities in the Age of Neuroscience." *Signs* 36 (4): 941–967.

Carey, Allison. 2014. "Parents and Professionals: Parents' Reflections on Professionals, Support Systems, and the Family in the Early Twentieth Century." In *Disability Histories*, edited by Susan Burch and Michael Rembis, 58–76. Champaign, IL: University of Illinois Press.

Frederick, Angela. 2014. "Mothering While Disabled." *Contexts* 13 (4): 30–35. (Well-written for an under-graduate audience).

Green, Sara. 2003. "They are Beautiful and They are Ours: Swapping Tales of Mothering Children With Disabilities Through Interactive

Interviewing." *Journal of Loss and Trauma* 8 (1): 1–13.

Saxton, Marsha. 2013. "Disability Rights and Selective Abortion." In *The Disability Studies Reader*, edited by Lennard Davis, (4th ed, 87-99). New York, NY: Routledge. (This reader also has two additional pieces exploring the issue of pre-natal testing and selective abortion, and Beginning with Disability has two pieces on this issue as well).

Shandra, Carrie L., and Penner, Anna. 2017. "Benefactors and Beneficiaries? Disability and Care to Others." *Journal of Marriage and Family* 79 (4): 1160–1185.

Academic Books

Blum, Linda. 2015. *Raising Generation Rx: Mothering Kids With Invisible Disabilities in an Age of Inequality.* New York, NY: New York University Press.

Lewiecki-Wilson C., and Cellio J., eds. 2011. *Disability and Mothering: Liminal Spaces of Embodied Knowledge.* Syracuse University Press.

Mauldin, Laura. 2016. *Made to Hear: Cochlear Implants and Raising Deaf Children.* Minneapolis, MN: University of Minnesota Press.

Memoirs and First-Person Accounts on Family

Ballou, Emily, daVanport, Sharon, & Onaiwu, Morénike G., eds. 2021. *Sincerely, Your Autistic Child: What People on the Autism Spectrum Wish Their Parents Knew about Growing Up, Accep-tance, and Identity.* Boston, MA: Beacon Press.

Bérubé, Michael. 2016. *Life as Jamie Knows It: An Exceptional Child Grows Up.* Boston, MA: Beacon Press.

Lindgren, Kristen. 2011. "Reconceiving Motherhood." In *Disability and Mothering: Liminal Spaces of Embodied Knowledge*, edited by Cynthia Lewiecki-Wilson, and Jen Cellio, 88–97. Syracuse, NY: Syracuse University Press.

Simon, Rachel. 2013. *Riding the Bus with My Sister.* Houghton Mifflin Harcourt.

Internet Resources

Disabled Parenting Project website at Disabledparenting.com.

National Research Center for Parents with Disabilities at https://heller.brandeis.edu/parents-with-disabilities/.

Parenting with a Disability: You're your Rights Toolkit https://www.nfb.org/sites/www.nfb.org/files/images/nfb/publications/brochures/blindparents/parentingwithoutsight.html.

Rocking the Cradle: Ensuring the Rights of Parents with Disabilities and Their Children (2012a) https://ncd.gov/sites/default/files/Documents/NCD_Parenting_508_0.pdf

Through the Looking Glass at https://www.lookingglass.org/.

Videos and Films

"The Challenges of Being a Disabled Mum" https://www.youtube.com/watch?v=neNkaIFeyIA (documentary, 56 minutes, follows two disabled mothers as they parent).

"I am Sam." (2001). Jesse Nelson (Director), Bedford Falls Company. A Hollywood film that depicts a father with intellectual disabilities).

"My Dad Matthew," a short video about a father with cerebral palsy and his son, https://www.youtube.com/watch?v=EsVzlyD7ArM (6 minutes).

"SSI Marriage Penalty," by self-advocates in New York, https://www.youtube.com/watch?v=sPqo0V9BGD8 (8 minutes).

ACTIVITIES

1. List and define four historical trends or ideologies that shape pregnancy or motherhood today. For each, explain how this trend or ideology has a particular impact on mothers of children with disabilities and/or mothers with disabilities. How might "cripping parenthood" challenge these trends/ideologies and offer new ways to parent? For an additional component, watch The Challenges of Being a Disabled Mum (see resources). What are the key themes of the video? Make at least four linkages between the chapter and the video, clearly explaining each link using the chapter and the video. Provide four examples of adaptive parenting. Discuss how parenthood is shaped by each woman's particular disability and social context.

2. *Rocking the Cradle: Ensuring the Rights of Parents with Disabilities and Their Children* (see resources) contains several chapters (Chapters 4–17) on policy related to parenting and disability. Each student/group should read a single chapter or set of chapters. Each student/group should report back on the key concerns and policy needs raised by their chapter(s). As a large group consider the breadth of policy and supports relevant to support parenting.

3. Read Angela Frederick's article (see resources) and/or *Parenting with a Disability: Your Rights Toolkit* (see resources). What obstacles do parents with disabilities face? How do parents address these obstacles on an individual level? How might they address these obstacles on a macro, social level (e.g., how might we change systems?)

CHAPTER 9

Economy and Politics

Chapter Synopsis

The economy and state independently and interactively play a role in producing disability, shaping our understandinqg of disability, and determining our response to disability. In the United States, a neoliberal response to disability values productivity and individualism such that those who attain self-sufficiency are rewarded with civil rights and resources. In contrast, those deemed unproductive often lose their rights, and the benefit system often channels them into segregated settings, poverty, and a devalued social status. International comparisons show that poverty and exclusion are products of policies, and alternative strategies might provide both rights and a safety net.

Learning Outcomes

9.1 Explain materialist and political economy theories.

9.2 Analyze the ways in which capitalism and the state contribute to the production of disability in the United States and globally.

9.3 Evaluate the landscape of disability policy to consider achievements and limitations in achieving equity for people with disabilities.

9.4 Apply the concept of productivism to American disability policy.

9.5 Reflect on the advantages and disadvantages of the commodification of disability services.

9.6 Debate the merits of alternative approaches to disability policy.

Materialist and Political Economy Theories

The economy and the state play a central role in disability and the inequality associated with disability, as groups of people compete for resources and institutionalize unequal patterns of access and power. Here we will draw on two key theoretical approaches—materialism and political economy—to frame this body of work.

Materialist theories, discussed in Chapter 1, argue that the resources needed to survive (the material environment) and the economy (a society's system for distributing resources) determine social relationships, culture, and disability. Historically, as the means of production changes, so do the relations of production. In feudal Europe, for instance, farming and agricultural production was the centerpiece of how people survived (i.e., agriculture was the means of production). The land provided food, shelter, materials for clothing, and resources for heat. However, only a small percentage of the population—the nobility—owned all the land. The majority of people had no choice but to labor as serfs for the nobles. Under these material conditions, life was hard for most people and disability was common, but in some ways disability was less meaningful than it is today. People were born into their social positions as nobles or serfs. Serfs were poor and labored alongside family members insofar as they were able to regardless of disability.

With the rise of capitalism, the mode of production changed. Goods were now mass produced in factories. **Capitalism** is characterized by private ownership of the mode of production (industry/factories), mass production, and the expansive commodification of resources for sale in the marketplace (i.e., almost all things, even essential resources, must be purchased). Capitalists own companies, while the workers, who have little independent access to the resources they need to survive, work to earn money to meet their needs. The imperative for profit is a defining feature of capitalism. Propelled by the drive for profit, capitalists may exploit the workers more and more, forcing the workers to work longer hours, work faster, live with fewer benefits/securities, and work in poorer conditions. Capitalists may replace workers with technology and move jobs overseas to hire more exploitable labor. Because capitalism is a competitive system, capitalists have little choice but to exploit their laborers. If they do not, other companies will exploit their workers, reap greater profits, and drive ethical companies into failure. Thus, the quest for profit erases almost all sense of obligation on the part of capitalists to care for the workers who produce the goods and wealth of the society. In this system, disability may matter a great deal (Rosenthal, 2019; Russell, 1998). For example, workers compete for jobs and wages, and capitalists may resist hiring people with disabilities due to stereotypes and concerns regarding liability and cost. They also may avoid providing disability accommodations if and when they can. For workers, working outside the home reduces the potential flexibility of work and access to caregivers who can provide support.

To add the government into the mix, the idea of **Political Economy** suggests that the government and economy are intertwined, such that state policies usually serve the interests of elites/capitalists. In this chapter, we will examine how capitalism and the state produce disability, shape the response to disability, and influence many of the social disadvantages experienced by people with disabilities.

The Production of Disability

Capitalism and the Production of Disability

Among many possible causes of disability, capitalism plays an important role in producing disability.

Unsafe and grueling work conditions produce disability. According to the Social Security Administration, "A substantial proportion of disability in the United States is caused by injuries and illnesses that arise because of an individual's work" (O'Leary et al., 2012). This includes, for instance, injuries and illnesses due to exposure to chemicals and substances, poor safety regulations and practices, machine-related accidents, vehicular accidents related to work, repetitive motion injuries, violence in the workplace, and mental stress. People in low-income households, immigrants, and people of color are particularly likely to work in low-pay and dangerous jobs.

According to Jonathon Karmel (2017) in his book *Dying to Work: Death and Injury in the American Workplace*, "the right to a safe and healthy workplace has been made difficult to achieve" (p. 5). Businesses enjoy access to a vast population of exploitable labor and the political power to ensure few regulations and avoid costly punishments. In this context, the cost-benefit analysis for American businesses becomes clear: worker injuries/illnesses are often cheaper than ensuring workplace safety. Historically, for example, from 1911 to 1997, approximately 103,000 coal miners died at work, and even more workers experienced disease and disability (CDC, 1999). Preventative measures were possible, but corporations decided not to dedicate the funds necessary for worker safety.

Compared to the early days of capitalism, work is now far safer in many ways (Karmel, 2017). Modern labor laws protect worker safety and encourage humane working conditions. In 1913, 37 of every 100,000 workers died due to work-related circumstances, but, by 1997, four workers per 100,000 died. That is good news! However, work is still far from safe. In 2015, 150 workers died each day because of their work (Karmel, 2017). Moreover, even as fatality rates decline, the risk of disability does not disappear. The National Safety Council (n.d.) reports that in 2018, a worker was injured on the job every seven seconds. For example, desk workers rarely experience workplace fatality, but they commonly develop back pain and repetitive motion injuries. Health care workers become sick and disabled through exposure to diseases and chemicals, injuries in the course of caregiving, and access to drugs. Service sector workers face high levels of injury and mental health conditions because they work in high stress jobs for little pay.

Consider an example of disability in the workplace that made the news headlines. In 2020, Facebook content moderators made the news when they sued Facebook. Moderators worked all day in isolation with few breaks while viewing horrific content, including violence, hate speech, and suicides. They argued that the content of their work and poor work conditions caused mental health conditions including depression, anxiety, and PTSD. Facebook settled the case and agreed to improve work conditions, provide on-site mental health care, and compensate employees who developed work-related mental health conditions (Newton, 2020).

Patterns of consumption driven by profit produce disability. Capitalism and mass production have offered people access to more products than ever before, and that has been good for the health of Americans in many ways. For example, greater access to food has all but eliminated some diseases, like Scurvy which is associated with a deficiency of vitamin C. However, modern patterns of consumption also cause disease and disability.

Tobacco and nicotine offer a clear example. Tobacco use is the *leading* cause of preventable disease, disability, and death in the United States (CDC, 2019a). By the 1960s, evidence clearly documented the dangers of tobacco; however, the tobacco industry covered up this information and continued to reap tremendous profits. In the 1990s, states won a series of successful

PHOTO 9.1
The rise in vaping will likely lead to higher rates of illness and disability

Credit: AleksandrYu (2021). Reproduced with permission from istock.com.

lawsuits against the industry, and cigarette use declined. Then e-cigarettes, marketed to youth by offering a range of fun flavors, provided a new revenue stream. Among high school students from 2011 to 2019, smoking traditional cigarettes declined (15.8%–5.8%), but the use of e-cigarettes rose from 1.5% to 27.5%. In 2019, 31% of high school students reported using tobacco products, despite evidence linking e-cigarettes to reduced brain development and increased risk of lung diseases (Bhatta & Glantz, 2019; CDC, 2019e).

Food has also changed dramatically due to industrialization. In order to heighten profits, companies produce ultraprocessed, "hyper-palatable" foods (e.g., soda, snack foods, french fries) (Steele et al., 2017). These foods tend to be low in vitamins, fiber, and protein, and high in sugar, salt, saturated fats, and calories. From 1970 to 2010, American's calorie consumption increased 23%, and, in 2010, 57.5% of the American diet consisted of ultraprocessed foods. These trends lead to obesity, high blood pressure, diabetes, and a host of other disabling conditions, especially in low-income households that tend to rely more heavily on less-expensive, ultraprocessed foods (Desilver, 2016).

Capitalism marginalizes people with bodies deemed nonstandardized and nonefficient from the workplace and defines those bodies as disabled. The unemployment rate of people with disabilities is persistently high. In 2019, only 38.9% of working age adults with disabilities living in the community were employed, compared to 78.6% of people without disabilities (Houtenville & Rafal, 2020). The wide gap in employment has persisted regardless of vocational rehabilitation programs and legislation like the Americans with Disabilities Act (ADA) aimed to increase employment.

Being able to work or not is not simply, or primarily, a matter of one's biology. Historically, in agricultural economies, most people contributed in some way. Family members worked alongside each other, benefitting from including all family members (even those who could only contribute minimally) and providing care while working. The shift to factories changed the economic calculation of work and relationships. Unlike families, capitalists focus on profitability, which demands they invest in the fastest, most efficient laborers. They may be reluctant to commit to accommodations, both due to cost and to resist the idea that they are obligated to meet worker's needs. The standardization of the work process (e.g., assembly lines, fixed and "efficient" production methods) further excludes atypical bodies and minds. Moreover, in capitalism, workers do not work alongside family who used to provide support.

Indeed, as people with disabilities face exclusion from the workplace, their family members must leave their homes to work, and they are unable to provide care to family members who are now increasingly excluded from paid labor. New responses to disability emerge, such as nursing homes and institutions, which commodify care while enabling nondisabled family members to work. Thus, as countries industrialize, some people come to be defined as disabled, and they are often excluded from paid labor and cast as dependents (Rose, 2017; Russell, 1998).

To fully understand the role of capitalism in producing disability, we also must discuss its role in producing inequality. However, because inequality is produced by capitalism in conjunction with government policies, let's first bring the state into this discussion.

The Production of Disability and the State

The state produces disability through war and state violence. Through the military, police, and other mechanisms, the state exerts legitimate (i.e., sanctioned by the state), although at times morally dubious, violence. This violence may disable those enacting the violence and/or those on whom the violence is enacted (Paur, 2017).

War is one of the causes of disability. As of 2019, 18.8 million people in America were veterans, equaling 8% of the adult population. Around 4.7 million (25%) veterans reported a service-related disability, and 44% of disabled veterans had a severe disability (US Bureau of Labor Statistics, 2020). The rate of service-related disability has increased for veterans who served in more recent conflicts. 41% of veterans of post 9/11 (2001) conflicts reported service-related disabilities, compared to 26% of veterans from the first Gulf War era (1990–2000), and 15% from earlier conflicts. As with industrial accidents, we see that higher survival rates lead to higher disability rates; veterans who would have died from their injuries in the past now survive with disabilities. There is also now greater awareness of disability, especially mental health conditions.

Globally, during the 20th century an estimated 191 million people died, and more became disabled, as the direct or indirect result of armed conflict. More than half of these fatalities were civilians (Sidel & Levy, 2008). In the 21st century, most armed conflict involves civil wars, often in low-income countries.

War's indirect effects also disable. Mass destruction devastates a country's infrastructure, leading to shortages of clean water, food, power, and health care. War creates refugees, some of whom have life-long disabilities, some of whom are disabled by war, and some of whom become disabled by displacement and forced migration. Furthermore, **militarism**—the national prioritization of the preparation for war—diverts money away from health care and human welfare. In 2019, the United States spent $697 billion, 16% of federal spending, on defense. This is a lot of money, but it also spent 23% of federal spending on social security and 25% on health insurance programs, leading to a debate about whether the United States spends too much or not enough on the military versus social welfare (Center on Budget and Policy Priorities, 2020a). Low-income nations, on the other hand, tend to spend much less overall on their militaries, but a much greater percentage of their limited budgets. In 1990, Ethiopia spent $16 per capita for the military and $1 for health. Sudan spent $25 per capita on the military and $1 on health (Sidel & Levy, 2008).

War is not the only expression of state violence. Police violence, incarceration, institutionalization, and compulsory sterilization provide other examples (Ben-Moshe, 2020; Chapman & Withers, 2019). Throughout the history of institutions, the state paid to segregate people with intellectual and mental disabilities, denying their rights and subjecting them to neglect and abuse. State laws permitted the compulsory sterilization of over 60,000 Americans, mostly poor women (Ladd-Taylor, 2017). Police violence disproportionately targets people of color, people with disabilities, and disabled people of color (Moore et al., 2016). As will be discussed in Chapter 11, prisons are some of the most violent and disabling sites in America today, disproportionately targeting America's poor and people of color, yet Americans often overlook or justify this violence (Ware et al., 2014).

The state creates/defines disability through its administrative categories, policies, and programs. With a stroke of the pen, the state creates or erases disability as it defines disability in relation to its numerous programs and laws (Stone, 1984). For example, in 1984, Congress passed amendments that led to the revision and expansion of the Social Security's definition of "mental disorders," leading to an increase in the number of people counted as disabled and eligible for disability benefits (Social Security Administration, n.d.).

Different state programs have different goals, and therefore create very different definitions of disability. Social Security ties definitions of disability directly to the inability to work. Special education law offers a much broader definition of disability associated with biological conditions that negatively affect learning. The Americans with Disabilities Act (ADA), which prohibits discrimination, uses yet another definition. In the ADA, a disability is "a physical or mental impairment that substantially limits one or more major life activities, a person who has a history or record of such an impairment, or a person who is perceived by others as having such an impairment." Thus, someone might count as disabled with regard to special education eligibility, but not by the standards of the ADA or Social Security. And, because the government operates on multiple levels and through many systems, policies and laws regarding disability do not align, leading to bizarre inconsistencies regarding who is defined as disabled and the consequences of that label (Grossman, 2019).

The Production of Disability Through Economic Inequality

Economic inequality and poverty produce disability. Because capitalism thrives on labor exploitation, it tends to produce a vast gulf in resources between capitalists and workers, especially when the government promotes laissez-faire economic policies (i.e., policies that promote freedom of the private market). More equal societies tend to have less disability, whereas more unequal societies have more disability (Torras, 2006).

Socioeconomic status is one of the strongest predictors of disability (Taylor, 2010). People with low incomes and little wealth live in neighborhoods with fewer resources; experience greater exposure to toxins, violence, and stress; and tend to have less access to high-quality, consistent medical care—all of which increase the risk of disability. Older Americans from socioeconomically disadvantaged backgrounds are up to three times more likely to report disability than older Americans from nondisadvantaged backgrounds (Schoeni et al., 2005). According to a longitudinal study of older Americans, respondents who reported difficulty meeting their expenses experienced a median age of the onset of disability seven years younger than those who reported no difficulty in meeting their expenses (Matthews et al., 2005). The impact of class has implications for racial inequality as well. African Americans experience higher rates of disability as compared with Whites, but much of this difference is explained by class. Indeed, according to a study by Fuller-Thomson and her colleagues (2009), 90% of the Black-White difference in disability rates among older men and 75% of the Black-White difference among older women were explained by differences in income and education.

The role of poverty and income inequality in producing disability is especially concerning because economic inequality has increased in the United States over the last 50 years. In 1968, people in the bottom 20th percentile of income earned 4.2% of all income, and people in the top 20% earned 42.6%. By 2018, those in the bottom 20% earned 3.1% of the nation's income, and the top 20% earned 52% (US Census Bureau, 2019).

Among industrialized nations, the United States has particularly high levels of inequality. One measure of inequality looks at how workers in the bottom 10th percentile of the earnings distribution fare in comparison to the median worker. Across 21 industrialized countries, American workers fare the worst on this measure (Gould & Wething, 2012). In the United States, workers in the bottom 10th percentile earned only 47% of the earnings of the median worker. In contrast, in the most equal countries including Ireland and Belgium, workers in the bottom 10th percentile earned 73%.

Adding disability into the mix, Figure 9.1 shows a comparison of the rate of poverty for people with and without disabilities in 29 industrialized nations. The United States had the *highest* level of poverty for people with disabilities (Schur et al., 2013). In three of the 29 nations (Sweden, Norway, and Slovak Republic), people with disabilities were no more likely to be poor than people without disabilities.

FIGURE 9.1 **Global Rates of Poverty for People With Disabilities, 2010 (Schur et al., 2013)**

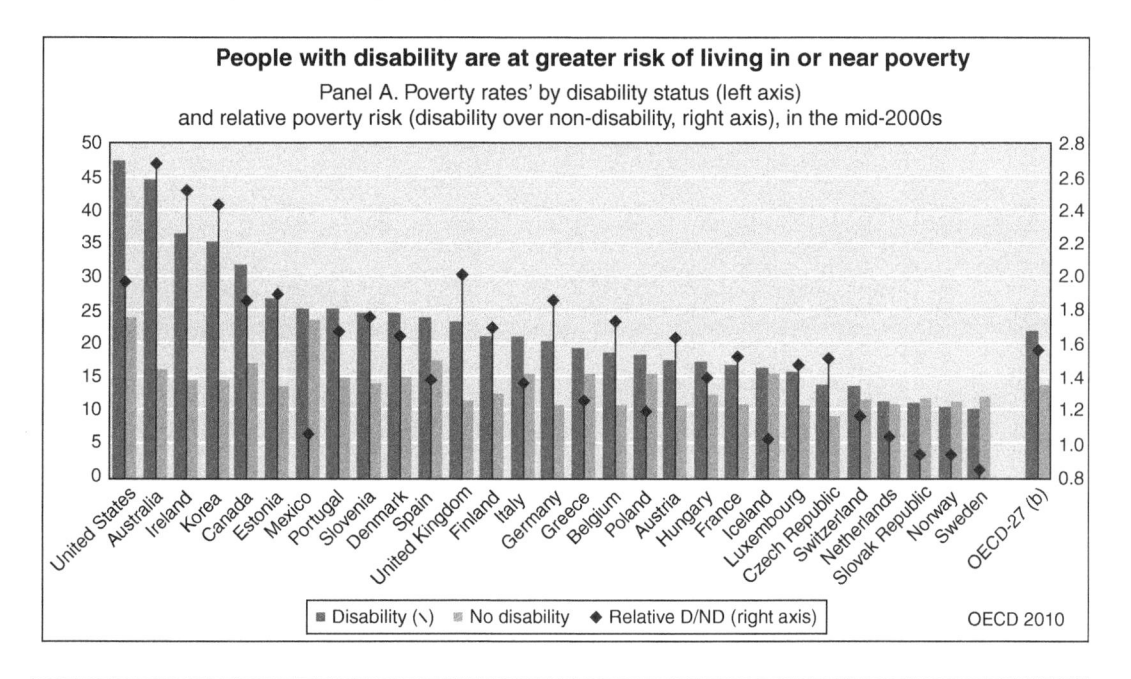

PART III Macro Social Structures and Disability

Why does the United States have such high rates of poverty compared to other industrialized countries? The United States has fewer regulations on capitalism than most industrialized countries. It embraces **neoliberalism**—a political and economic philosophy that promotes individual freedom based on a laissez-faire approach to capitalism with little government regulation or public provision of services (Fritsch, 2017; Giroux, 2008). People are encouraged to independently rely on their merit to attain success and discouraged from expecting public support. In neoliberalism, capitalists hold little responsibility to ensure that workers can afford to meet their basic needs, to address the systemic inequality that shapes access to opportunities, or to address the human harm resulting from work processes, pollution, or the products of capitalism. For example, in the United States even full-time workers struggle with poverty. In 2021, the federal minimum wage was $7.25 (the rate has held steady since 2009). Someone making $7.25 per hour, working 40 hours per week with no vacations for 52 weeks would earn $15,080, which is above the federal poverty line for one person but below it for a household of two or more people.

In addition to low wages and benefits through employment, the United States has fewer public social welfare programs than its industrialized peers. As shown in Figure 9.2, in 2019 the United States federal government spent

FIGURE 9.2 US Federal Budget Allocation, 2019

Most of Budget Goes Toward Defense, Social Security, and Major Health Programs

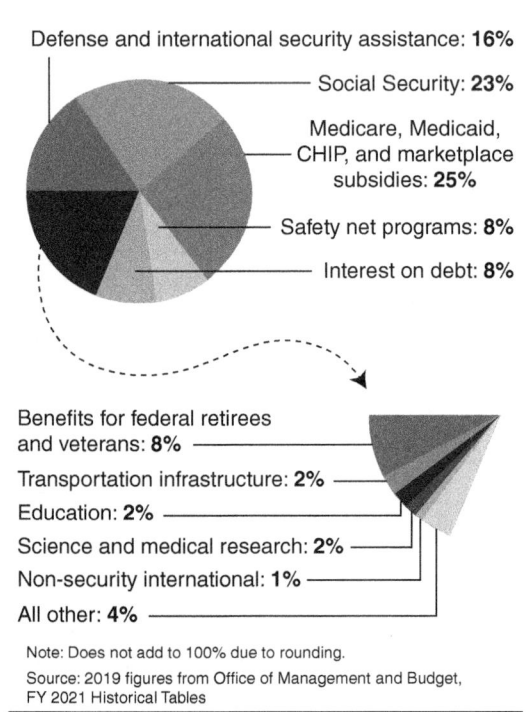

Defense and international security assistance: **16%**
Social Security: **23%**
Medicare, Medicaid, CHIP, and marketplace subsidies: **25%**
Safety net programs: **8%**
Interest on debt: **8%**

Benefits for federal retirees and veterans: **8%**
Transportation infrastructure: **2%**
Education: **2%**
Science and medical research: **2%**
Non-security international: **1%**
All other: **4%**

Note: Does not add to 100% due to rounding.
Source: 2019 figures from Office of Management and Budget, FY 2021 Historical Tables

CENTER ON BUDGET AND POLICY PRIORITIES I CBPP.ORG

25% of its national budget on public health programs, 23% on Social Security, 8% on safety net programs, and 2% on education. It is important to note that these programs help stem poverty. Analysis by the Center on Budget and Policy Priorities (2020b) indicates that, without the current income, health, and safety net programs, the American poverty rate would almost double. In 2018, the poverty rate would have been 24% instead of 12.8%. In comparison with Europe, though, the American spending priorities are very different. The US funds an "expansive security state," spending twice as much than Europe on the military, more on public safety (e.g., police and prisons), and less on social welfare programs (Giroux, 2008; Lowery, 2020).

The Production of Disability Through Economic Inequality on a Global Scale

Economic inequality and its association with disability becomes starker when we use a global lens. In 2017, the richest eight billionaires held the same wealth as the bottom 50% of the global population (Elliot, 2017). That is a pretty shocking statistic. Eighty percent of the world's people with disabilities live in low-income countries. These countries experience malnutrition and hunger, violence and warfare, lack of clean water and safe foods, unsanitary conditions, and inadequate health care systems. For example, a shocking 663 million people worldwide lack access to safe drinking water, and 2.4 *billion* people lack access to safe sanitation systems, including 70% of people in Sub-Saharan Africa and 53% of people in Southern Asia (CDC, 2017). These conditions encourage the spread of infection diseases, such as cholera, dysentery, hepatitis A, and polio, and result in disablement.

Using a metric referred to as **Disability Adjusted Life Years (DALY)**, in which each DALY is equivalent to the loss of one healthy year due to premature death, disease, or disability, Max Roser and Hannah Ritchie (2020) show a strong correlation between a nation's gross national income (GNI) and DALYs (see Figure 9.3).[1] Poorer nations lose far more years of healthy life than do wealthier nations. This effect is greatest when looking at the deaths and disabilities that result from communicable diseases. Nations in Africa tended to have the lowest GNIs and the highest loss of DALYs.

Since industrialization, high-income industrialized nations, concentrated in the Global North, have prospered, while low-income nations, concentrated in the Global South, have disproportionately suffered from mass poverty, disease, and disability. Immanuel Wallerstein (1974) developed World Systems Theory to explain this pattern. **World Systems Theory** asserts that there is a global economic system in which high-income industrialized nations grow rich through exploitative economic processes, such as converting the economies of poor countries into single crop export economies (e.g., sugar, coffee), using their vulnerable people as cheap labor, and extracting their resources, all while channeling profits back into the economies of high-income nations. This system constrains the economic development of low-income countries and leads to the poverty of their people. For instance, once Britain colonized Jamaica, the profits from the production and export of sugar flowed to Britain, while the local people had little access to essential resources, reaped little of the profits from their labor, and experienced higher disability rates and lower life

---

[1] Chart reproduced from Roser and Ritchie (2020).

FIGURE 9.3 GNI per Capita and DALY Loss, 2012

GNI per capita vs DALYs lost due to communicable and non-communicable diseases
Disability-Adjusted Life Years (DALYs) measure the number of years lost due to ill-health and early death. This is called the Burden of Disease. Gross National Income per capita is measured in International Dollars, which adjusts for price differences between countries.

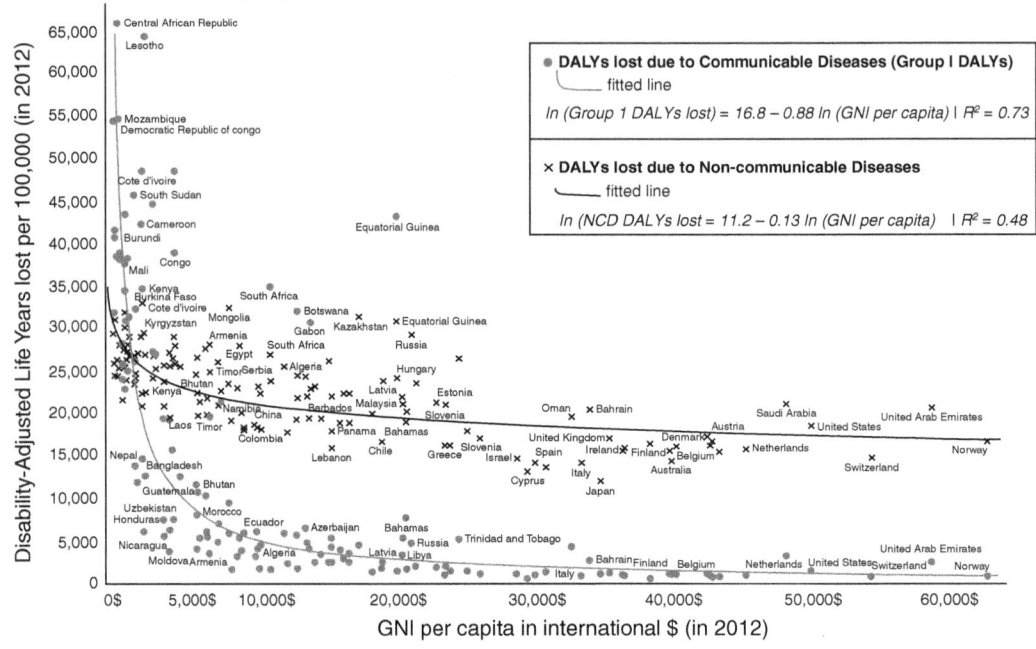

- DALYs lost due to Communicable Diseases (Group I DALYs) — fitted line
  ln (Group 1 DALYs lost) = 16.8 − 0.88 ln (GNI per capita) | $R^2 = 0.73$

× DALYs lost due to Non-communicable Diseases — fitted line
  ln (NCD DALYs lost = 11.2 − 0.13 ln (GNI per capita) | $R^2 = 0.48$

Data source: Sterck O., Roser, M., Ncube, M., Thewissen, S. 2017 - Allocation of development assistance for health: Is the predominance of national income justified? (forthcoming in Health Policy and Planning)
This dada visualization is available at OurWorldData.org where you find more research and visualization on this topic. Licenced under CC-BY-SA by the author Max Roser.

expectancies (see Chapter 3). Thus, the global system of labor exploitation and resource extraction disproportionately disables people, particularly people of color, from impoverished nations. Global inequality not only produces global disability; it also undercuts the ability of low-income nations to provide care and support to their people with disabilities (Charlton, 2000; Erevelles, 2011; Grech et al., 2016). As argued by scholars such as Nirmala Everelles (2011) and Patty Berne (2015), in the economic calculation of transnational capitalism, the disablement of Black/Brown and poor bodies is deemed an acceptable loss.

As already noted, in addition to poverty, war and violence also disabled people. The high prevalence of warfare in low-income countries result in part from the global economic systems of colonization and exploitation by high-income countries. Economic exploitation leaves low-income countries with little internal capacity for economic development, leading to political corruption and strife (Pisani & Grech, 2015). High-income countries also directly engage in military actions against low-income nations, often driven, at least in part, by economic concerns related to the needs of capitalism such as the need for resources and to protect investments. Moreover, economics shape military strategies. For example, it costs approximately $3 to produce a landmine, but as much as $1,000 to remove it. One of the most common consequences of landmines is loss of limbs. Eighty million landmines are still active in 78 countries, leading to 15,000–20,000 injuries or deaths per year (Sidel & Levy, 2008). Ninety percent of the victims of landmines are civilians and 25% are children. Long after conflicts such as the Vietnam War and

PHOTO 9.2 Landmine Survivors in Cambodia

Persian Gulf War are over, the damage continues (Unicef, n.d.), yet the countries and people responsible for laying the mines are usually not held responsible for clearing them.

Political Economy and National Responses to Disability

There are many possible responses to disability, such as economic and social policies, religious responses (e.g., prayer, healing ceremonies), and medical treatments. In this section, we will focus on how the state, in relation to economic interests, responds to disability. We will focus on three common political/economic responses: exclusion, the provision of benefits, and the promotion of civil rights and inclusion. First, we will describe each approach, and then we will provide an analysis of how these approaches are used, drawing on a political economy approach.

Response 1: Legal and Social Exclusion

Exclusion has been a common way to respond to disability. When establishing American democracy, the forefathers concluded that not all citizens were fit to participate in self-governance. They imagined the ideal citizen as both rational and independent. People labeled as intellectually and mentally disabled, slaves, women, and indigenous people were deemed too intellectually and mentally deficient, too incompetent, to be trusted to vote or exercise civil rights (Baynton, 2001; Minow, 1990; Nielsen, 2012). Instead of rights, they were placed in systems of **paternalism** in which people deemed competent (e.g., parents, husbands, slave owners, doctors) held the authority to make decisions for them. Disability labels intertwined with racism and sexism so that various marginalized populations were defined as disabled, and their political exclusion was justified on that basis (Baynton, 2001; Nielsen, 2012).

As America industrialized and eugenics flourished, increasingly people with disabilities were portrayed as a danger to society (see Chapter 3). This fueled the growth of policies focused on segregation and social control, such as custodial institutionalization (i.e., institutionalization focused on long-term segregation and social control instead of effective treatment), compulsory sterilization, and exclusion from public schools and the corresponding development of separate schools and classrooms for children with disabilities (Ferguson, 1994; Trent, 1994).

Today, exclusion, segregation, and the denial of rights continue to be used as a policy response to disability (Beckwith, 2016; Carey, 2009; Taylor, 2004). Data from 2011 indicate that almost 90,000 people with intellectual and developmental disabilities continue to live in institutional settings (NCD, 2012b). For people with psychiatric diagnoses, in 2014 almost 180,000 resided in hospital or other institutional settings, not counting the vast numbers who are in the nation's jails and prisons (National Association of State Mental Health Directors, 2017). Prisons have become the largest residential program for people with mental health conditions (Rembis, 2014). Looking across these numbers, institutionalization remains a key response to disability (Dowdall, 1996).

Exclusion continues in other realms of life as well. As already discussed, employment rates are low. As will be seen in the chapter on Education, many children with disabilities continue to receive an education in settings that are unnecessarily segregated. And, still to this day, parents with disabilities can lose custody of their children on the basis of disability without evidence of child abuse or neglect (NCD, 2012a).

Response 2: Benefits and Protections

People with disabilities often are provided with public benefits such as income maintenance programs and public health insurance. These benefits can serve positive and negative purposes. As a positive, they may provide the resources and services to enhance one's ability to participate in society. However, as a negative, they may serve to channel people out of the workforce, into segregated settings, and maintain people with disabilities in poverty (Hahn, 1983; Longmore, 2003; Russell, 1998).

Societies must determine how to distribute resources. In the United States, people are primarily expected to accrue resources through work, and the state seeks to encourage people to work. That said, the state also redistributes funds for a variety of purposes, such as assisting people in need or companies on the verge of bankruptcy. **Social welfare programs** are public programs, such as subsidized income, access to health insurance and health care, and subsidies for food and housing, set in place to assist people in meeting their basic needs.

Because American social welfare programs value the ideal of self-sufficiency through employment, they typically make sharp distinctions between the **"deserving poor,"** who are people who work, have a work history and/or are considered unable to work, and the **"undeserving poor"** who are portrayed as able but unwilling to work (Katz, 2013). This distinction is largely ideological, a product of American discourse that imagines that most poor people have sufficient opportunities to find work that will lift them out of poverty and overlooks issues of discrimination, unequal educational systems, insufficient employment opportunities in particular neighborhoods, and a low minimum wage. Setting aside the question of whether policy should distinguish between the deserving and undeserving poor, people with disabilities are often judged to be deserving. They are more likely than many other groups of people to be presumed to be unable to work through no fault of their own. Of course, there are distinctions made among people with disabilities. For example, people with intellectual disabilities are more likely to be seen as deserving than people with mental disabilities; and, people with clearly documented disabilities are more likely to be seen as deserving than people with invisible and difficult-to-document disabilities. But, overall, people with disabilities who are poor are often seen as more deserving of assistance than able-bodied poor men for instance. As such, the United States created several important social welfare programs that benefit people with disabilities. Below we will discuss (1) Social Security programs, (2) public health insurance programs, and (3) additional safety net programs.

Social Security. Social Security is America's primary social welfare policy. Created in 1935 as part of the New Deal, Social Security's primary function is to protect older Americans against poverty. Workers contribute to the Social Security system via a tax on their earnings, and, when they reach the eligible age to retire, they receive monthly income payments throughout their retirement. Those who earn more while working also pay more in social security taxes, and then they receive higher monthly income payments from social security once retired. Insofar as disability is more common among older Americans, social security programs play a significant role in supporting people with disabilities.

In addition, Social Security offers two important programs specifically for people with disabilities: Social Security Disability Insurance (SSDI) and Supplemental Security Income (SSI). **SSDI**, established in 1965, offers monthly income payments to people with a work history who have paid into the social security system and acquire disabilities before reaching retirement age. **SSI**, created in 1972, offers monthly income payments to people with disabilities who are low-income. SSI is "means-tested," which means that one does not need a work history, but one must be disabled and have an income below a certain threshold to qualify. In 2018, SSDI served approximately 10 million people with disabilities, and SSI served eight million people with disabilities. Social security programs have played an important role in reducing the rate of poverty for older and disabled Americans (Center on Budget and Policy Priorities, 2019).

Even within the public benefit system, those who have worked are rewarded compared to those who have not. The average monthly benefit in April 2020 for disabled workers receiving SSDI was $1,258, compared to $576 for SSI recipients (SSA, 2020). Thus, those who have not established a sufficient work history, even if due to significant disability, are economically punished and likely to live in chronic poverty. Moreover, the benefit levels of SSI, and means-tested programs in general, are purposefully kept at levels below the income of those working full-time at minimum wage, in order to encourage all those who can work to do so. Someone earning $7.25 for 35 hours of work per week would earn $1,015 per month, compared to only $576 for an SSI recipient. While it is valuable to encourage work, this practice keeps people unable to work in poverty.

Public Health Insurance Programs. Most industrialized nations consider health care to be a right, but the United States does not. The expectation in the United States is that people will receive health care insurance through their employer, but not all Americans work and not all employers offer health care benefits to all workers. To help address these gaps, the United States offers several public health care programs. **Medicare**, enacted in 1965, provides health insurance primarily to people who have a work history, paid into the social security system, and no longer work due to old age or disability. **Medicaid**, also enacted in 1965, is means-tested and provides health insurance to eligible people with low-incomes. Through Medicaid, some people with disabilities are eligible for community-based long-term services and supports (LTSS), which help disabled people live in and participate in the community.

Medicaid and Medicare are vitally important programs for many people with disabilities who tend to have significant health care needs, are disproportionately poor, and are far less likely to have private health care through employment. However, these programs also create barriers to employment. For people with disabilities to receive SSDI, SSI, and/or Medicare/Medicaid, they must prove that they are totally unable to work due to disability. Many people with disabilities could work, but they might not be able to work the full-time jobs that come with health insurance or, due to ableism, are not hired for these jobs. Since life without health insurance is not feasible for many disabled people, they are pushed out of the labor market and onto benefits. (We will discuss Medicaid and Medicare in greater length in Chapter 10.)

Additional Safety Net Programs. The United States also provides a range of safety net programs, such as Temporary Assistance for Needy Families (TANF), Supplemental Nutrition Assistance Program (SNAP), and housing subsidies, which assist people in meeting their basic needs. These programs are means-tested, focusing on low-income households. They are not specifically for people with disabilities, but because people with disabilities are disproportionately poor, these programs provide essential support to them. For example, one in five SNAP households contains a person with a disability (Jones, n.d.), and 29% of households receiving housing subsidies have a disabled member (Sard & Alvarez-Sánchez, 2011).

Response 3: Civil Rights, Employment, and Inclusion

A third strategy for addressing disability via public policy is to ensure freedom and opportunity through the provision of civil rights so that people with disabilities can be maximally productive and pursue their self-interests. This approach rose to prominence in the 1970s, as the Disability Rights Movement flourished and activists demanded rights and opportunities.

Conceptually, scholars often distinguish between two types of rights—negative and positive. Disability activists typically link them together and demand both types. **Negative rights** ensure the freedom to act as one wishes without state intervention. Many of the rights enshrined in the Bill of Rights, such as the rights to free speech, to assembly, and to religion, are negative rights. Disability activism includes negative rights such as the freedom to vote, to liberty (including being free from institutionalization), and to equal opportunities in the workplace. **Positive rights**, on the other hand, create an obligation on the part of the state or other entities to do or provide something. The right to a public education is a positive right because the state must organize and spend resources to deliver public education for its citizens. Disability activism also entails positive rights, such as obligating schools and employers to provide accessibility and accommodations, even if this imposes an extra effort or cost. The provision of positive rights is often essential for people with disabilities to enjoy negative rights. For example, a wheelchair user may not be able to enjoy equal opportunities in the workplace if the workplace does not ensure accessibility.

The rights approach emphasizes the importance of accessibility, opportunity, and self-determination. *Accessibility* is key to civil rights because people with disabilities can only experience equal opportunity if they have the same access as others enjoy. Civil rights open *opportunities* by prohibiting discrimination on the basis of disability. Civil rights also enable *self-determination* by ensuring that people may freely pursue their interests, such as where to live, what services to use, and with whom to associate.

As will be detailed in Chapter 12, many laws have been passed guaranteeing rights to people with disabilities. The most prominent of these is the Americans with Disabilities Act (ADA), a federal law which prohibits discrimination on the basis of disability and mandates accessibility and reasonable accommodations in the areas of employment, public accommodations and services, transportation and telecommunications. The rights approach treats people with disabilities as full-fledged citizens who hold all of the rights and privileges conferred to other Americans. The policy expectation is that, given these rights, people with disabilities will gain access to employment and become productive, self-supporting members of society (Russell, 1998).

The rights approach has revolutionized disability policy and shifted its focus to creating access, opportunities, and self-determination in all areas of life from employment to housing to sexuality (Scotch, 1984). Since the passage of rights legislation, people with disabilities have increasingly enjoyed access to public education, services in the community, and opportunities to take on valued roles in society. In a 2018 study on employment, Vidya Sundar and her colleagues found that 48% of employed people with disabilities use workplace accommodations and more than 70% felt comfortable discussing their

PHOTO 9.3 Some families create businesses to hire people with disabilities

disability with supervisors (Sundar et al., 2018). Some employers prioritize hiring and supporting employees with disabilities (Gould et al., 2020).

However, the rights approach has limitations. Rather than ensuring freedom for people with disabilities, rights-on-the-books may promote the illusion of opportunity while leading to very little change in people's lived experience. In his classic work on rights, Isaiah Berlin ([1969] 1984) argued that the lack of material resources undercuts an individual's ability to effectively use rights. For example, people are told that they are free to work, yet inadequate education, ableism and racism, poverty, and other barriers hinder access to paid employment. Under these conditions, despite the ADA's protection from employment discrimination, many are left behind, unable to overcome the myriad obstacles to working (Barnes & Mercer, 2005; Schur et al., 2017). Indeed, there has been no improvement in the employment gap between people with and without disabilities since the passage of the ADA (Maroto & Pettinicchio, 2015). Given that people with disabilities supposedly have rights, though, they are now blamed for their own failures to work while persistent systemic inequalities are largely ignored.

Balancing Responses Based on Productivity

American policy uses a blend of these three responses—exclusion, benefits, and civil rights—in its response to disability. This blend is influenced by the philosophy of **productivism**—the idea that people who are productive and contribute to society should be rewarded, while people who are deemed unproductive should be excluded and should receive only meager government benefits or no benefits (Dimitrova, 2020; McRuer, 2006; Rose, 2017; Russell, 1998; Scull, 2015).

Getting people to work is one of America's top policy priorities, and in the national discourse, becoming a productive, self-sustaining worker and tax-payer defines one as a success story (Rose, 2017). To elaborate on Figure 9.4, those who appear likely to become self-sustaining, productive tax-payers—the **"able-disabled"** (Titchkosky, 2003)—are more likely to be welcome in society and receive appropriate education, rehabilitation, and civil rights. Indeed, the passage of civil rights legislation such as the ADA was largely driven by the hopes that increasing access and prohibiting discrimination would enable people with disabilities to get jobs and get off public benefits (Davis, 2015; Russell, 1998; Scotch, 1984). Thus, people are included and enjoy rights insofar as they can become "predictably productive under neoliberalism and as such are rewarded and trumpeted as evidence of an inclusive society" (Fritsch, 2013, p. 142). When workers or former workers receive benefits, their benefits are more likely to be relatively generous and portrayed as deserved.

FIGURE 9.4 The Influences of Productivism on Disability Policy

Productivism
Goal = minimize social investment and maximize profit and self-sufficiency

For those seen as Productive
Effective Education
Treatment
Rehabilitation
Some services
Less stigmatizing benefits

For those Perceived as "Dependents"
Segregation (e.g., institutionalization)
Marginalization (e.g., denied jobs)
Poverty (benefits below minimum wage)
Minimal services, neglect, and abuse
Stigmatizing benefits

On the other hand, those who do not meet the standards of productivity often get pushed out of society, onto benefits, and into segregated and even dangerous settings such as institutions, sheltered workshops, and nursing homes. While some of these settings are far better than others, the drive to reduce the cost of care and the devaluation of populations defined as unproductive too often leads to custodial warehousing, where few supports are offered, rights are largely ignored, and neglect and violence are rampant. Benefits for those deemed unproductive often are stigmatized and maintain people in poverty. For people in poverty and without a job, rights-on-paper may do little to actually enable them to lead a self-determined life.

In the United States, the statuses of "contributing productive citizen" and "unproductive recipient of public benefits" are often defined as mutually exclusive (Fraser & Gordon, 1974). Those who are employed have little access to public health insurance, even if their work does not offer insurance or if the availability of work is unstable. To receive SSDI, SSI, or Medicaid/Medicare due to disability, one must be "totally unable to work." Thus, people with disabilities must too often *choose* between the valued but precarious status of worker OR the status of recipient of public benefits.

Many do not have this choice. The inflexible structure of full-time work, the lack of accommodations, discrimination (based on disability, race, gender, sexuality, etc...), poverty, lack of transportation, and other factors prevent many people with disabilities from getting full-time jobs that offer benefits, and they are reluctantly pushed onto benefits and/or into poverty without benefits. Even after the passage of the ADA, the lack of employment opportunities for people with disabilities is glaring. Rather than create an economic system that encourages people to contribute as they are able to and receive adequate pay, benefits, and support, American economic policy rewards those who attain full-time work with employer benefits and continues to marginalize those who do not.

Global Focus: Neoliberalism, Rights, and Safety Net in Bulgaria

In some ways, the United States is exceptional in its strident commitment to individualism and capitalism and its resistance to providing government support for its residents. Many other countries, though, experience dilemmas that are similar in some ways. Drawing on the work of Ina Dimitrova (2020), we consider Bulgaria, a postsocialist Eastern European country. Bulgaria's disability policy is based primarily on exclusion and benefits. Many people with disabilities are institutionalized or placed in segregated programs. The state offers benefits to people with disabilities which provide financial support but also enforce their exclusion from the workforce. When families began to fight for disability rights, they argued that access to rights would enable people with disabilities to work, and they criticized the system of public benefits and those on it. Activists explicitly framed rights and community services as an "investment" so that disabled people could become productive. One activist, for example, stated that programs to support the employment of people with disabilities cost money, but "all expenses that are made for people with disabilities, and for children with disabilities, and for their parents are a kind of investment. It pays back but you need to know where to invest, what activities to support in order to make them useful for the others. People with disabilities are not dependent, needy, they can be useful to society" (Dimitrova, 2020, p. 76).

(Continued)

Like in the United States, activists frame deservedness of rights and supports in terms of productivity. This encourages the employment of people with disabilities, but leaves those unlikely to be productive defined as unworthy of investment and excluded. Unlike in the United States, the Bulgarian state and state-connected organizations of people with disabilities have so far rejected this view and maintained the benefit system instead of opening opportunities for work. Interestingly, neither the United States nor Bulgaria offer a well-balanced way to simultaneously provide rights *and* a safety net.

The Disability Industry

Increasingly, disability care and services are provided through for-profit industries. Societies can meet the basic needs of its citizens in many ways: collective public policy available to most citizens (e.g., public education or universal health care), charity (e.g., food banks), government benefits for specific populations (e.g., Medicaid/Medicare), or private, for-profit companies. In Gary Albrecht's, 1992 path-breaking book, *The Disability Business*, he argues that the provision of care over time has shifted from being mostly freely given by loved ones or through charity to a set of **commodities**—anything that satisfies a need or desire, has a market value, and is sold on the market. The response to disability has become big business. In 2019, the physical therapy industries, including physical, occupational, and speech therapies, were a $34 billion dollar per year industry; drug, alcohol, and other addiction therapies were a $42 billion dollar per year industry; medical durable goods (e.g., wheelchairs, bath chairs) was a $49.9 billion dollar industry per year; and nursing homes were a $139 billion dollar per year industry.

When businesses are in charge of disability services and goods, this leads to positive and negative consequences. Some of these consequences are laid out in Table 9.1.

Let's consider a specific example, looking at the commodification of direct care and personal assistance. Increasingly, people with disabilities (or the state or their family members) pay for care. Transforming care into a commodity potentially offers many benefits. To the degree that people with disabilities control the transaction, they can hire who they choose to perform the services they choose in the settings they choose. It frees disabled people from a forced dependency on family. People with disabilities become positioned as an employer or "consumer" with purchasing power, which challenges stereotypes of incompetence and dependence.

The commodification of care, though, also has disadvantages. In the disability industry, health care workers, personal assistants, and direct care staff are exploited for profit. Direct care, for example, is one of the fastest growing occupations in America, but the average hourly wage in 2018 for direct care workers was $12.27 and the median annual earnings $20,200

TABLE 9.1 Positive and Negative Consequences of the Commodification of Disability Services

Positive Consequences of Commodification	Negative Consequences of Commodification
Profit-motive drives innovation in treatments, equipment, and services.	Innovation and marketing accelerates demands for services that many Americans cannot afford, driving up health care costs and increasing inequality.
Those who have money enjoy a vast array of products and services, like luxurious assisted living communities, accessibility features for their home, and safety devices.	The gap in care between the wealthy and others grows. America's poor are far more likely to be in nursing homes with fewer nurses, fewer aides, and worse inspection records (Rau, 2017).
People with disabilities potentially gain value in society via their role in producing profit as consumers and by creating a demand for goods (DePoy & Gilson, 2018).	People with disabilities are depersonalized and viewed primarily as the source of profit or costs.
	Health care workers, personal assistants, and direct care staff are exploited for profit.

(Scales, 2020). Fifteen percent of direct care workers live in poverty, 44% live in low-income households, and 42% use public assistance (e.g., Medicaid, food stamps, housing subsidies). Direct care work is performed largely by women (86% of the direct care workforce), people of color (59%), and immigrants (26% of direct care workers were born outside of the United States) (Scales, 2020). Low pay and meager benefits encourage high staff turnover and poor quality work. Wealthy people with disabilities have far more control over their services than people who are poor. People with disabilities, desperate for services they can afford, are pushed to engage in exploitative practices, such as purposefully hiring vulnerable workers who will work for less and hiring multiple part-time workers to avoid paying benefits to their employees. Seeking higher wages, exploited workers will seek out wealthier clients or move to more lucrative employment opportunities. Thus, the structure of paid personal assistance in the context of limited public funding creates conflict between people with disabilities and personal assistance (Chang, 2017; Cranford, 2020; Katzman, 2020).

Alternative Approaches

Disability activists have proposed alternative responses to disability that challenge neoliberalism and productivism. These include human rights and disability justice approaches.

Human Rights

Instead of pitting the provision of rights against the provision of a safety net, a human rights approach suggests that both are possible and necessary. **Human rights** approaches argue that all people, citizens and noncitizens, should have the rights *and* basic resources necessary to live dignified and fulfilling lives. Human rights may include, for example, freedoms of speech and religion, rights to education and health care, rights to housing and food, and the right to a minimum income.

The United Nations Convention on the Rights of Persons with Disabilities (CRPD, ratified in 2008) provides a framework by which to implement a human rights approach for people with disabilities. It serves "to promote, protect and ensure the full and equal enjoyment of all human rights and fundamental freedoms by all persons with disabilities, and to promote respect for their inherent dignity." The rights detailed in the CRPD include constitutional civil rights (e.g., freedom of assembly, freedom of speech), as well as rights specific for people with disabilities such as rights to access, personal mobility, assistive technology, supports and services, and participation in public and social life. One hundred and eighty states and the European Union (the vast majority of nations) have signed onto this treaty, committing themselves to implementing its goals. The United States, Bhutan, Cambodia, Lebanon, Solomon Islands, St. Lucia, Tajikistan, Tonga, and Uzbekistan have not signed (Disabled World, 2020). Without codification into national-level laws, human rights are challenging to implement.

Disability Justice

Disability Justice is a perspective and a movement that centers the experiences of the most marginalized people and aims to achieve collective access and liberation, leaving no one behind. Patty Berne (2015) argues that the Disability Rights Movement was led too often by White men with disabilities and "invisibilized the lives of people who lived at intersecting junctures of oppression—disabled people of color, immigrants with disabilities, queers with disabilities, trans and gender nonconforming people with disabilities, people with disabilities who are houseless, people with disabilities who are incarcerated, people with disabilities who have had their ancestral lands stolen, among others." Leaders of the Disability Rights Movement prioritized the pursuit of rights without focusing on intersectional oppression and the provision of a safety net, largely leaving oppressed populations behind—still segregated, still poor, and still demeaned as burdens.

By centering the voices of the most oppressed, disability justice activists aim to achieve collective liberation. In a capitalist calculation of productivity and profit, those who are chronically sick, who have significant care needs, who require significant accommodations, and who must face multiple forms of oppression are people easily disregarded. Disability justice activists argue that collective liberation must ensure rights *and* care, meeting the basic needs of all people *and* empowering them via rights (Piepzna-Samarasinha, 2018). Rights and social welfare do not have to be mutually exclusive; they are both needed to ensure the well-being of diverse people. Disability Justice imagines the social conditions that would enable us to value, include, and support all people with disabilities of all backgrounds (Erevelles, 2011; Piepzna-Samarasinha, 2018).

Conclusion

Although we often think of disability as a natural occurrence, the economy and state play a significant role in producing disability, shaping our understanding of disability, and determining our response to disability. In the United States, the value placed on productivity and individualism has encouraged a neoliberal response in which freedom and rights are tied to self-sufficiency and employment. In contrast, those deemed unproductive often lose their rights, and the benefit system channels them into segregated settings, poverty, and a devalued social status. This doesn't have to happen, though. International comparisons show that poverty and exclusion are products of policies, and alternative strategies might provide both rights and a safety net.

KEY TERMS

Able-disabled 204
Americans with Disabilities Act of 1990 203
Capitalism 190
Deserving poor 200
Materialist theories 189
Medicaid 202
Medicare 202
Militarism 193
Negative rights 202
Neoliberalism 196
Paternalism 199
Political Economy 190
Positive rights 202
Productivism 204
Social welfare programs 200
SSDI 201
SSI 201
Undeserving poor 200
World Systems Theory 197

RESOURCES

Readings

Berne, Patty. 2015. "Disability Justice – A Working Draft." *Sins Invalid*. Available at https://sinsinvalid.org/blog/disability-justice-a-working-draft-by-patty-berne (accessed October, 2018).

Piepzna-Samarasinha, Leah Lakshmi. 2018. *Care Work: Dreaming Disability Justice*. Vancouver: Arsenal Pulp Press.

Rosenthal, K. (Ed.) 2019. *Capitalism and Disability: Selected Writings by Marta Russell*. Chicago: Haymarket Books.

Russell, Marta. 1998. *Beyond Ramps: Disability at the End of the Social Contract*. Monroe, ME: Common Courage Press.

Shur, Lisa, Kruse, Douglas, and Blanck, Peter. 2013. *People With Disabilities: Sidelined and Mainstreamed?* Cambridge: Cambridge University Press. (Chapter 2)

United Nations, n.d., *Convention on the Rights of Persons with Disabilities*, Available at https://www.un.org/development/desa/disabilities/convention-on-the-rights-of-persons-with-disabilities/convention-on-the-rights-of-persons-with-disabilities-2.html

Videos

"Beyond Disability Rights; Disability Justice: Leah Lakshmi Piepzna-Samarashina," https://www.youtube.com/watch?v=n_sw6Hjtfg8 (26 minutes).

"Three Minute Theory: What Is Neoliberalism," https://www.youtube.com/watch?v=dzLv3rfnOVw (4 minutes).

ACTIVITIES

1. In small groups, consider: what *social conditions* are required for disability to be an acceptable or a valued state? Brainstorm what policies would break the connection between poverty and disability. Brainstorm what policies would break the connection between social exclusion and disability. The connections between poverty, exclusion, and disability are stronger for low-income households and racial minorities. Would your policies eliminate the inequality by race and class associated with disability? How might policies specifically address intersectional inequality regarding race, class, and disability?

2. The previous chapter on ableism and this chapter both discuss the fact that people with disabilities are still largely excluded from work, despite the ADA. What policies/laws might increase the employment of people with disabilities? Debate the merits of such policies.

3. Read the Convention on the Rights of Persons with Disabilities (CRPD). The United States failed to ratify the CRPD. Compare the view of rights in the CRPD with the view of rights in the Constitution/Bill of Rights. What are the similarities? What are the differences? Why has the United States rejected a human rights approach? Debate the merits of the rights approach that the United States uses versus a more expansive human rights approach.

CHAPTER 10

Health Care

Chapter Synopsis

This chapter opens by considering conceptualizations of health, illness, and disability. The chapter then turns to the implications of the medical model, which has been the dominant response to disability in the United States. Although disability activists critique the dominance of the medical model in disability policy, they also fight for access to equitable health care.

The dominant response to disability in industrialized countries tends to be medical. Medical professionals identify, treat, and try to cure disability. Disability activists and scholars have criticized the dominance of a medical approach and introduced the social model. In the social model of disability, the medical system is one component of the social environment, and, like any other component, it can potentially disable by contributing to stigma or enable by providing self-determination. People with disabilities fight for access to high quality, equitable, and self-determined health care, while resisting the imposition of treatment.

Conceptualizations of Health, Illness, and Disability

"Here's to your health!" is a traditional toast, but what does it mean to be healthy? One view of health rests in the **biomedical**

Learning Outcomes

10.1 Evaluate the approaches and terminology related to health, illness, disability, and mental illness.

10.2 Assess the positive and negative impacts of medicalization.

10.3 Evaluate community-based settings with regard to institutional versus person-centered services.

10.4 Apply the determinants of health and health access to explain poor health outcomes among people with disabilities.

approach. In this approach, health is defined as the absence of disease and disability, whereas the presence of disease and disability means that one is "unhealthy." While the biomedical approach is common, it has conceptual disadvantages. Because it defines all people who experience disease or disability as "unhealthy," it does not correspond well to the way many people perceive themselves. Someone who has autism, for example, does not necessarily see themselves as unhealthy. Even someone who receives medical treatment regularly, such as a person with diabetes, might not see themselves as unhealthy insofar as they participate in many activities and enjoy life.

A broader approach is a **multidimensional approach to health** (Ware, 1986). In this approach, the indicators of health may include, among others:

- the absence of biophysiological abnormalities and symptoms;
- engagement in physical activities (with or without support);
- a sense of emotional/and mental well-being and resiliency;
- social participation and access to valued social roles;
- the exercise of rights, choice, and self-determination; and
- positive self-perception and feelings of health.

Whereas the biomedical approach positions illness and disability as the opposite of health, a multidimensional approach suggests that people who are ill or disabled may or may not experience various indicators of health. In addition to or rather than cure, enhancing health may be achieved by addressing a range of factors such as expanding social opportunities and/or self-determination. A wellness approach offers greater flexibility in health promotion and is more amenable to the inclusion of people with disabilities in health policy.

Distinguishing Illness and Disability

Some disability activists and scholars have worked to disassociate disability from disease and illness. **Disease** is defined as a biological abnormality with a relatively clear biological or pathogenic cause, and **illness** is the social-psychological experience of disease (Parsons, 1972). For example, COVID-19 is a disease caused by a virus, and illness is the subjective experience of COVID-19, including experiencing symptoms, interpreting them, and making decisions about identification and treatment. Diseases are typically assumed to be undesirable, dangerous, and best cured by medical science if possible. Most people, including most disability activists, applaud the discovery of cures for diseases, such as polio or cancer.

Disability is often understood in a different light. When people think of disability, they often think of conditions that are long-term, relatively stable, and likely without a cure, like intellectual disability, paralysis, or blindness. Because disabilities are more likely to be long-term and relatively stable, they are more likely to be experienced as an integral and valued part of one's identity and human biodiversity (Scotch & Schriner, 1997). Michelle Garcia (2020), a disabled woman with cerebral palsy, distinguishes between illness and disability when she explains that it feels degrading when people treat her as if she's ill. She complains that her family members "keep saying that I'm sick and that I should stop working. But I'm not sick. I'm disabled. That's part of me. It's not just my family. It's the way society in general sees disability: *Oh, poor you, you're sick and you cannot do this."*

As Garcia's statement suggests, it may be useful to distinguish between illness and disability. However, the distinction is blurry at best (Couser, 2015; Shakespeare, 2010; Thomas, 2007). Disability and disease are often related. One might cause the other. For example, polio (disease) may lead to an inability to walk and the experience of inaccessible environments (disability). Moreover, the conditions associated with disability can be short-term, unstable, and/or curable.

The desire to distinguish disability from illness actually may be an ableist endeavor. Disability activists may try to gain social acceptance by portraying people with disabilities as healthy, vibrant, and capable—the "**healthy disabled**" (Wendell, 2001). In doing so, they distance themselves from the stigma of sickness, pain, and contagion and reinforce stigma against people who are ill. Vice versa, people who are ill may distance themselves from disabilities to show that they are on the road to recovery and are still (or will be upon recovery) fully capable people. A more inclusive approach values all bodies, including "the magnificence of a body that shakes, spills out, takes up space, needs help, moseys, slinks, limps, drools, rocks, curls over on itself" (Mingus, 2017, p. 140).

Mental Illness and Disability

How does mental illness fit in to this discussion? As noted, disease is caused by a pathogenic cause, and illness is the social-psychological experience of disease. Mental illness, however, does not neatly fit these definitions. Referring to mental diagnoses as "illness" is more of an ideological description than fact. As of yet, many mental illnesses cannot be diagnosed by clear biological markers nor can doctors reliably predict based on biological markers who will experience mental illness. For instance, many people say that depression is caused by chemical imbalances, but there's little evidence proving causation. Doctors cannot typically evaluate one's chemical balance and predict mental illness based on bloodwork or scans. Rather, they use medication to adjust brain chemistry *in response* to symptoms. Ashok Malla et al. (2015, p. 148) explain, "In the absence of any substantiated biological marker for mental disorders..., the hallmark defining features of mental disorders, at least for now, remain the changes in how the patients feel, think, and act and how these changes affect their relations to themselves and to others."

If there is not a clear pathogenic cause, why use the term illness? Many medical professionals *assume* there are underlying biological causes that have yet to be discovered. The term illness also asserts that doctors (not religious leaders, educators, police officers, etc.) are the appropriate profession to identify and treat mental conditions. Medical professionals may hope that framing mental conditions as an illness will reduce stigma. If you remember, people occupying the sick role are supposed to be excused from blame and provided access to treatment.

Interestingly though, several studies have shown that people who consider mental conditions to be an illness are not less likely to hold stigmatizing views of people with mental illness. Bernice Pescosolido et al. (2010) used national-level data from 1996 to 2006 to examine understandings of and responses to mental conditions. Over the ten-year span, Americans grew more likely to use biological explanations for mental conditions. They were more likely to say that schizophrenia, depression, and alcohol dependence were caused by neurobiological factors rather than "bad character," "ups and downs," or the "way someone was raised." Similarly, over the same period of time, a higher percentage of Americans embraced the use of medical treatment for mental conditions—85% in 2006 compared to 75% in 1996. Holding biological views and supporting medical treatment, however, *did not* correlate with reduced stigma, and at times was associated with increased stigma. People who held biological views were no more likely to feel comfortable with people with mental conditions as potential coworkers, neighbors, and romantic partners, nor were they less likely to believe that people with mental conditions were dangerous.

It may be that stigma toward people with mental conditions does not decrease over time, even as explanations shift, because *stigma is a defining feature of what becomes labeled as mental illness*. Mental conditions are defined as illnesses, not in relation to biomedical markers, but in relation to social norms and perceived violations of those norms (Szasz, 1961). In other words, something may only become identified as mental illness if it is stigmatized. The Diagnostic Statistical Manual (DSM) is filled with culturally relative terms like "inappropriate," "bizarre," and "unexpected." Since expectations vary by culture, so do diagnoses. For example, in some religious communities, communicating with angels and dead ancestors may be expected and valued, whereas in other communities such events may be interpreted as symptoms of mental illness (Horowitz, 2002). Thus, communicating with spirits only becomes diagnosed as mental illness when it is labeled as deviant and stigmatized.

As such, the term "mental disability" might be a more appropriate descriptor than "mental illness." **Mental disability** acknowledges that people live in a society that plays a role in producing particular mental states (e.g., depression, anxiety), neglects to meet the needs of people experiencing those mental states, labels those people as ill when they do not meet normative expectations, stigmatizes them and discriminates against them, and limits their opportunities (Price, 2013).

To consider the terms mental illness versus mental disability, let's consider the example of teen depression. As seen in Figure 10.1, the number of teens age 12–17 who report experiencing a major episode of depression in the past year has increased from 8% (2 million) in 2007, to 13% (3.2 million) in 2017 (Geiger & Davis, 2019). One in five girls (20%) reported a major depressive episode in the past year, compared to 7% of boys.

The increasing rate of depression and the gender difference in rates is not likely solely, or even primarily, due to the chemical pathology of young girls. Rather, increased social pressure in an age of social media, society's obsessive focus on body image, and heightened academic competition have placed teens in a situation of intense pressure, and they are suffering the effects of it. Teens with depression often experience *disability*, although few teens would use that word to describe their experience. They may face challenges in meeting expected goals and behaviors, are marked by society as unacceptable, and experience stigma. Teens in particular feel like they are expected to be enjoying their life, and they experience guilt and shame regarding depression. Medical professionals present depression, grief, and anxiety as individual

FIGURE 10.1 Depression by Gender, 2007–2017 (Geiger & Davis, 2019)

U.S. teen girls are more likely than boys to face depression, receive treatment

% of teens ages 12–17 who have had at least one major depressive episode in the past year, 2007–2017

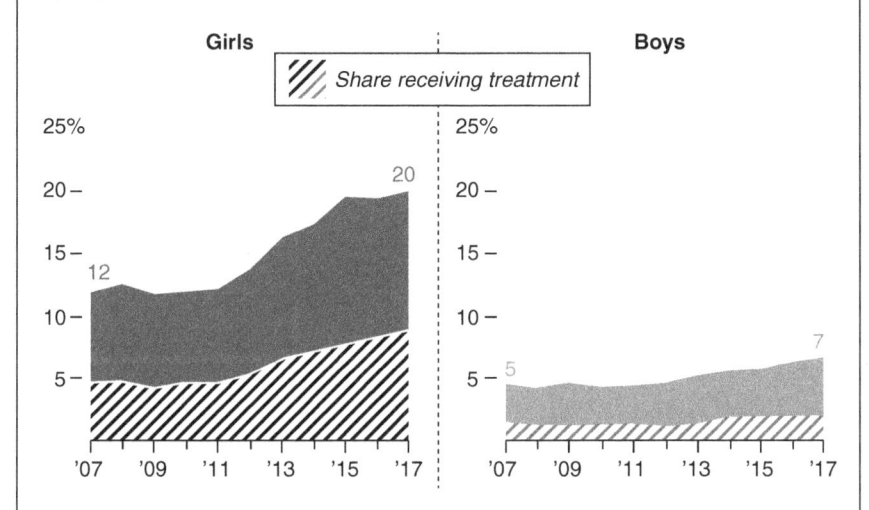

Girls | Boys

Share receiving treatment

Girls: 12 (2007) → 20 (2017)
Boys: 5 (2007) → 7 (2017)

Note: "Major depressive episode," as defined in the fifth edition of the Diagnostic and Statistical Manual of Mental Disorders, is used as proxy measure for depression. "Treatment" is defined as seeing or talking to a health or alternative service professional or using prescription medication for depression in the past year.
Source: 2017 National Survey on Drug Use and Health, Substance Abuse and Mental Health Services Administration (Department of Health and Human Services).

PEW RESEARCH CENTER

biological pathologies, overlooking that depression and anxiety may be common reactions to a turbulent and dangerous world.

Other alternatives to the descriptor "mentally ill" exist, including "mad" and "psychiatric survivors." **Mad activists** reclaim the derogatory idea of madness and use it as a double entendre—they have been labeled by society as mad/insane and they are mad/angered about the devastating consequences of the label, such as the loss of rights, stigma, and violence. Mad activists challenge the power of the psychiatric profession and seek alternative forms of care that respect human rights and diversity (Lewis, 2017a). As is often the case when derogatory words are reclaimed, "mad" is typically used in-group, by people who have experienced psychiatric diagnosis or by their political allies. Those who have experienced mental hospitalization and psychiatric treatment as traumatic and violent may refer to themselves as **psychiatric survivors**, highlighting the oppression and violence they have encountered from the psychiatric profession (Pelka, 2012). The terms Mad and Psychiatric Survivor both tend to be explicitly political labels of resistance.

The Growing Dominance of the Medical Model

The *medical model* regards disability as an individual deficit or limitation rooted in individual biology. Medical understandings of disability are one among many interpretations of particular conditions and behaviors, alongside explanations related to religion and human character/choice. In the early 20th century, however, doctors engaged in several political strategies to secure **professional sovereignty**—exclusive professional control over the body and the mind, including identifying and defining problems and delivering treatments. In the mid-1800s, doctors organized the American Medical Association (founded in 1847), secured control of medical education and licensure, transformed hospitals from charitable institutions that served the poor to centers of scientific research and education, and gained control over health care policy (Freidson, 1970; Navarro, 1984; Starr, 1982).

As doctors gained greater control and prestige, many aspects of life became medicalized. **Medicalization** is the process by which social phenomena come to be seen as a medical condition in need of medical intervention (Conrad, 2007). For better or worse, a wide array of conditions and behaviors, such as alcoholism, obesity, attention-deficit disorder, social anxiety, trans identities, acne, crooked teeth, and skin wrinkles, have all been medicalized. Despite this trend, some medicalized conditions have since been demedicalized. For example, same-sex sexual attraction was defined and treated as a mental illness until 1973, when it was removed from the Diagnostic Statistical Manual (DSM).

There are advantages and disadvantages to medicalizations, some of which are laid out in Table 10.1.

Debates about medicalization have been particularly fierce around childhood learning disabilities and mental health conditions such as attention-deficit/hyperactivity disorder (ADHD) (Blum, 2015). As shown in Figure 10.2, about 10% of school-age children are estimated to have ADHD, a rate increasing 5.5% each year (CDC, n.d.).

On the one hand, the medicalization of ADHD has increased awareness of this issue, led to the availability of a range of treatments and medications, and decreased the stigma faced by youth who find it difficult to succeed in particular settings such as those with a lot of distractions. On the other hand,

TABLE 10.1   Advantages and Disadvantages of Medicalization

Advantages	Disadvantages
Draws attention to potentially limiting, painful, or fatal conditions	May define natural human variation as a medical problem and increase stigma
Encourages research, treatment, and services	May impede the use of other interpretations and responses
May reduce shame/stigma	May lead to treatments with greater risk than the initial condition
May increase access to treatment and to health insurance coverage	May impose the mandate to be fixed
	May be driven by profit-motive, increasing costs while unequally distributing care

FIGURE 10.2 Growth of ADHD Rates, 1997–2017

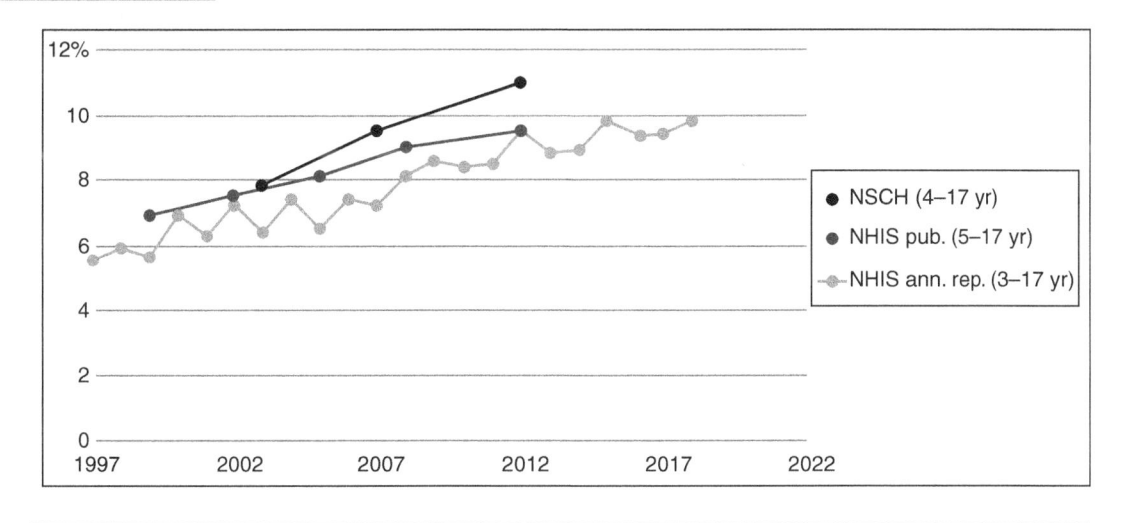

- NSCH (4–17 yr)
- NHIS pub. (5–17 yr)
- NHIS ann. rep. (3–17 yr)

Source: National Health Interview Survey 1997–2006 (CDC, n.d.)

some scholars and parents have worried that the quickly increasing rates of diagnosis reflect a desire to use medications to cope with an array of social pressures facing children and their families, in the absence of more time-consuming and expensive therapeutic responses and/or broader social policy responses.

As medical sovereignty grew and medicalization expanded, medical professionals focused disability policy on medical responses, including cure, rehabilitation, and institutionalization. Medical experts believed that people with physical disabilities were best served through medical treatment and therapy to enable them to meet the (inaccessible and unaccommodated) demands of the modern workforce (Jennings, 2016). For people seen as too ill or disabled to work in standard conditions, medical professionals advocated the expansion of a benefit system (with medical professionals in control of identifying who was disabled and unable to work), and congregate care for those with intellectual and mental disabilities as well as the aging populations (with medical professionals in charge of the institutions and nursing homes). They did this despite demands by disabled activists calling for opportunities and rights for people with disabilities (Jennings, 2016).

Treatment and Rehabilitation

Treatment and rehabilitation are meant to minimize limitations and maximize functioning and independence. As detailed in Chapter 9, the United States established public health insurance programs, increasing access to insurance for people with disabilities. These programs include:

- *Medicare*, which serves older people and people with significant disabilities who contributed to Social Security through working but are no longer expected to work due to age or able to work due to disability;

- *Medicaid*, which serves people who are poor or people who are disabled who do not meet the minimum contributions to the Social Security system through their work history;
- Children's Health Insurance Program (CHIP) which serves eligible low-income children and families who do not qualify for Medicaid/Medicare and do not have private insurance; and
- Subsidized health insurance programs associated with the Patient Protection and Affordable Care Act of 2010 (ACA, i.e., Obamacare).

People with disabilities have low rates of employment and, therefore, are far less likely to have private health insurance than people without disabilities (46% vs. 76%) (Houtenville & Rafal, 2020). Public health insurance programs are essential for addressing that gap. When public insurance is accounted for, people with disabilities ages 18–64 are slightly *more likely* to have health insurance than people without disabilities (90% vs. 87%).

Due to medical and public health advances, diseases like polio and smallpox have largely been eradicated in the United States, and some previously disabling conditions are now handled with relative ease. For example, cataracts—the clouding of the lens inside one's eye—are common as one ages, and it can greatly impair vision and hinder functionality. New procedures and technologies, including artificial lenses, have radically reduced the threat posed by cataracts and increased the independence of older Americans.

Rehabilitation, which focuses on restoring diminished functionality and skills, is often an important component of treatment. It may teach new disability skills, empower people to form positive disability identities, and enable the incorporation of assistive technology into people's lives and identities. Christina Papdimitriou (2008) frames the collaborative work between the physical therapist and the patient as the process of **re-embodiment**—the process by which one becomes comfortable with and attuned to one's new body after impairment. More specifically, she uses the term enwheeled to describe becoming a successful wheelchair user. In addition to learning the functional skills of moving the chair, people who are **enwheeled** learn to incorporate the chair as a "natural" part of themselves and to feel empowered in their chair (Stone & Papadimitriou, 2015). Before rehabilitation, newly disabled patients may feel cut off from their past identities and unable to imagine a new future, but, after rehabilitation, participants ideally emerge with a new sense of self and possibility (Stone & Papadimitriou, 2015).

While a valuable experience for many, rehabilitation can be problematic from a disability perspective. For example, *the underlying value system of rehabilitation valorizes a narrow view of independence* and, therefore, may demean life as a disabled person. Common rehabilitation goals regarding mobility illustrate this point. Rehabilitation envisions a continuum of outcomes from the least favorable to the most favorable. In this continuum, the least favorable mobility outcome would be being bedridden, and the continuum would proceed through being pushed in a chair, self-propelled in a chair, walking with equipment, or walking independently as the most favorable outcome. The value placed on walking independently, though, dismisses the advantages of using a wheelchair. A doctor who had never prescribed a wheelchair explained, "I've probably had shut-ins who could do a lot more if they were in a wheelchair. But there's a tendency on the patient's part, as well as on my part, to see wheelchairs as a last resort. I want to keep them ambulating independently rather than utilize a wheelchair, despite its benefits" (Iezzoni, 2003, p. 209). Here a narrow vision of independence reliant on a walking body is prioritized, even if it results in increasing the social isolation of and danger to the patient. The value of independence also disregards cultures that stress community and family interdependence (Thomas, 2009).

PHOTO 10.1
Physical therapy builds skills but can also rely on a narrow vision of independence

Therapists also tend to prize patients who are hardworking, motivated, and compliant. Critics charge that some therapies prioritize conformity more than functionality and self-fulfillment. Applied Behavioral Analysis (ABA), for example, encourages particular behavior and discourages other behavior through engaging in very intensive, highly structured, and repetitive exercises tied to clear rewards and punishments over hours and hours, maybe years and years. It was originally developed by Ole Lovaas to eradicate effeminate behavior in boys, and it was later adapted to produce "appropriate" behavior in children with autism (Lovaas, 1987). Today, ABA is highly recommended for autism, and it can be a valuable part of treatment. However, ABA is not well-regulated, and it can involve very long hours, negative reinforcements and even force, imposing stress and trauma on children (Carey et al., 2020). In a blog discussion, a person who experienced ABA stated, "There is also a high price that autistic children can pay when ABA is practiced in such a way that compliance itself is a goal—abuse, physical/sexual/emotional" (Whitt, 2014b; see also Whitt, 2014a). Thus, weighing the benefits and costs of treatment can be quite complex.

Institutionalization

While the pursuit of treatment and rehabilitation may have positive and negative outcomes, the negative consequences of medicalization become far more overwhelming when it involves long-term institutionalization. Institutionalization subjects one's whole life to medical authority for an extended period of time and results in a fundamental loss of rights, liberty, and dignity.

Early institutional settings in America—almshouses, poorhouses, jails—were not disability-specific and did not offer medical treatment. As medical professionals gained professional sovereignty in the 1800s, institutions became increasingly specialized and medicalized (Moran, 2000). The number of institutions for people with mental illness and people with intellectual disabilities grew. At first, there was hope that these would be places of treatment and education and that patients would return, newly cured, back to their families and communities. But these hopes quickly faded as institutional superintendents grappled with their inability to cure mental and intellectual disabilities and communities failed to offer the necessary supports and accommodations for people with disabilities to thrive. Increasingly institutions became *custodial*, housing people for life (Ferguson, 1994; Grob, 1994; Trent, 1994).

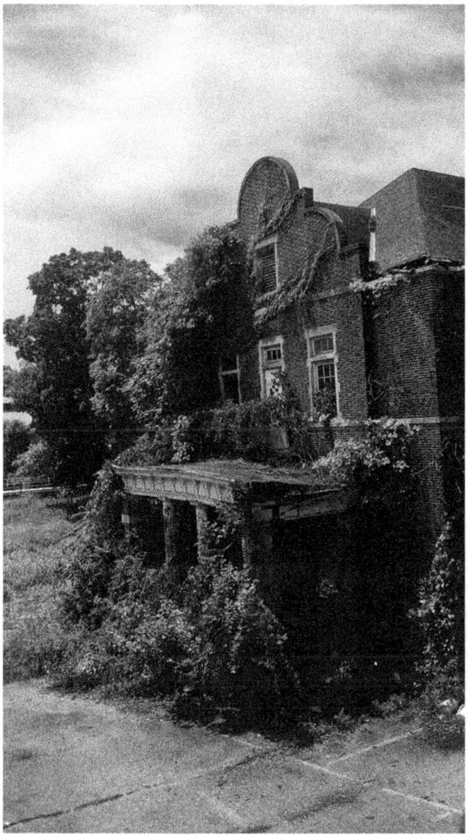

Credit: Sierra Gaglione (2019). Reproduced with permission from istock.com.

PHOTO 10.2 Abandoned institution, Pennhurst State School

As *eugenics* (a movement to improve population quality through selective breeding and population control) spread, communities sought to remove and isolate people with disabilities who were increasingly seen as dangerous and diseased. Institutional populations grew and state funding did not keep pace, leading to overcrowding, poor hygiene, abuse and neglect, and a failure to deliver treatment and education (Ferguson, 1994; Trent, 1994). In 1937, Pennsylvania Governor George H. Earle reported institutional conditions "so lacking in humaneness as to be almost unbelievable in the great civilized Commonwealth." Conditions continued to deteriorate (Earle, 1937). In 1965, after Senator Robert Kennedy toured New York's Willowbrook State School, he described it as a "snake pit."

Erving Goffman (1963) coined the term **total institutions** to refer to places where people are contained, isolated from external influences, held under a central authority encompassing all areas of life, and restricted to a formally administered life. Examples of total institutions include mental hospitals, prisons, boot camps, and cults. Goffman listed several characteristics of a total institution:

- All aspects of life are practiced in the same location and under a single authority.
- Individuals and their activities are subsumed into a group of "like" individuals who are required to do similar things and are treated similarly.
- Daily routine, activities, and ways of life are strictly scheduled, monitored, and enforced by authority figures.
- All activities are said to contribute to a plan toward the official aims of the institution and justified as such, regardless of whether they are effective or beneficial.
- Sharp inequality and group boundaries between "inmates" and administrators are enforced, and inmates have few ways to exercise any kind of individuality or power.

Why do total institutions embrace these characteristics? Sometimes total institutions use these strategies to strip away member's former identities and rebuild new ones with an intense sense of group solidarity and commitment to group goals. Institutions for people with intellectual and mental disabilities, though, rarely worked toward or achieved those ends. Instead, these strategies ensured bureaucratic efficacy and control over a disempowered population.

Although medical professionals claimed institutions would provide effective treatment, disability scholars have long argued that the stripping of rights, choices, access to valued roles, and individuality is not an effective way to help one learn to thrive in the outside world or to build strong and resilient mental capacity (Belknap, 1956; Goffman, 1961; Rothman, 1971). People with intellectual disabilities, for example, need access to *more* opportunities to learn and practice skills, not fewer. People with mental disabilities may benefit from short-term intensive treatment or removal from a crisis, but long-term segregation rarely addresses the factors contributing to crisis or builds the skills required to succeed in the community. Moreover, the sharp inequality and patients' powerlessness and isolation leave them highly vulnerable to abuse, with almost no mechanisms to protest or even to reveal that abuse (Burghardt, 2018; Johnson & Williams, 2002; Reaume, 2009).

Deinstitutionalization

Deinstitutionalization—the movement of people out of institutional settings and into the community—represents a significant shift in policy, reversing the growth of institutions that took place over the course of more than a century (Ben-Moshe, 2020). As shown in Figure 10.3, from 1970 to 2014, the institutional populations in public psychiatric hospitals declined by 89%, a reduction of over 300,000 patients (National Association of State Mental Health Directors, 2017). Across a similar period (1967–2007), the number of people with intellectual and developmental disabilities in public institutions declined by 81%, a reduction of 158,000 people (Scott et al., 2008).

FIGURE 10.3 Total Populations in State-Funded Public Institutions, 1967–2014

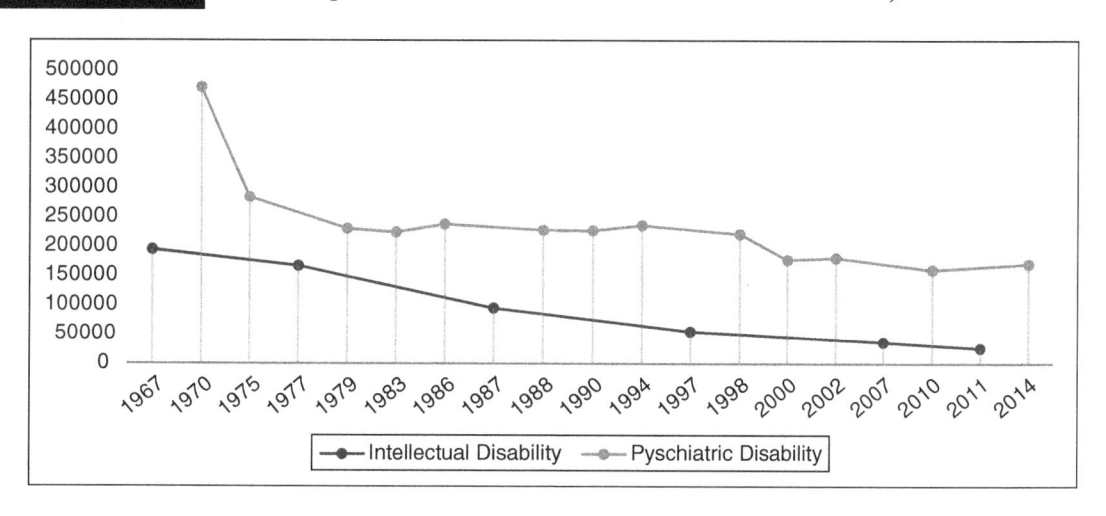

Data Source: Data published in Scott et al. (2008) and National Association of State Mental Health Directors (2017).

Chapter 12 on social movements will discuss how and why deinstitutionalization occurred. Here we will briefly note that disabled activists, parents, and their allies exposed the horrors and ineffectiveness of the institutions and created community alternatives. They demanded freedom and equal opportunities for people with disabilities in the community and demonstrated that supports and services could be provided more effectively in the community than in segregated settings (Pelka, 2012; Rothman & Rothman, 1984). Slowly, rights were gained and a community infrastructure emerged to support people living in the community, including home- and community-based services (HCBS), the redirection of federal and state funding from institutions to community services, the right to a public education (IDEA), and the rights to accessible environments and freedom from discrimination (ADA). In the shift from institution to community, society embraced a new view of people with disabilities, moving away from a politics of medicalized stigma to policies that envisioned people with disabilities as citizens with rights.

The Incomplete Process of Deinstitutionalization

Closing institutions alone does not ensure a fulfilling life in the community. Rights, opportunities, access, accommodations, and services must be in place. Unfortunately, some politicians used deinstitutionalization as a way to save money by shutting down institutions without investing in adequate community services (Ben-Moshe, 2020). Due to social problems like unaffordable and inaccessible housing, a lack of jobs that offer accommodations, and poor access to health care and community services, some people become homeless. Others experience **transinstitutionalization**—the movement from one institution to another type of institution, like a nursing home or prison.

Indeed, other forms of institutionalization have increased as deinstitutionalization has occurred. Data regarding people with intellectual and developmental disabilities show that, in addition to the 32,909 people who lived in state-funded facilities, 26,695 lived in private facilities and 29,608 live in nursing homes, suggesting much less progress toward deinstitutionalization than is often claimed (NCD, 2012b). For people with psychiatric diagnoses, in 2014, 39,907 lived in state-funded psychiatric hospitals (a decline since 1970), but the number in other institutional settings increased since 1970. 28,461 patients resided in private psychiatric hospitals (an increase of 160% from 1970), 109,646 in other residential settings (e.g., veterans homes, nursing homes), and a large number reside in jails and prisons (National Association of State Mental Health Directors, 2017). Estimates suggest that at least 20% of prisoners have mental health conditions, and American prison population has more than tripled since 1970. Thus, prisons have become the largest residential program for people with mental health conditions (Rembis, 2014). Looking across these numbers, institutionalization remains a key response to disability (Dowdall, 1996). The demographics of institutionalization have changed, though, as people of color have been disproportionately imprisoned (Ben-Moshe, 2020; Parsons, 2018).

Some people cite the perceived shortages of beds in psychiatric hospitals and the increasing prevalence of people with mental health conditions in prisons to argue that the United States should again expand institutions. Most leading disability scholars reject that argument. People with mental disabilities are usually better served by comprehensive, affordable, accessible home- and community-based services. Research suggests that investing in community services provides more effective care while respecting civil and human rights (Ben-Moshe et al., 2014).[1]

Home- and Community-Based Services

Home- and community-based services (HCBS) may include, for example, paid personal assistance, group homes, job coaches, health care and rehabilitation delivered in the community. In keeping with the goals of the disability rights movement, activists have striven to create systems of HCBS that are empowering (designed so that people with disabilities have the power to choose their services, staff, residence, treatment, etc.), person-centered (tailored to meet individualized goals and in accordance with individual preferences), and inclusive (delivered in settings that serve people with and without disabilities and that support participation in the community).

Access to an array of HCBS that are empowering, person-centered, and inclusive is crucial to the success of people with disabilities. The movement away from institutional models to HCBS models, though, is not attained simply with a change in attitudes or expectations. Rather, it requires a fundamental shift in policy, altering not only where services take place but also the relations of power within the service system and the funding of services (Kelly, 2016). Examples of policies that support the shift from institutional models to person-centered models include the following:

- Medicaid's "Money Follows the Person" and Home and Community-Based Waiver programs provide people with disabilities with a state-funded, flexible budget that they can allocate for the services of their choice. This enables people with disabilities to prioritize the services most important to them. They become "consumers" with the power to purchase services, rather than "clients" or "patients."

- Personal assistance and home health aides provide services directed by people with disabilities in their own home (paid for out-of-pocket, by Medicaid, or by private insurance). People with disabilities may hire and fire their aides and schedule aides to meet their needs. While constrained by the high cost and limited public funding, personal assistance and home health aides are a key resource for many who wish to live in the community (Kelly, 2016).

- Independent Living Centers are run by people with disabilities and offer a range of services to assist people in community living. These centers value the expertise of the disability community and provide services such as information on accessible housing and wheelchair repair, assistance applying for employment and/or benefits, and rights workshops.

---

[1]Studies show that typically the growth in alternative institutional sites is not driven by the people released from institutions (Ben-Moshe, 2020). For example, the demographics of those released from psychiatric hospitals (e.g., disproportionately White) and those imprisoned (e.g., disproportionately Black) are not the same. Rather, society is creating new strategies for how to impose institutional control and who will be subject to it (Parsons 2018).

Community-based care and their institutional underpinnings. HCBS models of care are not problem-free (Kelly, 2016). They assume that the person with a disability (or others in their network) has the capacity to manage their own staff. They require a community infrastructure including affordable housing and a labor pool of potential personal assistants. And it commodifies care in ways that lead to tensions between people with disabilities who are trying to maximize their services with limited funding and personal assistants who are often women of color working for low pay (Crawford, 2020; see Chapter 9 for a discussion of this tension). Despite these problems though, these policies strive to challenge institutionalization and re-design systems in ways that empower people with disabilities to live self-determined lives.

However, community services can themselves take on the characteristics of total institutions. In some ways, today's community services look nothing like the old institutions. For example, today's group homes are usually smaller, cleaner, and more likely to allow individuality among the residents. However, to look back at Goffman's framework, an institution is not defined sociologically simply by size or appearance, but rather by its patterns of authority. An institution is any setting in which the lives of people with disabilities are dominated by centralized authority, where people are grouped and treated based on their disability classification rather than as an individual, where they are surveilled and restricted and where their lives are structured according to bureaucratic needs and goals rather than their own preferences. *By these characteristics, many people with disabilities continue to live institutionalized lives even in the community.* One's diagnosis may determine where one lives, one's staff, and one's opportunities. Staff may monitor and document all aspects of the person's life and document progress toward medical goals. Moreover, services are often part of highly bureaucratized systems, and the goals of efficiency, cost reduction, and reducing agency liability may take precedence over individual needs (Dobransky, 2014).[2]

The institutional framework is maintained in community-based services in part because these services continue to be highly medicalized and bureaucratized (Dobransky, 2014). Medicaid—one of the nation's public health insurance programs—pays for many long-term community-based services including group homes, sheltered workshops, and day programs. To fund such services, Medicaid requires:

- Diagnosis, encouraging the identification, grouping, and serving of people based on diagnosis, rather than their individuals needs or preferences;

- Documentation of the provision of health-related services, thereby demanding that staff provide, monitor, and record health-related activities, orient the provision of services around health, and that "consumers" participate in these activities, invading the privacy of people with disabilities and undercutting their self-determination;

---

[2]To note, federal policies often define institutions for people with disabilities as residential service settings with more than 16 people, and community services are those that house fewer than 16 people with disabilities. This definition assumes that larger facilities tend to be more bureaucratic and restrictive and thereby more institutional.

- Documentation of health "progress," such that "healthy lifestyles" are imposed and "high-risk" behaviors (e.g., drinking, smoking, eating sugary foods, and sex) are avoided, although nondisabled adults can freely engage in these behaviors.

Goffman's framework of total institutions can serve as a guide to examine service settings across a number of factors to assess the *degree to which* they are institutionalized or person-centered (Table 10.2).

Sexuality in community settings with institutional underpinnings. To further consider the issue of the institutional underpinnings of community services, let's examine sexuality. Sexuality is a part of the human experience and a human right. Can people with disabilities engage in sexuality in today's service system?

In the early 20th century, one of the many goals of institutions was eugenic—to prevent procreation by people with disabilities. Gender segregation was often strictly enforced, and residents held no right to privacy. In today's world, much more respect is accorded to the sexuality of people with disabilities. People with disabilities have greater recognition of their rights, more privacy, and more control over their services, all of which enables them

TABLE 10.2 Comparison on Institutional Settings and Person-Centered Settings

Institutional Setting	Person-Centered Setting
People live/act in a single location or within a set of locations/services that are dominated by nondisabled authorities and standardizing bureaucracies.	People with disabilities interact in varied settings with varied levels and types of power; they may come and go as they please and choose which settings to participate in.
Disability serves as a master status, as the pre-defined basis for grouping people. People with similar diagnoses are expected to engage in group activities (group bowling, group shopping).	Disability is a potentially relevant trait, but people may come together based on other interests or needs (e.g., an interest in learning, a love of music, wanting to live in the city). People with disabilities may act as individuals (with support as needed).
Activities and ways of life are strictly scheduled and monitored. Compliance is expected, and progress is monitored and rewarded.	People with disabilities have privacy and choices regarding their schedule and activities. Activities are justified by individual interest, not to meet institutional goals such as documenting progress in health or habilitation.
Policies are created by nondisabled "experts" and staff, guided by bureaucratic needs and funding.	Individuals with disabilities have flexibility to determine and pursue their interests and the power to enact them.
Power is hierarchically arranged with nondisabled professionals in charge and clear distinctions between nondisabled staff and disabled clients.	There may be equal relationships, shifting power, or a hierarchical structure in which the person with a disability asserts control over their services and staff.

to act as empowered sexual beings. That said, the sexuality of many people with disabilities who live in facilities continues to be monitored and often denied (Achey, 2020; Gill, 2015; Santinele Martino, 2019).

Group homes often say that they respect residents' right to sexuality; however, the reality may be very different. Adults with disabilities may need to ask the staff's permission to date or to have sex, and permission can be denied or constrained based on a range of reasons, such as parent objections, staff religious objections, safety concerns, or household issues (e.g., staffing levels; privacy needs in a setting with roommates). Furthermore, when someone wants to engage sexually, their desire may become codified in their service plan, becoming the topic of conversation among myriad professionals and family members. Professionals and family members can determine what progress or goals must be achieved before a person can be sexual (e.g., completion of a sexual education course, a conversation with parents). Professionals also track "deviant" sexuality (e.g., having sex at work or in public) and establish behavioral plans to reduce such behaviors. Staff typically retain the authority to refuse to assist in sexuality, and people with disabilities who are LGBTQ+ may be particularly likely to be denied assistance (Santinele Martino, 2019). Thus, the human right to sexuality is often quickly denied to people with disabilities via power hierarchies and bureaucratic rationales, even while service providers claim to support the rights of their residents.

Access to Health Care and Health Equity

Health Differentials

While it is important to critique the medical model and its propensity toward institutionalization, access to respectful health care is crucial for people with disabilities. People with disabilities have poorer health than people without disabilities. They report a higher number of health conditions, fewer healthy days, lower rates of perceived good health, and higher health care expenditures (CDC, 2019b; Rimmer & Rowland, 2008). Thirty-seven percent of people with disabilities report being in poor health, compared to only 8% of people without disabilities (Altman & Bernstein, 2008).

People with disabilities are at high risk of developing secondary conditions. **Primary conditions** are the direct manifestation of a disease or disability. **Secondary conditions** are preventable conditions related to the disability. For example, a spinal cord injury may lead directly to paralysis, a primary condition. For people with paralysis, factors like social isolation, lack of accessible exercise, and increased risk of poverty can lead to secondary conditions like obesity, diabetes, and gastrointestinal problems. Adults with disabilities are far more likely than people without disabilities to be obese, have heart disease, and diabetes (see Figure 10.4).

Determinants of Health and Disability

Chapter Nine on political economy discussed the social production of disability and health as related to capitalism and state policy. Here, we draw on Ecosocial theory to explore the social and environmental factors that shape the distribution of disease and disability across groups in a population (Krieger, 2005). This theory connects the environment to embodiment as one's

FIGURE 10.4   Prevalence of Secondary Conditions, 2017

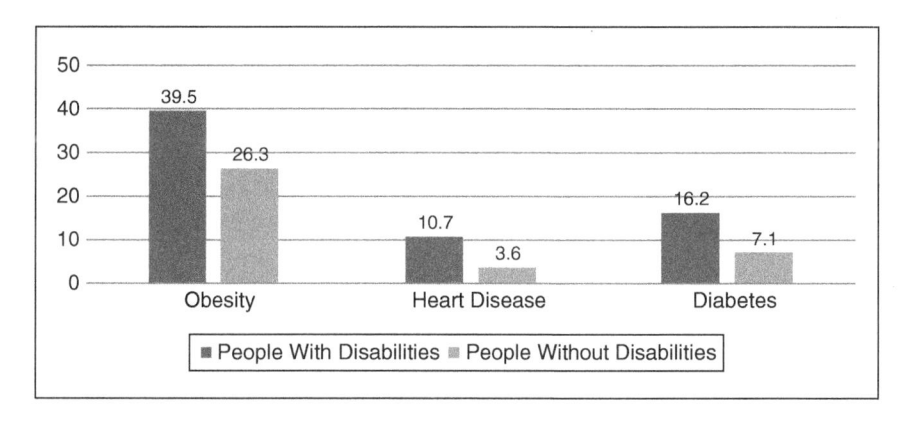

Condition	People With Disabilities	People Without Disabilities
Obesity	39.5	26.3
Heart Disease	10.7	3.6
Diabetes	16.2	7.1

Source: Centers for Disease Control (2017) Behavioral Risk Factor Surveillance System, published in CDC (2019a).

experience of the material, and social world shapes one's physical and mental being. Building on Healthy People (2020), we lay out seven key domains of the social determinants of health and briefly discuss how these may affect people with disabilities.

1. **Economic stability**—Social class and social inequality are among the leading predictors of health and disability (Robert & House, 2000; Syme & Berkman, 1976/2019, Wilkinson & Pickett, 2010). People in low-income households have less access to health care services and to a broad array of resources that promote health like healthy food and gym memberships. They are more likely to live in overcrowded, hazardous, and toxic environments, and they are more likely to experience unproductive stress (Masters et al., 2015). Even if their basic needs are met, being on the bottom of a social hierarchy is itself stressful and leads to poorer health outcomes (Marmot et al., 1978; Marmot et al., 1991; Wilkinson & Pickett, 2010). People with disabilities are more likely to live in chronic poverty and to be unemployed than people without disabilities, and, therefore, these factors affect their health.

2. **Education**—Along with income, education is a leading predictor of health. More education is associated with higher income. In addition, education has direct positive effects on health. Those with more education have greater ability to navigate complex health care bureaucracies, identify and understand medical conditions, and follow medical regimes (Hayward et al., 2015). People with disabilities, though, are less likely to graduate from high school or earn bachelor's degrees than people without disabilities, so again risk factors accumulate for people with disabilities.

3. **Health care insurance and services**—Access to health care can help prevent the onset of disease and disability through proactive monitoring of health. It can also minimize the long-term negative consequences of health conditions when they occur. Many Americans receive health insurance through their employer, but people with disabilities have a low rate of employment. *Medicare* and *Medicaid*, America's primary public health insurance programs, provide health insurance to many people with disabilities, and the Affordable Care Act (ACA) offers subsidies to purchase private health insurance for those

without employer insurance and who are not eligible for public programs. However, many Americans still lack sufficient access to affordable, high-quality health care. In 2018, although 89% of adults with disabilities 18–64 had insurance, 11% did not. The ACA reduced the uninsured from a peak of 18.2% of Americans in 2010 to a low of 10.3% in 2016 (CDC, 2019d). However, many people, such as those with disabilities that are mild, hard to diagnose or document, or who are still able to work, may not be eligible for Medicaid or Medicare and may fall through the cracks.

Moreover, even with insurance, people with disabilities may not receive the level of care they need. People with disabilities are 2.5 times more likely than people without disabilities to delay or skip health care due to cost (27% vs. 12.1%) (Krahn et al., 2015). People who use long-term services and supports experience a chronically underfunded system. As of 2016, 656,195 people were on waitlists to receive Medicaid funding for HCBS (Grossman, 2019).

Insurance and costs are not the only limited factors. Ableism hinders access. As discussed in Chapter 6, health care providers have surprisingly negative attitudes about living with chronic disability (Iezzoni et al., 2021; Pendo, 2008; Robey et al., 2006). Disability stereotypes, such as the asexuality of people with disabilities, diminish the quality of care. More than one-fifth of physician specialist offices are not accessible for people who use wheelchairs (Lagu et al., 2013). Sociologists Heather Dillaway and Catherine Lysack (2015) found inaccessibility to be a major barrier for women with physical disabilities seeking gynecological health care. Even without explicitly ableist attitudes, medical professionals may avoid the extra time, labor, and costs associated with serving people with disabilities (Ervin et al., 2014; Krahn et al., 2015). For example, many people with intellectual and developmental disabilities struggle to find a dentist who will provide appropriate care and work with patients who may be erratic, have behavioral challenges, and/or communication disabilities (NCD, 2017). Thus, even though people with disabilities on average need more medical care, they have difficulty accessing it.

Finally, policies hinder health access. For example, insurance companies typically cover mental health treatment at lower levels than physical health treatment. Disability activists are fighting for **mental health parity**—ensuring the same level of coverage, services, and supports for mental health conditions as provided for physical health conditions (NAMI, 2017). Another policy barrier, noted in Chapter 4 on Inequality and Ableism, is the *institutional bias*, which refers to funding systems that pay for services in large-scale, institutional settings rather than community settings, a funding bias that impedes the development of access to community-based health care.

4. **Neighborhood and build environment**—One's neighborhood affects exposure to violence, pollution, and disease, as well as the quality of education, access to affordable food and housing, transportation, and the availability of health care services. Due to poverty, people with disabilities tend to reside in areas with fewer resources, and inaccessibility further hinders access to food, gyms, parks, etc. In a study on access to food, a participant explained that she cannot drive due to epilepsy, and her neighborhood does not provide public transportation. She walks to the store, "But how do we get the stuff home? So that kind of limits where you can go, unless they're able to get a ride with someone" (Webber & Sobal, 2007).

5. **Social and community context**—Social capital affects health outcomes (Kawachi, 2010). James House and colleagues argue that "social relationships,

or the relative lack thereof, constitute a major risk factor for health—rivaling the effects of well-established health risk factors such as cigarette smoking, blood pressure, blood lipids, obesity, and physical activity" (House et al., [1988] 2019, p. 115). On an interpersonal level, one's social ties confer information, resources, and social support. On a community level, communities that foster equality, shared resources, and solidarity are healthier. People with disabilities, though, are more likely to be socially isolated than people without disabilities (Condeluci & Fromknecht, 2014; Pescolsolido et al., 2010). Community organizations such as schools and churches often continue to practice segregation and inaccessibility, effectively barring people with disabilities from the benefits of community solidarity.

6. Intersections of race and disability—African Americans and Native Americans are more likely than Whites to have disabilities, to experience a wide range of health conditions, and to die from those conditions. At birth, African Americans have a life expectancy three years fewer than White Americans (75.3 vs. 78.8). The gap increases if we look only at men (71.9 African American men vs. 76.4 White men) (Arias & Xu, 2019). Part of the gap is explained by SES; poverty negatively affects health, and African Americans are disproportionately poor. However, independent of SES, racism contributes to the poorer health outcomes of African Americans. Racism, for example, denies people access to community resources, blocks the development of some forms of social capital, leads to medical discrimination, and produces social-psychological stress (Phelan & Link, 2015; Williams & Mohammed, 2013). Thus, minorities are more likely to become disabled, and minorities with disabilities have greater difficulty accessing resources and care and, therefore, have worse health outcomes.

7. Health behaviors—People with disabilities are more likely to engage in some forms of high-risk behavior. For example, adolescents and adults with disabilities are more likely to use cigarettes and e-cigarettes (27.8% of adults with disabilities smoke cigarettes compared to 13.4% of adults without disabilities) (CDC, 2019b), and youth with disabilities are more likely to have unprotected sex (Blum, Kelly, & Ireland, 2001). People with disabilities are also less likely to engage in health promotion activities, such as exercise, routine health screenings or professional teeth cleanings (Office of Disease Prevention and Health Promotion, 2020).

Disability and Health Through the Lens of COVID-19

Beginning in 2020, the spread of COVID-19 and its variants caused massive social upheaval. As is so often the case, the disability community was hit especially hard. People with disabilities were infected with and died from COVID-19 at higher rates than the general population (Kennedy et al., 2020; Turk et al., 2020). In New York City, a region hit hard early in the pandemic, residents of group homes for people with intellectual and developmental disabilities were five times more likely than the general population to develop COVID-19 and almost five times more likely to die from it (Hakim, 2020). In New York state overall, between April 10 and July 10, 2020, people with intellectual disabilities had case rates 2.5 times higher than the state rate and case-fatality rates 2 times greater (Landes et al., 2020). The virus also tore through many nursing homes. The presence of underlying conditions, the inability to engage in social distancing due to the need for support, living in congregate settings, and poverty are several of the factors that greatly increased risk for people with disabilities.

Coronavirus exposed the heightened vulnerability of the disability community in so many ways. Economically, despite their low rates of employment pre-COVID-19, people with disabilities lost their jobs at greater rates. Between March and April 2020, employment fell by 18% for the general population and by 24% for people with disabilities (Brooks, 2020; Maroto & Pettinicchio, 2020). Job loss was particularly severe for White and Black women with disabilities, who tend to work in industries hardest hit by the pandemic (Schur et al., 2021). Moreover, people who receive disability benefits are often prohibited from saving money, so they are uniquely unprepared for emergencies.

Social isolation intensified for people with disabilities, while ironically social distancing was also difficult to achieve. State and agency policies regarding social distancing upended the established relationships of paid and unpaid support upon which people with disabilities relied. Some aides stopped working for many reasons, including the lack of protective equipment, the inability to social distance while providing care, and/or the need to provide care to their own children who were now home from school. Many programs such as recreational and worship opportunities went online or into hiatus, and many schools went online. People with disabilities rarely had input into how their services transformed or into the policies that affected their lives (Schormans et al., 2021), and the technology required for new modes of communication like Zoom were not easily accessible or available (Churgani & Houtrow, 2020). Although isolation increased, social distancing was also hard to achieve due to factors like poverty, jobs in the low-wage service sector, the need for support, and residence in congregate settings.

Shocking gaps in health care and long-term support were exposed. Many health services went online, including health care and mental health care, but people with disabilities have less access to computers and the internet. Medical care that was not COVID-19 related was deprioritized, leaving people who depend on ongoing therapies and treatments in the lurch. Without proper care in the community, many people with disabilities felt threatened with potential placement in nursing homes, the very places with some of the highest death rates. Disability rights organizations even had to sue several states to fight against medical discrimination when states issued plans that deprioritized the provision of care for those with shorter

PHOTO 10.3
Woman Working From Home During COVID-19 Outbreak

Credit: FG Trade (2021). Reproduced with permission.

expected life expectancies (Abrams, 2020; Fink, 2020; Kennedy et al., 2020). The combination of high needs and limited resources created a "thin margin of health" for people with disabilities, especially for disabled people of color and in poor communities, such that even meeting basic needs and accessing vital health services became uncertain (Lederer, 2020; Kennedy et al., 2020, p. 5; Prior, 2020).

As they have so often done, disability communities drew on their "crip wisdom" to provide one another with needed support (Bak, 2020; Carey et al., 2020; Sins Invalid, 2020). For example, the Disability Justice Culture Club in Oakland, California created a network for the provision of aid, and Disabled American Veterans assisted people with applying for benefits (Anderson, 2020). Some people hoped that the pandemic would heighten access to workplace accommodations like working from home (Schur & Kruse, 2020) and increase support for affordable health care for all. Yet, perhaps not surprisingly, others instead felt that their needs were disregarded as the nation focused instead on re-igniting the economy (Kukla, 2020; Ladau, 2020; Ne'eman, 2020).

Conclusion

People with disabilities in general have greater health needs than people without disabilities yet struggle to get the health care that they need. Simultaneously, the medical model pervades the lives of people with disabilities. Traditionally national disability policy drew on the medical model and focused on treatment, rehabilitation, and institutionalization. In response to activism, the United States now recognizes the rights of people with disabilities, including to live in the community. Because community services to support people with disabilities are largely funded through health programs, though, the medical model continues to dominate their lives, potentially undercutting their self-determination as adults.

KEY TERMS

Biomedical approach 211
Deinstitutionalization 221
Disease 212
Enwheeled 218
Healthy disabled 213
Illness 212
Mad activists 215

Medicalization 216
Mental disability 214
Mental health parity 228
Multidimensional approach to health 212
Primary condition 226
Professional sovereignty 216

Psychiatric survivors 215
Re-embodiment 218
Secondary conditions 226
Total institutions 220
Transinstitutionalization 222

RESOURCES

Academic Readings

Ben-Moshe, Liat. 2020. *Decarcerating Disability: Deinstitutionalization and Prison Abolition*. Minneapolis, MN: University of Minnesota Press.

Dillaway, Heather E., and Lysack, Catherine 2015. "'Most of them are Amateurs': Women with Spinal Cord Injury Experience the Lack of Education and Training Among Medical Providers while Seeking Gynecological Care."

Disability Studies Quarterly 35 (3): https://dsq-sds.org/article/view/4934.

LisaI., Rao, Sowmya R., Ressalam, Julie, Bolcic-Jankovic, Dragana, Agaronnik, Nicole, Donelan, Karen, ... Campbell, Eric G. 2021. "Physicians' Perceptions of People With Disabilities and Their Health Care." *Health Affairs* 40 (2): 297–306.

Kelly, Christine. 2016. *Disability Politics and Care*. Vancouver, BC: University of British Columbia Press.

Papadimitriou, Christina 2008. "Becoming En-Wheeled: The Situated Accomplishment of Re-Embodiment as a Wheelchair User After Spinal Cord Injury." *Disability and Society* 23 (7): 691–704.

Rembis, Michael 2014. "The New Asylums: Madness and Mass Incarceration in the Neoliberal Era." In *Disability incarcerated: Imprisonment and disability in the United States and Canada*, edited by Liat Ben-Moshe, Charles Chapman and Allison C Carey, 139–159. London: Palgrave Macmillan.

Popular Readings

Holohan, Meghan. 2020. "A Black Woman With a Disability Fights Back Against Racism and Ableism in the Doctor's Office." *Today*, https://www.today.com/health/being-black-disabled-woman-means-self-advocacy-t186708?fbclid=IwAR0b4v8m4zH0XZcU_tg91wtQsX1doU0mNsMLPOTrFaf99Y7nuniRY3IVR5U.

Op-Eds Related to Coronavirus by People With Disabilities

Kukla, Elliot. 2020, March 19. "My Life is More 'Disposable' During This Pandemic." *New York Time*. Retrieved from https://www.nytimes.com/2020/03/19/opinion/coronavirus-disabled-healthcare.html.

Ladau, Emily. 2020, March 25. "As a Disabled Person, I'm Afraid I May Not be Deemed Worth Saving From the Coronavirus." *HuffPost*. Retrieved from https://www.huffpost.com/entry/coronavirus-healthcare-rationing-medical-ethics-disability_n_5e7a2b0dc5b6f5b7c54bb117.

Ne'eman, Ari. 2020, March 23. "I Will Not Apologize for My Needs." *New York Times*. Retrieved from https://www.nytimes.com/2020/03/23/opinion/coronavirus-ventilators-triage-disability.html.

Health Policy

Healthy People. 2020. https://www.healthypeople.gov/2020/topics-objectives/topic/disability-and-health.

Websites

American Association on Health and Disability. https://www.aahd.us/.

CDC, Disability and Health Promotion. https://www.cdc.gov/ncbddd/disabilityandhealth/index.html.

Map of state variation in Medicaid HCBS Waiver Waitlists at https://centerondisability.org/ada_parc/utils/indicators.php?id=9-.

Films and Videos

"First Hand: Michelle Garcia." PBS. Michelle Garcia, a Latinx activist with disabilities, discusses how Coronavirus makes her situation even more precarious. (4 minutes) PBS. https://www.pbs.org/video/michelle-garcia-afzi2p/.

"Heavy Load." 2008. (1 hour 30 min)—a documentary about men with disabilities and their support staff in a punk rock band constrained by the social service system and/or Paul Richard's Tedx talk on the Stay Up Late Campaign "Imagine Leaving Every Night Out at 9:30." https://stayuplate.org/about/ (15 minutes).

"How Health Care Makes Disability a Trap." 2018. Disabled filmmaker Jason DaSilva describes the barriers in moving and pursuing his dreams created by heath care bureaucracies and Medicaid funding for community supports. https://www.youtube.com/watch?v=7Lfxle9UwCI.

"Improving Health Care Access for People With Disabilities, The Independence Center," 2019. People with disabilities speak about challenges and solutions regarding accessibility of medical care, 12 minutes. https://www.youtube.com/watch?v=KKyzZVpWezw.

ACTIVITIES

1. Institutional versus Person-Centered Settings. Consider the degree to which residential services in your geographic area are institutional or person-centered. This might entail having the class tour a nursing home and/or group home, assigning groups of students to tour different facilities on their own time, and/or relying on students in the class to discuss their experiences with various settings. What would need to happen for institutional settings to become person-centered?

2. Politics of the Healthy Disabled and a More Inclusive Approach. Watch Aimee Mullins' Ted Talk I Have Twelve Pairs of Legs https://www.ted.com/talks/aimee_mullins_my_12_pairs_of_legs?language=en (12 minutes) and Cheryl Marie Wade's Disability Culture Rap https://www.youtube.com/watch?v=-KnJwUMTP8s&has_verified=1 (22 minutes). What approach to acceptance does Mullins use? How does her approach potentially rely on attractiveness, ability, and health? What approach to acceptance does Wade use? How does she broaden her politics to include a wide range of people and abilities? Which political approach might be more effective? For what?

3. Impact of Coronavirus. Read the section of the chapter on the Coronavirus, the Op-eds listed above under resources and watch Michelle Garcia's video. Explain how the experience of the Coronavirus for people with disabilities reflects broader structural inequities.

CHAPTER 11

Education and Criminal Justice

Learning Outcomes

11.1 Explain the goals of the Individuals with Disabilities Education Act and various indicators of its success or failure.

11.2 Assess the evidence regarding the impact of labeling in special education.

11.3 Build an intersectional analysis of the benefits of special education considering class and race.

11.4 Compare and contrast the educational experience in K-12 grade education versus higher education for students with disabilities.

11.5 Examine the reasons for the high rate of incarceration for people with disabilities.

11.6 Analyze incarceration as an intersectional issue.

The United States responds to disability in various ways. Employment policy encourages the employment of some while channeling others out of the labor market and onto public benefits. Health care is a primary response, which may lead to treatment and services for some and long-term institutionalization for others. In this chapter, we look at two more responses to disability: education and criminal justice.

Education

Thirteen percent of America's school children receive **special education**, defined as educational services and instruction designed to enhance the academic success of students with disabilities. Despite the fact that special education is a longstanding part of the education system that serves a large portion of students, it is often overlooked in sociology. Sociology has too often *naturalized* special education, viewing it as a service for children with biological deficits instead of as a complex social phenomenon tied to intersectional inequality. In this chapter, we will look at education as one of the primary social responses to disability, focusing on the roots, purpose, and effects of constructing a largely separate system of education for children with disabilities, the impact of labeling, and the unequal distribution of the benefits of special education.

The Rise of Special Education

Education, institutions, and medical care for people with disabilities emerged as prominent responses to disability in the mid-1800s. In this time, educators developed innovative techniques to teach diverse children. For instance, Louis Braille created the dot code named after him, Thomas Gallaudet brought European advances in sign language to the United States, and Samuel Gridley Howe opened a school for children who were blind and then for children with intellectual disabilities. Each of these reformers believed in the power of education to open opportunities and transform disabled people into productive citizens.

The optimistic potential of education, though, was undercut by many factors. Disability was heavily stigmatized in the United States, and the rise of medical specialization fueled the idea that people with disabilities needed distinct and separate systems of treatment and education. Eugenics portrayed people with disabilities as deviant threats to the very moral fiber of the nation and further encouraged segregation. And, in a society with an abundant supply of unskilled labor, capitalists had little incentive to hire disabled workers who potentially needed extra time or support. Given this context, many schools—especially those for children with intellectual disabilities—abandoned their educational mission and instead morphed into custodial institutions. Rather than providing education, institutions imposed lifelong segregation and control.

From its outset, the field of special education embraced a dual and contradictory agenda: (1) to confer skills to those seen as able to become productive; and (2) to segregate, control, and minimize the burden of those deemed unable to be productive. *Both* agendas were and are deeply rooted in special education. Today, both agendas continue to guide the delivery of special education. For some students, special education offers a useful set of resources and services to enhance educational success. For other students, special education is a stigmatized educational track with low expectations and poor outcomes. For some it's a blend. The experience and benefits of special education depend heavily on one's diagnosis, school, class, race, gender, and other factors.

Before addressing inequality, though, let's cover some basics of special education, starting with the growth of special education. The field of special education grew through the 1900s and expanded at a dramatic rate after the passage of the 1975 Education for All Handicapped Children Act, now called the **Individuals with Disabilities Education Act (IDEA). IDEA** is a civil rights law which mandates the provision of a free appropriate education to all children with disabilities. Before IDEA, many children with disabilities were excluded from school. As laid out in Table 11.1, IDEA guarantees, among other things, the following rights:

PHOTO 11.1
Samuel Gridley Howe, an early leader in education for people with disabilities

TABLE 11.1   The Provisions of the Individuals With Disabilities Education Act

A free appropriate public education (FAPE)	All children have a right to a public education. Moreover, the education must be "appropriate," i.e., accessible and beneficial for the child.
An Individualized Education Program (IEP)	All children eligible for special education must receive an educational plan, specifying their individual needs, goals, supports, and services to ensure their educational needs are met.
Least Restrictive Environment (LRE)	IDEA asserts that children with disabilities should be educated alongside children without disabilities—in the same settings and modalities as children without disabilities—to the maximum degree beneficial for the disabled child.
Parent Participation	Parents have a right to be involved in the IEP process.
Right to Appeal	Parents have a right to appeal decisions made by the school regarding diagnosis, placement, services, and supports.
Transition Services	As the student nears graduation, the IEP must support the student in planning for life after graduation.

Since the passage of IDEA, the percentage of American students who receive special education services has increased. As shown in Figure 11.1, in 1976, 8.3% of school children had a special education label. This percentage increased steadily until 2000, when the percentage hit 13.3%. Since then, enrollment has been relatively stable. In 2017, 13.7% of students received special education services.

Educational Achievements and Concerns

The United States has made tremendous strides in the education of students with disabilities in the past 50 years, and it is a testament to the potential for broad social change.

- Whereas before IDEA many children sat at home or in institutions with few educational opportunities, now most children with disabilities attend school.
- The rate of inclusion has improved over time; 95% of students with disabilities now attend neighborhood schools that serve children with and without disabilities. Furthermore, the percent of students with disabilities who spend 80% or more of their school day in a general

FIGURE 11.1   Percentage of Students in Special Education, 1976–2018

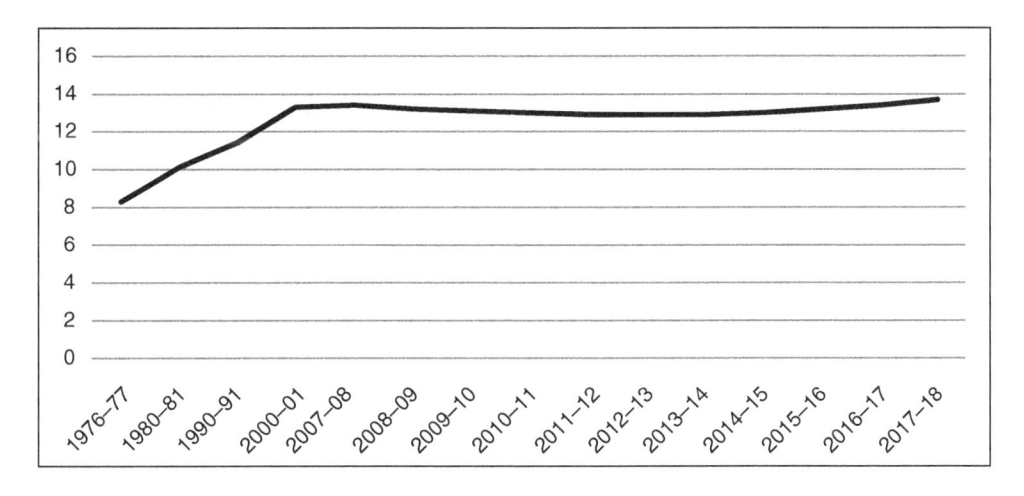

Source: U.S. Department of Education, National Center for Education Statistics. (2019a). *Digest of education statistics, 2018* (NCES 2020-009).

education classroom increased from 47% in 2000 to 64% in 2018 (Hussar et al., 2020).

- The high school graduation rate of students with disabilities has improved dramatically over time, as has the likelihood of attending college (see Figure 11.2).

There is still cause for alarm, however.

- Although graduation rates have improved over time, the gap between people with and without disabilities who graduate high school has remained relatively steady (Houtenville & Boege, 2019). In 2008, 23.4% of young adults with disabilities did not have a high school diploma, compared to 12.7% of young adults without disabilities, a difference of 10.7 percentage points. By 2018, 16.7% of young adults with disabilities did not have a high school diploma compared to 7.7% of young adults without disabilities, a difference of 9 percentage points. Both groups improved their rate of high school graduation, but the gap stayed relatively steady, only improving by 1.7 percentage points (see Figure 11.3). The same trend exists among those who attain a bachelor's degree or more. Both students with and without disabilities are now more likely to attain a bachelor's degree, but the gap between the two groups *widened* a little over time (see Figure 11.4).

- Studies have consistently found that children with disabilities experience stigma and low expectations from teachers and parents, regardless of their actual academic performance.

FIGURE 11.2 Percentage of Students With Disabilities Served Under the IDEA Graduating With a Regular High School Diploma, 1995–2015

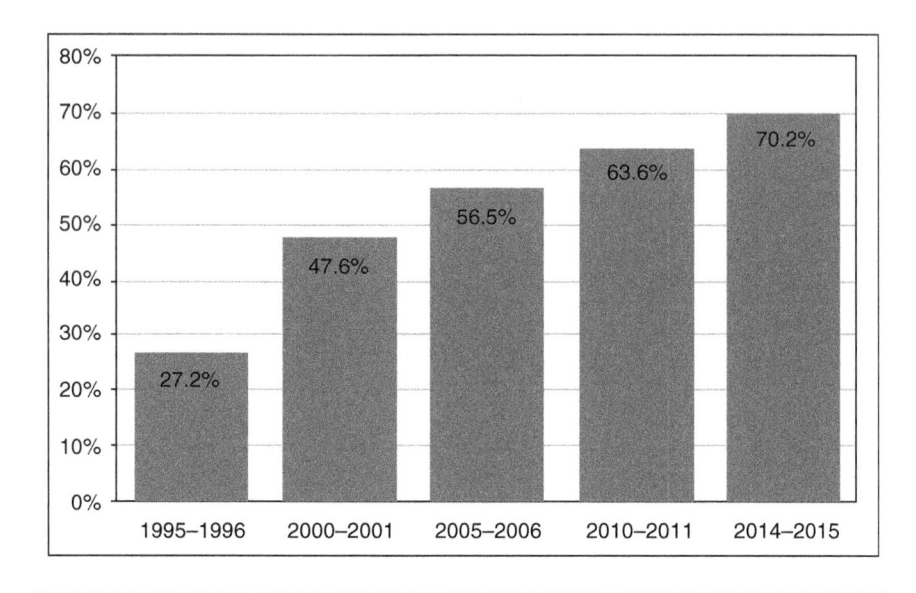

Year	Percentage
1995–1996	27.2%
2000–2001	47.6%
2005–2006	56.5%
2010–2011	63.6%
2014–2015	70.2%

Source: "Students with Disabilities Graduating from High School and Entering Postsecondary Education: In Brief." 2017. *Everycrsreport.com.* Available at https://www.everycrsreport.com/reports/R44887.html. CRS analysis using data from the US Department of Education, Office of Special Education Programs, Data Analysis System (DANS), "Children with Disabilities Exiting Special Education."

FIGURE 11.3 Percentage of Adults Ages 25–32 Without a High School Diploma, 2008–2018

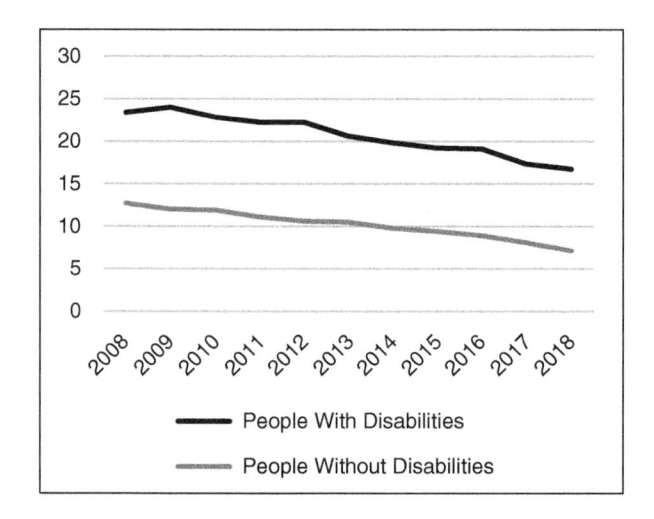

Source: American Community Survey data 2008–2018, compiled in Houtenville, A. and Boege, S. 2019. *Annual Report on People With Disabilities in America: 2018.* Durham, NH: University of New Hampshire, Institute on Disability.

FIGURE 11.4 Percentage of Adults Ages 25–32 With a Bachelor's Degree or Higher, 2008–2018

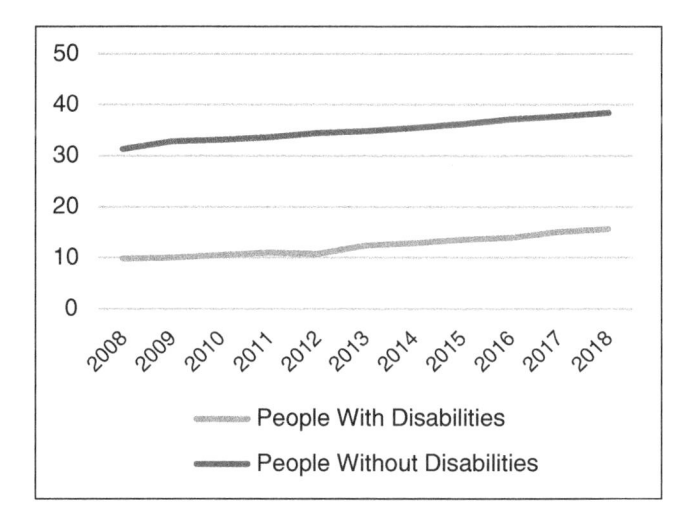

Source: American Community Survey data 2008–2018, compiled in Houtenville, A. and Boege, S. 2019. *Annual Report on People With Disabilities in America: 2018*. Durham, NH: University of New Hampshire, Institute on Disability.

- Inclusion (defined as attending 80% of more of one's class time in the same school and classes as students without disabilities)—a central goal of the IDEA—varies widely by social factors such as state, zip code, race, and disability category (NCD, 2018).
- Children with disabilities from minority and low-income backgrounds are more likely to experience educational segregation and out-of-school discipline than White children with disabilities (NCD, 2018).

Labeling Theory, Rising Rates, and Shifting Diagnoses

One of the central dilemmas in special education is tied to the advantages and disadvantages of labeling children as disabled. **Labeling theory** (Becker, 1966) explains that labels have their own power to create consequences, regardless of whether the labels reflect reality or not. For instance, among those who engage in drug use, those labeled "drug addicts" may be more likely to incorporate drug use into their identity and face punishment, regardless of whether they actually use drugs more than those who remain unlabeled. Disability, like other labels, is created for particular purposes and then applied to a group of people, and the label itself results in various consequences. Some of these consequences are positive and some are negative.

Labeling and Stigma

In special education, labels are supposed to serve a positive function. Ideally, they provide access to a range of services and accommodations that benefit students. For example, students may gain access to extended time, assistive technologies, and therapies. Thus, the label *should* benefit children.

However, a disability label may also cause negative consequences, such as low expectations and bullying (Swearer et al., 2012). Students with disabilities experience *stigma*, especially in the form of low expectations. A 2013 study by sociologist Dara Shifrer offers evidence of this effect. Using a national database, Shifrer compared students with similar academic performance, motivation, behaviors, and family backgrounds. She found that, among youth with similar academic and social backgrounds, teachers and parents held lower educational expectations for youth with disabilities than for similarly achieving and behaving youth without disabilities. In fact, Shifrer found that the odds of teachers expecting students with disabilities to earn a college degree were 82% lower than for students without disabilities, even when all other factors describing the children were similar. The odds of parents expecting children with disabilities to achieve a college degree were 48% lower than for students without disabilities, even when all other factors are similar. Other studies using experimental methods similarly reveal that teachers hold lower expectations and negative stereotypes of children with disabilities. For example, when teachers were given randomly assigned vignettes of various children, they described the children with disabilities in more negative terms and saw less potential in them (Allday et al., 2011; Ohan et al., 2011).

Lower expectations hinder academic progress. Stella Chatzitheochari and Lucinda Platt (2019) studied advancement in the British educational system into academic or vocational programs. They found that students with disabilities were less likely to advance into academic programs and college for two reasons. The more important reason—the *primary effect*—was that students with disabilities on average performed more poorly in school and therefore were less likely to be placed in college tracks. But, *secondary effects*—the effects of the *label* rather than performance—existed as well. Students with disabilities who achieved good grades and were qualified for a college track were still less likely to be placed in that track as compared to their similarly achieving, nondisabled peers. They were disadvantaged by their disability *label*, mostly due to lower expectations, thereby creating a *self-fulfilling prophecy* (Scheff, 1966; see too Shandra & Hogan, 2009).

Inclusion and Segregation

Disability labels may also affect one's educational placement. The label and its associated services may enable a student with disabilities to be successful in an inclusive classroom alongside their peers, or the label may lead to the placement of children in segregated, disability-specific settings. IDEA asserts that children with disabilities should be educated in the least restrictive environment. Therefore, they should be provided the accommodations and supports necessary to be appropriately educated in their neighborhood school and in general education classes alongside children without disabilities unless there are clear educational benefits for the child to be placed in a more restrictive, disability-specific, setting.

An inclusive education is more than the physical placement of children with disabilities in the same school or classroom. **Inclusive education** involves a philosophy and a set of practices in which children with disabilities, in the same schools and classes as their nondisabled peers, are "valued and active participants, and where they are provided supports needed to succeed in the academic, social, and extra-curricular activities of the school" (McLeskey et al., 2014, p. 4). Because it is difficult to measure a school's philosophy and practices, though, researchers often measure inclusion in terms of time and place. Most commonly, inclusive education is defined as students who spend 80% or more of their class time in general education classes.

PHOTO 11.2
Children in Inclusive Art Class

In theory, all students can be included. For some students, the accommodations needed for successful inclusion might be minimal, like extended test time or materials in an alternative format. For other students, the accommodations may be more extensive, such as in class aides and the fundamental rethinking of classwork to meet the goals of an individual student. Let's consider a hypothetical example. Kierra is a 17-year-old student with an intellectual disability who reads at a second-grade reading level. She can still be included in 12th grade English, though, with appropriate accommodations. When the class reads *Pride and Prejudice,* for example, she might read a simpler, shorter version, listen to the audiobook, and/or watch the movie and read short excerpts. She could still participate in class discussion. As some students write an analysis of *Pride and Prejudice,* she might do an individualized project that builds on her specific skills and academic goals.

When we think about inclusion, for some students we may need to reframe "success." From a traditional perspective, if Kierra cannot meet the same goals as her classmates, she is failing. However, let's consider Kierra's individual progress instead. From her starting point, if she attains *more skills* in the inclusive classroom than she would in the disability-specific classroom, then inclusion is a success. According to the evidence, it is likely that by participating in an inclusive class Kierra will better build skills. Evidence suggests the benefits of inclusion are extensive and that, overall and when implemented well, inclusive education is usually a more effective educational strategy than segregation by disability/ability. A 2018 report by the National Council on Disability (NCD) summarizes the research and concludes that students with disabilities in inclusive settings accrued many benefits as compared to students with disabilities in disability-specific settings. They achieved greater academic success, improved their communication skills at greater rates, had more satisfying and diverse friendships, gained more social skills, had fewer absences, had fewer behavioral problems, were less likely to be formally disciplined, felt more engaged, *and* had better post-secondary education outcomes including higher rates of employment and attending college. In contrast, in a disability-specific classroom, Kierra might never gain exposure to *Pride and Prejudice,* discuss the constraints of gender roles, or engage in meaningful conversation with nondisabled students (see Figure 11.5).

What about students who need extensive supports or accommodations, like Kierra in the example above? Research shows that students who use extensive accommodations and supports benefit *more* from inclusion than students who use fewer supports (NCD, 2018). And what about students without disabilities? Does inclusion drain time and resources away from them and hinder their progress? The evidence does not support this theory. Students without disabilities who attend inclusive schools do no worse on average than those who attend schools with extensive segregation by disability (NCD, 2018). Overall, inclusive educational environments tend to offer more educational opportunities, foster higher expectations, and lead to better educational and post-educational outcomes for students with disabilities without harming students without disabilities.

As noted already, the rate of inclusion has improved over time. Given this evidence, we might expect inclusion to be the standard practice in schools. While schools have increased the use of inclusion, there is still resistance to it. Why?

FIGURE 11.5 Considering Success and Failure in the Inclusive Classroom

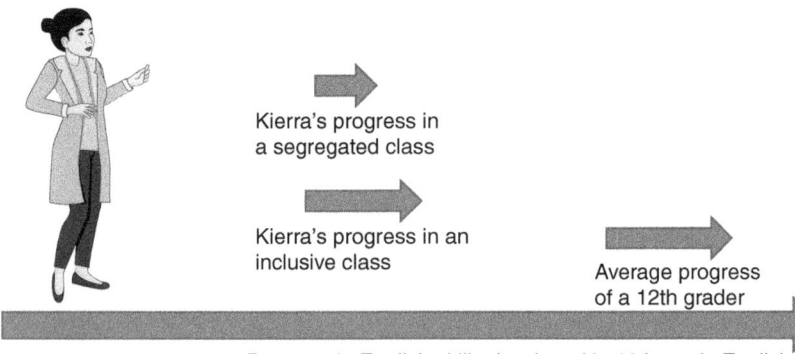

Kierra's progress in a segregated class

Kierra's progress in an inclusive class

Average progress of a 12th grader

Progress in English skills developed in 12th grade English

- Some of the resistance may be due to **institutional inertia**—the tendency of big bureaucracies to reproduce the same practices, even after those practices become ineffective or counter-productive (Hannan & Freeman, 1984). Some school districts built specific buildings for disabled children; many teachers were taught to be *either* general education *or* special education teachers; and school administrators created distinct tracks of children. Because these investments in segregated education have already been made, there is now a massive infrastructure that would need to be radically altered to achieve inclusion. However, bureaucracies tend to resist large-scale, rapid change.

- Some of the resistance may due to active **institutional interests**—the array of goals and needs of an organization. Segregation by disability may serve institutional needs, even if it is detrimental to some children. For example, administrators may use special education classrooms as a management tool to channel students perceived as problematic out of the general education classroom.

- Some children may benefit from disability-specific educational programs, and school districts may overgeneralize these needs in order to deliver services in a cost-efficient manner. For example, a school district may have two children who benefit more from education and intensive therapy delivered outside of the general education classroom. To meet these needs in an efficient manner, the school district may create a *class* for children with disabilities and send many students to that class, including students who could succeed in the general education classroom. Or, students may have a specific educational need or accommodation, and districts may decide it is more efficient to create a distinct school with these programs and services rather than providing them across all district schools. This approach prioritizes the efficient use of resources, rather than meeting the individualized needs of students supported in the most inclusive settings, as set forth by IDEA.

- Some of the resistance may be due to stigma and outmoded beliefs. School officials and parents may assume, for example, that disabled children are best served in separate programs, despite evidence to the contrary (Connor & Ferri, 2007).

Building an Intersectional Analysis of Special Education

Special education labels may benefit students, or they may lead to negative consequences such as low expectations and segregation. The advantages and disadvantages of special education are unequally distributed. Research shows that type of diagnosis, race, and class play a significant role in whether special education confers advantages or disadvantages.

"Promising" and Less Promising Diagnoses

Diagnoses are labels, and as such they reflect values, create meanings, and lead to consequences. As we know, the proportion of children labeled as disabled has increased over time. The overall increase in special education, though, masks different trends for various diagnoses. Figure 11.6 shows that some diagnoses have become more common among students, while others have become less common. Intellectual disability has decreased significantly, by 65% over time. As intellectual disability diagnoses declined, other diagnoses increased, especially autism, "specific learning disabilities," and "other health conditions" which includes attention-deficit hyperactivity disorder (ADHD). Meanwhile, visual disabilities and speech and language disabilities remained relatively stable.

To think about why these shifts occurred, let's consider the consequences of particular labels and the resources they confer or exclude one from. Historically, a wide range of children were assumed to have low IQs. Children with deafness, speech disabilities, and learning disabilities, for instance, all risked being labeled as having intellectual disabilities. This label primarily led to exclusion from public school, rather than the provision of high quality educational services. As such, parents had little incentive to seek out a diagnosis for their child.

Later in history, learning disability emerged as a label distinct from intellectual disability. Intellectual disability is characterized by a subaverage IQ. In contrast, learning disability is a label used to identify children with

FIGURE 11.6 Number of Special Education Students (in Thousands) in Diagnosis Categories, 1976–2018

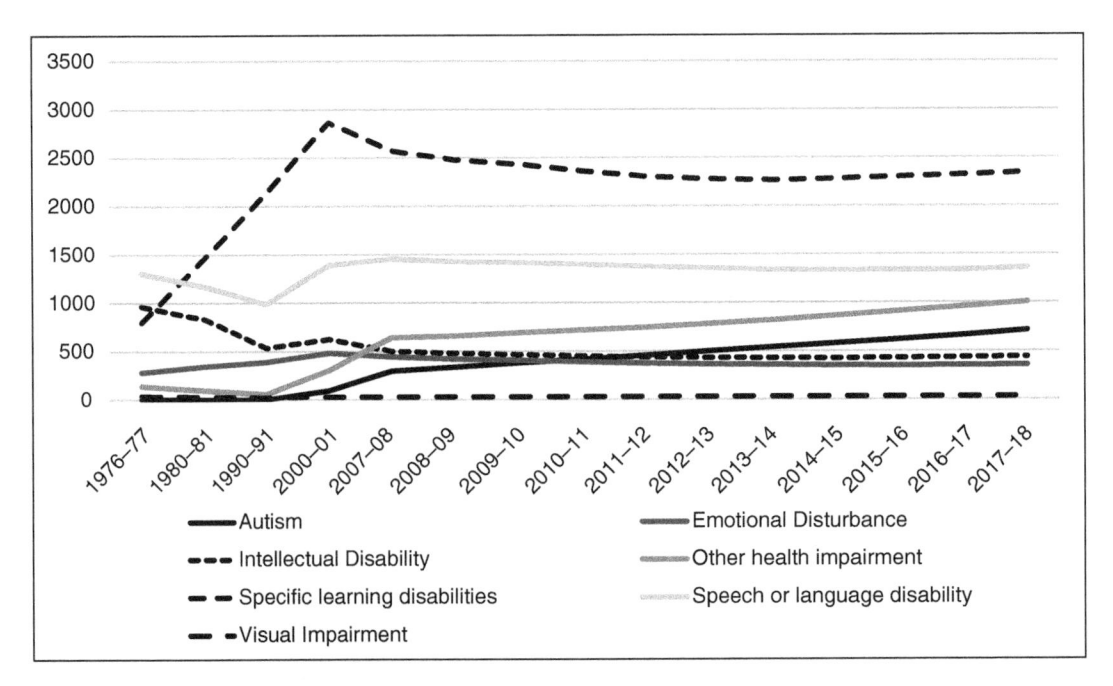

Source: U.S. Department of Education, National Center for Education Statistics. (2019a). *Digest of education statistics, 2018* (NCES 2020-009).

academic achievement lower than expected given their IQs. For example, a child with dyslexia might struggle in school due to specific differences in the ways that they process language, not due to low intelligence. Once teachers accommodate these differences, children with dyslexia should succeed on par with children of similar IQ. Because the label of learning disability does not imply lower intelligence, it carries less stigma. Children with learning disabilities came to be seen as potentially productive and worthy of an investment in their education. Therefore, they were given services and accommodations, in contrast with the exclusion often experienced by children labeled intellectually disabled. Thus, learning disability became a **promising diagnosis**—a diagnosis that potentially leads to beneficial services, often in inclusive settings alongside nondisabled children. Parents started seeking out ways to diagnose their children who were struggling in school as learning disabled. The learning disability label became a pathway to secure individualized services for struggling students in an otherwise impersonal bureaucratic setting (Blum, 2015; Ong-Dean, 2009).

Autism also emerged as a label distinct from intellectual disability. In the 1980s and 1990s, therapies emerged specifically for autism. Media attention increasingly focused on autistic savants and geniuses, indicating the untapped potential in this population. As services for children with learning disabilities and autism increased, children with intellectual disabilities were largely left behind. Children with intellectual disabilities are still more likely to be placed in segregated settings and are given less access to high-quality educational programming.

From 2005–2006 to 2015–2016, the rate of inclusion increased from 53.6% of special education students to 62.7% (NCD, 2018). As Figure 11.7 shows, though, inclusion varies significantly by diagnosis. Those most likely to be included are students with speech and language impairments (86.7%), specific learning disabilities (69.2%), visual impairments (67.2%), and other health impairments (which includes ADHD). Students with intellectual disabilities

FIGURE 11.7 Percentage of Students in Inclusive Settings by Diagnosis, 2015–2016

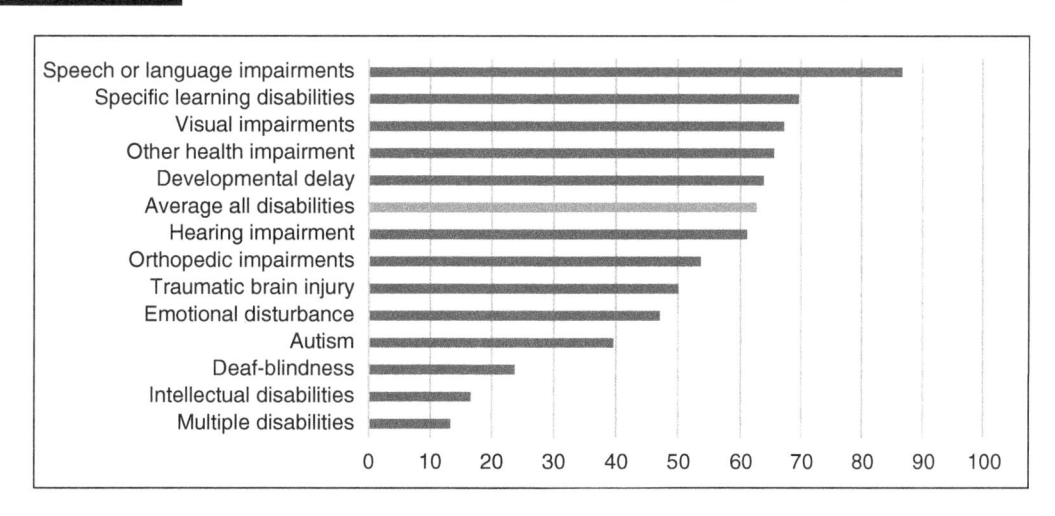

Source: NCD (2018), drawing on 2016 U.S. Department of Education data.

(17%) and multiple disabilities (13%) are least likely to be included. For students with intellectual disabilities, their rates of inclusion have barely changed in the last decade. Thus, access to inclusion varies by diagnosis.

Bringing in SES

Socioeconomic status (SES) plays a significant role in shaping the advantages and disadvantages of special education. The processes involved in securing a high-quality special education—including diagnosis, the IEP, and potentially legal proceedings—advantage families with higher incomes and more education.

Sociologist Pierre Bourdieu (1984) created the concept of **cultural capital**—the exclusive or particular cultural knowledge enacted in relationships through which one accrues resources and benefits. Schools reproduce inequality by valuing some cultural capital and the students who have that capital over other cultural capital. A wealthy student might speak French, be a trained debater, and have an appreciation for literary classics. A student from a low-income background may know how to care for her aging grandmother, shop for food on a budget, and use public transportation to cross the city in the most efficient manner. Both have skill sets, but one is more valued by the educational system than the other. Anette Lareau (2003), drawing on Bourdieu, further showed that SES shapes parenting styles. High-income parents are more likely to engage in **concerted cultivation**—the provision by parents of attention and organized activities to help ensure their children's success in life. High-income parents use their resources to help their children acquire the cultural capital valued by the education system and the workplace.

Securing special educational services is a complicated process, and high-income families use their cultural capital, as well as direct economic resources and social capital, to try to ensure their children gain access to services that will benefit them (Trainor, 2010). In the diagnosis process, high-income parents are more likely to have the resources to secure a private disability evaluation, through which they can exert influence and secure a promising diagnosis which is more likely to lead to services and less likely to lead to intense stigma (Blum, 2015; Holt et al., 2019; Ong-Dean, 2009). Once a student is diagnosed, schools are not always readily forthcoming with a full range of services. Parent advocacy is central to the process, and this also favors parents with higher education, more comfort with bureaucracy, and more money (Leiter, 2012; Ong-Dean, 2009). IDEA gives parents the right to appeal school decisions, but this legal and bureaucratic process again entails resources. Thus, the processes of special education are highly reliant on parent advocacy and resources, which ensures inequality by class (Voulgarides, 2018).

Meryl Alper's (2017) study of youth who use assistive technology demonstrates the role of class privilege in accessing the benefits of special education. Many students benefit from, or could benefit from, technology. Alper studied technology related to augmentative and alternative communication—devices that assist a student in communication. She found that high-income parents could more easily identify beneficial technology, advocate for its provision by the school, and support its use at home. In contrast, low-income parents had less knowledge about technology, felt more intimidated by school officials and more reluctant to advocate for technology, and worried more about their child using technology owned by the school because they worried it might break and they would be held financially responsible. High-income parents facilitated technology use in other ways too. For instance, they paid for high-speed internet at home and supplemented school technology, such as buying additional entertainment software. Thus, children from wealthy families had a broader range of technology, received more support in using it, and enjoyed the integration of their technology across areas of their life, such as school, family, and recreation.

Credit: "The main page of an AAC device layout for Portuguese speakers" (2014). Obtained from Wikimedia Commons. https://commons.wikimedia.org/wiki/File:The_main_page_of_an_AAC_device_layout_for_English_speakers.png

PHOTO 11.3
Example Layout of Child's AAC Device

Household wealth is not the only way that SES influences special education. The resources of the neighborhood and school also matter. Schools are funded in part through local property taxes, which means that wealthy districts can afford to provide a comprehensive range of services, whereas poor districts struggle to provide even the most basic of services. Comparing students in wealthy and poor neighborhoods, Louise Holt and her colleagues (2019) found that children in poor neighborhoods were more likely to receive disability *labels*, but children in wealthy neighborhoods were more likely to receive disability *services*. In poor neighborhoods, disability labels often led to segregation and low expectations; in wealthy neighborhoods, disability labels were more likely to lead to useful services that helped children succeed.

Bringing in Race

Shawn Anthony Robinson, a Black man with a learning disability, modified lyrics by Tupac Shakur to describe his experience in special education as "Me Against the World" (2017). He depicts feeling trapped in a system designed for his failure, where he succeeded *despite* special education, not because of it. "Me Against the World" begins:

It's me against deficit thinkers

Oh-hahhh

Stuck in special education

Me against the world bro

The death of Black male's creativity is a result of some teacher's objectivity;

Sociological analysis can situate Robinson's personal experience in a broader system of inequality in which race and its intersection with class are highly salient. According to the National Center for Education Statistics (Hussar et al., 2020), in the 2018–2019 school year, Black and Native American children were the racial/ethnic groups most likely to be placed in special education. 18% of Native American children, 16% of Black children, 14% of White children, 13% of Hispanic, and 7% of Asian children were placed in special education. African American students were more likely to be labeled with "unpromising" diagnoses such as intellectual disability (9% of Black children in special education vs. 6% of White children in special education) (U.S. Department of Education, 2019b). Race also shapes educational outcomes. As shown in Figure 11.8, Black children in special education were 12 percentage

FIGURE 11.8 Percentage of Students Served by IDEA in 2015–2016 by Race and Exit Path for High School

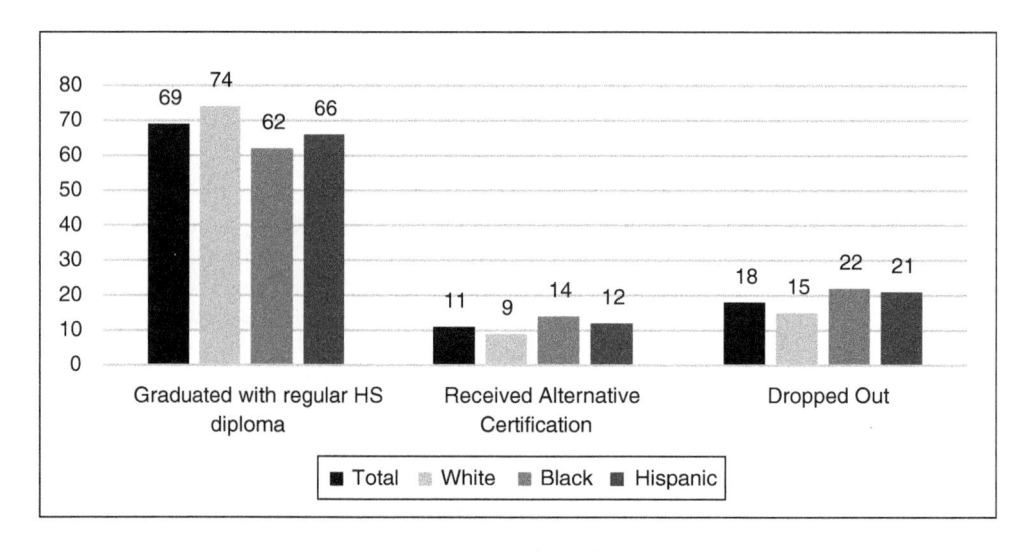

Exit Path	Total	White	Black	Hispanic
Graduated with regular HS diploma	69	74	62	66
Received Alternative Certification	11	9	14	12
Dropped Out	18	15	22	21

Source: National Center for Education Statistics, 2019, compiling data from U.S. Department of Education, Office of Special Education Programs, Individuals with Disabilities Education Act (IDEA) *Digest of Education Statistics 2017.*

points less likely to graduate with a regular high school diploma (74% of White students in special education vs. 62% of Black students in special education) and more likely to drop out of high school (15% of White children in special education vs. 22% of Black children in special education).

The statistics show that Black students are disproportionately labeled disabled and placed in special education. There is fierce debate as to *why* these patterns occur and whether Black children are overclassified or underclassified as disabled.

The **overclassification** argument suggests that Black youth are inappropriately and disproportionately labeled as disabled and channeled into special education, thereby increasing segregation and decreasing the quality of education provided to them. Ferri and Connor's (2006) study shows that, after racial segregation in schools was struck down by the Supreme Court, special education came to play an important role in enforcing racial distance through educational segregation and suspension. In school, Black youth experience racialized interpretations of their behavior, leading to increased diagnosis of intellectual, learning, and emotional disabilities. For example, Aydin Bal and colleagues (2019) found that African American and Native American students were two to three times more likely to be labeled as emotionally disturbed than White students. Black students in special education are more likely to be in classrooms segregated by disability/ability as compared to White students. As shown in Figure 11.9, in 2015–2016, 65.5% of White students were included in general education at least 80% of the time, compared to only 58% of Black students, a gap of 7.5 percentage points. Furthermore, data from Wisconsin show that African American students in special education were seven times more likely to receive exclusionary discipline (e.g., suspension) than White students in special education (Bal et al., 2019) (Figure 11.9).

The **underclassification** argument, though, suggests that African American children are more likely to have disabilities due to factors such as poverty, discrimination, and lack of health care, and that, based on higher rates of disability, they may be *underserved* by special education. Paul Morgan and his

FIGURE 11.9 Percentage of Students Included in General Education at Least 80% of Class-Time by Race, 2015–2016

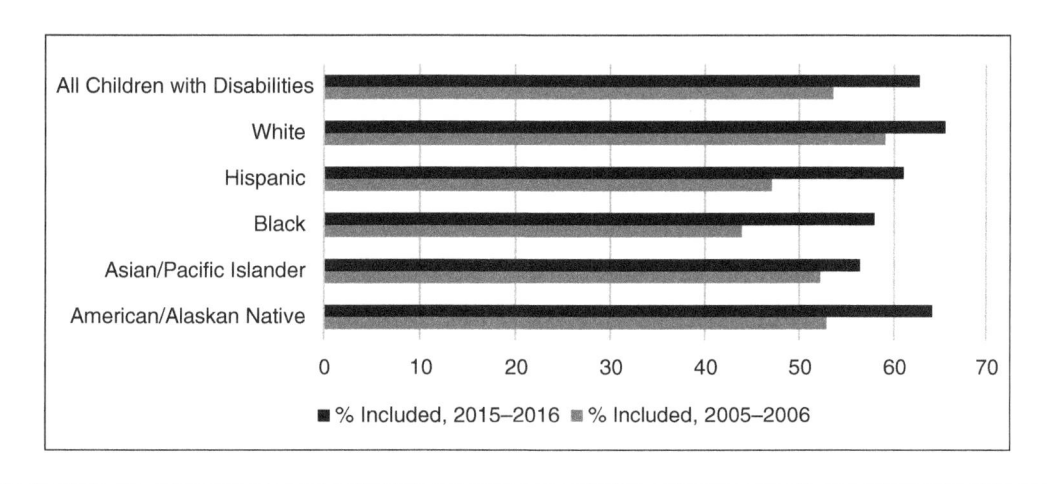

Source: NCD (2018), compiling data from U.S. Department of Education, 29th Report to Congress, 2010 Table 2.2, pp. 210–219 and U.S. Department of Education, EDFacts Data Warehouse (EDW), "IDEA Part B Child Count and Educational Environments Collection," 2015–2016.

colleagues (2019) compared White and Black students with similar academic achievement, income, and other factors, and found that Black students were *less likely* to receive special education given their needs. They argued that White and high-income parents may be more successful in advocating for diagnoses and services.

Ironically perhaps, both arguments may be true. Dara Shifrer (2018) argues that broad systems of social inequality inside and outside of school—such as racism, increased poverty, residential segregation, and lack of health care—leads to gaps in educational performance. Classifying minority youth as disabled potentially provides services but also masks these social inequalities. Instead of addressing systemic racial inequality, special education too often labels Black youth as deficient and provides individual-level services and/or leads to low expectations and segregation.

While the issue of overrepresentation versus underrepresentation in special education is important, the better question may be: how well does special education serve the students labeled as disabled? In general, special education seems to serve White students better than minority students. For White and higher SES youth, special education is more likely to offer a valuable set of services that enable their inclusion and success, and parents may fight to attain these services. On the other hand, Black and lower SES youth may be more likely to find that the special education system works against them and is less responsive to the advocacy of their parents.

Two studies shed light on how special education may be experienced differently by people of different races. Rachel Fish (2019) examined how the racial composition of schools affected the placement of students of various races in special education. She found that **racial distinctiveness**—being a minority in terms of the specific racial composition of the school—affected special education placement. As the proportion of White students in a school increased, Black students were increasingly at risk of "less promising" diagnoses, such as intellectual disability and emotional disturbance. In comparison, as the proportion of minority students increased, White students were increasingly at risk of "promising" diagnoses, like speech/language impairment. Thus, students in the racial minority (both White and Black) were at higher risk of special education placement, but students of color were more likely to experience a less promising diagnosis leading to more segregation and fewer educational opportunities, whereas White students were more likely to experience a more promising diagnosis that increased access to helpful services.

Let's also discuss Catherine Voulgarides's 2018 ethnographic study of special education in three different schools that varied in their income and racial composition. *School 1* was rated a high-achieving district due to high test scores and its 100% graduation rate. It served a predominantly White (92%) and wealthy neighborhood, where only 15% of the students qualified for free and reduced-price lunches (FRPL). In this school, school administrators were committed to delivering high-quality special education, parents felt like they had input into the IEP, and the school even "overaccommodated"—giving children more services than required by law.

School 2 had test scores that placed it as "average achieving." Seventy-nine percent of the local residents were White, and 33% of its students qualified for FRPL. Given that the neighborhood had less money, the school had a more limited budget. School administrators restricted access to special education services, often by predetermining the services each child would receive prior to the IEP meeting and providing less expensive services. Parental advocacy met resistance by administrators.

School 3 was rated as "low-achieving." Its neighborhood had a lower percentage of White residents (41%), and 65% of the students qualified for FRPL. This school offered only the bare minimum for special education and often failed at that. They, for example, sent notices of IEP meetings to the wrong home address and did not work closely with parents. With their limited resources, they spent their energy meeting the basic requirements of legal compliance, such as documenting annual IEP meetings, rather than actually providing special education.

Vougarides concludes that neighborhood resources and school culture create distinct experiences of special education in each school, ultimately perpetuating inequality. Upper-class and White children disproportionately benefited from more resources and a school culture geared to promote their success. Students from low-SES neighborhoods were more likely to experience schools struggling to meet the basic needs of their students and without capacity to meet "additional" needs. Like Shifrer, Vougarides argues that, by focusing on individual children, special education ignores systemic educational and social inequality and, as such, too often fails to remedy persistent racial and class inequality.

Higher Education

The final section on education addresses higher education. As noted earlier in this chapter, students with disabilities are increasingly attending and graduating from college, but there is still a significant gap in college graduation rates for students with and without disabilities. In 2018, 38.4% of young adults without disabilities aged 25–34 had attained a bachelor's degree or higher, compared with 15.6% of young adults with disabilities. Thus, students without disabilities were more than twice as likely to attain a BA or more.

Why might that be? We already discussed primary and secondary effects. The primary effect shows that, for a range of reasons, students with disabilities on average perform less well academically than students without disabilities, which hinders their advancement to college. The secondary effect shows that, even for students with the same academic performance, students with disabilities experience lower expectations and more stigma, so that their label hinders their progress.

For students who attend college, they have lower graduation rates from four-year schools. Let's consider the experience once one gets to college.

Differences in the Disability Services and Accommodations in High School and College

The experience of being a college student with a disability is very different from being a high-school student. Irene Ingersoll (2016) laid out the following differences, listed in Table 11.2.

High school students operate in a system in which school administrators and teachers are responsible for the identification of students who may have disabilities, development of the IEP, implementation of the IEP in the classroom, assessment of student success, and adjustment of the services as needed. Parents have a legal right to input in this process, and parent advocacy can shape the outcome. In contrast, college students must engage in

TABLE 11.2 Disability Services in High School and College

High School	College
The school is responsible for identifying disability.	The student must provide documentation of disability.
School is responsible for identifying the student's needs and goals and creating and implementing a system of individualized disability services.	Colleges must have the capability to deliver a host of services and accommodations, but the student must self-identify and request accommodations, requiring student self-advocacy.
Modifications can and should be made as appropriate to the curriculum.	Colleges offer accommodations, but they are not obligated to modify the essential elements of the curriculum or learning expectations.
Parents have a legal right to participate and to challenge school decisions.	Parents have no legal right to participate. In fact, privacy laws shield student records from parents.
IEP plans are reviewed each year.	Student goals, progress, and services are not systematically monitored or assessed.

self-advocacy—the identification and promotion of one's own interests and rights. Colleges must have disability services and accommodations available to eligible students, but students must apply for such services, request accommodations, and decide when/if they want to use their accommodations. Parents are largely shut out of the process.

Given the choice of whether to use accommodations or not, many students do not. This may be due to several reasons. Valerie Leiter (2012) describes a **developmental mismatch** in which colleges expect students to engage in self-advocacy without first building the required skills. Moreover, college students may worry about stigma and resist self-identifying as disabled. In a qualitative study of college students with disabilities (Wood, 2017b), one student explained, "I don't want people to identify me by my disability because I'm in [pre-med]; it's a really hard major and there's already a stigma of being a girl" (p. 82). The accommodations process in college also creates a lot of work for students with disabilities, and the work involved may not be seen as leading to sufficient benefits. In a study by Carroll-Miranda (2017), a student described the accommodations process, saying: "The experience is difficult. It is difficult because you have to make more effort to be the same as the rest" (p. 281). The same student continued: "Sometimes there are not that many benefits when compared with all the burdens faced, like all the difficulties that come with having to take the documents, that you have to get them here or there… it takes time and in the end it is not as effective for all the struggles you go through" (p. 284).

Ableism in Higher Education

College students report many experiences of ableism on college campuses. Many college campuses are physically inaccessible, even if they comply with the ADA. Campuses are physically vast, and students may only be given 10 or 15 minutes between classes. Social spaces like dorms and fraternities are not held to the same accessibility standards as learning spaces. ADA parking and entrances may be inconveniently located or poorly identified. The cost of higher education makes it financially inaccessible for many people with disabilities, who tend to have higher rates of poverty and higher costs of living. The culture of higher education also exudes ableism (Price, 2011). Higher education is an institution that values intelligence, productivity, efficiency, and independence. As such, there may be far greater willingness to accommodate physical differences than intellectual and mental differences. For example, students who cannot attend class due to depression may face more resistance regarding accommodations than students who cannot attend class due to asthma or a medical appointment related to paralysis.

Disability service systems on campuses typically do not foster disability pride. Instead, disability is medicalized and individualized, and students must ask for individual accommodations. There is little concerted effort on most campuses to build connections among students with disabilities or to foster positive disability identities. Sociologist Tanya Titchkosky (2011) argues that college administrators still act as if students with disabilities are out of the norm, and they justify the continued lack of accessibility based on budget and ignorance. They treat disability primarily as an administrative, logistical issue, rather than as an equity issue.

That said, some colleges do intentionally foster disability pride and inclusion. For example, Syracuse University in New York has a disability community center, which provides a hub for community-building and disability programming. Millersville University in Pennsylvania and Syracuse University are among a growing number of universities that offer inclusive college programs for students with intellectual disabilities. Through these programs, students with intellectual disabilities gain access to campus life and classes with a range of supports like academic and life skills coaching. And, as a final example, Texas A&M offers adaptive sports, including wheelchair basketball, wheelchair football, wheelchair soccer, and sitting volleyball.

PHOTO 11.4 College Adaptive Sports are one way to build opportunities on campuses

Credit: VM (2019). Reproduced with permission from istock.com.

Wrapping Up Education

In a meritocracy, education is one of the most important ways to attain social mobility. Historically, children with disabilities were largely shut out of education. The rise of special education offered ways to promote the education and opportunities of students with disabilities. However, special education is enmeshed with other systems of inequality, and some children benefit from it far more than other children.

Criminal Justice and Carceral Responses to Disability

Education in its ideal form envisions people with disabilities as worthy of investment and as a valuable part of the community. Incarceration, on the other hand, imposes social control and segregation.

Disability is intricately associated with deviance. For example, historically in some cultures people who had seizures were believed to be possessed by demons, and women with mental illness risked being labeled as witches. In the late 1800s and early 1900s, some American cities passed "ugly laws" which made it illegal for "any person, who is diseased, maimed, mutilated or deformed in any way, so as to be an unsightly or disgusting object, to expose himself or herself to public view" (quoted in Albrecht, 2006, pp. 175–176; Schweik, 2009). While some people may believe that negative views of disability are a thing of the past, it is not true. Behaviors like staying in bed all day, drooling in public, or self-soothing by rocking back and forth are often seen as violating social expectations and are often met with stigma. Because disability is tied to cultural norms, disability labels and rates vary tremendously depending on the nation and culture.

Society can respond to deviance in varied ways. Two of the most common ways related to disability are medicalization and criminalization. *Medicalization* is the process by which social phenomena come to be seen as a medical condition in need of medical intervention (Conrad, 2007). **Criminalization** is the process by which social phenomena come to be seen as a crime worthy of significant punishment. Drug use, for example, might be seen as a health crisis driven by biological addiction which requires medical treatment and/or as an act of deviance driven by disregard for social norms which requires punishment. Either way drug use is seen as deviant—a problem that violates the norms of society in need of remedy or response. Thomas Szasz (1961) famously argued that mental illness was nothing more than social deviance controlled via medicalization rather than criminal justice.

Of these responses (medicalization or criminalization), medicalization is often presented as a kinder, "softer" way to respond to social deviance (Tausig et al., 2004). For example, if one's child is misbehaving at school, a label of ADHD might be less stigmatizing and more beneficial than a label of delinquent.

However, as we've seen, disability labels are not without negative consequences, and they do not protect one from criminalization. This is particularly true for mental illness. In fact, Dr. E. Fuller Torrey and colleagues (2014) estimates that 20% of inmates in jails and 15% of inmates in state prisons—a

FIGURE 11.10   Mental Health of Inmates, 2011–2012

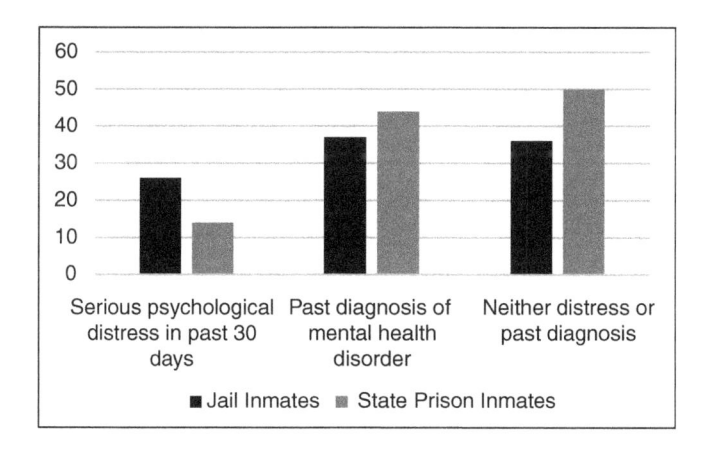

[Bar chart showing percentages for Jail Inmates and State Prison Inmates:
- Serious psychological distress in past 30 days: Jail ~26%, State Prison ~14%
- Past diagnosis of mental health disorder: Jail ~37%, State Prison ~44%
- Neither distress or past diagnosis: Jail ~36%, State Prison ~50%]

Source: Jennifer Bronson and Marcus Berzofsky (2017). Indicators of Mental Health Problems Reported by Prisoners and Jail Inmates, 2011–2012. Bureau of Justice Statistics.

total of approximately 356,000 people—have a serious mental illness. This figure is 10 times more than the current number of patients with serious mental illness in state hospitals. More people with serious mental illness reside in the Los Angeles County Jail, Chicago's Cook County Jail, or New York's Rikers Island Jail than in any psychiatric hospital in the United States (Rembis, 2014; Torrey et al., 2010).

Using data from 2011 to 2012, Jennifer Bronson and Marcus Berzofsky (2017) examined mental health in jails and prisons. As shown in Figure 11.10, approximately one in four (26%) jail inmates and one in seven (14%) prison inmates experienced serious psychological distress in the last 30 days, compared to only 5% of the general (nonincarcerated) population. 37% of jail inmates and 44% of prison inmates had been told in the past that they had a mental health disorder. Looking at the two measures together, only 36% of jail inmates and 50% of prison inmates experienced neither psychological distress in the past 30 days nor past diagnosis.

Why Incarcerate People With Disabilities?

Why are so many people with disabilities incarcerated? To answer this question, we need a broad lens. We must consider first why the United States imprisons so many people in general. The United States imprisons a higher rate of its people than any other country in the world. According to the World Prison Brief (n.d.), in 2018 the United States incarcerated 639 per 100,000 people. The next highest countries were El Salvador (566/100,000), Turkmenistan (552), Thailand (546), Palau (522), and Rwanda (511). Countries like England and Canada were far down on the list, incarcerating 133 and 107 persons per 100,000, respectively. Looking at adults in the United States in 2018, 6,613,500 people (roughly one in 38 adults) were under correctional supervision, which includes people who are incarcerated or in programs for parole or probation (Kaeble & Cowhig, 2018).

PHOTO 11.5
Silhouette of Prison and Barbed Wire Fencing

Credit: Gatsi (2017). Reproduced with permission.

The uniquely punitive stance of the United States as compared to other Western industrialized nations demonstrates the dominance of **carceral logic**—the ideology that incarceration is an appropriate response to a wide array of social issues such as deviance, poverty, homelessness, and racial strife (Ben-Moshe, 2020; Chapman et al., 2014). As noted in previous chapters, the United States has a high rate of poverty, does not provide universal health insurance, and has a meager social safety in comparison to most European nations. Instead of providing affordable housing or housing subsidies, homelessness is often criminalized via anti-begging and anti-vagrancy laws. Instead of providing access to safe, prescribed, and affordable medication, those who self-medicate using illegal drugs face long prison sentences. This ideology supports the **Prison Industrial Complex**—the alliance between government and the private businesses that run prisons and the associated services which accrue profit from surveillance and imprisonment.

The administration and outcomes of criminal justice in the United States are also very unequal. Looking by race, White men were incarcerated at a rate of 312 per 100,000, Hispanic men at a rate of 820 per 100,000, and Black men at a rate of 1,824 per 100,000 (Carson & Anderson, 2016). Minority and poor communities are more heavily policed. Laws punish street crime more severely than White collar crime, focusing punishment on defendants from lower SES backgrounds. Moreover, the processes from arrest through sentencing (and after) are shaped by access to resources and racism, disadvantaging the least well off.

But how does disability enter in?

First, carceral logics directly target people with disabilities, intersecting with greater targeting of poor and minority communities (Ben-Moshe, 2020). From poorhouses in early America to the rise of psychiatric hospitals and institutions after the Industrial Revolution to the modern day prison, each of these settings has segregated and controlled people with disabilities (Chapman et al., 2014). Specialized institutions at times conferred treatment, but primarily they served to warehouse people with disabilities and therefore as sites of incarceration which relied on a facade of treatment (Ben-Moshe, 2020). As institutional abuses were exposed and activists demanded change, policy makers promised to rectify the abuses by creating a host of community-based services for people with disabilities. Some institutions closed, and some community services emerged, but sufficient funding was not channeled into community services. Instead, the closure of institutions coincided with the rise of mass incarceration in prisons (Ben-Moshe, 2020; Parsons, 2018). Either way—in institutions or in prison—people with disabilities have been segregated.

Second, the implementation of a carceral logic to address social problems deeply impacts people with disabilities because people with disabilities are disproportionately poor and marginalized. Let's consider the examples offered above of the criminalization of homelessness and drug use. Homelessness is criminalized through a variety of laws against loitering, vagrancy, begging, and public indecency. We know from prior chapters that people with disabilities are disproportionately poor, and we know that the stock of accessible housing is very limited and more expensive than inaccessible housing. We also know that 29% of households receiving housing subsidies have a disabled member (Sard & Alvarez-Sánchez, 2011). Because people with disabilities are disproportionately homeless, they then suffer disproportionately from the criminalization of homelessness. They are more likely to be arrested for minor offenses related to homelessness and less able to pay associated fees and bail. Similarly, we know in the absence of affordable health care, including mental health care, people with disabilities may turn to illegal drug use to self-medicate. Thus, the war on drugs disproportionately affects people with disabilities. Overall, people with mental health conditions are mostly arrested for minor violations and "nuisance crimes," such as loitering and trespassing, and subsistence crimes motivated by basic needs for food, shelter, and hygiene, not for major or violent crimes (Slate, 2017).

Third, ableism pervades the criminal justice process. If we proceed through each stage of the criminal justice process, people with disabilities are disadvantaged.

Police officers take note of people who act and move in unexpected ways. They may interpret someone with autism as someone on drugs, and someone with cerebral palsy as someone who is drunk. In interactions between the police and those suspected of a crime, people with disabilities may not act as expected, leading to arrest and, at times, police violence (Perry & Carter-Long, 2016; Moore et al., 2016). As examples, Connor Leibel, a White autistic teenager, died after an altercation with the police. Connor was walking and playing with a piece of string, and the police officer thought he was on drugs. When Connor did not respond to police orders as expected, the police officer pushed him against a tree and then forced him to the ground where he was forcibly restrained (Perry & Carter-Long, 2016; Kahn, 2018). Migdiel Sanchez, a 35-year-old Deaf Latino man, died on his own front porch when police called out to him and he did not follow orders. In a study of media reports from 2013 to 2015, David Perry and Lawrence Carter-Long (2016) found that one-third to one-half of all people killed by police had a disability.

Once arrested, people with disabilities are disproportionately poor, reducing their access to high-quality lawyers. Disabilities such as intellectual disability may diminish a defendant's understanding of Miranda rights. Juries may interpret the manifestations of disability—such as lack of eye contact or fidgeting—as evidence of the defendant's guilt. While many states have some protections for people with mental illness accused of crimes, other states have eliminated the insanity defense (Totenberg, 2020).

Once in prison, prisons are notoriously inaccessible. Counseling and educational programs, which may facilitate early release, are often not accessible. Sign language interpretation and communication technology are rare, leading deaf inmates to experience extreme isolation and longer sentences (Lewis, 2017b). Prisoners with disabilities are likely victims of abuse in prison, and they serve longer sentences than prisoners without disabilities (James & Glaze, 2006).

Finally, incarceration is itself a disabling institution. Not only are people with disabilities disproportionately represented in prison, but prisons create and exacerbate disability (Ware et al., 2014). Due to overcrowding and poor sanitation, acute infectious diseases spread rapidly. For example, infections and deaths from COVID-19 occurred at high rates in prisons (Marshall Project, 2020). Prisons also create and exacerbate mental health disorders such as depression, anxiety, and post-traumatic stress disorder. Drawing on national data of prisoners, Andrew Wilper and his colleagues (2009) found that prisoners (federal, state, and jails) had higher age-adjusted rates of many conditions, including diabetes, hypertension, heart disease, asthma, and HIV than the general population. Yet, among prisoners with chronic medical conditions, 14% of federal prisoners, 20% of state prisoners, and 68% of jail inmates had received no medical examination since incarceration. More than one in five were taking prescription medications upon entering prison/jail, but, of these, 26% of federal prisoners, 29% of state prisoners, and 42% of jail inmates stopped taking their medication. Despite these statistics documenting the inadequate care, prisons may actually provide more health care than available to the poor and marginalized in the community. Wilper and his colleagues (2009) found that mental health treatment was more common in prison/jail compared to the access individuals had in the community at the time of their arrest.

The School-to-Prison Pipeline

The **school-to-prison pipeline** refers to the policies and practices that push America's school children, especially the most at-risk children, out of classrooms and into the juvenile and criminal justice systems. In 1999, the Columbine school shooting shocked the nation, but it turned out not to be an isolated event. In the next 20 years (1999–2019), 68 school shootings occurred, and the average number of days between them decreased (Melgar, 2019). Ironically, though, although school shootings have become a part of our national consciousness, violence and victimization at schools has actually declined significantly. Between 1992 and 2013, victimization at school decreased by 70%, a trend that began well *before* the increased security presence (Robers et al., 2015).

Despite the general trend toward decreasing victimization in schools, schools around the nation hired security guards, increased police presence, and passed stricter disciplinary measures including greater use of out-of-school suspension and expulsion. Thus, schools have paralleled America's carceral logic, increasing punishment even as delinquency decreases. Also parallel, America's schools have criminalized a wide range of behaviors from fighting and drug use to skipping class and carrying aspirin, much of which used to be dealt with through in-school discipline. Inattention, acting out, and alcohol and drug use among adolescents are often tied to children's experience of poverty, family dysfunction, and other issues, yet schools increasingly channel their funding toward security rather than counseling and social programs.

Also parallel to America's criminal justice system, discipline is not meted out equally. Although most mass shootings in schools have been in White communities, the policing of children has been concentrated in inner-city schools where poor children of color reside. Disability presents another, often intersectional, form of inequality. Despite IEPs and behavioral plans, children with disabilities may be punished for disability-related behaviors and responses. According to Samantha Calero and her colleagues (2017), in the 2011–2012 school year, students with disabilities constituted 12% of the school population but 25% of those arrested and referred to law enforcement. Students with disabilities were twice as likely to receive out-of-school suspension as their nondisabled peers. Moreover, many disabilities go unidentified and unaccommodated, especially mental health and other "invisible" disabilities, and disability-related behaviors may be met with punishment instead. Minority children are disproportionately labeled as disabled, segregated by ability/disability, and subject to harsher punishments for the same violations as White children (NCD, 2018). Indeed, some scholars argue that special education plays a crucial role in channeling minority children out of the general education classroom and into the school-to-prison pipeline (Erevelles, 2014).

The consequences of the school-to-prison pipeline are significant. Students who experience out-of-school suspensions have lower graduation rates. Once in the criminal justice system, minor violations of probation such as missing school can lead to arrest. Students with arrest records then have difficulty finding a job and establishing a successful adult life.

Therapeutic Jurisprudence, Alternative Sentencing, Social Services, and Disability Justice

Alternatives to incarceration are possible. Some people suggest returning to the days of large psychiatric hospitals, but disability activists usually emphatically reject that option. Returning to large-scale institutionalization ignores the history of institutional abuse, their ineffectiveness, and the civil rights of people with disabilities.

Instead of incarceration/institutionalization, several other strategies have been proposed. Some solutions, like therapeutic jurisprudence and alternative sentencing, create options within the criminal justice system that recognize disability and seek to ensure access to treatment, rehabilitation, and support rather than punishment (Slate et al., 2013). Other approaches, such as Disability Justice and defunding/diverting funding, propose diverting money from the processes of mass incarceration to instead strengthen the safety net, social services, and health care.

Conclusion

In many ways, great strides have been made toward including people with disabilities in education. However, the education system demonstrates the continued use of segregation and the role of low expectations in blocking opportunities for people with disabilities, especially those from poor and minority communities. The prevalent use of criminal justice responses to disability even more dramatically shows that segregation and social control remain a dominant response to disability in today's society.

KEY TERMS

Carceral logic 256
Concerted cultivation 246
Criminalization 254
Cultural capital 246
Developmental mismatch 252
Inclusive education 241
Individuals with Disabilities Education Act (IDEA) 235
Institutional inertia 243
Institutional interests 243
Labeling theory 239
Overclassification 249
Prison Industrial Complex 256
Promising diagnosis 245
Racial distinctiveness 250
School-to-prison pipeline 258
Self-advocacy 251
Special education 234
Underclassification 249

RESOURCES

Scholarly articles

Chapman, Chris, Allison C. Carey, and Liat Ben-Moshe. 2014. "Reconsidering Confinement: Interlocking Locations and Logics of Incarceration." In *Disability incarcerated: Imprisonment and disability in the United States and Canada*, ed. Liat Ben-Moshe, Chris Chapman, and Allison C. Carey, 3–24. New York City: Palgrave Macmillan.

Fish, Rachel. 2019. "Standing Out and Sorting In: Exploring the Role of Racial Composition in Racial Disparities in Special Education." *American Educational Research Journal* 56, no. 6: 2573–2608.

Robinson, Shawn A. 2017. "'Me Against the World': Autoethnographic Poetry." *Disability and Society* 32, no. 5: 748–752.

Shifrer, Dara. 2013. "Learning Disabilities and Inequality." *Sociology Compass* 7/8: 656–669.

Ware, Syrus, Joan Rusza, and Dias Giselle. 2014. "It Can't Be Fixed Because It's Not Broken: Racism and Disability in the Prison Industrial Complex." In *Disability incarcerated: Imprisonment and disability in the United States and Canada*, ed. Liat Ben-Moshe, Chris Chapman, and Allison C. Carey, 164–184. New York City: Palgrave Macmillan.

Books

Alper, Meryl. 2017. *Giving voice: Mobile communication, disability, and inequality*. Cambridge, MA: MIT Press.

Ben-Moshe, Liat. 2020. *Decarcerating disability: Deinstitutionalization and prison abolition*. Minneapolis, MN: University of Minnesota Press.

Bérubé Michael. 2016. *Life as Jamie knows it: An exceptional child grows up*. Boston, MA: Beacon. (Memoir).

Leiter, Valerie. 2012. *Their time has come: Youth with disabilities on the cusp of adulthood*. New Brunswick, NJ: Rutgers University Press.

Voulgarides, Catherine Kramarczuk. 2018. *Does compliance matter in special education? IDEA and the hidden inequities of practice*. New York, NY: Teachers College Press.

Films and Videos

Deaf in Prison. 2014. BEHEARDDC. Discusses abuse and discrimination against deaf prisoners. 25 minutes. https://www.youtube.com/watch?v=AstF5kMaH_w.

Deej. 2017. Directed by Robert Rooy, Rooy Media. A documentary about DJ Savarese ("Deej"), a young adult who types on a text-to-voice synthesizer, as he makes his way through high school and his dreams of college. 72 minutes.

Intelligent Lives. 2019. Directed and produced by Dan Habib. Institute on Disability, University of New Hampshire. A documentary exploring the stories of three young adults, each of whom are navigating the transition into a variety of inclusive adult roles and settings. 70 minutes.

On the Outs: Reentry for Inmates with Disabilities. 2016. Disability Rights Washington. Follows three inmates with varied disabilities upon their release from prison. 34 minutes. https://www.youtube.com/watch?v=7WukbvDKTdk.

Rethinking the Mental Health and Criminal Justice Systems." 2019. Disability Rights Washington. Uses a specific story to discuss problems in the criminal justice system. 6 minutes. https://www.youtube.com/watch?v=tKzFfqq95QE.

ACTIVITIES

1. Watch *Intelligent Lives*. (a) Identify the varied supports/services in place that facilitate inclusion. (b) Discuss how inclusion may look different for different people, different settings, and at different life stage transitions. (c) Drawing on the film's narration, examine the reasons for the long history of educational segregation by disability.

2. Read Shawn Anthony Robinson's "Me Against the World" (full reference in resources). (a) Pull out the main points Robinson is making about his experience in special education. (b) Using the sociological imagination, situate his experience in an intersectional analysis of special education. In other words, use the text to provide a broader context to his discussion of race, segregation, and ableism in special education.

3. Read Bérubé's memoir about his son, Jamie, growing up and transitioning from special education to the adult world. (a) Where and how was Jamie included? (b) What forms of economic, social, and cultural capital did Jamie's family use to open opportunities for him? (c) What barriers to inclusion, and to a fulfilling life for Jamie, did the Jamie and his family encounter?

4. Consider each step of the criminal justice process and how people with diverse disabilities may experience disadvantage.

5. Consider how social control and segregation become part of each social response to disability (health care, social services and benefits, education, criminal justice). Consider how each contributes to inequality by race. What does social equality and justice look like for people with disabilities and how might we attain it?

CHAPTER 12

Social Movements and Social Change

Learning Outcomes

12.1 Identify examples of social change and stasis in the social experience of disability.

12.2 Apply sociological theories of social movements to explain the rise of disability activism and the tactics used.

12.3 Examine how people become activists and the barriers to activism.

12.4 Explain how change may occur even in the absence of activism, and how inequality may persist despite activism.

Chapter Synopsis

In this last chapter, we examine the factors shaping social change and stasis. Much of the chapter is dedicated to disability activism, explaining why social movements arise, their tactics, and their impacts. We then briefly discuss other structural factors that cause change, and why, in the face of so much change, issues like the high rate of poverty among people with disabilities remain resistant to change.

Introduction

Disability history is filled with remarkable transformations; however, statistics also reveal persistent systemic inequalities. Indeed, both trends—tremendous social change *and* the persistence of grave inequality—are true over time. In this chapter, we provide an overview of some of the major sources of change. We first examine disability activism using sociological theories of social movements. Then, we consider broader causes of social change such as technology and culture. Finally, we consider the idea of stasis and why some patterns endure across time.

Examples of Social Change and Stasis

Sociologists are deeply concerned with why certain aspects of societies change, as well as **stasis**-stability over time. Disability has changed tremendously over time. Some examples of major areas of change include the following:

- Definitions and the prevalence of disability—Some diseases and disabilities have been eradicated or are now curable. For example, cataracts, which used to be a disabling vision impairment, often now can be cured. Some phenomena, such as acne, wrinkles, weight, anxiety, and depression, have been medicalized and are now treated as medical "conditions." And other phenomena medicalized in the past—like same-sex sexual attraction—are no longer seen as medical conditions.
- Identities and lived experiences—Before the 1970s, people with varied impairments did not commonly see themselves as a collective group. Now, vibrant disability communities engage in collective activism, art, and intellectual enterprises.
- Disability policy—Prior to the 1970s, disability policy focused on institutionalization, vocational rehabilitation, and the provision of benefits. People with disabilities were often viewed as objects of pity and charity. In the latter twentieth century, policies shifted toward community-based services, disability rights, and accessibility.

Despite these changes, much has remained consistent over time.

- Poverty and economic marginalization—Despite the passage of the Americans with Disabilities Act (ADA), people with disabilities continue to be disproportionately poor.
- Cultural devaluation and stigma—Many people continue to imagine that the world would be better without disability in it. *Compulsory ablebodiedness*—the intense pressure to erase or minimize disability and attain the socially determined expectations regarding normalcy and productivity—remains a central experience in the lives of many people with disabilities.
- Policy barriers and second-class citizenship—Despite much legal progress, people with disabilities face policy barriers to, among other things, immigration, marriage, parenting, working, and moving across state lines and even to different counties without losing services.

Explaining Social Change: Social Movements and Disability Activism

How do sociologists explain social change? Here we look at the role of activism and social movements in creating change. The next section will then turn to broader factors contributing to social change including economic change, cultural diffusion, and technology.

The Disability Rights Movement and Disability Activism

Some social change is provoked by **activism**—intentional action directed toward creating social change. Activism may be individual or collective, although sociologists often focus on collective organizing.

Historically, many of the activists who focused on disability-related issues were nondisabled professionals and family members. Instead of supporting people with disabilities, some early activism focused on imposing the segregation and social control of people with disabilities. For example, the proponents of *eugenics*—a movement to improve population quality—advocated for legislation to allow compulsory sterilization and prevent immigration among those deemed "unfit" (Kline, 2005; Trent, 1994). Others, though, fought to improve the quality of life experienced by people with disabilities. For example, parent activism grew substantially in the 1950s and 1960s. They tended to focus on the development and funding of services for people with congenital and developmental disabilities (Carey et al., 2020). Parents created many of today's largest nonprofit disability organizations, including The Arc, the National Alliance on Mental Illness (NAMI), and United Cerebral Palsy (UCP). Over time, some parent-led organizations incorporated civil rights for people with disabilities into their mission, and parents continue to be important in disability activism today.

While professionals and parents have been involved in disability activism for a long time, the heart of modern disability activism is led by people with disabilities. Single-disability organizations and movements tended to emerge first. The Deaf community and the blind community were among the first to engage in activism for their respective populations; the National Association of the Deaf formed in 1880 and the National Federation of the Blind in 1940 (Fleischer & Zames, 2011; Nielsen, 2012). People with physical disabilities organized in 1935 into the League of the Physically Handicapped to protest discrimination in employment policy. Other movements grew as well. For example, the **psychiatric survivor movement** criticizes psychiatric professions and presents patients and ex-patients as survivors of an oppressive system that uses confinement and abuse (e.g., electroshock therapy, overmedication) with impunity. Psychiatric survivors argue that, instead of damaging therapies, people instead need their basic human and civil rights recognized (Pelka, 2012). **Self-advocacy movements** emerged among people with intellectual disabilities and, separately, autistics who have fought to wrest control of policy and practices from professionals and parents and, instead, to exercise control over their own lives.

Over time, activism shifted from single-disability activism toward cross-disability activism. For example, the American Coalition of Citizens with Disabilities was founded in 1975 to foster cooperation and organizing across various disability groups. Dr. Frank Bowe, the first executive director, explained, "Instead of fighting over each group's slice of the pie, it made more sense for us as a group to fight for a larger pie…" (Pelka, 2012, p. 248). The Disability Rights Education and Defense Fund, founded in 1979, is a national-level, cross-disability law and policy center focused on ensuring the civil rights of disabled people. And, the American Association of People With Disabilities describes itself as a "convener, connector, and catalyst for change, increasing the political and economic power of people with disabilities" (American Association of People With Disabilities, n.d.).

Scholars often group these organizations and movements into the Disability Rights Movement. **The Disability Rights Movement** encompasses many loosely aligned organizations and movements within a decentralized structure, all fighting to improve the lived experience of people with disabilities (Charlton, 2000; Fleischer & Zames, 2011). As noted, the organizations vary. They may target a single disability or work across disabilities; they may pursue services, rights, justice, or other issues; they may be local, state-level, national, or international in scope; they may limit their tactics to legitimate channels of political influence, while others engage in civil disobedience and radical protest (Charlton, 2000; Barnartt & Scotch, 2001). These organizations at times work independently and, at other times, they build alliances to work toward shared goals (Van Dyke & McCammon, 2010; Zald & McCarthy, 1997).

While not cohesive, several common goals encouraged collaboration across disability organizations, including the following (Charlton, 2000; Longmore, 2003b; Nielsen, 2012; Pelka, 2012):

- "Nothing About Us Without Us"—people with disabilities should be empowered to live self-determined lives and have a voice in decisions affecting their lives.
- Civil and human rights—people with disabilities, individually and collectively, should enjoy the full range of civil and human rights.
- Social reform, accessibility, and inclusivity—vast social changes must occur in attitudes, policies, law, and physical structures for people with disabilities to fully participate in society.

Most Americans have little awareness of disability activism, but they are aware of its outcomes. Indeed, disability activism has been very successful in some ways. It fostered deinstitutionalization, the funding of community-based services, and the passage of many pieces of legislation securing accessibility and rights for people with disabilities. The *Americans with Disabilities Act of 1990* (ADA), which prohibits discrimination based on disability and mandates public accessibility, is often considered its crowning achievement.

Increasingly, disability activists resist the focus on rights and instead use a justice or liberation framework. *Disability Justice* activists focus their activism on challenging the overlapping systems of oppression such as racism, poverty, and colonialism that feed into and off of ableism. They tend to be explicitly critical of capitalism and neoliberal policies that devalue people with bodies and minds that do not conform to the interests of capitalists, and instead they call for policies and practices that position all people as inherently valuable. Disability justice prioritizes the leadership, perspectives, and needs of those most marginalized, especially people who experience multiple forms of oppression. Embracing the interdependence and creativity common in disability communities, they call for a reorganization of social policy and institutions in ways that value, include, empower, and support the most vulnerable (Berne, 2015; Mingus, 2017; Piepzna-Samarasinha, 2018).

The Emergence of the Disability Activism

Examples of disability activism can be found through history, but disability activism led by people with disabilities blossomed in the 1970s. Why the 1970s?

To casual observers, it seems like movements arise when people share a grievance. Clearly though, that explanation alone does not suffice. People with disabilities experienced marginalization before the 1970s, but a large-scale, effective, collective movement did not emerge until then. In fact, overwhelming oppression—such as when the state is repressive, poverty and violence threaten survival, and stigma devalues one's humanity—often hinders effective collective activism (Morrison, 1971).

Rather than rising from the individual experience of oppression alone, social movements arise when there are certain social elements present. We will draw on sociological theories of social movements to examine four relevant elements: a frame identifying a collective problem with a collective solution, the availability of political opportunities, a sense of collective identity, and the mobilization of resources.

Social Movement Frames. In the social movement literature, a **frame** refers to the ways in which social movements construct meaning to identify particular problems, explain those problems, and advocate particular solutions (Snow, 2013; Snow et al., 1986). The emergence of the Disability Rights Movement was in part due to the success of other rights movements, particularly the Civil Rights Movement led by Black activists. Disability activists drew on and adapted the civil rights frame for their own purposes (Charlton, 2000; Fleischer & Zames, 2011; Scotch, 1984). In contrast to seeing disability as a personal tragedy, the **civil rights frame** reimagined the problems of disability as resulting from a system of oppression which denied people with disabilities rights and opportunities and proposed that the solution to disability oppression was the eradication of ableism and the establishment of disability rights. This frame served to unite people across different impairments. Although a blind person may not have the same needs or skills as a person with a mental disability, they both suffer from stigma and discrimination. The civil rights frame focused their collective energies on securing rights and access.

Political opportunity. Political opportunity theory argues that movements tend to flourish when the political structure is open to or vulnerable to change (McAdam, 1982, 1996). Through the mid to late-1900s, frustration regarding disability policy grew. The public cost of institutions grew, while exposé after exposé revealed shocking neglect and abuse experienced by people with disabilities in institutions. The cost of public benefit programs also grew, as inaccessibility and lack of opportunity barred the path to self-sufficiency. This situation troubled politicians in both the Democratic and Republican parties. Democrats wanted to ensure equity, rights, and human dignity. Republicans wanted to minimize government benefits and provide opportunities for people to become self-supporting. Thus, across the political aisle, both parties saw the potential value of providing rights to people with disabilities. According to sociologist David Pettinicchio (2019), state officials, ahead of and largely independent of activists, passed early rights legislation such as the Architectural Barriers Act and Section 504 of the 1973 Vocational Rehabilitation Act (see too Davis, 2015; Scotch, 1984).

Section 504 offers a particularly interesting example of legislative change. The 1973 Rehabilitation Act was designed to fund vocational rehabilitation, and a few Congressional staffers inserted language prohibiting discrimination on the basis of disability—which became Section 504—because they believed that vocational rehabilitation would be more successful if disabled people experienced greater accessibility and opportunity in the workplace. Sociologist Richard Scotch notes that "Although its importance to millions of Americans is now evident, Section 504 began as an inconspicuous segment of routine legislation" (1984, p. 3).

Supportive politicians played a key role in advancing disability policy throughout American history. President Franklin Delano Roosevelt, a polio survivor, established Social Security in 1935, which protected older Americans (many of whom have disabilities) from poverty. John F. Kennedy, whose sister had an intellectual disability, helped bring the idea of civil rights for people with intellectual disabilities to the forefront of national policy. And, George H. W. Bush supported the 1990 Americans with Disabilities Act as part of his platform of "compassionate conservatism," a Republican ideal of helping people become self-supporting (Davis, 2015; Pettinicchio, 2019).

In addition to opening opportunities for the passage of legislation, some politicians actually fostered activist involvement and the growth of disability organizations (Pettinicchio, 2019; Scotch, 1984). Beginning in the 1970s, the federal government funded training and technical assistance programs for disabled activists. Politicians invited people with disabilities to review drafts and to serve as a channel of communication between the government and constituencies of disabled citizens. Moreover, legislation referring to "people with disabilities" encouraged people with diverse disabilities to see themselves as a collective and to collectively promote and defend their rights. Civil rights legislation in effect helped create the disability identity.

These examples do not mean that all politicians were supportive of disability rights, however. As we know, politicians hold diverse beliefs. Many politicians resisted mandates for accessibility and rights. They saw disability rights as costly and burdensome for employers, public service providers, transportation systems, and others. Indeed, the passage of disability rights legislation led to a political **backlash**—a political countermovement intended to dismantle disability rights and ensure their impotency (Krieger, 2003; Pettinicchio, 2019). State resistance, though, tended to further energize disabled activists and gave them a target to protest. Thus, disability activism developed in response to both state encouragement and resistance.

To show this effect, we will continue with the example of Section 504. Although the Nixon administration passed the 1973 Vocational Rehabilitation Act including Section 504, it refused to publish regulations. Regulations provide guidelines for interpreting, implementing, and enforcing the law. Without the regulations, Section 504 was just a symbolic nod expressing the value of rights, but it had little real impact. Years passed without regulations. Armed with rights legislation but denied the regulations, activists organized. When the Carter administration came into office, activists demanded regulations. Soon after, in April 1977, they organized the **504 sit-ins** at the department offices of Health, Education and Welfare (HEW) in several cities. In San Francisco, Judy Heumann and others led a sit-in that lasted 25 days, setting a record for the longest sit-in at a federal building (Fleischer & Zames, 2011; Heumann & Joiner, 2020; Pelka, 2012). Thus, support from some political actors opened opportunities for disabled activists to demand their rights, while resistance from other political actors energized activists and created a target for their protests (Pettinicchio, 2019).

PHOTO 12.1 President Bush Signing the 1990 Americans with Disabilities Act

Credit: "President Bush Signing the Americans with Disabilities Act, July 26, 1990" Photograph by George Bush Presidential Library and Museum. Obtained from Wikimedia Commons. https://commons.wikimedia.org/wiki/File:Bush_signs_ADA.jpg

Constructing a collective identity. Movements rely on people working to-gether, and this requires a collective identity and an oppositional (or critical) consciousness. **Collective identity** involves a sense of belonging to a group (Taylor & Whittier 1999; Snow & Corrigall-Brown, 2015). As part of the group, activi-sts often gain an **oppositional consciousness**—the framing of an individuals' experiences as a collective phenomenon of shared oppression best addressed through challenging the status quo (Barnartt & Scotch, 2001; Groch, 1994; Mansbridge, 2001). For people with disabilities, the collective identity and oppositional consciousness achieved through engaging in activism often transformed their prior views from disability as tragedy to disability as oppression (Darling, 2013). The 504 sit-ins, for example, cultivated a collective identity rooted in the shared experience of ableism and a sense of political efficacy among participants, many of whom had experienced social isolation and dependence (Fleischer & Zames, 2011; Pelka, 2012). Activist Kitty Cone recalled a young girl who participated in the 504 sit-ins. She had always been ridiculed for her use of crutches, and she longed to be beautiful, which in her mind meant no longer needing her crutches. After bonding with other disabled activists and recognizing her own political power, though, she said, "I've always wanted to be beautiful, but now I know I *am* beautiful" (Pelka, 2012, p. 276). Cone explained that the 504 sit-ins were a transformational experience for many participants who now felt powerful and proud of themselves *as* disabled people, not *in spite of* their disability (Pelka, 2012, p. 282).

Resource mobilization theory. Resource Mobilization Theory argues that social movements tend to be successful to the extent that they effectively gather and deploy resources, including funding, members, and political support (McCarthy & Zald, 1977). People with disabilities are disproportionately poor and socially marginalized, which hinders their social activism. That said, disabled activists have marshalled significant resources. Some leaders, like Justin Dart, who is best known for his leadership role in achieving the passage of the ADA, had extensive personal resources. Dart came from a wealthy family with connections to Ronald Regan and George Bush, and he used his personal economic and political capital to advance disability rights. Other activists used varied strategies to gather key resources.

One key way to mobilize resources is to use the media. For example, in the 1990 "Capitol Crawl" about 60 disabled activists crawled up the steps of the nation's Capitol building. This dramatic display vividly enacted the consequences of inaccessibility and the painstaking work required of people with disabilities to achieve basic access to their own elected officials. It achieved national media coverage and raised awareness of the fight to pass the ADA.

Alliance-building is another way to secure resources (Carey et al., 2020). Common allies of disabled activists include veterans, parents of children with disabilities, older people, minority communities, and LGBTQ+ communities, as well as organizations focused on particular issues such as civil rights, health care, and poverty policy (Barnartt, 2020).

Tactics of Disability Activism

The scope of tactics that fall within activism is quite broad. It includes activities like participating in rallies and marching, signing a petition, writing a blog advocating a political position, communicating with political representations regarding a social issue, or even just speaking up for oneself or others. We will discuss in-system tactics, contentious tactics, disability culture, and the idea of existence as resistance.

In-system tactics are those that use conventional social and political channels of influence. One of the most common is the awareness campaign. For example, organizations led by professionals developed telethons and poster child campaigns designed to raise awareness and money by provoking sympathy for children with disabilities (Longmore, 2016). In contrast, disabled activists tend to reject appeals based on pity and instead raise awareness of the abilities of people with disabilities and the pressing need for rights, opportunities, and accessibility (Lisicki, 2018). Other in-system tactics include, for example, political lobbying and the use of the legal system. Court cases played a key role in fighting for rights and were especially important in deinstitutionalization and securing the right to education.

Contentious tactics are those that provoke conflict or cause disruption in the lives of those in the opposition. These tactics include, as examples, rallies, marches, sit-ins, and boycotts. Although they are often seen as "illegitimate" tactics, many are now legally recognized and increasingly common. For example, groups can now apply for permits to march or protest, and these tactics are now part of mainstream activism. Between 2016 and 2018, one in five Americans protested in the streets or attended a rally, 19% of whom had never done so before (Jordan & Clement, 2018).

Sociologists studying social movements have found that protest and other contentious tactics may increase the likely success of the movement (Gamson, 1990; Piven & Cloward, 1971). This may seem counter-intuitive, but disruptive tactics draw media attention, create unpleasant conditions for dominant groups, and make working with less disruptive groups more appealing. Disruptive groups therefore may shift the conversation and make compromise

PHOTO 12.2
Disability Activists

Credit: "The celebration of the 20th anniversary of the ADA brought several attendees." Photograph by Oregon Department of Transportation (2008). Obtained from Wikimedia Commons. https://commons.wikimedia.org/wiki/File:Celebration_attendees_(4863686300).jpg

with moderate groups appealing. Once contentious tactics become common, though, their effectiveness may decline (Barnartt & Scotch, 2001).

Sociologists Sharon Barnartt and Richard Scotch (2001) studied disability protests dating from 1970 to 1999. They found that 45% of protests focused on demands related to disability services, including ending forced treatment for mental illness, ending electroshock therapy, resisting cuts to Medicaid and disability benefits, and demanding funding for personal assistance in the community. Forty-one percent of protests focused on rights, including accessibility in public transportation, accessibility in buildings and programs, and laws such as Section 504 and the ADA. Disability protests tended to be nonviolent, and arrests occurred at 35% of the protests. The typical protest involved a large group of people gathered near government buildings, carrying signs and chanting. Even with relatively little disruption, disability protests attracted media attention. The cultural predisposition to feel sympathy for people with disabilities and the media interest in covering disability protests may lend to their success even without causing major disruption. The majority of protests were not immediately successful in attaining their short-term goals. In the long run, however, disability protests likely had positive impacts such as encouraging the growth of disability activism, raising the public consciousness of disability issues, and helping to change the image of people with disabilities.

Disability Culture offers another type of tactic to promote social change. Paul Longmore (2003) referred to disability culture as the "second phase" of the Disability Rights Movement. He argued that rights legislation would not be sufficient to transform the cultural disregard for people with disabilities. Cultural transformation would require disabled artists, writers, comedians, and others to express and explain the disability perspective. Engagement with disability culture—such as watching *Crip Camp* on Netflix, reading Alice Wong's blog about Disability Visibility (https://disabilityvisibilityproject.com/about/), or seeing Sins Invalid perform—may challenge prejudices and increase understanding about disability. Disability culture also raises the critical consciousness of people with disabilities. In his book, *Black Disabled Art History 101*, artist Leroy Moore Jr. recalls discovering disabled artists and musicians, saying "I didn't realize it then, but these records gave me the strength to face teachers and other adults who constantly told me that there were no artists who were Black and disabled like me" (2017, pp. 1–3).

"Existence Is Resistance" is the fourth type of tactic we will discuss. The saying "Existence is Resistance" (Egner, 2018; Wong, 2017) argues that, in a world that demeans people with disabilities and seeks to eradicate them, everyday actions—such as proudly claiming disability, demanding accommodations, resisting compulsory ablebodiedness, admitting vulnerability, expressing sexuality, providing care to each other, loving oneself and each other, and living every day - all become acts of resistance (Piepzna-Samarasinha, 2018; Wood, 2014). The visible presence of disabled people in the world is itself an act of resistance (Mingus, 2017; Wong, 2020). This sensibility that survival itself is resistance is heightened for people in intersecting marginalized communities, such as LGBTQ+, indigenous, and African-American disabled persons (Caldwell, 2010).

Becoming a Disability Activist

Ed Roberts and Judy Heumann offer two examples of early leaders in disability activism. **Ed Roberts** is considered one of the founders of the Independent Living Movement. Roberts became a quadriplegic due to polio, and he used a large machine—referred to as an iron lung—to assist him with breathing. Despite his academic qualifications, he had to fight to attend the University of California at Berkeley. Once admitted, the administration required Roberts to reside in the university health center rather than the dorms. Alongside other activists, Roberts helped to establish UC Berkeley's Physically Disabled Students Program and the broader Independent Living Movement (Nielsen, 2012). The **Independent Living Movement** seeks to ensure that people with disabilities have the resources, services, and supports necessary to live valued lives in the community and to retain maximal control over their own lives (Pelka, 2012). From this small beginning, there are now over 400 Centers for Independent Living throughout the United States (National Council on Independent Living, n.d.). Roberts' success demonstrated that people with significant disabilities could work, marry, and live fulfilling lives.

Judy Heumann also encountered disability discrimination, including the denial of her teacher's license because she used a wheelchair (Heumann, 2020). She sued and won. Beyond her personal success, Heumann and others formed **Disabled in Action** in 1970, an organization with a mission to fight against disability discrimination and for the full rights of disabled people. Disabled in Action gained notoriety for using protest tactics, such as their participation in the *504 sit-ins* to ensure that regulations for the 1973 Rehabilitation Act were established (Heumann, 2020; Pelka, 2012). Heumann came to represent an emboldened disability community, aware of their own power and effective at wielding it. Both Roberts and Heumann initially were **charismatic leaders**—leaders who exercise authority because they are seen by others as exceptional and worthy of being followed (Weber, [1922] 1968). They then built organizations and took on leadership roles in organizations that reinforced their authority as representatives of disability communities. While just two examples of leaders in disability activism, both Roberts and Heumann transformed what might have been seen as a personal tragedy into a collective fight against disability discrimination.

Leadership studies often focuses on the individual attributes of leaders, but sociologists also look at the deeper, structural factors that encourage or discourage activism. As already noted, the experience of oppression does not always lead to activism. What factors encourage people to become activists? While many factors come into play, we will focus on two: network connections and resources. Sociologists have found that network connections to activists play a key role in becoming an activist. These connections may be a product of "push-pull" factors. In her study of parent activists, sociologist Rosalyn Darling (1988) found that parents of children with disabilities confronted myriad problems for which they had little preparation. They had medical worries, faced uncooperative school officials, and lacked access to the services needed for their children to thrive. Parents often turned first to their networks established prior to disability, but their extended family, friends, and doctors were often not helpful, or even unsupportive. This *pushed* them away from their already established networks. Instead, they were *pulled* toward new sources of information and assistance, often toward other parents of disabled children fighting for services. In these new networks, parents could comfortably share their concerns, find acknowledgment, and learn useful information such as what laws existed, which professionals were best to work with, and how to advocate for services. For many parents, their activism only focused on their own family's needs. For others, though, they built activist careers and engaged in activism beyond the scope of their own family's needs and interests (Jones, 2010; Panitch, 2008).

Network connections also play a vital role for activists with disabilities. In his memoir *Lost in a Desert World* (2002), Roland Johnson describes his path to self-advocacy. Johnson was institutionalized as a child. When he was released, he worked at a sheltered workshop. Someone he knew from the workshop handed him a flyer and suggested he attend a conference on self-advocacy. He went and, for the first time, heard people with disabilities talking about changing the system. He met activists and others who helped him build self-advocacy skills. Before long, Johnson started talking publicly about the devastating impact of institutionalization. People with and without disabilities mentored him, helping him build his skills in leadership and advocacy.

Network connections are most effective for activism when they occur in free spaces controlled by people with disabilities (Groch, 2001), rather than spaces controlled by nondisabled people. For example, Deaf culture and activism often took root in Deaf residential schools led by Deaf administrators and Deaf teachers. These schools brought deaf children together for the first time into an ASL-rich environment where they could develop their political identity and oppositional consciousness. As another example, the Rolling Quads, placed together in the health center at UC Berkeley with minimal supervision or social control, developed friendships and hatched their plans for activism. In contrast, people in institutions for intellectual and mental disabilities faced almost complete domination by nondisabled staff, had few rights, received little to no education, feared sexual and physical abuse, and had little access to the outside world. These conditions shut down most opportunities for self-advocacy.

PHOTO 12.3
Self-advocate Roland Johnson, With President Bush

Credit: Wikimedia Commons

In addition to connections and control of one's space, a range of resources enable activism. People with education, money, time, and access to travel, for example, have more opportunities to engage in activism. Education enables one to articulate pressing concerns, to assess possible solutions, and to engage in activist strategies like writing an opinion piece or testifying at a public hearing. Access to technology and social media offers new opportunities for organizing that may be particularly valuable for people who often experience social isolation and inaccessibility. The potential of social media to foster activism has expanded greatly as posts go "viral" and people "follow" disability activists and organizations with the click of a button. While resources open opportunities for activism, many people with disabilities lack access to basic resources, and therefore these resources become a barrier rather than an opportunity.

Barriers to Activism

The Disability Rights Movement has been very successful, but there are significant barriers to activism for people with disabilities (Scotch, 1988). These include, among others:

- People with disabilities experience considerable social and political isolation. Since networks are one of the key paths into activism, social isolation hinders this path.
- People with disabilities also on average have lower incomes and less education. This makes it harder to join organizations with membership dues, travel to events, take time to engage in politics, and understand and articulate positions on complex social issues.
- Physical inaccessibility limits travel and attendance at meetings. Events held in people's homes may be particularly inaccessible.
- Due to stigma, many people resist identifying as disabled, which undercuts the potential for collective action.

As a brief exercise, consider the barriers to engaging in collective protest. Protests require travel, but not all people with disabilities have freedom of movement, and parents or staff may decide against allowing participation. Travel also requires funding and accessible transportation, which may or may not be available. Once at the protest, participants often must stand for long periods of time and march. The route may or may not be fully wheelchair accessible. The availability of accessible bathrooms and places to rest is not guaranteed. The threat of arrest or violence is daunting if one relies on personal assistance, technology, and/or medication. Protest organizations do not always provide ASL interpretation or other accommodations that would support active participation in the protest. Thus, access to the range of activism tactics is potentially limited, and therefore the likelihood that one may develop an identity as an activist may also be hindered.

Inequality in Activism

Because activism is based on access to human and social capital, social movements are themselves often unequal and lead to unequal benefits. Several forms of inequality are evident in disability activism. One form of inequality is based on type of disability. The Disability Rights Movement often positioned people with physical and sensory disabilities as the leaders of the movement, too often leaving people with intellectual and mental disabilities and chronic illnesses behind. This inequality leads to several consequences. In demanding civil rights, activists with physical and sensory disabilities may assert that they are just as intelligent and rational as other citizens and therefore deserve rights. This argument is compelling, but what does it mean for people who experience limitations in intelligence and/or rationality? Are they undeserving of rights? As another example, more attention has been paid to physical accessibility than to intellectual or emotional accessibility. The international accessibility symbol features a wheelchair, prioritizing physical disability and access (Ben-Moshe & Powell, 2007). Thus, people with intellectual and mental disabilities may feel excluded and even stigmatized by activists with physical disabilities and the focus on physical access (Pelka, 2012).

Intersections with race, class, and other axes of privilege/oppression constitute another type of inequality. White, educated, middle or upper class, heterosexual people have often positioned themselves as leaders of the Disability Rights Movement, which again leads to certain consequences. Their demands for access and inclusion may be based on other forms of privilege. For example, White, middle-class parents at times based their demands for education and community services for their children on their own status as "good, tax-paying citizens." While successful in building sympathy, this framing stigmatizes and excludes poor and immigrant families (Carey, 2009). Furthermore, White disabled leaders too often disregard leadership by people of color and the need to confront the ways ableism intersects with racism, heterosexism, and other forms of oppression (Berne, 2015; Erkulwater, 2018; Moore et al., 2016). Instead, they often focus on disability, as if race, class, gender, and sexuality are tangential. Describing the Center for Independent Living (CIL) at Berkeley in the 1970s, Corbett OToole (2015) explains that White activists focused on achieving accessibility, but in doing so, they ignored the range of access needs across diverse populations. She writes, "While the local independent living center fought hard for access to the library, they rarely fought for access to a battered women's shelter or for interpreters for the Gay Pride Parade and English-as-a-second-language classes. Many disabled people of color and disabled queers were left on their own to fight for their access rights" (2015, p. 101).

The focus on rights itself has been critiqued as catering to middle-class and well-educated people with disabilities. Rights are of course important, but to formally claim rights one needs access to the legal system and a lawyer. As seen in Chapter 11, not only are privileged families more successful in pursuing disability rights in education, but schools in higher-SES neighborhoods tend to offer more accommodations. White, disabled leaders often overlook the fact that disability communities further marginalized by race, poverty, and other factors face specific and intersectional barriers such as poor educational systems and prejudice. The Disability Rights Movement has provided the greatest opportunities to those most easily integrated into society, while minimizing, or even ignoring, the pressing needs of people who have complex medical needs, need extensive supports, and/or belong to communities impacted by multiple vectors of oppression (Berne, 2015; Fritsch, 2013; Mingus, 2017; Russell, 1998).

Inequality also pervades alliances with nondisabled groups. Alliance-building is a beneficial strategy for many social movements, because it increases access to resources while also connecting to and raising awareness among new populations (Carey et al., 2021). In disability activism though, allies often have more power and resources than disabled activists do, which both opens opportunities and poses risks. Allies with more power may shape the goals, message, and tactics of the movement, in effect undercutting the leadership of disabled activists (Russell & Bohan, 2016). For example, parents can be useful and effective allies in disability activism. They bring considerable resources and symbolic authority to the fight. However, they also tend to see themselves as not only allies but as leaders in disability activism, and their leadership may subvert the self-determination and empowerment of people with disabilities (Carey et al., 2019, 2020; McGuire, 2016; Rottier & Gernsbacher, 2020). Scholars and researchers are also important allies. They may conduct research valuable to achieving social change, contribute expertise, and connect activists with the substantial resources of universities and research institutes (Pombier, 2020). However, scholars may have their own priorities that complicate alliances, like the desire to pursue grant funding and to publish in academic journals. People with disabilities who are not academics may not have access to peer-reviewed articles and they may not benefit from academic research (Barnes, 2008). Nondisabled allies may also act in deeply ableist ways. For example, civil rights and feminist organizations may not provide sufficient accessibility or they may invite a token-disabled leader for symbolic diversity rather than truly committing to disability rights and justice. Thus, disability organizations may struggle to balance the needs of their disabled members with the desire to work with potential allies (Gillespie-Lynch et al., 2020; Piepzna-Samarasinha, 2018; Moore et al., 2016). Overall, disability activism strives to challenge inequality, but inequality creates barriers to activism, and disability activists and their allies are susceptible to reproducing inequality.

The Never-Ending Cycle of Activism

A final point about disability activism—it is a continual cycle. The passage of legislation is not an end point. Rather, it launches a cycle in which activists must fight to translate laws into actual social changes. This may include raising awareness about a new law, working with local organizations to help make changes in communities, and suing when people refuse to recognize their rights. Political backlash is common. Cuts to funding, unfriendly court decisions, and threats of legislative changes pose constant risks. Thus, disability activists must remain ever vigilant and engaged, continually fighting for and defending their rights (Davis, 2015; Krieger, 2003; Pettinicchio, 2019).

Global Focus: Disability Activism in China

The passage of the ADA in 1990 and the 2006 United Nation Convention on the Rights of Persons with Disabilities (CRPD) helped foster a global "disability revolution" as nations around the world shifted their disability policy to focus on rights (Heyer, 2015). International nongovernmental organizations (NGOs) based largely in the West funded global training and advocacy to spread the rights model and foster local activism around the globe (Charlton, 2000).

Transplanting a Western model of disability rights in myriad countries with different government systems, economic opportunities, and cultures, though, has been a challenge. Here drawing most directly on research by Shixin Huang (2019, 2020), we look briefly at the development of disability rights activism in China. China's population includes more than 83 million people with disabilities. Twenty-one percent live below the poverty line, and almost half are illiterate (Huang, 2020). China's disabled population faces stigma, rampant discrimination and inaccessibility, and a school system that still segregates and excludes children with disabilities.

Transnational advocacy organizations serve an important role in encouraging rights activism in China by providing training and funding (Huang, 2020). Grassroots disability advocacy organizations grew, and their activism yielded some results, including a 2015 national mandate to provide reasonable accommodations on the national college entrance exam.

(Continued)

Global Focus: Disability Activism in China (Continued)

However, the growth and efficacy of disability activism in China has been hindered by several factors. First, China's authoritarian government exerts significant control over how and if its citizens can organize. Activists protesting the Chinese government risk long-term imprisonment and state violence. A 2016 law prohibited Chinese individuals and organizations from accepting funding from overseas NGOs, essentially blocking a key funding source (Huang, 2019). Second, the successes of rights activism tend to be narrow and undercut by broader structural inequalities. For example, although students gained the right to reasonable accommodations on the college entrance exam, it did not change the system of segregated education prior to the exam, so most students with disabilities are not prepared for the exam. Nor are universities required to accept students with disabilities or provide accommodations once a student is enrolled. Not surprisingly then, a very small number of students with disabilities have taken the college entrance exam (Ma & Ni, 2020).

Furthermore, the everyday problems of poverty and exclusion are not necessarily best dealt with through rights activism. As a disability rights activist explained to Huang, "In 2012, I went to a remote village in the countryside to deliver a disability awareness training. In the training I was challenged by a disabled farmer in that village. He said, 'Do not talk about rights and awareness to me! Can rights buy me rice and oil?' From then on, I started to realize that the rights that I was talking about cannot solve people's everyday life challenges. I even asked myself, 'Why am I doing this job?'" (2020, p. 30). Western models of civil and political rights that leave unaddressed economic and social rights (e.g. rights to a minimum income, to work, to education, and to health care) too often fail to provide the means for people to actually thrive in society (Charlton, 2001; Huang, 2020).

This is not to argue that disability activism has had no positive impact in China. Services are increasingly delivered with rights-models in mind and empower people with disabilities in their everyday lives (Huang, 2019). People's awareness that they may hold rights has increased (Huang, 2019). Despite this shift toward disability rights, though, most disabled people remain poor and marginalized.

Structural Change and Stasis

Some changes in disability have resulted from purposeful efforts by individuals and organizations to create change. Many of the changes through time, though, resulted from structural shifts that often had little to do with disability activism. As systems change, they often cause both anticipated and unanticipated changes in other systems. A full discussion of structural changes and their effects on disability is beyond the scope of this book. Here, instead, we briefly present a few examples of broad social changes in the economy, technology, and culture to illustrate the ways in which changes in one social structure may have unanticipated consequences for disability. We then similarly discuss how the persistence of structural factors preserves ableism despite activists' efforts to challenge it.

Structural Changes

According to *materialist theories*, the economy and the resources we need to survive (our material environment) shape our social relationships, culture, and disability. Without directed activism or purposeful action regarding disability, the economic shift from agriculture to capitalism radically transformed the meaning of and response to disability (Oliver, 1990; Russell, 1998; Scull, 2015). In capitalism, the economy is driven by profit, the speed and efficiency of workers become paramount, and disability becomes seen as a threat to profit. Workers leave their families to work among strangers who hold no moral obligations toward them. They also leave behind family members who need care, who increasingly are positioned as "burdens." Health care itself becomes a commodity out of reach for many Americans. Profits are made by marketing new ailments and drugs to cure them, while ignoring the basic health needs of those without health insurance. Many of the changes in disability can be seen as a by-product of the rise of capitalism.

Other shifts in the material environment also have an impact on disability. Technology is one of the most important. Technology has the capacity for both uplift and oppression. New technologies, such as speech-to-text software and chirping crosswalk signals, have improved access. Technology has expanded opportunities to work from home and to network with people across vast distances. More problematic, though, technology has created the potential for great inequality as some people have more money and skills to benefit from technology, and as technology itself creates new forms of inaccessibility. Given the **digital divide**—the gap in access to and use of technology—many people with disabilities are left behind in the technological revolution.

Cultural shifts also impact disability, even when they are not primarily focused on disability. For example, Emile Durkheim (2014 [1893]) was one of the first sociologists to argue that, in a modern society with a high division of labor, respect for diversity would grow. In essence, if society wants people to do different work across the industrialized economy, it must allow them to be different. The growing value placed on diversity provides a cultural opportunity for disability activism as people embrace the advantages of diverse bodies and minds. However, the appreciation for diversity is largely tied to the one's contributions to society in terms of economic productivity, and those who are seen as not contributing still often remain stigmatized. As another broad cultural trend, mass media has valorized youth and beauty. In social media today, there's pressure to appear happy, successful, and popular. Again, this kind of society creates opportunities and challenges. On the one hand, people with disabilities can use social media to promote more inclusive understandings of success and beauty. On the other hand, people who do not meet the ideals of youth and beauty may feel demeaned and silenced, thereby increasing the marginalization of people with disabilities while also producing mental health disabilities.

Social Stasis

In this final section, we address the issue of stasis—stability over time. Although there has been so much change, people with disabilities remain disproportionately in poverty and marginalized. Even an achievement as monumental as the ADA has led to little improvement in the economic situation of people with disabilities. Sociologists examine resistance to change and consider why some social phenomena are so stable over time. Again, our goal is not to explore all of the reasons why inequality persists, but rather to introduce the importance of structural factors in the perpetuation of inequality despite activism.

Discussing the persistence of racial inequality over time despite changes in attitudes and laws, sociologist Eduardo Bonilla-Silva (2003) develops the idea of racialized social systems. He argues that racial inequalities are embedded within and across social institutions, even while each institution claims to be "color-blind." As an example, public schools receive funding based on local revenue. Since minority communities are disproportionately poor, this leads to racial inequality. However, because the funding mechanism (local revenue) appears race-neutral, this system is protected from and resistant to change via race activism. In fact, when activists advocate equalizing the educational system, they are often accused of injecting race into a color-blind system.

In a similar fashion, and interwoven with racism, *institutional ableism* means that ableism is built into and across social structures. Although aspects of the system may change, the system overall still reproduces ableism. For example, a society may establish a new law that prohibits employment discrimination based on disability, but it may not undo the ableism common within capitalism and the workplace (Maroto & Pettinicchio, 2015). The drive for profit still tends to position nonstandardized workers as potential liabilities. The bureaucratic structure of many workplaces hinders the flexibility required to individualize jobs. Moreover, there are myriad inequalities faced by people with disabilities as they try to compete for work, including segregated school systems, the lack of accessible transportation, expectations regarding productivity and standardized work processes, and disability benefit systems which potentially cut life-sustaining health benefits when people try to work. Those who are marginalized across multiple dimensions will be further disadvantaged. Thus, a single law cannot address all of these barriers, and employment rates remain low.

Most disability policies focus on reducing the public "burden" of disability or increasing the self-sufficiency of people with disabilities. *They do not fundamentally shift economic or political power.* Policies may try to decrease the barriers to employment, but the profits of capitalism still flow to a small percentage of people. As people with disabilities enter the workforce, they often lose public benefits, so they may not be better off economically. Employment may even put people with disabilities in a more economically precarious position since, if they are fired, they will lose income and health care. People with disabilities may gain access to vote, but if the candidates do not prioritize disability issues, voting may have little impact. Voting and employment are still important and valued activities; however, they may do surprisingly little to address broader systemic issues confronting people with disabilities such as poverty.

In addition, *ableism is still widely seen as legitimate*. Whereas many Americans acknowledge that it is wrong to be explicitly racist, they are surprised by the very idea of ableism and that it would be wrong to consider that being able is better than being disabled. People commonly toast to one's health and feel sympathy when people become disabled. In employment, some employers believe that their right to choose the best candidate includes selecting the candidate one who will be fastest, most easily integrated into the workplace, and the least costly. Educational segregation in schools by disability is widely upheld. Despite evidence regarding the benefits of inclusion, parents, teachers, and administrators commonly argue that educational segregation is better for students with disabilities, students without disabilities, and the school district as a whole. Despite the long history of abuse, neglect, and medical ineffectiveness of institutions, many people still argue that we need more long-term institutions to house people with mental and intellectual disabilities. Moreover, many of America's central values—independence, wealth, beauty, productivity, success—undercut the value of people with disabilities. Disability has been and continues to be seen as a justifiable reason for inequality (Baynton, 2001; Titchkosky, 2011).

Conclusion

In conclusion, in many ways, the lives of people with disabilities have vastly improved over the last 100 years, and much of this is due to activism. Institutionalization and compulsory sterilization are no longer dominant policy responses to disability; families rarely hide their disabled offspring; and people with disabilities have rights to education, voting, and access. On the other hand, many people with disabilities continue to be institutionalized in centers, prisons, nursing homes, and community services that deny them choice and control over their lives; many families continue to struggle to adequately support their disabled family members; people with disabilities continue to face policies that hinder marriage and parenting; and they continue to be disproportionately in poverty, unemployed, and socially isolated. Thus, much has changed, but there is more work to be done.

KEY TERMS

504 sit-ins 267
Activism 264
Backlash 267
Charismatic leaders 271
Civil rights frame 266
Collective identity 268
Contentious tactics 269
Digital divide 277
The Disability Rights Movement 265

Disabled in Action 271
Ed Roberts 270
"Existence is Resistance" 270
Frame 266
Independent Living Movement 271
In-system tactics 269
Judy Heumann 271
Oppositional consciousness 268

Political opportunity theory 266
Psychiatric survivor movement 264
Resource Mobilization Theory 268
Self-advocacy movements 264
Stasis 263

RESOURCES

Books on Disability Activism

Charlton, James. 2000. *Nothing about us without us: Disability oppression and empowerment.* Berkeley, CA: University of California Press.

Fleischer Doris and Frieda Zames. 2011. *The disability rights movement: From charity to confrontation.* Philadelphia, PA: Temple University Press.

Pelka, Fred. 2012. *What we have done: An oral history of the disability rights movement.* Amherst, MA: University of Massachusetts Press.

Pettinicchio, David. 2019. *Politics of empowerment: Disability rights and the cycle of American policy reform.* Stanford, CA: Stanford University Press.

Articles

Berne, Patty. 2015. "Disability Justice—A Working Draft." *Sins Invalid.* Available at sinsinvalid.org/blog/disability-justice-a-working-draft-by-patty-berne (accessed October 2018).

Carey, Allison C., Pamela Block, and Richard Scotch. 2019. "Sometimes Allies: Parent-Led Disability Organizations and Social Movements." *Disability Studies Quarterly* 39, no. 1, https://dsq-sds.org/article/view/6281.

Mingus, Mia. 2017. "Moving Toward the Ugly: A Politic Beyond Desirability." In *Beginning with disability: A primer,* ed. Lennard Davis, 137–141. New York: Routledge. [adapted from a 2011 speech].

Schweik, Susan M. 2011. "Lomax's Matrix: Disability, Solidarity, and the Black Power of 504." *Disability Studies Quarterly* 31, no. 1. https://dsq-sds.org/article/view/1371/1539.

Scotch, Richard K. 1988. "Disability as the Basis for a Social Movement: Advocacy and the Politics of Definition." *Journal of Social Issues* 44, no. 1: 159–172.

Memoirs of Disability Activists

Heumann, Judith. 2020. *Being Heumann: An unrepentant memoir of a disability rights activist.* Boston, MA: Beacon Press.

Johnson, Roland and Karl Williams. 2002. *Lost in a desert world.* Plymouth Meeting, PA: Speaking for Ourselves.

Linton, Simi. 2006. *My body politic: A memoir.* Ann Arbor, MI: University of Michigan Press.

O'Toole, Corbett J. 2015. *Fading scars: My queer disability history.* Fort Worth, TX: Autonomous Press.

Wong, Alice, ed. 2020. *Disability visibility: First-person stories from the 21st century.* New York: Vintage Books. And Alice Wong's blog The Disability Visibility Project at https://disability-visibilityproject.com/about/.

Films and Videos

"Crip Camp: A Disability Revolution." 2020. Netflix. 1 hour, 48 minutes. Camp Jened offered a freewheeling utopia where teens with disabilities experienced liberation, inclusion, and built community. Their bonds endured as many realized that civil disobedience and political participation could change the future.

"Lives Worth Living." 2011. Public Broadcasting Company. (time). Traces the evolution of the Disability Rights Movement, climaxing with the passage of the ADA, told by the movement's mythical heroes and drawing on archival footage.

"Leroy F. Moore Jr. Black disabled art history 101." 2014. YouTube video of Moore presenting on his book and the importance of black disabled art. 37 minutes. https://www.youtube.com/watch?v=9lSdblDv34o&t=1315s

"Piss on pity: We will ride." Roustabout Media. 61 minutes. Piss on Pity explores the power of a grassroots, disability rights network called ADAPT that is working to create a barrier-free, inclusive society.

Podcasts

Judi Chamberlin: Psychiatric Survivor Movement, Madness Radio, 45 minutes. https://www.madnessradio.net/madness-radio-judi-chamberlin-psychiatric-survivor-movement/.

Judy Heumann. The Heumann Perspective. https://judithheumann.com/heumann-perspective/, A series of conversations with disability change-makers and their allies.

Collections of First-Person Accounts of Disability Activism

Disability Rights and Independent Living Movements, Berkeley Oral History Collection, a collection of oral histories of those involved in these movements. https://www.lib.berkeley.edu/libraries/bancroft-library/oral-history-center/projects/drilm.

Nothing About Us Without Us: Stories of Self-advocates, a collection of oral histories of self-advocates with developmental disabilities, collected by Nicki Pombier, https://nickipombier.com/self-advocate-stories.

Visionary voices, video interviews with leaders of the Pennsylvania movement for civil rights for people with intellectual disabilities, https://disabilities.temple.edu/voices/.

ACTIVITIES

1. Choose an interview or set of interviews from the collections above (this could also include *What We Have Done*) and analyze it. In doing so, consider how the interviewee became an activist, what goals they had, how they framed their goals, what organizations they joined, and what tactics they used. Consider what privileges and/or barriers they faced on their activism. If possible, consider how successful their activism has been—what if anything has changed as a result of their activism?

2. Follow the social media account of a disabled activist or an organization led by disabled activists. Document the key themes that emerge from their social media postings.

3. Analyze the website of a disability organization that is led by people who are not disabled (e.g., parents, pro-fessionals, church) and the website of a disability organization that is led by disabled activists. What similarities and differences do you see in (a) the goals, (b) the language, (c) the tactics, and (d) the imagery? Why do you think that is?

4. Research disability activism in a different country. What are the key organizations, goals, and framing for disability activism? If possible, consider if/how they are influenced by Western models of disability rights. How is disability activism unique in that country and why?

Glossary

As a note, the meaning of concepts varies across time, different theoretical traditions, and scholars. The following definitions are not exclusive of other definitions or understandings. They represent the way these ideas are used in the context of this text.

504 Sit-in. Demonstrations in 1977 during which hundreds of disabled people occupied the 10 regional offices of the Department of Health, Education and Welfare to demand regulations for Section 504 of the 1973 Rehabilitation Act.

Able-disabled. A disabled person who appears as, or likely to become, a self-sustaining, productive taxpayer.

Ableism. A worldview that assumes the superiority of able bodies and minds and the inferiority of those who do not fit in within the normative expectations.

Access. The power and opportunity to enter, use, participate in, and have a sense of belonging or control over a social space, interaction, role, or resource.

Activism. Intentional action directed toward creating social change.

Agents of socialization. The people, groups, and social institutions that teach a person the culture's way of life and shape how that person comes to see themselves as fitting into the culture.

Ambivalent medicalization. The double-edged sword of medicalization that might both empower and constrain people with disabilities and their families, who then may have conflicting feelings and practices regarding their use of the medical model.

Anticipated value of earnings and costs. An aspect of the marital value theory which argues that the risk of divorce increases when disability causes an unanticipated and sharp decline in the economic value of partnership.

Backlash. A political countermovement intended to dismantle and ensure the impotency of a movement, in this case to undercut disability rights activism.

Biased sampling. Sampling error that occurs when decisions about sampling lead to an incongruence between the sample and the population.

Bio-medical approach to health. An approach to understanding health in which health is the absence of disease and disability.

Blind work. The strategies used by blind people to navigate and enjoy the world around them.

Capital. A resource which can be used to accrue more resources or advantage.

Capitalism. An economic system characterized by private ownership of the mode of production (industry/factories), mass production, and the expansive commodification of resources for sale in the marketplace.

Carceral logic. An ideology that embraces incarceration as an appropriate response to a wide array of social issues.

Caste system. A stratification system in which one's social position is assigned at birth (an ascribed status) and there is very little social mobility.

Charismatic leaders. Leaders who exercise authority because others see them as exceptional and worthy of being followed.

Civil rights frame. A frame which posits the problems of disability as resulting from a system of oppression and proposes that the solution to disability oppression require the eradication of ableism and the establishment of disability rights.

Class system. A stratification system that allows social mobility across economic positions and confers status based on achievement.

Collective identity. A sense of belonging to a group.

Collective political disability identity. A shared identity tied to political action; in this case, an identity which frames disability as a social construct, rejects narratives of disability as individual tragedy, unites people with disabilities on the basis of their shared experience as an oppressed minority, and demands access and rights.

Colonization. The process of establishing settlements and control over an area and its indigenous people while retaining strong ties to the settler's country of origin.

Color-blind racism. The use of subtle ideologies, such as meritocracy, to distinguish among people in ways that mask yet also perpetuate racial stratification.

Compulsory able-bodiedness. The demand that people with disabilities perform as able-bodied people or risk exclusion.

Concerted cultivation. The provision by parents of the attention and activities geared to help ensure their children's success in life.

Confucianism. A philosophy founded by Confucius that proposes a series of teachings and social guidelines to attain social order and harmony.

Contentious tactics. Activist tactics that provoke conflict or cause disruption in the lives of those in the opposition.

Counterculture. A culture that actively challenges the dominant culture and seeks to usurp it.

Courtesy stigma. Stigma caused by one's association with stigmatized individuals.

Criminalization. The process by which social phenomena come to be seen as a crime worthy of punishment.

Crip theories. A set of theories which centers the experience of disability, explains the world from the perspective of disability, and strives for liberation.

Critical theory. Theory that seeks to develop knowledge that reveals and challenges unjust power structures.

Cultural capital. The set of knowledge, behaviors and skills that indicate a particular lifestyle (usually associated with prestige) and helps one attain social mobility and/or resources.

Culture. A people's "way of life," encompassing their symbols, values, customs, artifacts, and rituals.

Curative violence. Violence committed in the attempt to cure, hide, and/or eradicate people with disabilities.

Cure culture. A culture in which the value of cure surpasses consideration of other risks or costs.

Cyborg. The melding of body, mind, and technology in ways that disrupt traditional dichotomies of ability/disability and natural/unnatural to create limitless possibility.

Deinstitutionalization. The movement of people out of institutional settings and into the community.

Deserving poor. Poor people who are defined as worthy of assistance, usually because they work, have a work history, and/or are considered legitimately unable to work.

Developmental mismatch. An incongruity between one's physical/mental capacity tied to life course and the demands one faces; in this case, the expectations placed on college students to self-advocate without first building the skills required for self-advocacy.

Deviance. The violation of social norms or laws.

Digital divide. The gap across groups in access to and use of technology.

Disability. There are many definitions of disability. One of the broadest is a label and experience produced through the *social processes* by which some bodies/minds are identified, categorized, and treated as disabled. See Chapter 2.

Disability activist role. A social status in which people with disabilities are expected to fight for empowerment and social justice.

Disability cliff. The loss of services upon high school graduation, when young adults with disabilities lose access to a host of services provided through public schools and enter adulthood facing a far more precarious, unsupportive, and fragmented service environment.

Disability culture. The creation of a way of life that embraces and centers disability and the disability perspective, created by people with disabilities.

Disability display. The purposeful public presentation of disability identity and traits.

Disability identity. The part of identity that relates to disability and interprets the meaning of disability for oneself in relation to society.

Disability identity development. A theory by Carol Gill, which lays out four types of integration to be achieved in order to build a positive disability identification.

Disability justice. A strand of disability activism that is committed to ending intertwining systems of oppression (e.g., ableism, racism, sexism, homophobia) and empowering and addressing the needs and interests of those most impacted by the violence of oppression.

Disability marriage penalty. The use of a married couple's combined income/assets to determine eligibility for public benefits (rather than the disabled individual's income/assets), which can result in the loss of public benefits upon marriage.

Disability pride. The evaluation of one's disability as value-added, having pride *because of* disability, not *despite* it.

Disability Rights Movement. A movement that encompasses many loosely aligned organizations and movements within a decentralized structure, all fighting to improve the lived experience of people with disabilities by ensuring rights and opportunities.

Disabled in action. An organization with a mission to fight against disability discrimination and for the full rights of disabled people.

Discourse. The organization of meaning in ways that constitute knowledge and inform our behavior.

Discrimination. The unequal treatment of people based on a group membership such as gender, race, or disability.

Disease. A biological abnormality with a relatively clear biological or pathogenic cause.

Dis-identification. The explicit rejection of the label of disability, disability identity, and group membership based on disability.

Drapetomania. A diagnosis labeling the rebellious act of slave escape as mental illness.

Emancipatory research. A research methodology which empowers disabled people throughout the research process to inform political and social change.

Embodiment. A theoretical perspective which argues that one's body mediates one's experience and understanding of the world.

Enwheeled. The process of becoming a successful and empowered wheelchair user.

Essentialism. The belief that social phenomena are biological, individual-level traits and that social outcomes flow as the natural outcomes of biological traits.

Eugenics. The science (or pseudo-science) of population improvement through selective breeding.

"Existence is resistance". A saying which means that in a world that demeans people with disabilities and tries to eradicate them, everyday actions and even survival become acts of resistance.

Feminist disability studies. A theoretical framework that aims to document and explain the intersecting experiences of and inequalities by gender and disability and to pursue social justice for women with disabilities.

Feminist intersectional disability framework. Feminist approach that expands feminist disability studies to address additional intersecting systems of inequality.

Feminist methodology. A research methodology committed to prioritizing women's voices in research, empowering women through research, and challenging gendered power differentials.

Feudalism. A social system in which a small number of lords controlled the land, and serfs lived and worked the lord's land.

Frame. The construction of meaning by social movements to identify particular problems, explain those problems, and advocate particular solutions.

Freak shows. Shows which presented a wide assortment of people as exhibits for entertainment.

Gender binary. The cultural construction of gender as only two, mutually exclusive, genders—male and female.

Gender queer identities. Identities that blur or reject the gender binary.

Gender roles. The norms, beliefs, and behaviors associated with masculinity and femininity.

Generalized other. A stage of socialization where people internalize broad social values and expectations and learn to evaluate themselves from the standpoint of the general community.

Globalization. The influence of individuals, companies, and governments across national and cultural borders.

Graying of America. The increase proportion of the population that is 65+.

Habitus. The deeply ingrained habits, skills, and dispositions that one develops due to life experiences shaped with the context of social structures including inequality.

Healthy disabled. People with disabilities who are not ill or in need of frequent medical care; an activist strategy to depict people with disabilities as healthy, vibrant, and capable and thereby minimize stigma.

Hegemony. The pervasive and secure social dominance of a set of ideas promoted by the ruling class, such that the ideas are widely accepted as true, natural, and inevitable.

Heteronormativity. Society's construction of heterosexual orientation, behaviors, and relationships as the norm and as valued above other sexualities.

Heumann, Judy (1947–). A disability rights activist, co-founder of Disabled in Action and a leader in the Independent Living Movement and the 504 sit-ins.

Hierarchies of disadvantage. The pattern of stratification in which groups who experience multiple forms of oppression also experience greater disadvantage.

Hippocrates. A Greek physician considered to be the "Father of Medicine" (460–377 B.C.).

Historical comparative analysis. The examination of a social phenomenon as it occurs across time and place in order to assess causal relationships.

Humanism. The belief in the inherent capacity of humans and societies to attain excellence through reason and empirical observation.

Identity. One's idea of self-understood within and against the social context.

Identity first language. A language convention that places the disability in the forefront (e.g., disabled person, autistic activist, blind woman).

Identity Politics. Social activism organized around a social identity, often seeking to alter the cultural understanding of and response to people in that identity group and to transform the identities of its movement participants.

Ideology. A belief system; in Marxist approaches, a belief system constructed by the ruling class to legitimate and support the means and relations of production.

Illness. The social–psychological experience of disease.

Impairment. Physical and mental traits determined to be atypical and often deemed undesirable.

Implicit bias. Unconscious attitudes and stereotypes that shape actions.

Impression management. The use of performative strategies to actively display one's identity and evoke desired feedback.

Impression management techniques. The host of strategies used to present a particular self to the world, receive acceptable feedback, and enable a positive self-identity.

Inclusive education. A philosophy and a set of practices in which children with disabilities are valued and active participants in the same schools and classes as their nondisabled peers.

Independent Living Movement. A social movement which began in 1960s Berkeley, California, to ensure the rights, supports, and access for people with disabilities to control their own lives.

Individuals with Disabilities Education Act (IDEA). A civil rights law, originally passed in 1975, which mandates the provision of a free and appropriate education to all children with disabilities.

Inspiration porn. The objectification of disabled people for the motivation and inspiration of nondisabled people.

Institution. A setting which operates around a centralized and hierarchical authority structure, enforces standardized rules, demands conformity, and erases individual difference; often used to refer to a large congregate site for people with disabilities in which they are disempowered and segregated.

Institutional ableism. Disproportionate disadvantage or harm to people with disabilities caused by and embedded within institutional patterns such as policies, procedures, and funding systems.

Institutional bias. The channeling of people with disabilities into large-scale, segregated settings rather than community settings due to national laws and policies such as Medicaid funding.

Institutional inertia. The tendency of bureaucracies to reproduce the same practices, even after those practices become ineffective or counterproductive.

Institutional interests. The array of goals and needs of an organization.

Institutional review boards. Committees established in 1974 to proactively monitor research on human subjects and ensure its adherence to ethical guidelines.

In-system tactics. Tactics seen as legitimate because they rely on conventional social and political channels of influence.

Intensive motherhood. A trend where mothers are increasingly expected to provide intensive engagement with their child.

International Classification of Functioning, Disability and Health (ICF) Model. A model in which disability is defined by functional limitations in at least one of three domains—body structure and function, activities, and participation—in interaction with impairments and the social environment.

Intersectionality. An approach which examines the construction and experience of oppression as intertwined across multiple systems of power.

Intimate citizenship. The rights and practices associated with people's most personal decisions, which are structured by public discourses and policies.

Justifiably excluded type. A set of people for whom exclusion is largely accepted.

Labeling theory. A theory that views social phenomena as understood through the process by which a label is socially created and applied to a group of people, often resulting in various consequences.

Language. People's most important symbol set, the way in which humans create and communicate complex systems of meaning.

Looking glass self. The theory by George Cooley in which the self is defined through the feedback received from society.

Mad activism. Activism that directly challenges the power of the psychiatric professions and seeks alternative forms of care that respect human rights and diversity.

Marital value. A theory that suggests that marriage is often a rational choice made when the perceived benefits of marriage outweigh the benefits of being unmarried.

Master status. A status that dominates the ways in which others think about, interact with, and confer or deny opportunities to a person.

Material culture. The tangible products made in a culture and the tools and processes of producing those items.

Material hardship. A measure of the difficulty one experiences economically in meeting one's needs.

Materialist theories. A theoretical approach that prioritizes the role of the economy and the resources we need to survive (our material environment) as the primary determinants of our social relationships, culture, and disability.

Maternal activism. Activism conducted as part of the maternal role to ensure the safety and well-being of their families.

Mead's theory of socialization. A theory which lays out three stages of role-taking through which people learn to fit into and succeed in society.

Means of production. The processes and technologies by which a society produces the resources its members need and use.

Medicaid. A public health insurance program that is means-tested and provides health insurance to eligible people with low incomes.

Medical discourse. A discourse which presents disability and illness as biological problems to be defeated through medical cure.

Medicalization. The process by which social phenomena come to be seen as a medical condition in need of medical intervention.

Medical model. An overarching view of disability that regards it as resulting from an individual deficit or limitation rooted in individual biology.

Medical sociology. A subfield of sociology that studies the social constructions and institutional practices related to health, illness and well-being.

Medicare. A public health insurance program that provides health insurance primarily to people who have a work history, have paid into the social security system, and no longer work due to old age or disability.

Mental disability. A descriptor that acknowledges that society plays a role in producing particular mental states and the disadvantages that flow from them.

Mental health parity. The provision of the same level of coverage, services, and supports for mental health conditions as for physical health conditions.

Meritocracy. An ideology that suggests that one's social position should be based on one's earned accomplishments.

Militarism. The national prioritization of war and the preparation for war.

Minority group. A group that experiences profound and long-term disadvantage in relation to a majority group who exercises greater power and holds more resources.

Minority model. An overarching view of disability that regards it as a product of systematic disadvantage and views people with disabilities as a minority group with inferior access to power and resources.

Monotheistic religion. A religion centered on one god.

Moral entrepreneurship. The creative and time-consuming work performed by activists as they seek and create novel solutions to problems.

Mother blame. Blame placed on mothers for disability and, more broadly, for any negative outcomes experienced by their children.

Multidimensional approach to health. An approach to defining health encompassing a variety of physical, psychological, and social indicators.

Narratives. The stories created and shared that serve to construct meaning.

Negative right. A right that ensures freedom from state intervention (e.g., freedom of speech).

Neoliberalism. A political and economic philosophy that promotes individual freedom based on a laissez-faire approach to capitalism with little government regulation or public provision of services.

Neuroqueer Movement. A movement that rejects conformity, affirms people's right to be visibly autistic and/or neurodivergent, and embraces the fluidity of identity in gender, sexuality, and ability.

Norm. Socially expected behavior.

Normalization. The process by which people with disabilities are socialized into expected behaviors with the goal of participating in and taking on valued roles in society.

Occupational structure. The patterns of the distribution of work, earnings, and employment inequality.

Operationalization. The process by which concepts are transformed into measurable variables.

Oppositional consciousness. The framing of experiences as a collective phenomenon of shared oppression best addressed through challenging the status quo.

Overclassification. Disproportionate labeling of people into a group; in this case, an argument that suggests that minority and low-SES youth are disproportionately labeled as disabled and channeled into special education.

Participatory Action Research (PAR). A methodology that addresses issues identified by specific communities, in ways that are useful to the community, with the full and active participation of all relevant stakeholders.

Passing. The concealment of a stigmatizing trait.

Paternalism. A system in which people deemed competent hold authority over those deemed incompetent.

Performativity. A theoretical perspective which argues that identity is constituted through repeated, enacted performances.

Person-first language. A convention which places the person before the disability (e.g., person with a disability).

Political economy. A theoretical perspective focusing on the intersection of economic and political systems in shaping resource distribution and class stratification.

Political opportunity theory. A theory that argues that movements tend to flourish when the political structure is open to or vulnerable to change.

Polytheistic religion. A religion which focuses on the belief in multiple gods.

Positive right. A right that creates an obligation on the part of the state or other entity to do or provide something (e.g., the right to an education).

Positivism. The view that asserts there is an objective world to be discovered through scientific research methods conducted by unbiased researchers.

Poster child campaigns. Fundraising campaigns depicting cute, helpless children who, with the gift of charity, could access medical treatment and thereby cure.

Praxis. The use of theory and research to achieve social justice.

Prejudice. A set of preconceived negative attitudes and beliefs about a social group.

Primary condition. A condition resulting from the direct manifestation of a disease or disability.

Prison industrial complex. The alliance between the government and the private businesses that run prisons and their services which accrue profit from surveillance and imprisonment.

Productivism. A philosophy which posits that people who are productive and contribute to society should be rewarded, while people who are deemed unproductive should be excluded and/or receive only meager government benefits.

Professional sovereignty. Exclusive professional control, in this case over problems related to the body, the mind and the delivery of treatments.

Promising diagnosis. A diagnosis that leads to beneficial services, often in inclusive settings.

Protestant Reformation. A movement that challenged the hold of the Catholic Church and advocated a personal relationship between individuals and god without mediation by priests.

Proxy respondent. A person who participates in research on behalf of another person.

Psychiatric survivor. A person who describes their experience of mental hospitalization and psychiatric treatment as traumatic and violent.

Psychiatric Survivor Movement. A movement of psychiatric patients, former patients, and their allies that criticizes psychiatric professions and treatments as an oppressive system.

Qualitative research. A research method that foregoes the goal of counting or standardizing measurements, and instead dives deeply into examining meaning through techniques such as open-ended survey questions, fieldwork, and observation.

Quantitative research. A method of research that gathers data in a way that transforms data into numbers.

Racial distinctiveness. Being a minority in terms of the specific racial composition of the setting (e.g., a school).

Racialization of diagnosis. The infusion of racialized values and stereotypes into patterns of diagnosis, leading to differential diagnosis by race.

Reclamation. To take a derogatory term and instill it with group pride.

Reembodiment. The process by which one becomes comfortable with and attuned to one's body after impairment.

Relations of production. The pattern of social relationships created through the structure of inequality in ownership and control of the means of production.

Representations. Symbolic imagery which create and reflect the meaning of a social phenomenon.

Research gatekeepers. People other than the research subjects themselves whose approval is necessary for participation in research.

Resource Mobilization Theory. A theory that argues that social movements tend to be successful to the extent that they effectively gather and deploy resources, including funding, members, and political support.

Risky mothers. A label assigned to disabled mothers who are perceived as destined to pass on their own incapacity via hereditary passage of "defective" traits and/or through the social and economic disadvantages.

Rituals. Opportunities to engage in routinized behavior in order to socialize and unify people within a culture.

Roberts, Ed (1939–1995). A disability rights activist who is considered one of the founders of the Independent Living Movement.

Role. An expected behavior associated with any given status.

Role disruption. Upending established relational patterns and expectations.

Role-taking. The interactional skill of seeing oneself from a given social position.

Rooting. The choice by young adults with disabilities to remain at their parents' home because it provides a desirable level of accessibility and supports for an increasingly independent life.

Sandwich Generation. Middle-aged Americans who provide financial support to both children and aging parents.

Sapir–Whorf thesis. The theory that language shapes our understanding and experience of the world.

Scholar-activist. Scholars who use research and knowledge production to advance social justice.

School-to-prison pipeline. The policies and practices that channel America's schoolchildren, especially the most at-risk children, out of classrooms and into the juvenile and criminal justice systems.

Scientific motherhood. The expectation placed upon mothers to use medical and scientific information to maximize the health and potential of their child.

Second shift. The dual responsibilities of women who work and hold responsibility for childcare and housework.

Secondary conditions. Conditions indirectly related to a disability that are at times preventable.

Section 504. A section of the 1973 Vocational Rehabilitation Act which prohibited discrimination on the basis of disability by programs or activities receiving federal funds.

Self-advocacy. The act of identifying and promoting one's own interests individually or in collective action with others.

Self-advocacy movements. Movements led by people with disabilities to exercise control over their own lives; often used to describe activism among people with intellectual disabilities and, separately, autistics.

Self-fulfilling prophecy. A phenomenon where expectations lead to the outcome expected.

Sexual ableism. The system of establishing qualifications to be sexual based on criteria of ability, intellect, morality, physicality, appearance, age, race, social acceptability, and/or gender conformity and thereby hindering the expression of sexuality by people with disabilities.

Sexual rights. Rights which confer control over one's body and freedom to engage in private, intimate acts.

Sexuality. One's sexual identity, orientation, behavior, and relationships.

Sick role. The social expectations of a sick person, including that the sick person recognize their illness and comply with medical treatment and that others will exempt the sick from their standard responsibilities.

Sighted ways. The cultural conventions and norms highly reliant on sight.

Sitala. A Hindu goddess of sores, pustules, and diseases who, according to believers, would visit villages and bring either wrath or auspicious tidings.

Social capital. The ways in which relationships serve as resources.

Social construction. The process by which people create the meaning of the world around them through social interaction.

Social Darwinism. A cultural discourse centered on the maxim of the survival of the fittest, such that the human race and society evolve toward perfection when unhindered competition is allowed.

Social death. The denial of legal and social personhood.

Socialization. The process by which one learns the values, beliefs, and practices of their culture, including how they fit into the web of statuses and relationships.

Social model. An overarching view of disability that regards it as a social construct rooted in the physical and social environment.

Social Security Disability Income (SSDI). A public program which offers monthly income payments to disabled people with a work history who have paid into the social security system and acquire disabilities before reaching retirement age.

Social stratification. The ways in which a society groups people and ranks them within a social hierarchy.

Social welfare programs. Public programs to assist people in meeting their basic needs.

Sociological imagination. The process by which people recognize the broader social context shaping individual experiences.

Sociology of Disability. A subfield in Sociology which seeks to examine a broad range of social experiences, processes, and outcomes in relation to disability as a social concept and identity category.

Special education. Educational accommodations, services and instruction designed to enhance the academic success of students with disabilities.

Standpoint theory. A theoretical perspective that argues that knowledge is produced from a person's or a group's particular social position in society.

Stasis. Stability in social patterns and outcomes over time.

State-centered theories. A set of theories that center the role of the state in creating, defining, and affecting disability.

Status. A socially recognized position.

Stereotype. Generalizations which are often false, simplified, and/or negative, about a group, which may be used to judge individual people.

Stereotype Content Model. A model that predicts based on two types of traits—warmth and competence—the content and outcomes of stereotypes.

Stereotype threat. A phenomenon in which the anxiety produced by negative stereotypes leads to poor performance.

Stigma. A discounted and discredited social standing based on the social perception of a personal attribute.

Stratification system. The ways in which a society groups people and ranks them within a social hierarchy, leading to systematically different access to resources.

Stuck in transition. The experience of young adults who want to establish independent lives but must stay or return to their parent's home for a variety of reasons.

Subculture. A group united by shared beliefs and practices, distinguished from the mainstream but not in opposition to it.

Successful aging. An ideology which presents ideal aging as aging with maximal functionality and the absence of disease and disability.

Superstructure. The range of social institutions which support and legitimate capitalism and the needs of the capitalists.

Supplemental Security Income (SSI). A public program which offers monthly income payments to people with disabilities who have low income.

Symbol. Anything that serves as a referent for some object or idea.

Symbolic interactionism. A theoretical perspective which argues that through everyday social interactions, people create and share symbols and meanings.

Tabula rasa. A concept used by John Locke to posit that humans are born with a cognitive blank slate and accumulate knowledge through sensory experience.

Temporarily able-bodied. A term that calls attention to the fact that most people one day will enter the status of disabled.

The Americans with Disabilities Act of 1990. An act which prohibits discrimination against people with disabilities in employment, the provision of public services, public transportation, and telecommunications.

Total institutions. As conceptualized by Erving Goffman, settings where people are contained, isolated from external influences, held under a central authority encompassing all areas of life, and restricted to a formally administered life.

Transhumanism. A philosophy that advocates the development and use of technology to enhance the human mind and body.

Transinstitutionalization. The movement from one institution to another type of institution.

Tuskegee experiments. Experiments conducted in 1932–1966 in which the US Public Health Service denied treatment to 600 black men with syphilis in order to track the progression of the disease.

Twelve tables. The first legal code of the Roman Republic (451 & 450 BC).

Typology of disability orientations. A typology developed by Rosalyn Darling showing the complexity of how people think about their disability identity and the factors influencing disability identity.

Ugly laws. Laws which banned people with visible disabilities and deformities from public spaces.

Underclassification. An argument that suggests that African American children may be under-identified as disabled and underserved by special education.

Undeserving poor. Poor people who are portrayed as able but unwilling to work and therefore seen as undeserving of public assistance.

United Nations Convention on the Rights of Persons with Disabilities (2008). An international treaty in which countries agree to uphold a broad range of human rights for people with disabilities.

Values. Collective ideals about right and wrong.

Verstehen. The German word for understanding, used by Max Weber to emphasize that the central task of sociologists is to understand the world from the point of view of those being studied.

Vulnerable populations. Groups who, based on a history of abuse and continued vulnerability, are protected by Institutional Review Board protocols.

Western medicine. A view of medicine in which the body is treated like a machine with independent parts with specialized doctors working on specific parts; highly reliant on science.

World Systems Theory. A theory that asserts that there is a global economic system in which high-income industrialized nations grow rich through exploiting the economic resources and labor of low-income countries.

References

Abbott, A. (1988). *The system of professions: An essay on the division of expert labor.* University of Chicago Press.

Abraham, L. K. (1993). *Mama might be better off dead: The failure of health care in urban America.* University of Chicago Press.

Abrahams, A. (2020, April 24). "This is really life or death": For people with disabilities, Coronavirus is making it harder than ever to receive care. *Time.* time.com/5326098/coronavirus-people-with-disabilities/

"Access Points": A conversation with Bethany Stevens on disability, sexuality, and technology. (2017). *Logic Magazine.* https://logicmag.io/sex/bethany-stevens-on-disability-sexuality-and-technology/

Achey, N. (2020). *Direct support professionals' perspective of sexuality of adults with intellectual disabilities: A qualitative analysis of interviews with providers in Maine* (Doctoral dissertation, University of Maine).

Administration for Community Living (ACL). (2018). *2018 profile of older Americans.*

Albrecht, G. L. (1992). *The disability business: Rehabilitation in America.* SAGE.

Albrecht, G. L. (2006). *Encyclopedia of disability.* SAGE.

Alexander, J. C. (2003). *The meanings of social life: A cultural sociology.* Oxford University Press.

Allday, A. R., Duhon, G. J., Blackburn-Ellis, S., & Van Dycke, J. L. (2011). The biasing effect of labels on direct observation by preservice teachers. *Teacher Education Quarterly,* 34(1), 35–38.

Alper, M. (2017). *Giving voice: Mobile communication, disability, and inequality.* MIT Press.

Altman, B. M. (2001). Exploring theories and expanding methodologies: Where we are and where we need to go. In B. Altman (Ed.), *Definitions of disability, and their operationalization, and measurement in survey data: An update. Research in social science and disability* (vol. 2, pp. 77–100). Elsevier Science.

Altman, B. M., & Bernstein, A. (2008). *Disability and health in the United States, 2001–2005.* National Center for Health Statistics.

American Association of People With Disabilities. (n.d.). *AAPD home page.* https://www.aapd.com/

Anand, S. (2013). Historicising disability in India: Questions of subject and method. In R. Addlakha (Ed.), *Disability studies in India: Dialectic between global discourses and local realities* (pp. 35–60). Routledge.

Anand, S. (2015). Corporeality and culture: Theorizing difference in the South Asian context. In S. Rao & M. Kalyanpur (Eds.), *South Asia and disability studies: Redefining boundaries and extending horizons* (pp. 154–170). Peter Lang.

Anderson, B. (2020, April 1). How disability activists are fighting isolation, collectively. *In These Times.* https://inthesetimes.com/article/disabled-queer-activists-isolation-mutual-aid-bay-area-covid-19

Anderson, L., Hewitt, A., Pettingell, S., Lulinski, A., Taylor, M., & Reagan, J. (2018). *Family and individual needs for disability supports (v.2) community report.* Research and Training Center on Community Living, Institute on Community Integration.

Angell, A. M., & Solomon, O. (2017). "If I was a different ethnicity, would she treat me the same?": Latino parents' experiences obtaining autism services. *Disability & Society,* 32(8), 1142–1164.

Anspach, R. (1979). From stigma to identity politics: Political activism among the physically disabled and former mental patients. *Social Science & Medicine,* 13, 765–773.

Apple, R. D. (2006). *Perfect motherhood: Science and childbearing in America.* Rutgers University Press.

Arias, E., & Xu, J. (2019). National vital statistics reports. *Center for Disease Control.* https://www.cdc.gov/nchs/data/nvsr/nvsr68/nvsr68_07-508.pdf

Bak, J. (2020, March 26). Coronavirus shows care work isn't just for disabled communities any more. *BitchMedia.* https://www.bitchmedia.org/

article/care-work-disability-framework-becomes-coronavirus-response

Bal, A., Betters-Bubon, J., & Fish, R. E. (2019). A multilevel analysis of statewide disproportionality in exclusionary discipline and the identification of emotional disturbance. *Education and Urban Society*, 51(2), 247–268.

Ballou, E.P., daVanport, S., & Onaiwu, M.G. (Eds.). (2021). *Sincerely, your autistic child: What people on the autism spectrum wish their parents knew about growing up, acceptance, and identity*. Beacon Press.

Banks, J. (2018). Invisible man: Examining the intersection of disability, race, and gender in an urban community. *Disability & Society*, 33(6), 894–908.

Barclay, J. L. (2014). Mothering the 'useless': Black motherhood, disability, and slavery. *Women, Gender, and Families of Color*, 2, 115–140.

Barclay, J. L. (2021). *The mark of slavery: Disability, race, and gender in antebellum America*. University of Illinois Press.

Barnartt, S. N. (2010). *Disability as a fluid state. Research in social science and disability* (vol. 5). Emerald Press.

Barnartt, S. (2020). Allyship changes in American disability protests over five decades: An empirical analysis. In A. C. Carey, J. Ostrove, & T. Fannon (Eds.), *Disability alliances and allies: Opportunities and challenges. Research in social science and disability* (vol. 11, pp. 111–132). Emerald Press.

Barnartt, S., & Scotch, R. (2001). *Disability protests: Contentious politics 1970-1999*. Gallaudet University Press.

Barnartt, S., & Seelman, K. (1988). A comparison of federal laws toward disabled and racial/ethnic groups in the USA. *Disability, Handicap & Society*, 3(1), 37–47.

Barnes, C. (2008). An ethical agenda in disability research: Rhetoric or reality? In D. M. Mertens & P. E. Ginsberg (Eds.), *The handbook of social research ethics* (pp. 458–473). SAGE.

Barnes, E. (2016). *The minority body: A theory of disability*. Oxford University Press.

Barnes, C., & Mercer, G. (Eds.). (1997). *Doing disability research*. The Disability Press.

Barnes, C., & Mercer, G. (2005). Disability, work, and welfare: Challenging the social exclusion of disabled people. *Work, Employment & Society*, 19(3), 527–545.

Basile, K., Breiding, M., & Smith, S. (2016). Disability and the risk of sexual violence in the United States. *American Journal of Public Health*, 1–6(5), 928–933.

Bassey, E., Ellison, C., & Walker, R. (2019). Social capital, social relationships and adults with acquired visual impairment: A Nigerian perspective. *Disability and Rehabilitation*, 41(10), 1169–1176.

Baynton, D. (2001). Disability and the justification of inequality in American history. In P. K. Longmore & L. Umansky (Eds.), *The new disability history: American perspectives* (pp. 33–57). New York University Press.

Bearden, E. (2019). *Monstrous kinds: Body, space, and narrative in Renaissance representations of disability*. University of Michigan Press.

Becker, H. (1966). *Outside: Studies in the sociology of deviance*. The Free Press.

Beckwith, R. (2016). *Disability servitude: From peonage to poverty*. Palgrave Macmillan.

Beitz, J. (2006). Disappointment. In C. Dowling, N. Nicoll, & B. Thomas (Eds.), *A different kind of perfect: Writings by parents on raising a child with special needs* (pp. 18–19). Trumpeter.

Belknap, I. (1956). *Human problems of a state mental hospital*. McGraw-Hill.

Bell, C. (Ed.). (2011). *Blackness and disability: Critical examinations and cultural interventions*. Michigan State University Press.

Bell, S. (2016). Bringing our bodies and ourselves back in: Seeing Irving Kenneth Zola's legacy. In S. E. Green & S. N. Barnartt (Eds.), *Sociology looking at disability: What did we know and when did we know it?* (pp. 143–158). Emerald.

Ben-Moshe, L. (2020). *Decarcerating disability: Deinstitutionalization and prison abolition*. University of Minnesota Press.

Ben-Moshe, L., Chapman, C., & Carey, A. (Eds.). (2014). *Disability incarcerated: Disability and imprisonment in the United States and Canada*. Palgrave Macmillan.

Ben-Moshe, L. & Powell, J. J. W. (2007). Revis(it)ing the International Symbol of Access. *Disability & Society*, 22(5), 489–505.

References

Bentley, S. (2017). The silencing invisibility cloak. In L. X. Z. Brown, E. Ashkenazy, & M. G. Onaiwu (Eds.), *All the weight of our dreams: On living radicalized autism* (pp. 299–305). Dragon Bee Press.

Berger, R. (2009). *Hoop dreams on wheels: Disability and the competitive wheelchair athlete*. Routledge.

Berger, R. (2013). *Introducing disability studies*. Lynn Rienner.

Berger, P., & Luckmann, T. (1966). *The social construction of reality: A treatise in the sociology of knowledge*. Anchor Books.

Berlin, I. ([1969] 1984). Two concepts of liberty. In M. Sandel (Ed.), *Liberalism and its critics* (pp. 15–36). Basil Blackwell.

Berne, P. (2015). Disability justice—A working draft. *Sins Invalid*. sinsinvalid.org/blog/disability-justice-a-working-draft-by-patty-berne

Bérubé, M. (2016). *Life as Jamie knows it: An exceptional child grows up*. Beacon.

Bérubé, M. (2018, April 2). Don't let my son plunge off the "disability cliff" when I'm gone. *USA Today*. https://www.usatoday.com/story/opinion/2018/04/02/dont-let-my-son-plunge-off-disability-cliff-column/443138002

Bhatia, A. (2017). Transitioning from one culture to another. In M. Jarman, L. Monoghan, & A. Q. Harkin (Eds.), *Barriers and belonging: Personal narratives of disability* (pp. 37–42). Temple University Press.

Bhatta, D., & Glantz, S. (2019). Association of e-cigarette use with respiratory disease among adults: A longitudinal analysis. *American Journal of Preventive Medicine*, 58(2), 182–190.

Bianchi, S., Robinson, J., & Milkie, M. (2006). *Changing rhythms of American family life*. Basic Books.

Biklen, D. (2005). *Autism and the myth of the person alone*. New York University Press.

Bingham, S., & Green, S. (2015). Aesthetic as analysis: Synthesizing theories of humor and disability through stand-up comedy. *Humanity & Society*, 40(3), 278–305.

Bingham, S., & Green, S. (2016). *Seriously funny: Disability and the paradox of humor*. Lynne Rienner.

Black, T., Black, M., & Monaghan, L. (2017). Conversation with a mother and son. In M. Jarman, L. Monaghan, & A. Q. Harkin (Eds.), *Barriers and belonging: Personal narratives of disability* (pp. 77–80). Temple University Press.

Block, P., & Fátima, G. (2014). Historical perspectives of autism in Brazil: Professional treatment, family advocacy, and autistic pride, 1943-2010. In S. Burch & M. Rembis (Eds.), *Disability histories* (pp. 77–97). University of Illinois Press.

Blum, L. (2007). Mother-blame in the Prozac nation: Raising kids with invisible disabilities. *Gender & Society*, 21(2), 2020–2026.

Blum, L. (2011). "Not this big, huge, racial-type thing, but...": Mothering children of color with invisible disabilities in the age of neuroscience. *Signs*, 36(4), 941–967.

Blum, L. (2015). *Raising generation Rx: Mothering kids with invisible disabilities in an age of inequality*. New York University Press.

Blum, L. M. (2020). Gender and disability studies. In N. A. Naples (Ed.), *Companion to women's and gender studies* (pp. 175–194). Wiley.

Blum, R., Kelly, A., & Ireland, M. (2001). Health-risk behaviors and protective factors among adolescents with mobility impairments and learning and emotional disabilities. *Journal of Adolescent Health*, 28(6), 481–490.

Boardman, F. (2011). Negotiating discourses of maternal responsibility, disability, and reprogenetics: The role of experiential knowledge In C. Lewiecki-Wilson & J. Cellio (Eds.), *Disability and mothering: Liminal spaces of embodied knowledge* (pp. 34–48). Syracuse University Press.

Bogdan, R. (1990). *Freak show: Presenting human oddities for amusement and profit*. University of Chicago Press.

Bolden, C. (2016, June 7). Mental illness is not just a 'white person's disease'. *Huffington Post*. https://www.huffpost.com/entry/mental-illness-is-not-a-white-persons-disease_b_10309790

Bonilla-Silva, E. (2003). *Racism without racists: Color-blind racism and the persistence of racial inequality in the United States*. Rowan & Littlefield.

Bossen, L., & Gates, H. (2017). *Bound feet, young hands: Tracking the demise of footbinding in village China*. Stanford University Press.

Bourdieu, P. (1984). *Distinction: A social critique of the judgement of taste*. Harvard University Press.

Braddock, D., & Parish, S. (2001). An institutional history of disability. In G. L. Albrecht, K. D. Seelman, & M. Bury (Eds.), *Handbook of disability studies* (pp. 11–68). SAGE.

Brashear, R. (Director). (2013). *Fixed: The science/fiction of human enhancement (Film)*. Making Change Media.

Bregain, G. (2013). An entangled perspective on disability history: The disability protests in Argentina, Brazil and Spain, 1969–1982. In A. Klein, P. Verstaete, & S. Barsch (Eds.), *The imperfect historian: Disability histories in Europe*. Peter Lang.

Bronson, J., & Berzofsky, M. (2017). *Indicators of mental health problems reported by prisoners and jail inmates, 2011–2012*. Department of Justice, Bureau of Justice Statistics.

Brooks, J. (2020). *Workers with disabilities may remain unemployed long after the Covid-19 pandemic*. Lerner Center for Public Health Promotion, Issue Brief #30. Syracuse University.

Brown, A. (2019a). *Pleasure activism: The politics of feeling good*. AK Press.

Brown, K. (2019b). *The pretty one: On life, pop culture, disability, and other reasons to fall in love with me*. Atria.

Brown, K. (2016, April 27). Love, disability, and movies. *Catapult*. https://catapult.co/stories/love-disability-and-movies

Brown, R. L., & Batty, E. (2020). The impact of internalized stigma on physical health indicators and health care utilization over a three-year period. *Stigma and Health*, 6(2), 143–150.

Brown, R. L., & Moloney, M. (2019). Intersectionality, work, and well-being: The effects of gender and disability. *Gender & Society*, 33(1), 94–122.

Brown, S. (2002). What is disability culture? *Disability Studies Quarterly*, 22(2), 34–50.

Brown, S. (2003). *Movie stars and sensuous scars*. iUniverse Publishers.

Brune, J., & Wilson, D. (Eds). (2013). *Disability and passing: Blurring the lines of identity*. Temple University Press.

Burch, S., & Joyner, H. (2007). *Unspeakable: The story of Junius Wilson*. University of North Carolina Press.

Burch, S. & Nielsen, K. (2015). History. In R. Adams, B. Reiss, & D. Serlin (Eds.), *Keywords for disability studies* (pp. 95–97). New York University Press.

Burghardt, M. (2018). *Broken: Institutions, families, and the construction of intellectual disability*. McGill-Queen University Press.

Burke, P. (2004). *Brothers and sisters of disabled children*. Jessica Kingsley.

Burke, C., & Byrne, B. (Eds.). (2020). *Social research and disability: Developing inclusive research spaces for disabled researchers*. Routledge.

Butler, J. (1990). *Gender trouble: Feminism and the subversion of identity*. Routledge.

Caldwell, K. (2010). We exist: Intersectional in/visibility in bisexuality and disability. *Disability Studies Quarterly*, 30(3-4). https://dsq-sds.org/article/view/1273

Caldwell, K., Harris, S., & Renko, M. (2020). Inclusive management for social entrepreneurs with intellectual disabilities. *Journal of Applied Research in Intellectual Disabilities* 33(2), 204–218.

Calero, S., Kopić, K., Lee, A., Nuevelle, T., Spanjaard, M., & Williams, T. (2017). *On the problematization and criminalization of children and young adults with non-apparent disabilities*. Ruderman Family Foundation.

Campbell, F. (2009). *Contours of ableism: The production of disability and abledness*. Palgrave Macmillan.

Campbell, E. (2017). Beating the odds: Life with an invisible and chronic disability. In M. Jarman, L. Monaghan, & A. Q. Harkin (Eds.), *Barriers and belongings: Personal narratives of disability* (pp. 64–71). Temple University Press.

Caplan, A. (1989). The meaning of the Holocaust for bioethics. *Hastings Center Report*, 19(4), 2–3.

Carey, A. (2009). *On the margins of citizenship: Intellectual disability and civil rights in twentieth century America*. Temple University Press.

Carey, A. (2013). The sociopolitical contexts of passing and intellectual disability. In J. A. Brune & D. J. Wilson (Eds.), *Disability and passing* (pp. 142–166). Temple University Press.

Carey, A. (2014). Parents and professionals: Parents' reflections on professionals, support systems, and the family in the early twentieth century. In S. Burch & M. Rembis (Eds.), *Disability histories* (pp. 58–76). University of Illinois Press.

Carey, A., Block, P., & Scotch, R. (2019). Sometimes allies: Parent-led disability organizations and social movements. *Disability Studies Quarterly*, 39(1). http://dsq-sds.org/

Carey, A., Block, P., & Scotch, R. (2020). *Allies and obstacles: Disability activism and parents of children with disabilities*. Temple University Press.

Carey, A., Ostrove, J., & Fannon, T. (Eds.). (2020). *Disability alliances and allies: Opportunities and challenges. Research in social science and disability* (vol. 11). Emerald Press.

Carlson, L. (2009). *The faces of intellectual disability: Philosophical reflections*. Indiana University.

Carroll-Miranda, M. (2017). Access to higher education mediated by acts of self-disclosure: "It's a hassle." In S. L. Kerschbaum, L. T. Eisenman, & J. M. Jones (Eds.), *Negotiating disability: Disclosure and higher education* (pp. 275–290). University of Michigan Press.

Carson, E., & Anderson, E. (2016). *Prisoners in 2015*. Bureau of Justice Statistics.

Cassell, J. (2005). *Life and death in the intensive care*. Temple University Press.

Cassiman, S. (2011). Mothering, disability, and poverty: Straddling borders, shifting boundaries, and everyday resistance. In C. Lewiecki-Wilson & J. Cellio (Eds.), *Disability and mothering: Liminal spaces of embodied knowledge* (pp. 289–301). Syracuse University Press.

Castles, K. (2004). "Nice, average Americans": Postwar parents, groups, and the defense of the normal family. In J. W. Trent & S. Noll (Eds.), *Mental retardation in America* (pp. 351–370). New York University Press.

Center for an Accessible Society. (n.d.). *The "institutional bias" in long-term care policy*. http://www.accessiblesociety.org/topics/persasst/instbias.htm

Center on Budget and Policy Priorities. (2019, September 6). *Chart book: Social security disability insurance*. cbpp.org/research/social-security/chart-book-social-security-disability-insurance

Center on Budget and Policy Priorities. (2020a). *Most of budget goes towards defense, social security, and major health programs*. cbpp.org/most-of-budget-goes-towards-defense-social-security-and-major-health-programs-2

Center on Budget and Policy Priorities. (2020b). *Policy basics: Where do our federal tax dollars go*. https://www.cbpp.org/research/federal-budget/policy-basics-where-do-our-federal-tax-dollars-go

Centers for Disease Control and Prevention (CDC). (1999). *CDC achievements in public health, 1990-1999: Improvements in workplace safety: Improvement in workplace safety – United States, 1900-1999*. https://www.cdc.gov/mmwr/preview/mmwrhtml/mm4822a1.html

Centers for Disease Control and Prevention (CDC). (2017). *Assessing access to water and sanitation*. cdc.gov/healthywater/global/assessing.html

Centers for Disease Control and Prevention (CDC). (2018). *CDC: 1 in 4 US adults live with a disability*. https://www.cdc.gov/media/releases/2018/p0816-disability.html

Centers for Disease Control and Prevention (CDC). (2019a). *Cigarette smoking among adults with disabilities*. cdc.gov/ncbddd/disabilityandhealth/smoking-in-adults.html

Centers for Disease Control and Prevention (CDC). (2019b). *Disability and health related conditions*. https://www.cdc.gov/ncbddd/disabilityandhealth/relatedconditions.html

Centers for Disease Control and Prevention (CDC). (2019c). *Infant mortality statistics from the 2017 period linked birth/infant death data set*. https://www.cdc.gov/nchs/data/nvsr/nvsr68/nvsr68_10-508.pdf

Centers for Disease Control and Prevention (CDC). (2019d). *National Health Interview Survey: Long-term trends in health insurance coverage, table 1*. https://www.cdc.gov/nchs/data/nhis/health_insurance/TrendHealthInsurance1968_2018.pdf

Centers for Disease Control and Prevention (CDC). (2019e). *Smoking and tobacco use: Data and statistics*. cdc.gov/tobacco/data_statistics/index.htm

Centers for Disease Control and Prevention (CDC). (n.d.). *ADHD throughout the years*. https://www.cdc.gov/ncbddd/adhd/timeline.html

Chang, G. (2017). Inevitable intersections: Care, work, and citizenship. In M. Rembis (Ed.), *Disabling domesticity* (pp. 163–194). Palgrave Macmillan.

Chapman, C., Carey, A., & Ben-Moshe, L. (2014). Reconsidering confinement: Interlocking locations and logics of incarceration. In L. Ben-Moshe, C. Chapman, & A. C. Carey (Eds.), *Disability incarcerated: Imprisonment and disability in the United States and Canada* (pp. 3–24). Palgrave Macmillan.

Chapman, C., & Withers, A. (2019). *A violent history of benevolence: Interlocking oppression in the moral economies of social working*. University of Toronto Press.

Charlton, J. (2000). *Nothing about us without us: Disability oppression and empowerment*. University of California Press.

Chatzitheochari, S., & Platt, L. (2019). Disability differentials in educational attainment in England: Primary and secondary effects. *British Journal of Sociology*, 70(2), 505–525.

Chib, M. (2011). *One little finger*. SAGE.

Chouinard, V. (1997). Making space for disabling differences: Challenging ableist geographies. *Environment and Planning D: Society and Space*, 15(4), 379–387.

Chugani, C. D., & Houtrow, A. (2020). Effect of COVID-19 pandemic on college students with disabilities. *American Journal of Public Health*, 110(2), 1722–1723.

Clare, E. (2017). *Brilliant imperfection: Grappling with cure*. Duke University Press.

Cohen, P. (2014). Marriage rates among people with disabilities. *Council on Contemporary Families*. thesocietypages.org/ccf/2014/11/24/marriage-rates-among-people-with-disabilities-save-the-data-edition

Collins, P. (1990). *Black feminist thought: Knowledge, consciousness, and the politics of empowerment*. Routledge.

Condeluci, A. (2009). *The essence of interdependence*. Lash & Associates.

Condeluci, A., & Fromknecht, J. (2014). *Social capital: The key to macro change*. Lash & Associates.

Connolly, K. (2009). *Double take*. Harper Publishing.

Connor, D., & Ferri, B. (2007). The conflict within: Resistance to inclusion and other paradoxes in special education. *Disability & Society*, 22(1), 63–77.

Connors, C., & Stalker, K. (2003). *The views and experiences of disabled children and their siblings: A positive outlook*. Jessica Kingsley.

Connors, C., & Stalker, K. (2007). Children's experiences of disability: Pointers to a social model of childhood disability. *Disability & Society*, 22(1), 19–33.

Conrad, P. (2007). *On the medicalization of society*. Johns Hopkins University Press.

Cooley, C. ([1902] 1983). *Human nature and the social order*. Transaction.

Couser, T. (2015). Illness. In R. Adams, B. Reiss, & D. Serlin (Eds.), *Keywords for disability studies* (pp. 105–107). New York University Press.

Cox, P. (2013). Passing as sane, or how to get people to sit next to you on the bus. In J. A. Brune & D. Wilson (Eds.), *Disability and passing* (pp. 99–110). Temple University Press.

Coyle, C., Kramer, J., & Mutchler, J. (2014). Aging together: Sibling carers of adults with intellectual and developmental disabilities. *Journal of Policy and Practice in Intellectual Disabilities*, 11(4), 302–312.

Crawford, C. J. (2020). *Home care fault lines: Understanding tensions and creating alliances*. Cornell University Press.

Crenshaw, K. (1989). Demarginalizing the intersection of race and sex: A black feminist critique of antidiscrimination doctrine, feminist theory, and antiracist politics. *University of Chicago Legal Forum*, 1989(1), 139–167.

Daen, L. (2017). Revolutionary war invalid pensions and the bureaucratic language of disability in the early republic. *Early American Literature*, 52(1), 141–167.

Danieli, A., & Woodhams, C. (2005). Emancipatory research methodologies and disability: A critique. *International Journal of Social Research Methodology*, 8(4), 281–296.

Daniels, J. N. (2019). Disabled mothering? Outlawed, overlooked, and severely prohibited: Interrogating ableism in motherhood. *Social Inclusion*, 7(1), 114–123.

Darling, R. B. (1988). Parental entrepreneurship: A consumerist response to professional dominance. *Journal of Social Issues*, 44(1), 141–158.

Darling, R. B. (2013). *Disability and identity: Negotiating self in a changing society*. Lynne Rienner.

David, R. (2016). Egyptian medicines and disabilities: From pharaonic to Greco-Roman

Egypt. In C. Laes (Ed.), *Disability in antiquity* (pp. 75–89). Routledge.

Davis, L. (1997a). Constructing normalcy: The bell curve, the novel, and the invention of the disabled body in the nineteenth century. In L. Davis (Ed.), *The disability studies reader* (pp. 9–28). Routledge.

Davis, L. (1997b). Universalizing marginality: How Europe became deaf in the eighteenth century. In L. J. Davis (Ed.), *The disability studies reader* (pp. 110–127). Routledge.

Davis, L. (2013). The end of identity politics: On disability as an unstable category. In L. Davis (Ed.), *The disability studies reader, fourth edition* (pp. 263–277). Routledge.

Davis, L. (2015). *Enabling acts: The hidden story of how the Americans with disabilities act gave the largest US minority its rights*. Beacon Press.

Davis, D., & Craven, C. (2016). *Feminist ethnography: Thinking through methodologies, challenges and possibilities*. Rowman & Littlefield.

de Carvalho, L. V., Áfio, A. C. E., Rodrigues Jr., J. C., de Almeida Rebouças, C. B., & Pagliuca, L. M. F. (2014). Advances in health promotion for people with disabilities and the law in Brazil. *Health*, 6, 2365–2374.

DePoy, E., & Gilson, S. (2011). *Studying disability: Multiple theories and responses*. SAGE.

DePoy, E., & Gilson, S. (2018). *Branding and designing disability*. Routledge.

Desilver, D. (2016). *What's on your table? How America's diet has changed over the decades*. PEW Research Center. pewresearch.org/fact-tank/2016/12/13/whats-on-your-table-how-americas-diet-has-changed-over-the-decades

DeVault, M. L. (1991). *Feeding the family: The social organization of caring as gendered work*. University of Chicago.

Dillaway, H., & Lysack, C. (2015). "Most of them are amateurs": Women with spinal cord injury experience the lack of education and training among medical providers while seeking gynecological care. *Disability Studies Quarterly*, 35(3). https://dsq-sds.org/article/view/4934

Dimitrova, I. (2020). Impasses of disability alliance-building in Bulgaria: Successful phantom activism and toxic grassroots mobilizations. In A. C. Carey, J. Ostrove, & T. Fallon (Eds.), *Disability alliances and allies: Opportunities and challenges. Research on social science and disability* (vol. 12, pp. 67–86). Emerald Press.

Disability Day of Mourning. N.d. https://disability-memorial.org/

Disabled Persons in India: A Statistical Profile, 2016. (2016). *Social statistics division, Government of India*. http://mospi.nic.in/sites/default/files/publication_reports/Disabled_persons_in_India_2016.pdf

Disabled World. (2020). *CRPD list of countries by signature*. https://www.disabled-world.com/disability/discrimination/crpd-milestone.php

Dobransky, K. (2014). *Managing madness in the community*. Rutgers University Press.

Dolmage, J. (2018). *Disabled upon arrival: Eugenics, immigration, and the construction of race and disability*. The Ohio State University Press.

Dorfman, D. (2016). The blind justice paradox: Judges with visual impairments and the disability metaphor. *Cambridge Journal of International and Comparative Law*, 5(2), 272–305.

Dorfman, D. (2020). [Un]usual suspects: Deservingness, scarcity and disability rights. *UC Irvine Law Review*, 10(2), 557–618.

Douglass, F. ([1850] 2009). The nature of slavery. In H. Brontz (Ed.), *African-American social and political thought: 1850–1920* (pp. 215–220). Transaction Publishers.

Dowdall, G. (1996). *The eclipse of the state mental hospital: Policy, stigma, and organization*. State University of New York Press.

Drew, J. (2015). Disability, poverty, and material hardship since the passage of the ADA. *Disability Studies Quarterly*, 35(3). https://dsq-sds.org/article/view/4947/4026

Du Bois, W. ([1903] 1994). *The souls of black folk*. Dover Publications.

Durkheim, E. ([1938] 2013). *The rules of sociological method and selected texts on sociology and its method* (2nd ed.). Palgrave.

Durkheim, E. ([1893] 2014). *The division of labor in society*. The Free Press.

Dwojuxigbe, M., Bolorunduro, M., & Busari, D. (2017). Female genital mutilation as sexual disability: Perceptions of women and their spouses in Akure, Ondo State, Nigeria. *Reproduction Health Matters*, 25(50), 80–91.

Earle, G. (1937). Remarks of Governor George H. Earle, Governor of Pennsylvania, at Ground-Breaking Ceremonies, Laurelton State Village, Thursday 23, 1937, at 11am est. Papers of the Governor George Howard Earle III, Pennsylvania State Archives, Manuscript Group 342, Official Papers, Speeches 1937–1938, box 15, 3-page document.

Edgerton, R. ([1967] 1993). *The cloak of competence: Stigma in the lives of the mentally retarded* (2nd ed.). University of California Press.

Edwards, M. (1997). Deaf and dumb in ancient Greece. In L. Davis (Ed.), *The disability studies reader* (pp. 29–51). Routledge.

Egner, J. (2018). *An intersectional examination of disability and LGBTQ+ identities in virtual spaces* (Graduate dissertation, University of South Florida). http://scholarcommons.usf.edu/etd/7149

Egner, J. (2019). 'The disability community was never mine': Neuroqueer disidentification. *Gender & Society*, 33(1), 123–147.

Elliott, L. (2017). World's eight richest people have same wealth as poorest 50%. *The Guardian*. www.theguardian.com/global-development/2017/jan/16/worlds-eight-richest-people-have-same-wealth-as-poorest-50

Engelman, D. (2018). *Endings and beginnings: A father's journey through his son's madness, loss, and a quest for meaning, an autoethnography*. Unpublished paper.

Engel, D., & Munger, F. (2003). *Rights of inclusion: Law and identity in the life stories of Americans with disabilities*. University of Chicago Press.

Eppard, L., Rank, M., & Bullock, H. (2020). *Rugged individualism and the misunderstanding of American inequality*. Lehigh University Press.

Erevelles, N. (2011). *Disability and difference in global contexts: Enabling a transformative body politic*. Palgrave Macmillan.

Erevelles, N. (2014). Crippin' Jim Crow: Disability, dis-location, and the school-to-prison pipeline. In L. Ben-Moshe, C. Chapman, & A. C. Carey (Eds.), *Disability incarcerated: Imprisonment and disability in the United States and Canada* (pp. 88–100). Palgrave Macmillan.

Erevelles, N., & Minear, A. (2013). Unspeakable offenses: Untangling race and disability in the discourses of intersectionality. In L. J. Davis (Ed.), *The disability studies reader* (4th ed., pp. 354–369). Routledge.

Erkulwater, J. (2018). How the nation's largest minority became white: Race politics and the disability rights movement, 1970-1980. *Journal of Policy History*, 30(3), 367–388.

Ervin, D., Hennen, B., Merrick, J., & Morad, M. (2014). Healthcare for people with intellectual and developmental disabilities in the community. *Frontiers in Public Health*, 2, 83.

Estreich, G. (2019). *Fables and futures: Biotechnology, disability, and the stories we tell ourselves*. MIT Press.

Etieylbo, E., & Omiegbe, O. (2016). Religion, culture, and discrimination against persons with disabilities in Nigeria. *African Journal of Disability*, 5(1), 192–198.

European Women's Lobby. (2011). *Women more prone to disability than men, and particularly vulnerable to discrimination and violence*. https://www.womenlobby.org/Women-more-prone-to-disability-than-men-and-particularly-vulnerable-to

Fannon, T. (2016). Out of sight, still in mind: Visually impaired women's embodied accounts of ideal femininity. *Disability Studies Quarterly*, 36(1). https://dsq-sds.org/article/view/4326

Farber, B. (1968). *Mental retardation: Its social context and social consequences*. Houghton Mifflin.

Fazio, M. (2019). Why those with disabilities wait years for programs they need to live on their own. *Disability Scoop*. https://www.disabilityscoop.com/2019/12/10/why-disabilities-wait-years-programs-need-live-own/27553/

Fegan, L., Rauch, A. & McCarthy, W. (1993). *Sexuality and people with intellectual disability*. Paul H. Brookes Publishing.

Ferguson, P. (1994). *Abandoned to their fate: Social policy and practice toward severely disabled people in America, 1820-1920*. Temple University Press.

Ferri, B., & Connor, D. (2005). Tools of exclusion: Race, disability, and (re)segregated education. *Teachers College Record*, 107(3), 453–474.

Ferri, B., & Connor, D. (2006). *Reading resistance: Discourses of exclusion in desegregation and inclusion debates*. Peter Lang.

Field, J. (2017). The governor's two bodies: Polity and monstrosity in Winthrop's Boston. *Early American Literature*, 52(1), 29–52.

Fine, M., & Asch, A. (1988). *Women with disabilities: Essays in psychology, culture and politics*. Philadelphia, PA: Temple University Press.

Finger, A. (1992). Forbidden fruit. *New Internationalist*, 223, 8–10.

Fink, S. (2020). Who gets lifesaving care? Tennessee changes rules after federal complaint. *New York Times*. nytimes.com/2020/06/26/US/coronavirus-rationing-tennessee.html

Fish, R. (2019). Standing out and sorting in: Exploring the role of racial composition in racial disparities in special education. *American Educational Research Journal*, 56(6), 2573–2608.

Fiske, S., Cuddy, A., Glick, P., & Xu, J. (2002). A model of (often mixed) stereotype content: Competence and warmth respectively follow from perceived status and competence. *Journal of Personality and Social Psychology*, 82(6), 878–902.

Fleischer, D., & Zames, F. (2011). *The disability rights movement: From charity to confrontation*. Temple University Press.

Foucault, M. (1965). *Madness and civilization: A history of insanity in the age of reason*. Random House.

Foucault, M. ([1975] 1995). *Discipline and punish: The birth of the prison*. Vintage.

Foucault, M. ([1978] 1990). *The history of sexuality: An introduction volume one*. Vintage.

Foucault, M. (1980). *Power/knowledge: Selected interviews and other writings, 1972–1977*. Pantheon.

Franzese, R. (2009). *Sociology of deviance: Differences, tradition, and stigma*. Charles C. Thomas.

Fraser, N., & Gordon, L. (1974). A genealogy of dependency: Tracing a keyword in the U.S. welfare state. *Signs*, 19(2), 309–336.

Frederick, A. (2015). Between stigma and mother-blame: Blind mothers' experiences in USA hospital post-natal care. *Sociology of Health and Illness*, 37(8), 117–1141.

Frederick, A. (2017). Risky mothers and the normalcy project: Women with disabilities negotiate scientific motherhood. *Gender & Society*, 31(1), 74–95.

Frederick, A., & Shifrer, D. (2019). Race and disability: From analogy to intersectionality. *Sociology of Race and Ethnicity*, 5(2), 200–214.

Fredriksen-Goldsen, K., Kim, H., & Barken, S. (2012). Disability among lesbian, gay and bisexual adults: Disparities in prevalence and risk. *American Journal of Public Health*, 102(1), 16–21.

Freidson, E. (1970). *The profession of medicine: A study of the sociology of applied knowledge*. University of Chicago Press.

Friedman, L. J. (1999). *Identity's architect: A biography of Erik H. Erikson*. Scribner/Simon & Schuster.

Friedman, C., & Rizzolo, M. (2018). Friendship, quality of life, and people with intellectual and developmental disabilities. *Journal of Developmental and Physical Disabilities*, 30(1), 39054.

Fritsch, K. (2013). The neoliberal circulation of affects: Happiness, accessibility and the capacitation of disability as wheelchair. *Health, Culture and Society*, 5(1), 135–149.

Fritsch, K. (2017). Contesting the neoliberal affects of disabled parenting: Toward a relational emergence of disability. In M. Rembid (Ed.), *Disabling domesticity* (pp. 243–267). Palgrave Macmillan.

Fuller-Thomson, E., Nuru-Jetere, A., Minkler, M., & Guralnick, J. (2009). Black-white disparities in disability among older Americans: Further untangling the role of race and socioeconomic status. *Journal of Aging and Health*, 21(5), 677–698.

Gabel, S., Vyan, S., Patel, H. & Swapnil, P. (2001). Problems of methodology in cross-cultural disability studies: An Indian immigrant example. In S. N. Barnartt & B. M. Altman (Eds.), *Exploring theories and expanding methodologies: Where we are and where we need to go. Research in social science and disability* (vol. 2, pp. 209–228). Elsevier Science.

Gallo-Silver, L., Bimbi, D., & Rembis, M. (2017). Reclaiming the sexual rights of LGBTQ people with attendant care dependent mobility impairments. In M. Rembis (Ed.), *Disabling domesticity* (pp. 195–214). Palgrave Macmillan.

Galvin, R. (2004). Challenging the need for gratitude: Comparisons between paid and unpaid care for disabled people. *Journal of Sociology*, 40(2), 137–155.

Gamson, W. (1990). *The strategy of social protest, subsequent edition*. Wadsworth Publishing.

Garcia, M. (2020). I want to spread my wings too. In P. Justesen (Ed.), *From the periphery: Real life stories of disability*. Lawrence Hill Books.

Gardiner, F. (2017). A letter at the intersection of autism and race. In L. X. Z. Brown, E. Ashkenazy, & M. Onaiwu (Eds.), *All the weight of our dreams: On living racialized autism* (pp. 11–18). DragonBee Press.

Garland-Thomson, R. (1996). *Freakery: Cultural spectacle of the extraordinary body*. New York University Press.

Garland-Thomson, R. (1997). *Extraordinary bodies: Figuring physical disability in American culture and literature*. Columbia University Press.

Garland-Thomson, R. (2015). Eugenics. In R. Adams, B. Reiss, & D. Serlin (Eds.), *Keywords for disability studies* (pp. 74–79). New York University Press.

Garland-Thomson, R. (2019). Becoming disabled. In P. Catapano & R. Garland-Thomson (Eds.), *About us: Essays from the disability series of the New York Times* (pp. 3–8). Leveright.

Geertz, C. (1973). *The interpretation of cultures: Selected essays*. Basic Books.

Geiger, A., & Davis, L. (2019). A growing number of American teenagers – Particularly girls – Are facing depression. *FactTank*. https://www.pewresearch.org/fact-tank/2019/07/12/a-growing-number-of-american-teenagers-particularly-girls-are-facing-depression/

Geiger, A., & Livingston, G. (2018). *8 facts about love and marriage in America*. Pew Research Center. https://www.pewresearch.org/fact-tank/2019/02/13/8-facts-about-love-and-marriage/

Gerschick, T. (2000). Toward a theory of disability and gender. *Signs*, 25(4), 1263–1268.

Gerschick, T., & Miller, A. (1995). Coming to terms: Masculinity and physical disability. In D. F. Sabo & D. F. Gordon (Eds.), *Men's health and illness: Gender, power, and the body. Research on men and masculinities series* (vol. 8, pp. 183–204). SAGE.

Gerschick, T., & Stevens, D. (2016). Invisibility, visibility, vilification, and near silence: The framing of disability in the early years of the American sociological society. In *Sociology looking at disability: What did we know and when did we know it. Research in social science and disability* (vol. 9, pp. 1–27). Emerald Group.

Gibson, M. (2014). Upsetting experience: Disability, mothering, and queer resistance. In M. F. Gibson (Ed.), *Queering motherhood: Narrative and theoretical perspectives* (pp. 203–218). Demeter Press.

Gill, C. (1997). Four types of integration in disability identity development. *Journal of Vocational Rehabilitation*, 9(1), 39–46.

Gill, C. (2000). Health professionals, disability, and assisted suicide: An examination of relevant empirical evidence and reply to Batavia. *Psychology, Public Policy, and Law*, 6(2), 526-545.

Gill, M. (2015). *Already doing it: Intellectual disability and sexual agency*. University of Minnesota Press.

Gillespie-Lynch, K., Dwyer, P., Constantino, C., Kapp, K., Hotez, E., Riccio, A., … Endlich, E. (2020). Can we broaden the neurodiversity movement without weakening it?: Participatory approaches as a framework for cross-disability alliance building. In A. C. Carey, J. Ostrove, & T. Fannon (Eds.), *Disability alliances and allies: Opportunities and challenges. Research in social science and disability* (vol. 12). Emerald Press.

Giroux, H. (2008). *Against the terror of neoliberalism: Politics beyond the age of greed*. Routledge.

GLAAD. (2020). *2018-2019: Where we are on TV*. GLAAD Media Institute. http://glaad.org/files/WWAT/WWAT_GLAAD_2018-2019.pdf

Glick, P., & Fiske, S. (2001). An ambivalent alliance: Hostile and benevolent sexism as complimentary justifications for gender equality. *American Psychologist*, 56(2), 109–118.

Goffman, E. (1956). *The representation of self in everyday life*. Doubleday Books.

Goffman, E. (1961). *Asylums: Essays on the social situation of mental patients and other inmates*. First Anchor Books.

Goffman, E. (1963). *Stigma: Notes on the management of spoiled identity*. First Anchor Books.

Goldberg, S., Killeen, M., & O'Day, B. (2005). The disclosure conundrum: How people with psychiatric disabilities navigate employment. *Psychology, Public Policy, and Law*, 3, 463–500.

Goode, D., Reiss, J., & Bronston, W. (2013). *A history and sociology of the Willowbrook State School*. American Association on Intellectual and Developmental Disabilities.

Goodman, N., Morris, M., & Boston, K. (2017). *Financial inequality: Disability, race and *poverty in America*. National Disability Institute. https://www.nationaldisabilityinstitute.org/wp-content/uploads/2019/02/disability-race-poverty-in-america.pdf

Gould, R., Harris, S. P., Caldwell, K., Fujiura, G., Jones, R., Ojok, P., & Enriquez, K. (2015). Beyond the law: A review of knowledge, attitudes, and perceptions in ADA employment research. *Disability Studies Quarterly*, 35(3). https://dsq-sds.org/article/view/4935/4095

Gould, R., Harris, S. P., Mullin, C., & Jones, R. (2020). Disability, diversity, and corporate responsibility: Learning from recognized leaders in inclusion. *Journal of Vocational Rehabilitation*, 52(1), 29–42.

Gould, E., & Kroeger, T. (2017). *Women can't educate their way out of the gender gap*. Economic Policy Institute.

Gould, E., & Wething, H. (2012). *U.S. poverty rates higher, safety net weaker than in peer countries*. Economic Policy Institute. https://www.epi.org/publication/ib339-us-poverty-higher-safety-net-weaker/

Gramsci, A. ([1889] 1971). *Selections from the prison notebooks*. International Publishers.

Granovetter, M. (1974). *Getting a job: A study of contacts and careers*. Harvard University Press.

Gray, D. E. (2003). Gender and coping: The parents of children with high functioning autism. *Social Science & Medicine*, 56, 631–642.

Grech, S. (2012). Disability, communities of poverty, and the global south. In A. Azzopardi & S. Grech (Eds.), *Inclusive communities: A critical reader* (pp. 69–84). Sense Publishers.

Grech, S., & Soldatic, K. (Eds.). (2016). *Disability in the global south: The critical handbook*. Springer International.

Greely, L. (1994). *Autobiography of a face*. Houghton Mifflin.

Green, S. (2003). They are beautiful and they are ours: Swapping tales of mothering children with disabilities through interactive interviewing. *Journal of Loss and Trauma*, 8(1), 1–13.

Green, S., & Barnartt, S. (2016). *Sociology looking at disability: What did we know and when did we know it? Research in social science and disability* (vol. 9). Emerald Press.

Green, S., Darling, R., & Wilbers, L. (2016). Struggles and joys: A review of research on the social experience of parenting disabled children. In S. E. Green & S. N. Barnartt (Eds.), *Sociology looking at disability: What did we know and when did we know it? Research in social science and disability* (vol. 9, pp. 261–285). Emerald.

Green, S., & Loseke, D. (2020). *New narratives of disability: Constructions, clashes, and controversies. Research in social science and disability* (vol. 11). Emerald.

Grob, G. N. (1994). *The mad among us: A history of the care of America's mentally ill*. The Free Press.

Groce, N. (2006). Cultural beliefs and practices that influence the type and nature of data collected on individuals with disability through national census. In B. M. Altman & S. N. Barnartt (Eds.), *International views on disability measures: Moving toward comparative measurement. Research in social science and disability* (vol. 4, pp. 41–54). Elsevier Science.

Groch, S. (1994). Oppositional consciousness: Its manifestations and development. The case of people with disabilities. *Sociological Inquiry*, 64(4), 369–395.

Groch, S. (2001). Free spaces: Creating oppositional consciousness in the disability rights movement. In J. Mansbridge & A. Morris (Eds.), *Oppositional consciousness: The subjective roots of social protest* (pp. 65–98). University of Chicago Press.

Grossman, B. (2019). Disability and corporeal (im)mobility: How interstate variation in Medicaid impacts the cross-state plans and pursuits of personal care attendant service users. *Disability and Rehabilitation*, 41(25), 3079–3089.

Grossman, B., & Mullin, C. (2020). Beneficiary work: The hidden labor of Medicaid users pursuing cross-state moves. *Sociological Forum*, 35(1), 50-72.

Guba, E., & Lincoln, Y. (2005). Paradigmatic controversies, contradictions, and emerging confluences. In N. K. Denzin & Y. S. Lincoln (Eds.), *The SAGE handbook of qualitative research* (3rd ed., pp. 191–215). SAGE.

Gurza, A. (2017). Queer and cripple in the 6ix. *DisabilityAfterDark*. http://www.andrewgurza.com/blog/2017/6/11/queer-and-cripple-in-the-6ix

Hahn, H. (1983). Paternalism and public policy. *Society*, 20, 36–46.

Hahn, H. (1985). Introduction: Disability policy and the problem of discrimination. *American Behavioral Scientist*, 28(3), 293–318.

Hahn, H. (1987). Civil rights for disabled Americans: The foundations for a political agenda. In A. Gartner & T. Joe (Eds.), *Images of the disabled, disabling images* (pp. 181–204). Praeger.

Hahn, H. (1989). Masculinity and disability. *Disability Studies Quarterly*, 9(9), 54–56.

Hakim, D. (2020). "It's hit our front door": Homes for the disabled see a surge of COVID-19. *New York Times*. https://www.nytimes.com/2020/04/08/nyregion/coronavirus-disabilities-group-homes.html

Hall, K. (Ed.). (2011). *Feminist disability studies*. Indiana University Press.

Haller, B., & Becker, A. (2014). Stepping backwards with disability humor? The case of NY gov. David Paterson's representation on 'Saturday Night Live'. *Disability Studies Quarterly*, 34(1). https://dsq-sds.org/issue/view/113

Hannan, M., & Freeman, J. (1984). Structural inertia and organizational change. *American Sociological Review*, 49, 149–164.

Haraway, D. J. (1991). *Simians, cyborgs, and women: The reinvention of nature*. Routledge.

Harding, S. (1987). *Feminism and methodology*. Indiana University Press.

Hays, S. (1996). *The cultural contradictions of motherhood*. Yale University Press.

Hayward, M., Hummer, R., & Sassoon, I. (2015). Trends and group differences in the association between educational attainment and U.S. adult mortality: Implications for understanding education's causal influence. *Social Science & Medicine*, 127, 8–18.

Heller, T. (2010). People with intellectual and developmental disabilities growing old: An overview. *Impact*, 23(1), 2–3.

Heller, T., & Harris, S. (2012). *Disability through the life course*. SAGE.

Hernandez, B., Keys, C., & Balcazar, F. (2004). Disability rights: Attitudes of private and public sector representatives. *Journal of Rehabilitation*, 70(1), 28–37.

Herzog, A. (2017). *The social contexts of disability ministry: A primer for pastors, seminarians, and lay leaders*. Cascade Books.

Heumann, J. and Joiner, K. (2020). *Being Heumann: An unrepentant memoir of a disability rights activist*. Beacon Press.

Heyer, K. (2015). *Rights enabled: The disability revolution from the US, to Germany and Japan, to the United Nations*. University of Michigan Press.

Hillary, A. (2014). Erasure of queer autistic people. In C. Wood (Ed.), *Criptiques* (pp. 121–146). Word Press. https://criptiques.files.wordpress.com/2014/05/crip-final-2.pdf

Hinshaw, S. (2007). *The mark of shame: Stigma of mental illness and an agenda for change*. Oxford University Press.

Hirschmann, N. (2013). Freedom and (dis)ability in early modern political thought. In A. P. Hobgood & D. H. Wood (Eds.), *Recovering disability in early modern England* (pp. 167–186). The Ohio State University Press.

Hitselberger, K. (2020, December 11). Why fashion and beauty are such important parts of my life. *Claiming Crip*. https://www.claimingcrip.com/blog/why-fashion-and-beauty-are-such-important-parts-of-my-life

Hochschild, A. (1989). *The second shift*. Viking Press.

Hoffman, E. A. (2021). *Lactation at work: Expressed milk, expressing beliefs, and the expressive value of law*. Cambridge University Press.

Hogan, D. (2012). *Family consequences of children's disabilities*. Russell Sage Foundation.

Hollinrake, S., Spencer, S., & Dix, G. (2019). Disabled citizens as researchers: Challenges and benefits of collaboration for effective action and change. *European Journal of Social Work*, 22(5), 749–762.

Holt, L., Bowlby, S., & Lea, J. (2019). Disability, special education needs, class, capitals, and segregation in schools: A population geography perspective. *Population, Space & Place*, 25(4). https://onlinelibrary.wiley.com/doi/10.1002/psp.2229

Horowitz, A. (2002). *Creating mental illness*. University of Chicago.

House, J., Landis, K., & Umberson, D. (1988). Social relationships and health. Science, 241(4865), 540-545. In P. Conrad & V. Leiter. (2019). The Sociology of Health and Illness, 10th Edition. (pp. 114–124). SAGE.

Houtenville, A., & Boege, S. (2019). *Annual report on people with disabilities in America: 2018*. University of New Hampshire, Institute on Disability.

Houtenville, A., & Rafal, M. (2020). *Annual report on people with disabilities in America: 2020*. University of New Hampshire, Institute on Disability. https://disabilitycompendium.org/annualreport

Huang, S. (2019). Ten years of the CRPD's adoption in China: Challenges and opportunities. *Disability & Society*, 34(6), 1004–1009.

Huang, S. (2020). International rights and local realities: Transnational allies of the disability rights movement in China. In A. C. Carey, J. Ostrove, & T. Fannon (Eds.), *Disability alliances and allies: Opportunities and challenges. Research in social science and disability* (vol. 11, pp. 19–40). Emerald Press.

Hughes, E. (1945). Dilemmas and contradictions of status. *American Journal of Sociology*, 50, 353–354.

Hughes, K., Bellis, M., Jones, L., Wood, S., Bates, G., Eckley, L., … Officer, A. (2012). Prevalence and risk of violence against adults with disabilities: A systematic review and meta-analysis of observational studies. *Lancet*, 379(9826), 1621–1629.

Human Rights Watch. (2018). Brazil: People with disabilities confined in terrible conditions. *Human Rights Watch*. https://www.hrw.org/news/2018/05/23/brazil-people-disabilities-confined-terrible-conditions#

Hussar, B., Zhang, J., Hein, S., Wang, K., Roberts, A., Cui, J., … Dilig, R. (2020). *The condition of education 2020 (NCES 2020-144)*. U.S. Department of Education.

Iezzoni, L. I. (2003). *When walking fails: Mobility problems of adults with chronic conditions*. University of California Press.

Iezzoni, L. I., & McCarthy, E. P. (2000). Mobility problems and perceptions of disability by self-respondents and proxy respondents. *Medical Care*, 38, 1051–1057.

Iezzoni, L. I., Rao, S. R., Ressalam, J., Bolcic-Jankovic, D., Agaronnik, N., Donelan, K., … Campbell, E. G. (2021). Physicians' perceptions of people with disabilities and their health care. *Health Affairs*, 40(2), 297–306.

Ingersoll, I. (2016). *College success for students with disabilities: A guide to finding and using resources, with real-world stories*. McFarland and Company.

Ishizuka, P. (2019). Social class, gender, and contemporary parenting standards in the United States: Evidence from a national survey experiment. *Social Forces*, 98(1), 31–58.

Jackson, A. J. (2021). *Worlds of care: The emotional lives of fathers caring for children with disabilities*. University of California Press.

Jacob, J., Kirshbaum, M., & Preston, P. (2017). Mothers with physical disabilities caring for young children. *Journal of Social Work in Disability & Rehabilitation*, 16(2), 95–115.

James, D. J., & Glaze, L. E. (2006). *Mental health problems of prison and jail inmates*. Bureau of Justice Statistics.

Jemmott, J. (2013). Institutional care of the mentally ill in nineteenth century Jamaica, *International Journal of Education and Research*, 1(6), 1–12.

Jemta, L., Fugl-Meyer, K. S., Öberg, K., & Dahl, M. (2009). Self-esteem in children and adolescents with mobility impairment: Impact on wellbeing and coping strategies. *Acta Paediatrica*, 98(3), 567–572.

Jennings, A. (2016). *Out of the horrors of war: Disability politics in World War II America*. University of Pennsylvania Press.

Johnson, N. E. (2017). *Images of an invisible disability: Framing hearing limitation in film and television*. Peeled Eyes Press.

Johnson, R. and Williams, K. (2002). *Lost in a desert world*. Speaking for Ourselves.

Jones, M. (2008). The most cruel and revolting crimes: The treatment of the mentally ill in mid-nineteenth century Jamaica. *The Journal of Caribbean History*, 42(2), 290.

Jones, L. A. (2010). *Doing disability justice*. Lulu.com.

Jones, D. (n.d.). SNAP matters to people with disabilities. *Food Research and Action Center*. https://frac.org/blog/snap-matters-people-disabilities#:~:text=In%20an%20average%20month%20in,5%20of%20all%20SNAP%20households

Jones-Garcia, W. (2011). My mother's mental illness. In C. Lewiecki-Wilson & J. Cellio (Eds.), *Disability and mothering: Liminal spaces of embodied knowledge* (pp. 210–217). Syracuse University Press.

Jordan, M., & Clement, S. (2018). Rallying nation. *Washington Post*. https://www.washingtonpost.com/news/national/wp/2018/04/06/feature/in-reaction-to-trump-millions-of-americans-are-joining-protests-and-getting-political/

Juette, M., & Berger, R. J. (2008). *Wheelchair warrior: Gangs, disability, and basketball.* Temple University Press.

Kaeble, D., & Cowhig, M. (2018). *Correctional populations in the United States, 2016.* Department of Justice, Bureau of Justice Statistics.

Kafer, A. (2013). *Feminist, queer, crip.* Indiana University Press.

Kahana, J. S., & Kahana, E. (2017). *Disability and aging: Learning from both to empower the lives of older adults.* Lynne Rienner.

Kahn, R. (2018, June 7). Brutal police officer knew nothing of autism, parents say. *Courthouse News Service.* https://www.courthousenews.com/brutal-police-officer-knew-nothing-of-autism-parents-say/

Kalyanpur, M. (2015). Mind the gap: Special education policy and practice in India in the context of globalization. In S. Rao (Ed.), *South Asia and disability studies: Redefining boundaries and extending horizons* (pp. 49–72). Peter Lang.

Karmel, J. D. (2017). *Dying to work: Death and injury in the American workplace.* Cornell University Press.

Katz, P. (1998). *The scalpel's edge.* Pearson.

Katz, M. B. (2013). *The undeserving poor: America's enduring confrontation with poverty.* Oxford University Press.

Katzman, E. (2020). Nothing about "us" without whom? (Re)cognizing alliance between disabled people and care workers in direct-funded attendant services. In A. C. Carey, J. Ostrove, & T. Fannon (Eds.), *Disability alliances and allies: Opportunities and challenges. Research in social science and disability* (vol. 11). Emerald Press.

Kawachi, I. (2010). Social capital and health. In C. Bird, P. Conrad, A. Fremont, & S. Timmermans (Eds.), *Handbook of medical sociology* (pp. 18–32). Vanderbilt University Press.

Kaye, H. S., Jans, L. H., & Jones, E. C. (2011). Why don't employers hire and retain workers with disabilities? *Journal of Occupational Rehabilitation*, 21(4), 526–536.

Kelly, C. (2016). *Disability politics and care.* University of British Columbia Press.

Kennedy, J., Frieden, L., Dick-Mosher, J., & Curtis, B. (2020). COVID-19 related needs of centers for independent living, CIL staff, and consumers. *Collaborative on Health Reform and Independent Living.* https://www.chril.org/

Kennedy, S., & Newton, M. J. (2016). The hauntings of slavery: Colonialism and the disabled body in the Caribbean. In S. Grech & K. Soldatic (Eds.), *Disability in the global south: The critical handbook* (pp. 379–392). Springer.

Kessler Foundation and National Organization on Disability (NOD). (2010). *Survey of Americans with disabilities: The ADA, 20 years later.* Harris Interactive. https://www.socalgrantmakers.org/sites/default/files/resources/Suvery%20of%20Americans%20with%20Disabilities.pdf

Kim, E. (2017). *Curative violence: Rehabilitating disability, gender, and sexuality in modern Korea.* Duke University Press.

Kimmel, M. S. (1996). *Manhood in America: A cultural history.* Free Press.

Kimmel, M., & Aronson, A. (2009). *Sociology now: The essentials.* Allyn & Bacon.

King, G. A., Zwaigenbaum, L., King, S., Baxter, D., Rosenbaum, P., & Bates, A. (2006). A qualitative investigation of changes in the belief systems of families of children with autism or Down Syndrome. *Child: Care, Health and Development*, 32, 353–369.

Kirakosyan, L. (2016). Promoting disability rights for a stronger democracy in Brazil: The role of NGOs. *Nonprofit and Voluntary Sector Quarterly*, 45(1_suppl), 114S–130S.

Kline, W. (2005). *Building a better race: Gender, sexuality, and eugenics from the turn of the century to the baby boom.* University of California Press.

Kohen, D. E., Dahinten, V. S., Leventhal, T., & McIntosh, C. N. (2008). Neighborhood disadvantage: Pathways of effects for young children. *Child Development*, 79(1), 156–169.

Krahn, G. L., Walker, D. K., & Correa-Araujo, R. (2015). Persons with disabilities as an unrecognized health disparity population. *American Journal of Public Health*, 105(S2), S198–S206.

Krane, D., & Hanson, K. W. (2004). *2004 N.O.D./Harris survey of Americans with disabilities.* Harris Interaction.

Kraus, L., Lauer, E., Coleman, R., & Houtenville, A. (2018). *2017 disability statistics annual report.* University of New Hampshire. https://disability

compendium.org/sites/default/files/useruploads/ 2017_AnnualReport_2017_FINAL.pdf

Kres-Nash, I. (2016). *Racism and ableism*. American Association of People With Disabilities (AAPD). https://www.aapd.com/racism-and-ableism/

Krieger, L. H. (Ed.). (2003). *Backlash against the ADA: Reinterpreting disability rights*. University of Michigan Press.

Krieger, N. (Ed.). (2005). *Embodying inequality: Epidemiologic perspectives*. Routledge.

Kukla, E. (2020, March 19). My life is more 'disposable' during this pandemic. *New York Times*. https://www.nytimes.com/2020/03/19/opinion/coronavirus-disabled-health-care.html

Kuuliala, J. (2016). *Childhood disability and social integration in the Middle Ages*. Brepols Publishers.

Ladau, E. (2020, March 25). As a disabled person, I'm afraid I may not be deemed worth saving from the coronavirus. *HuffPost*. https://www.huffpost.com/entry/coronavirus-healthcare-rationing-medical-ethics-disability_n_5e7a2b0dc5b6f5b7c54bb117

Ladd-Taylor, M. (2017). *Fixing the poor: Eugenic sterilization and child welfare in the twentieth century*. Johns Hopkins University Press.

Ladd-Taylor, M., & Umanski, L. (Eds.). (1998). *Bad mothers: The politics of blame in twentieth-century America*. New York University.

Laes, C. (2018). *Disabilities and the disabled in the Roman world: A social and cultural history*. Cambridge University.

Lagu, T., Hannon, N. S., & Rothberg, M. B. (2013). Access to subspecialty care for patients with mobility impairment. *Annals of Internal Medicine*, 158(6), 441–446.

Landes, S. D., Turk, M. A., Formica, M. K., & McDonald, K. E. (2020). *COVID-19 trends among adults with intellectual and developmental disabilities (IDD) living in residential group homes in New York state through July 10, 2020*. Research Brief #32. Learner Center for Public Health Promotion. Syracuse University. http://surface.syr.edu/cgi/viewcontent.cgi?article=1013&context=lerner

Landsman, G. (2009). *Reconstructing motherhood and disability in an age of "perfect" babies*. Routledge.

Lanier, H. K. (2015). Breaking Up with Dr. Normal. *Star in Her Eye*. https://starinhereye.wordpress.com/2014/01/05/breaking-up-with-doctor-normal/

Lareau, A. (2003). *Unequal childhoods: Class, race, and family life*. University of California Press.

Laughlin, H. H. (1922). *Eugenical sterilization in the United States*. Psychopathic Laboratory on the Municipal Court of Chicago.

Leavy, P., & Harris, A. (2019). *Contemporary feminist research from theory to practice*. Guilford Press.

Lederer, E. (2020, May 6). UN leader says 1B people with disabilities hard hit by virus. *Associated News*. https://apnews.com/c753de7283390477e007b0aeb4d09e3c

Lee, T. (2019, February 27). Black Hollywood: The struggle to include disability. *RespectAbility*. https://www.respectability.org/2019/02/black-hollywood-the-struggle-to-include-disability/

Lehrer, R. (2014). Beauty in exile. In C. Wood (Ed.), *Criptiques* (pp. 151–166). May Day. https://criptiques.files.wordpress.com/2014/05/crip-final-2.pdf

Leiter, V. (2012). *Their time has come: Youth with disabilities on the cusp of adulthood*. Rutgers University Press.

Lewiecki-Wilson, C., & Cellio, J. (Eds.). (2011). *Disability and mothering: Liminal spaces of embodied knowledge*. Syracuse University Press.

Lewis, B. (2017a). A mad fight: Psychiatry and disability activism. In L. J. Davis (Ed.), *The disability studies reader* (5th ed., pp. 102–118). Routledge.

Lewis, T. A. (2017b). In the fight to close Rikers, don't forget about deaf and disabled people. *Truthout*. https://truthout.org/articles/in-the-fight-to-close-rikers-don-t-forget-deaf-and-disabled-people/

Lewis, T. A. (2020). Ableism 2020: An updated definition. *Talila A. Lewis*. https://www.talilalewis.com/blog/ableism-2020-an-updated-definition

Liebowitz, C. (2014). A mixed-up, muddled journey into size and disability. In C. Wood (Ed.), *Criptiques* (pp. 59–66). May Day. https://criptiques.files.wordpress.com/2014/05/crip-final-2.pdf

Liebowitz, C. (2015). I am disabled: On identity-first versus person-first language. *The Body is Not an Apology*. https://thebodyisnotanapology.com/magazine/i-am-disabled-on-identity-first-versus-people-first-language/

Lightfoot, E., Hill, K., & LaLiberte, T. (2010). The inclusion of disability as a condition for termination of parental rights. *Child Abuse & Neglect*, 34(12), 927–934.

Lindgren, K. (2011). Reconceiving motherhood. In C. Lewiecki-Wilson & J. Cellio (Eds.), *Disability and mothering: Liminal spaces of embodied knowledge* (pp. 88–97). Syracuse University Press.

Linton, S. (1998). *Claiming disability: Knowledge and identity.* New York University Press.

Linton, S. (2006). *My body politic: A memoir.* University of Michigan Press.

Li, H., Parish, S. L., Mitra, M., & Nicholson, J. (2017). Health of U.S. parents with and without disabilities. *Disability and Health Journal*, 10(2), 303–307.

Lisicki, B. (2018). Block telethon 1992—The day we "pissed on pity." *National Disability Arts Collection and Archive*. https://medium.com/@theNDACA/block-telethon-1992-the-day-we-pissed-on-pity-69117b03825a

Li, L., & Singleton, P. (2016). The dynamic effect of disability on marriage: Evidence from the Social Security disability insurance program. *Center for Policy Research*, 217. https://surface.syr.edu/cpr/217

Longmore, P. K. (2003a). Screening stereotypes: Images of disabled people in television and motion pictures. In P. Longmore (Ed.), *Why I burned my book and other essays* (pp. 131–146). Temple University Press.

Longmore, P. K. (2003b). The second phase: From disability rights to disability culture. In P. Longmore (Ed.), *Why I burned my book and other essays*. Temple University Press.

Longmore, P. K. (2016). *Telethons: Spectacle, disability and the business of charity.* Oxford University Press.

Lorde, A. (1980/2020). *The cancer journals.* Penguin Books.

Losen, D. J., & Orfield, G. (2002). *Racial inequality in special education.* Harvard Education Press.

Lovaas, I. O. (1987). Behavioral treatment and normal educational and intellectual functioning in young children with autism. *Journal of Consulting and Clinical Psychology*, 1, 3–9.

Löw, M. (2016). *The sociology of space: Materiality, social space, and action.* Palgrave Macmillan.

Lowery, A. (2020, June). Defund the police. *The Atlantic.* https://www.theatlantic.com/ideas/archive/2020/06/defund-police/612682/

Lukin, J. (2013). Disability and blackness. In L. J. Davis (Ed.), *The disability studies reader, fourth edition* (pp. 308–315). Routledge.

MacInnes, M. D. (2011). Altar-bound? The effect of disability on the hazard of entry into first marriage. *International Journal of Sociology*, 41(1), 87–103.

Mahran, H., & Kamal, M. (2001). Physical disability in old kingdom tomb series. *Athens Journal of History*, 2(3), 169–192.

Mairs, N. (1986). *On being a cripple.* Arizona Board of Regents. https://docs.google.com/viewer?a=v&pid=sites&srcid=am95Y2VoYXZzdGFkLmNvbXxjbGFzc2VzfGd4OjRlNjM2YTI5ZjIyNDRiM2M

Mairs, N. (1996). *Waist-high in the world: A life among the nondisabled.* Beacon Press.

Malacrida, C. (2009). Performing motherhood in a disablist world: Dilemmas of motherhood, femininity, and disability. *International Journal of Qualitative Studies in Education*, 22(1), 99–117.

Malla, A., Joober, R., & Garcia, A. (2015). "Mental illness is like any other illness": A critical examination of the statement and its impact on patient care and society. *Journal of Psychiatry & Neuroscience*, 40(3), 147–150.

Ma, Z., & Ni, Z. (2020). Hero with zeroes? Tensions of using an anti-discrimination framework and an impact case approach for disability rights advocacy in China. *Disability Studies Quarterly*, 40(4), https://dsq-sds.org/article/view/7039

Manning, L. (2009). The magic wand: A poem by Lynn Manning. *International Journal of Inclusive Education*, 13(7), 785.

Mansbridge, J. (2001). The making of oppositional consciousness. In J. Mansbridge & A. Morris (Eds.), *Oppositional consciousness: The subjective roots of social protest* (pp. 1–19). University of Chicago.

Mansfield, C., Hopfer, S., & Marteau, T. M. (1999). Termination rates after prenatal diagnosis of Down syndrome, spina bifida, anencephaly, and Turner and Klinefelter syndromes: A systematic literature review. *Prenatal Diagnosis*, 19, 808–812.

Marmot, M. G., Rose, G. Shipley, M., & Hamilton, P. J. (1978). Employment grade and coronary heart disease in British civil servants. *Journal of Epidemiology and Community Health*, 32(4), 244–249.

Marmot, M. G., Smith, G. D., & Stansfield, S. (1991). Health inequalities among British civil servants: The Whitehall II study. *Lancet*, 337(8754), 1387–1393.

Maroto, M., & Pettinicchio, D. (2015). Twenty-five years after the ADA: Situating disability in America's system of stratification. *Disability Studies Quarterly*, 35(3), 1. https://dsq-sds.org/article/view/4927/4024

Maroto, M., & Pettinicchio, D. (2020). *An unequal labor market means that COVID-19 has been especially harmful for vulnerable groups including people with disabilities*. London School of Economics US Centre. https://blogs.lse.ac.uk/usappblog/2020/05/21/an-unequal-labor-market-means-that-covid-19-has-been-especially-harmful-for-vulnerable-groups-including-people-with-disabilities/

Maroto, M., Pettinicchio, D., & Patterson, A. C. (2019). Hierarchies of categorical disadvantage: Economic insecurity at the intersection of disability, gender, and race. *Gender & Society*, 33(1), 64–93.

Marshall Project. (2020, September 23). *A state-by-state look at Coronavirus in prisons*. https://www.themarshallproject.org/2020/05/01/a-state-by-state-look-at-coronavirus-in-prisons

Marx, K. ([1888] 1978). Theses on Feuerbach. In R. C. Tucker (Ed.), *The Marx-Engels reader* (2nd ed., pp. 143–145). W. W. Norton.

Marx, K. ([written 1845-6, published 1932] 1978). The German ideology: Part I. In R. C. Tucker (Ed.), *The Marx-Engles reader* (2nd ed., pp. 146–201). W. W. Norton.

Masters, R. K., Link, B. G., & Phelan, J. C. (2015). Trends in educational gradients of 'preventable mortality': A test of fundamental cause theory. *Social Science & Medicine*, 127, 19–28.

Matthews, R., Smith, L., Hancock, R., Jagger, C., & Spiers, N. (2005). Socioeconomic factors associated with the onset of disability in older age: A longitudinal study of people aged 75 years and over. *Social Science and Medicine*, 61(1), 1567–75.

Matysiak, B. (2001). Interpretive research and people with intellectual disabilities: Politics and practicalities. In S. N. Barnartt & B. M. Altman (Eds.), *Exploring theories and expanding methodologies. Research in social science and disability* (vol. 2, pp. 185–208). Elsevier Science.

Mauldin, L. (2016). *Made to hear: Cochlear implants and raising deaf children*. University of Minnesota Press.

Mauldin, L. (2017). A feminist, technoscientific approach to disability and caregiving in the family. In M. Rembis (Ed.). *Disabling domesticity* (pp. 139–161). Palgrave Macmillan.

Mazumdar, S., & Geis, G. (2001). Case study method for research on disability. In S. N. Barnartt & B. M. Altman (Eds.), *Exploring theories and expanding methodologies: Where we were and where we need to go. Research in social science and disability* (vol. 2, pp. 255–276). Elsevier Science.

McAdam, D. (1982). *Political process and the development of black insurgency, 1930–1970*. University of Chicago Press.

McAdam, D. (1996). Political opportunities: Conceptual origins, current problems, future directions. In D. McAdam, J. D. McCarthy, & M. N. Zald (Eds.), *Comparative perspectives on social movements* (pp. 20–40). Cambridge University Press.

McCarthy, J. D., & Zald, M. N. (1977). Resource mobilization and social movements: A partial theory. *American Journal of Sociology*, 82(6), 1212–1241.

McGuire, A. (2016). *War on autism: On the cultural logics of normative violence*. University of Michigan Press.

McLaren, C., Rosenblum, D., DeDona, M., Swick, S., & Tamborino, J. (2021). *Spotlight on women with disabilities*. US Department of Labor, Office of Disability Employment Policy.

McLeskey, J., Waldron, N.L., Spooner, F., & Algozzine, B. (2014). What are effective inclusive schools and why are they important? In J. McLeskey, N. L. Waldron, F. Spooner, & B. Algozzine (Eds.), *Handbook of effective inclusive schools* (pp. 3–16). Routledge.

McQuade, J. (2017). Colonialism was a disaster and the facts prove it. *The Conversation*. https://theconversation.com/colonialism-was-a-disaster-and-the-facts-prove-it-84496

McRuer, R. (2006). *Crip theory: Cultural signs of queerness and disability*. New York University Press.

McRuer, R. (2015). Sexuality. In R. Adams, B. Reiss, & D. Serlin (Eds.), *Keywords for disability studies* (pp. 167–169). New York University Press.

Mead, G. H. (1934). *Mind, self, and society*. University of Chicago Press.

Melgar, L. (2019, May 21). Are school shootings becoming more frequent? We ran the numbers. *KCUR/National Public Radio*. https://www.kcur.org/community/2019-05-21/are-school-shootings-becoming-more-frequent-we-ran-the-numbers

Me, A., & Mbogoni, M. (2006). Review of practices in less developed countries on the collection of disability data. In B. M. Altman & S. N. Barnartt (Eds.), *International views on disability measures: Moving toward comparative measurement. Research in social science and disability* (vol. 4, pp. 63–88). Elsevier Science.

Metzl, J. (2009). *The protest psychosis*. Beacon Press.

Metzl, J. (2018). Let's talk about guns, but stop stereotyping the mentally ill. In L. Davis (Ed.), *Beginning with disability: A primer* (pp. 165–169). Routledge.

Metzler, I. (2013). *A social history of disability in the Middle Ages: Cultural considerations of physical impairments*. Routledge.

Metzl, I. (2016). *Fools and idiots? Intellectual disability in the Middle Ages*. Manchester University Press.

Michalko, R. (2002). *The difference that disability makes*. Temple University Press.

Mietola, R., Miettinen, S., & Vehmas, S. (2017). Voiceless subjects?: Research ethics and persons with profound intellectual disabilities. *International Journal of Social Research Methodology*, 20(3), 263–274.

Miles, M. (2015). Studying responses to disability in South Asian histories: Approaches personal, prakrital and pragmatical. In S. Rao & M. Kalyanpur (Eds.), *South Asia and disability studies: Redefining boundaries and extending horizons* (pp. 127–149). Peter Lang.

Miles, A. L. (2019). "Strong black women": African American women with disabilities, intersecting identities, and inequality. *Gender & Society*, 33(1), 41–63.

Miller, D. A. (1981). The "sandwich" generation: Adult children of the aging. *Social Work*, 26(5), 419–423.

Mills, C. W. (1959). *The sociological imagination*. Oxford University Press.

Mingus, M. (2017). Moving toward the ugly: A politic beyond desirability. In L. David (Ed.), *Beginning with disability: A primer* (pp. 137–141). Routledge.

Minow, M. (1990). *Making all the difference*. Cornell University Press.

Mintz, S. W. (1985). *Sweetness and power: The place of sugar in modern history*. Penguin.

Mitchell, D. T., & Snyder, S. L. (1995). *Vital signs: Crip culture talks back* [Motion picture]. United States of America: Fanlight Productions.

Mitchell, D. T., & Snyder, S. L. (2000). *Narrative prosthesis: Disability and the dependencies of discourse*. University of Michigan Press.

Mitra, M., Mouradian, V. E., Fox, M. H., & Pratt, C. (2016). Prevalence and characteristics of sexual violence against men with disabilities. *American Journal of Preventive Medicine*, 50(3), 311–317.

Mog, A. & Swarr, A. L. (2008). Threads of commonality in transgender and disability studies. *Disability Studies Quarterly*, 28(4). https://dsq-sds.org/article/view/152/152*modified

Molina, N. (2006). *Fit to be citizens? Public health and race in Los Angeles, 1979–1939*. University of California Press.

Mollow, A. (2006). "When black women start going on Prozac": Race, gender, and mental illness in Meri Nana-Ama Danquah's Willow Weep for Me. *Melus*, 31(3), 67–99.

Molloy, E., & Nario-Redmond, M. R. (2007). College faculty perceptions of learning disabled students: Stereotypes, group identity and bias. In M. L. Vance (Ed.), *Disabled faculty and staff in a disabling society: Multiple identities in higher education* (pp. 253–268). Association on Higher Education and Disability.

Molton, I. R., & Yorkston, K. M. (2017). Growing older with a physical disability: A special application of the successful aging paradigm. *Journals of Gerontology*, 72(2), 290–299.

Mong, S. N. (2020). *Taking care of our own: When family caregivers do medical work*. Cornell University Press.

Mont, D. (2007). *Measuring disability prevalence*. The World Bank.

Moore, Jr., L. F. (2014). Droolilicious. In C. Wood (Ed.), *Criptiques* (pp. 225–226). Word Press. https://criptiques.files.wordpress.com/2014/05/crip-final-2.pdf

Moore, L. F. (2017). *Black disabled art history 101*. Xóchitl Justice Press.

Moore, L. F., Lewis, T. A., & Brown, L. X. Z. (2016). Accountable reporting on disability, race, and police violence: Community response to the Ruderman white paper on the media coverage of use of force and disability. *Harriet Tubman Collective.* https://docs.google.com/document/d/117eoVeJVP594L6-1bgL8zpZrzgojfsveJwcWuHpkNcs/edit

Moran, J. E. (2000). *Committed to the state asylum: Insanity and society in nineteenth-century Quebec and Ontario.* McGill-Queen's University Press.

Morgan, P. L., Woods, A. D., Wang, Y., Hillemeier, M. M., Farkas, G., & Mitchell, C. (2019). Are schools in the U.S. south using special education to segregate students by race? *Exceptional Children,* 86(3), 255–275.

Morris, J. (1991). *Pride against prejudice.* Women's Press.

Morris, J. (1993). Feminism and disability. *Feminist Review,* 43, 57–70.

Morris, M., & Asante-Muhammad, D. (2017, July 27). Race, wealth and disability in America. *Huffington Post.* https://www.huffpost.com/entry/race-wealth-and-disabilit_b_11194954

Morrison, D. E. (1971). Some notes toward theory on relative deprivation, social movements, and social change. *American Behavioral Scientist,* 14(5), 675–690.

Nair, A. (2017). 'They shall see his face': Blindness in British India, 1850–1950. *Medical History,* 61(2), 181–199.

NAMI. (2017). *Parity for mental health coverage.* www.nami.org/Learn-More/Public-Policy/Parity-for-Mental-Health-Coverage

Naples, N., Mauldin, L., & Dillaway, H. (2019). From the guest editors: Gender, disability and intersectionality. *Gender & Society,* 33(1), 5–18.

Narayan, J. (2004). Persons with disabilities in India: A special educator's personal perspective. *Disability Studies Quarterly,* 24(2). https://dsq-sds.org/issue/view/26

Nario-Redmond, M. R. (2010). Cultural stereotypes of disabled and non-disabled men and women: Consensus for global category representations and diagnostic domains. *British Journal of Social Psychology,* 49(3), 471–488.

Nario-Redmond, M. R. (2020). *Ableism: The causes and consequences of disability prejudice.* Wiley.

National Association of State Mental Health Directors. (2017). *Trends in psychiatric inpatient capacity, United States and each state, 1970 to 2014.*

National Center for Education Statistics (NCES). (2016). *Disability rates and employment status by educational attainment.* US Department of Education, NCES. https://nces.ed.gov/programs/coe/indicator_tad.aspnces.ed.gov/programs/coe/pdf/coe.tad.pdf

National Council on Disability (NCD). (2000). *Transition and post-school outcomes for youth with disabilities: Closing the gaps to post-secondary education and employment.* https://ncd.gov/publications/2000/Nov12000

National Council on Disability (NCD). (2009). *The current state of health care for people with disabilities.* https://www.ncd.gov/rawmedia_repository/0d7c848f_3d97_43b3_bea5_36e1d97f973d.pdf

National Council on Disability (NCD). (2012a). *Rocking the cradle: Ensuring the rights of parents with disabilities and their children.*

National Council on Disability (NCD). (2012b). *Institutions in brief.* https://ncd.gov/publications/2012/DIToolkit/Institutions/inBrief

National Council on Disability (NCD). (2017). *Neglected for too long: Dental care for people with intellectual and developmental disabilities.*

National Council on Disability (NCD). (2018). *IDEA series: The segregation of students with disabilities.* https://ncd.gov/sites/default/files/NCD_Segregation-SWD_508.pdf

National Council on Independent Living. (n.d.). *About independent living.* https://www.ncil.org/about/aboutil/

National Institute on Mental Health. (2019). *Mental illness.* https://www.nimh.nih.gov/health/statistics/mental-illness.shtml

National Organization on Disability. (2000). *National organization on disability/Harris survey of Americans with disabilities.* Harris Interactive.

National Safety Council. (n.d.). Work injury costs. *Injury Facts.* https://injuryfacts.nsc.org/work/costs/work-injury-costs/

Navarro, V. (1984). Medical history as justification rather than explanation: A critique of Starr's: The social transformation of American

Medicine. *International Journal of Health Services*, 14, 511–527.

Neely-Barnes, S. L., Hall, H., Roberts, R. J., & Graff, C. (2011). Parenting a child with an autism spectrum disorder: Public perceptions and parental conceptualizations. *Journal of Family Social Work*, 14(3), 208–225.

Neely-Barnes, S., Zanskas, S., Delavega, E. M., & Evans, T. K. (2014). Parenting with a disability and child mental health: A propensity score analysis. *Journal of Social Work in Disability & Rehabilitation*, 13(3), 226–246.

Ne'eman, A. (2020, March 23). I will not apologize for my needs. *New York Times*. https://www.nytimes.com/2020/03/23/opinion/coronavirus-ventilators-triage-disability.html

Nelson, A. (2011). *Body and soul: The Black Panther Party and the fight against medical discrimination*. University of Minnesota Press.

Newton, C. (2020, May 12). Facebook will pay $52 million in settlement with moderators who develop PTSD on the job. *The Verge*. TheVerge.com/2020/5/12/21255870/facebook-content-moderator-settlement-scola-ptsd-mental-health

Nielsen, K. E. (2012). *A disability history of the United States*. Beacon Press.

Nishida, A. (2016a). Understanding political development through an intersectionality framework: Life stories of disability activists. *Disability Studies Quarterly*, 36(2). https://dsq-sds.org/article/view/4449/4302

Nishida, A. (2016b). *Affecting neoliberal public health care: Interdependent relationality between disabled care recipients and their care providers* (Unpublished doctoral dissertation). The City University of New York, New York.

Nosek, B. A., Smyth, F. L., Hansen, J. J., Devos, T., Lindner, N. M., Ranganath, K. A., ... Banaji, M. R. (2007). Pervasiveness and correlates of implicit attitudes and stereotypes. *European Review of Social Psychology*, 18, 36–88.

Nyangweso, M. (2018). Disability in Africa: A cultural/religious perspective. *Research Gate*. https://www.researchgate.net/publication/325642373_Disability_in_Africa_A_CulturalReligious_Perspective

Office of Disease Prevention and Health Promotion. (2020). *Healthy people 2020*. Healthy People. https://www.healthypeople.gov/2020/topics-objectives/topic/disability-and-health

Office of Victims of Crime. (2018). *Crimes against people with disabilities*. https://ovc.ncjrs.gov/ncvrw2018/info_flyers/fact_sheets/2018NCVRW_VictimsWithDisabilities_508_QC.pdf

Ohan, J. L., Visser, T. A. W., Strain, M. C., & Allen, L. (2011). Teachers' and education students' perceptions of and reactions to children with and without the diagnostic label "ADHD." *Journal of School Psychology*, 49(1), 81–105.

Ólafsdóttier, L. B., Egilson, S. T., Árnadóttir, U., & Hardonk, S. C. (2019). Child and parent perspectives of life quality of children with physical impairments compared with non-disabled peers. *Scandinavian Journal of Occupational Therapy*, 26(7), 496–504.

O'Leary, P., Boden, L. I., Seabury, S. A., Ozonoff, A., & Scherer, E. (2012). Workplace injuries and the take-up of social security disability benefits. *Social Security Bulletin*, 72(3). ssa.gov/policy/docs/ssb/v72n3/v72n3p1.html

Oliver, M. (1990). *The politics of disablement*. Macmillan Education.

Oliver, M. (1992). Changing the social relations of research production. *Disability, Handicap & Society*, 7(2), 101–114.

Oliver, M. (2002). Using emancipatory methodologies in disability research. Conference Presentation, First Annual Disability Research seminar. https://disability-studies.leeds.ac.uk/wp-content/uploads/sites/40/library/Oliver-Mikes-paper.pdf

Olkin, R. (2000). Are children of disabled parents at risk for parentification? *Through the Looking Glass*. https://www.lookingglass.org/pdf/Are-Children-of-Disabled-Parents-at-Risk-for-Parentification-TLG.pdf

Olsen, R., & Clarke, H. (2003). *Parenting and disability: Disabled parents' experiences of raising children*. Polity Press.

Ong-Dean, C. (2009). *Distinguishing disability: Parents, privilege, and special education*. University of Chicago Press.

Ostrander, N. R. (2008). When identities collide: Masculinity, disability, and race. *Disability & Society*, 23(6), 585–597.

OToole, C. J. (2002). Sex, disability and motherhood: Access to sexuality for disabled mothers. *Disability Studies Quarterly*, 22(4). https://dsq-sds.org/article/view/374/495

OToole, C. J. (2015). *Fading scars: My queer disability history*. Autonomous Press.

Panitch, M. (2008). *Disability, mothers and organization: Accidental activists*. Routledge.

Papadimitriou, C. (2008). Becoming en-wheeled: The situated accomplishment of re-embodiment as a wheelchair user after spinal cord injury. *Disability & Society*, 23(7), 691–704.

Parker, K., & Patten, E. (2013). *The sandwich generation: Rising financial burden for middle-aged Americans*. PEW Research Center. https://www.pewsocialtrends.org/2013/01/30/the-sandwich-generation/

Parsons, T. (1951). *The social system*. The Free Press.

Parsons, T. (1972). Definitions of health and illness in light of American values and social structure. In E. G. Jaco (Ed.), *Patients, physicians and illness* (2nd ed., pp. 165–187). Free Press.

Parsons, A. E. (2018). *From asylums to prisons: Deinstitutionalization and the rise of mass incarceration after 1945*. University of North Carolina Press.

Parsons, J. A., Baum, S., Johnson, T. J., & Hendershot, G. (2001). Inclusion of disabled populations in interview surveys: Review and recommendations. In S. N. Barnartt & B. M. Altman (Eds.), *Exploring theories and expanding methodologies. Research in social science and disability* (vol. 2, pp. 167–184). Elsevier Science.

Patel, S. (2014). Racing madness: The terrorizing madness of the post-9/11 terrorist body. In L. Ben-Moshe, C. Chapman, & A. C. Carey (Eds.), *Disability incarcerated* (pp. 201–216). Palgrave Macmillan.

Patterson, O. (1982). *Slavery and social death: A comparative study*. Harvard University Press.

Paur, J. (2017). *The right to main: Debility, capacity, disability*. Duke University Press.

Pelka, F. (2012). *What we have done: An oral history of the disability rights movement*. University of Massachusetts Press.

Pendo, E. (2008). Disability, equipment barriers, and women's health: Using the ADA to provide meaningful access. *Saint Louis University Journal of Health Law & Policy*, 2, 15–56.

Penrose, W. D. (2015). The discourse of disability in ancient Greece. *Classical World*, 108(4), 499–523.

Perry, D. M., & Carter-Long, L. (2016). *Media coverage of law enforcement use of force and disability*. Ruderman Family Foundation. https://rudermanfoundation.org/white_papers/media-coverage-of-law-enforcement-use-of-force-and-disability/

Pescosolido, B. A., Martin, J. K., Long, S. J., Medina, T. R., Phelan, J. C., & Link, B. G. (2010). "A disease like any other"?: A decade of change in public reactions to schizophrenia, depression, and alcohol dependence. *American Journal of Psychiatry*, 167(11), 278–284.

Pettinicchio, D. (2019). *Politics of empowerment: Disability rights and the cycle of American policy reform*. Stanford University Press.

Pettinicchio, D., & Maroto, M. (2021). Who counts? Measuring disability cross-nationally in census data. *Journal of Survey Statistics and Methodology*. 9(2), 257–284.

Phelan, J. C., & Link, B. G. (2015). Is racism a fundamental cause of inequalities in health? *Annual Review of Sociology*, 41, 311–330.

Phelan, J. C., Link, B. G., Stueve, A., & Pescosolido, B. A. (2000). Public conceptions of mental illness in 1950 and 1996: What is mental illness and is it to be feared? *Journal of Health and Social Behavior*, 41(2), 188–207.

Piepzna-Samarasinha, L. L. (2018). *Care work: Dreaming disability justice*. Arsenal Pulp Press.

Pisani, M., & Grech, S. (2015). Disability and forced migration: Critical intersections. *Disability and the Global South*, 2(1), 421–441.

Pitts-Taylor, V. (2010). The plastic brain: Neoliberalism and the neuronal self. *Health*, 14(6), 635–652.

Piven, F. F., & Cloward, R. A. (1971). *Poor people's movements: Why they succeed, how they fail*. Vintage Books.

Plummer, K. (2003). *Intimate citizenship: Private decisions and public dialogues*. University of Washington Press.

Pombier, N. (2018). Personal interview with Allison Carey.

Pombier, N. (2020). A different story: Narrative allyship across ability. In A. C. Carey, J. Ostrove, & T. Fannon (Eds.), *Disability alliances and allies: Opportunities and challenges. Research in social science and disability* (vol. 12, pp. 225–257). Emerald Press.

Portman, M. (2006). The why of it. In C. Dowling, N. Nicoll, & B. Thomas (Eds.), *A different kind of perfect: Writings by parents on raising a child with special needs* (pp. 57–60). Trumpeter.

Powell, R., Mitra, M., Smeltzer, S., Long-Bellil, L., Smith, L., Rosenthal, E., & Iezzoni, L. (2019). Adaptive parenting strategies used by mothers with physical disabilities caring for infants and toddlers. *Health & Social Care in the Community* 27(4), 889–898.

Price, M. (2011). *Mad at school: Rhetorics of mental disability and academic life.* University of Michigan Press.

Price, M. (2013). Defining mental disability. In L. J. Davis (Ed.), *The disability studies reader* (4th ed., pp. 283–303). Routledge.

Priestly, M. (2001). *Disability and the life course: Global perspectives.* Cambridge University Press.

Priestly, M. (2003). *Disability: A life course approach.* Polity Press.

Pring, J. (2016). Activists protest outside premiere of "disability snuff movie." *Disability News Service.* https://www.disabilitynewsservice.com/activists-protest-outside-premiere-of-disability-snuff-movie/

Prior, R. (2020, April 8). Coping with disease and disability in the time of coronavirus. *CNN.* https://www.cnn.com/2020/04/08/health/coronavirus-disability-and-chronic-illness-wellness/index.html

Pruett, S. R., & Chan, F. (2006). The development and psychometric validation of the disability attitude association test. *Rehabilitation Psychology,* 51(3), 202–213.

Prussing, E., Sobo, E. J., Walker, E., & Kurtin, P. S. (2005). Between 'desperation' and disability rights: A narrative analysis of complementary/alternative medicine use by parents for children with down syndrome. *Social Science & Medicine,* 60(3), 587–598.

Putnam, R. (2000). *Bowling alone: The collapse and revival of American community.* Simon and Schuster.

Ralph, L. (2018). What wounds enable: The politics of disability and violence in Chicago. In L. J. Davis (Ed.), *Beginning with disability: A primer* (pp. 142–161). Routledge.

Rau, J. (2017). Why huge quality gaps among nursing homes are likely to grow if Medicaid is cut. *National Public Radio.* npr.org/sections/health-shotes/2017/09/28/554-3-740/why-huge-quality-gaps-among-nursing-homes-are-likely-to-grow-if-medicacid-is-cut

Ray, V. (2019). A theory of racialized organizations. *American Sociological Review,* 84(1), 26–53.

Reaume, G. (2009). *Remembrance of patients past: Patient life of the Toronto hospital for the insane, 1870–1940.* University of Toronto Press.

Reich, J. A. (2016). *Calling the shots: Why parents vaccinate.* New York University.

Reilly, P. R. (1991). *The surgical solution: History of involuntary sterilization in the United States.* Johns Hopkins University Press.

Reinharz, S. (1992). *Feminist methods in social research.* Oxford University Press.

Rembis, M. (2011). *Defining deviance: Sex, science, and delinquent girls.* University of Illinois Press.

Rembis, M. (2014). The new asylums: Madness and mass incarceration in the neoliberal era. In L. Ben-Moshe, C. Chapman, & A. C. Carey (Eds.), *Disability incarcerated: Imprisonment and disability in the United States and Canada* (pp. 139–159). Palgrave Macmillan.

Richards, P. L. (2004). 'Beside her sat her idiot child': Families and developmental disability in mid-nineteenth century America. In S. Noll & J. W. Trent, Jr. (Eds.), *Mental retardation in America* (pp. 65–84). New York University Press.

Richardson, J., Wu, J., & Judge, D. M. (2019). *Global convergence of vocational and special education: Mass schooling and modern educability.* Routledge.

Richter, Z. A. (2016). Melting down the family unit: A neuroqueer critique of table-readiness. In M. Rembis (Ed.), *Disabling domesticity* (pp. 335–348). Palgrave Macmillan.

Ridolfo, H., & Ward, B. W. (2013). *Mobility impairment and the construction of identity.* Lynne Rienner.

Rimmer, J. H., & Rowland, J. L. (2008). Health promotion for people with disabilities: Implications for empowering the person and promoting disability-friendly environments. *American Journal of Lifestyle Medicine,* 2(22), 409–420.

Rinaldi, J. (2013). Reflexivity in research: Disability between the lines. *Disability Studies*

Quarterly, 33(2). https://dsq-sds.org/issue/view/102

Rizzolo, M., Hemp, R., Braddock, D., & Schindler, A. (2009). *Family support services in the United States: 2008. Policy Research Brief.* Research and Training Center of Community Living. University of Minnesota.

Ro, C. (2019, July 27). Racial stereotypes are making Americans sicker. *Forbes.* https://www.forbes.com/sites/christinero/2019/07/27/racial-stereotypes-are-making-americans-sicker/?sh=57321541207b

Robers, S., Zhang, A., Morgan, R. E., & Musu-Gillette, L. (2015). *Indicators of school crime and safety.* National Center for Education Statistics and Bureau of Justice Statistics.

Robert, S. A., & House, J. S. (2000). Socioeconomic inequalities in health: An enduring problem. In C. E. Bird, P. Conrad, & A. M. Fremont (Eds.), *Handbook of medical sociology* (5th ed., pp. 79–97). Prentice Hall.

Robey, K. L., Beckley, L., & Kirschner, M. (2006). Implicit infantilizing attitudes about disability. *Journal of Developmental and Physical Disabilities*, 18(4), 441–453.

Robinson, B. B. (1928). Problems of community management of non-institutionalized feeble-minded and delinquent. *Proceedings of the National Conference of Social Work*, 367–372.

Robinson, S. A. (2017). "Me against the world": Autoethnographic poetry. *Disability & Society*, 32(5), 748–752.

Rodas, J. M. (2015). Identity. In R. Adams, B. Reiss, & D. Serlin (Eds.), *Keywords for disability studies* (pp. 103–104). New York University Press.

Rogers, C. (2011). Mothering and intellectual disability: Partnership rhetoric? *British Journal of Sociology of Education*, 32(4), 563–581.

Rohmer, O., & Louvet, E. (2018). Implicit stereotyping against people with disability. *Group Processes & Intergroup Relations*, 21(1), 127–140.

Rolnick, A. C. (2019). Defending white space. *Cardozo Law Review*, 40(4), 1639. http://cardozolawreview.com/defending-white-space-self-defense/#:~:text=For%20White%20people%20living%20in%20White%20spaces%2C%20a,duty%E2%80%94to%20protect%20one%E2%80%99s%20home%20and%20neighborhood%20from%20intruders

Rose, M. L. (2003). *The staff of Oedipus: Transforming disability in Ancient Greece.* University of Michigan Press.

Rose, S. F. (2017). *No right to be idle: The invention of disability, 1840s–1930s.* University of North Carolina Press.

Rosenhan, D. L. (1973). On being sane in insane places. *Science*, 179(4070), 250–258.

Rosenthal, K. (Ed.). (2019). *Capitalism and disability: Selected writings by Marta Russell.* Haymarket Books.

Roser, M., & Ritchie, H. (2020). Burden of disease. *OurWorldInData.org.* https://ourworldindata.org/burden-of-disease

Rossiter, K., & Rinaldi, J. (2018). *Institutional violence and disability: Punishing conditions.* Routledge.

Rothman, D. J. (1971). *The discovery of the asylum.* Little, Brown.

Rothman, D. J., & Rothman, S. M. (1984). *The Willowbrook Wars.* Harper and Row.

Rottier, H., & Gernsbacher, M. A. (2020). Autistic adult and non-autistic parent advocates: Bridging the divide. In A. C. Carey, J. Ostrove, & T. Fannon (Eds.), *Disability alliances and allies: Opportunities and challenges. Research in social science and disability* (vol. 12, pp. 155–166). Emerald Press.

Rousso, H. (2013). *Don't call me inspirational: A disabled feminist talks back.* Temple University Press.

Rowe, J. W., & Kahn, R. L. (1997). Successful aging. *The Gerontologist*, 37, 433–440.

Russell, M. (1998). *Beyond ramps: Disability at the end of the social contract.* Common Courage Press.

Russell, G. M., & Bohan, J. S. (2016). Institutional allyship for LGBT equality: Underlying processes and potentials for change. *Journal of Social Issues*, 72(2), 335–354.

Ryan, A. A., & Scullion, H. F. (2000). Nursing home placement: An exploration of the experiences of family carers. *Journal of Advanced Nursing*, 32(5), 1187–1195.

Sakakibara, K. (2018). The disablement score: An intersubjective severity scale of the social exclusion of disabled people. *Societies*, 8(1), 12. https://www.mdpi.com/2075-4698/8/1/12

Samuels, E. (2015). Passing. In R. Adams, B. Reiss, & D. Serlin (Eds.), *Keywords for disability studies* (pp. 135–136). New York University Press.

Samuels, E. (2017). Six ways of looking at crip time. *Disability Studies Quarterly*, 37(3). https://dsq-sds.org/article/view/5824/4684

Sanchez, M. (2016). The sibling disability experience: An analysis of studies concerning non-impaired siblings of individuals with disabilities from 1960–1990. In S. E. Green & S. N. Barnartt (Eds.), *Sociology looking at disability: What did we know and when did we know it?* (pp. 241–259). Emerald.

Santinele Martino, A. (2019). Power struggles over the sexualities of individuals with intellectual disabilities. In K. Malinen (Ed.), *Dis/consent: Perspectives on sexual consent and sexual violence* (pp. 98–107). Fernwood Publishers.

Santinele Martino, A. (2020). *The romantic and sexual lives of adults with intellectual disability in Ontario, Canada* (Doctoral dissertation, McMaster University).

Santinele Martino, A. (2021). "I don't want to get in trouble": A study of how adults with intellectual disabilities convert and navigate intellectual disability sexual fields. *Culture, Health & Sexuality*. https://doi.org/10.1080/13691058.2021.1942552

Santinele Martino, A., & Schormans, A. F. (2018). When good intentions backfire: University research ethics review and the intimate lives of people labeled with intellectual disability. *Qualitative Social Research*, 19(3), 375–392.

Sard, B., & Alvarez-Sánchez, T. (2011). *Large majority of housing voucher recipients work, are elderly, or have disabilities*. Center on Budget and Policy Priorities. https://www.cbpp.org/research/large-majority-of-housing-voucher-recipients-work-are-elderly-or-have-disabilities

Sátyro, G. D., & Cunha, E. S. M. (2014). The path of Brazilian social assistance policy post-1988: The significance of institutions and ideas. *Brazilian Political Science Review*, 18(1), 80–108.

Saxton, M. (1987). Prenatal screening and discriminatory attitudes about disability. *Women & Health* 13(1–2), 217–224.

Scales K. (2020). It's time to care: A detailed profile of America's direct care workforce. *Phi National*. https://phinational.org/wp-content/uploads/2020/01/Its-Time-to-Care-2020-PHI.pdf

Scheff, T. J. (1966). *Being mentally ill: A sociological theory*. Aldine.

Schoeni, R. F., Martin, L. G., Andreski, P. M., & Freedman, V. A. (2005). Persistent and growing socioeconomic disparities in disability among the elderly. *American Journal of Public Health*, 95(11), 2065–2070.

Schormans, A. F., Hutton, S., Blake, M., Earle, K., & Head K. (2021). Social isolation continued: COVID-19 shines a light on what self-advocates know too well. *Qualitative Social Work*, 20(1/2), 83–89.

Schrad, Mark Lawrence (2015, September 5). Does down syndrome justify abortion. *New York Times*. www.nytimes.com

Schur, L. (2003). Barriers or opportunities? The causes of contingent and part time work among people with disabilities. *Industrial Relations: A Journal of Economy and Society*, 42(4), 589–622.

Schur, L., Han, K., Andrea, K., Mason, A., Blanck, P., & Krause, D. (2017). Disability at work: A look back and forward. *Journal of Occupational Rehabilitation*, 27(4), 482–497.

Schur, L., & Kruse, D. (2020). Coronavirus could revolutionize work opportunities for people with disabilities. *The Conversation*. https://theconversation.com/coronavirus-could-revolutionize-work-opportunities-for-people-with-disabilities-137462

Schur, L., Kruse, D., & Blanck, P. (2013). *People with disabilities: Sidelined or mainstreamed*. Cambridge University Press.

Schur, L., van der Meulen Rodgers, Y., & Kruse, D. (2021). COVID-19 and employment losses for workers with disabilities: An intersectional approach. The center for women and work working paper series. Rutgers University. http://smlr.rutgers.edu/sites/default/files/Documents/Centers/CWW/Publications/draft_covid19_and_disability_report.pdf

Schweik, S. M. (2009). *The ugly laws: Disability in public*. New York University Press.

Schweik, S. M. (2011). Lomax's matrix: Disability, solidarity, and the black power of 504. *Disability Studies Quarterly*, 31(1). https://dsq-sds.org/article/view/1371/1539

Scotch, R. K. (1984). *From good will to civil rights*. Temple University Press.

Scotch, R. K. (1988). Disability as the basis for a social movement: Advocacy and the politics of definition. *Journal of Social Issues*, 44(1), 159–172.

Scotch, R. K. (2000). Models of disability and the Americans with Disabilities Act. *Berkeley*

Journal of Employment and Labor Law, 21, 213–222.

Scotch, R. K., & Schriner, K. (1997). Disability as human variation: Implications for policy. *The Annals of the American Academy of Political and Social Science*, 549(1), 148–159.

Scott, E. K. (2010). "I feel as if I am the one who is disabled": The emotional impact of changed employment trajectories on mothers caring for children with disabilities. *Gender & Society*, 24(5), 672–696.

Scott, N., Lakin, K. C., & Larson, S. A. (2008). The 40th anniversary of deinstitutionalization in the United States: Decreasing state institutional populations, 1967-2007. *Intellectual and Developmental Disabilities*, 46(5), 402–405.

Scull, A. (2015). *Madness in civilization*. Thames & Hudson.

Secmezsoy-urquhart, J. (2016). *Did disabled people have a place at Renaissance royal courts?* University of Glasgow.

Shakespeare, T. (2010). The social model of disability. In L. J. Davis (Ed.), *The disability studies reader* (pp. 266–273). Routledge.

Shakespeare, T., Gillespie-Sells, K., & Davies, D. (1996). *The sexual politics of disability*. Cassell.

Shandra, C. L., & Hogan, D. P. (2009). The educational attainment process among adolescents with disabilities and children of parents with disabilities. *International Journal of Disability, Development and Education*, 56(4), 363–379.

Shandra, C. L., Hogan, D. P., & Short, S. E. (2014). Planning for motherhood: Fertility attitudes, desires, and intentions among women with disabilities. *Perspectives on Sexual and Reproductive Health*, 46(4), 203–210.

Shandra, C. L., & Penner, A. (2017). Benefactors and beneficiaries? Disability and care to others. *Journal of Marriage and Family*, 79(4), 1160–1185.

Sherry, M. (2016). *Disability hate crimes: Does anyone really hate disabled people?* Palgrave Macmillan.

Shifrer, D. (2013). Stigma of a label: Educational expectations for high school students with learning disabilities. *Journal of Health and Social Behavior*, 54(4), 462–480.

Shifrer, D. (2018). Classifying the social roots of the disproportionate classification of racial minorities and males with learning disabilities. *The Sociological Quarterly*, 59(3), 384–406.

Shifrer, D., Muller, C., & Callahan, R. (2011). Disproportionality and learning disabilities: Parsing apart race, socioeconomic status, and language. *Journal of Learning Disabilities*, 44(3), 246–257.

Shildrick, M. (2015). Sex. In R. Adams, B. Reiss, & D. Serlin (Eds.), *Keywords for disability studies* (pp. 164–166) New York University Press.

Shuttleworth, R., Wedgewood, N., & Wilson, N. J. (2012). The dilemma of disabled masculinity. *Men and Masculinities*, 17(2), 174–194.

Sidel, V. W., & Levy, B. S. (2008). The health impact of war. *International Journal of Injury Control and Safety Promotion*, 15(4), 189–195.

Siebers, T. (2008). *Disability theory*. University of Michigan Press.

Silberman, S. (2016, May 17). The invisibility of Black autism. *Undark*. https://undark.org/2016/05/17/invisibility-black-autism/

Silverman, A. M., & Cohen, G. L. (2014). Stereotypes as stumbling-blocks: How coping with stereotype threat affects life outcomes for people with physical disabilities. *Personal and Social Psychology Bulletin*, 40, 1330–1340.

Simmel, G. (1971). *George Simmel: On individuality and social forms*. University of Chicago Press.

Singh, I. (2013). Brain talk: Power and negotiation in children's discourse about self, brain, and behavior. *Sociology of Health and Illness*, 35(6), 813–827.

Singleton, P. (2012). Insult to injury: Disability, earnings, and divorce. *Journal of Human Resources*, 47(4), 972–990.

Sins Invalid. (2015). 10 principles of disability justice. *Sins Invalid*. https://www.sinsinvalid.org/blog/10-principles-of-disbility-justice

Sins Invalid. (2020, March 19). Social distancing and crip survival: A disability centered response to COVID-19. *Sins Invalid*. https://www.sinsinvalid.org/news-1/2020/3/19/social-distancing-and-crip-survival-a-disability-centered-response-to-covid-19

Slate, R. N. (2017). Deinstitutionalization, criminalization of mental illness, and the principle of therapeutic jurisprudence. *Southern California Interdisciplinary Law Journal*, 26, 341–356.

Slate, R. N., Buffington-Vollum, J. K., & Johnson, W. W. (2013). *The criminalization of mental illness: Crisis and opportunity for the justice system* (2nd ed.). Carolina Academic Press.

Smith, D. E. (2005). *Institutional ethnography: A sociology for people.* AltaMira Press.

Smith, D. E. (2007). Women's perspective as a radical critique of sociology. *Sociological Inquiry,* 44(1), 7–13.

Smith, V. (2012). North Carolina's institutional bias: Enforcing the ADA's integration mandate. *North Carolina Medical Journal,* 73(3), 219–221.

Smith, S. L., Choueiti, M., & Pieper, K. (2016). *Inequality in 800 popular films: Examining portrayals of gender, race/ethnicity, LGBT, and disability from 2007–2015.* Media, Diversity and Social Change Initiative. https://annenberg.usc.edu/sites/default/files/2017/04/10/MDSCI_Inequality_in_800_Films_FINAL.pdf

Snow, K. (2001). People first language. *Disability is Natural.* https://nebula.wsimg.com/1c1af57f9319dbf909ec52462367fa88?AccessKeyId=9D6F6082FE5EE52C3DC6&disposition=0&alloworigin=1

Snow, D. A. (2013). Framing and Social Movements. In D. Snow, D. Della Porta, B. Klandermans, & D. McAdam (Eds.), *Encyclopedia of social and political movements.* Wiley/Blackwell.

Snow, D. A., & Corrigall-Brown, C. (2015). Collective identity. In J. D. Wright (Ed.), *International encyclopedia of the social and behavioral sciences* (2nd ed.). Elsevier.

Snow, D. A., Rochford, E. B., Worden, S. K., & Benford, R. D. (1986). Frame alignment processes, micromobilization, and movement participation. *American Sociological Review,* 51(4), 464–481.

Snyder, M., Kleck, R., Strenta, A., & Mentzer, S. (1980). Avoidance of the handicapped: An attributional ambiguity analysis. *Journal of Personality and Social Psychology,* 37(12), 2297–2306.

Snyder, S. L., & Mitchell, D. T. (2005). *Cultural locations of disability.* University of Chicago Press.

Snyder, S. L., & Mitchell, D. T. (2006). Eugenics and the racial genome: Politics at the molecular level. *Patterns of Prejudice,* 40(4–5), 399–412.

Social Security Administration (SSA). (2020). *Monthly statistical snapshot, April 2020.* https://www.ssa.gov/policy/docs/quickfacts/stat_snapshot/

Social Security Administration (SSA). (n.d.). *Trends in the social security and supplemental security income disability programs.* https://www.ssa.gov/policy/docs/chartbooks/disability_trends/sect04.html

Sohail, Z., Bailey, R. K., & Richie, W. D. (2014). Misconceptions of depression in African Americans. *Frontiers in Psychiatry,* 5(65), 1–3.

Solomon, A. (2013). *Far from the tree: Parents, children, and the search for identity.* Scribner.

Solomon, A. (2019). Mental illness is not a horror show. In P. Catapano & R. Garland-Thomson (Eds.), *About us: Essays from the disability series of the New York Times* (pp. 11–17). Leveright.

Sonik, R. A., Parish, S. L., Mitra, M., & Nicholson, J. (2018). Parents with and without disabilities: Demographics, material hardship, and program participation. *Review of Disability Studies,* 14(4), 1–20.

Sousa, A. (2011). From refrigerator mothers to warrior-heroes: The cultural identity transformation of mothers raising children with intellectual disabilities. *Symbolic Interaction,* 34(2), 220–243.

Souza, C. N. (2020). Reframing the story of Helen Keller and Anne Sullivan: Resisting (dis)ability stereotypes through an analysis of children's literature. In S. E. Green & D. R. Loseke (Eds.), *New narratives of disability: Constructions, clashes, and controversies. Research in social science and disability* (vol. 11, pp. 11–26). Emerald.

Spillman, L. (Ed.). (2002). *Cultural sociology.* Blackwell.

Starr, P. (1982). *The social transformation of American medicine: The rise of a sovereign profession and the making of a vast industry.* Basic Books.

Stasio, B. J. (2010). People with disabilities and the federal marriage penalties. *Impact,* 32(2). University of Minnesota, Institute on Community Integration.

Steele, E. M., Popkin, B. M., Swinburn, B., & Monteiro, C. A. (2017). The share of ultra-processed foods and the nutritional quality of diets in the United States: Evidence from a nationally representative cross-sectional study. *Population Health Metrics,* 15, 1–11.

Stephens, F. (2018). *I am a man with Down syndrome and my life is worth living*. [Speech]. https://www.youtube.com/watch?v=1d8ocuPrlT8

Stern, A. M. (2016). *Eugenic nation: Faults and frontiers of better breeding in modern America*. University of California.

Stern, C. (2019). Forced to divorce: Americans with disabilities must pick marriage or health care. *OZY*. ozy.com/the-new-and-the-next/forced-to-divorce-americans-with-disabilities-must-pick-marriage-or-healthcare/92284

Stevens, B. (2011). *Structural barriers to sexual autonomy for disabled people*. American Bar Association. https://www.americanbar.org/groups/crsj/publications/human_rights_magazine_home/human_rights_vol38_2011/human_rights_spring2011/structural_barriers_to_sexual_autonomy_for_disabled_people/#:~:text=Myriad%20problems%20could%20be%20presented,and%20culturally%20competent%20sexual%20and

Stevens, B. (2015, March 4). There was no access into her vagina… monologue. *Crip Confessions*. https://cripconfessions.com/there-was-no-access-into-her-vagina-monologue/

Stevens, J. D. (2020). Stuck in transition with you: Variable pathways to in(ter) dependence for emerging adult med with mobility impairments. In S. E. Green & D. R. Loseke (Ed), *New narratives of disability: Constructions, clashes, and controversies. Research in social science and disability* (vol. 11, pp. 169–184). Emerald.

Stiker, H. (1999). *A history of disability*. University of Michigan Press.

Stobee, M. (2011). Ugly past of US human experiments uncovered. *NBC News*. http://www.nbcnews.com/id/41811750/ns/health-health_care/t/ugly-past-us-human-experiments-uncovered/#.XW6fe2N7nIU

Stone, D. (1984). *The disabled state*. Temple University Press.

Stone, E. V. (1998). *Reforming disability in China: A study in disability and development* (PhD dissertation, Department of Sociology and Social Policy, University of Leeds).

Stone, A. (2017). Lunacy and liberation: Black crime, disability and the production and eradication of the early national enemy. *Early American Literature*, 52(1), 109–140.

Stone, D. A., & Papadimitriou, C. (2015). Rehab as an existential, social learning process: A thought experiment. In K. McPherson, B. E. Gibson, & A. Leplege (Eds.), *Rethinking rehabilitation: Theory and practice*. CRC Press.

Stone, E., & Priestly, M. (1996). Parasites, pawns, and partners: Disability research and the role of non-disabled researchers. *The British Journal of Sociology*, 47(4), 699–716.

Stroman, D. F. (2003). *The disability rights movement: From deinstitutionalization to self-determination*. University Press of America.

Students with disabilities graduating from high school and entering postsecondary education: In brief. (2017). *Everycrsreport.com*. https://www.everycrsreport.com/reports/R44887.html

Sundar, V., O'Neill, J., Houtenville, A. J., Phillips, K. G., Keirns, T., Smith, A., & Katz, E. E. (2018). Striving to work and overcome barriers: Employment strategies and successes of people with disabilities. *Journal of Vocational Rehabilitation*, 48(1), 93–109.

Swearer, S. M., Wang, C., Maag, J. W., Siebecker, A. B., & Frerichs, L. J. (2012). Understanding the bullying dynamic among students in special and general education. *Journal of School Psychology*, 50(4), 503–520.

Swedish Disability Federation. (2007). *The Swedish disability movement's alternative report on UN international covenant on civil and political rights*. United Nations Human Rights Treaty Bodies. https://tbinternet.ohchr.org/Treaties/CCPR/Shared%20Documents/SWE/INT_CCPR_NGO_SWE_93_10092_E.pdf

Swindler, A. (1986). Culture in action: Symbols and strategies. *American Sociological Review*, 51(2), 273–286.

Switzer, J. V. (2003). *Disabled rights: American disability policy and the fight for equality*. Georgetown University Press.

Syme, S. L., & Berkman, L. F. (2019 [1976]). Social class, susceptibility, and sickness. In P. Conrad & V. Leiter (Eds.), *The sociology of health and illness: Critical perspectives* (pp. 43–50). SAGE.

Szasz, T. S. (1961). *The myth of mental illness: Foundations of a theory of personal conduct*. Harper & Row.

Sze, S., & Valentin, S. (2007). Self-concept and children with disabilities. *Education*, 127(4), 552–557.

Tabatabai, A. (2020). Neoliberalism and the fight for the child: Narratives of queer mothering. In

S. E. Green & D. R. Loske (Eds.), *New narratives of disability: Constructions, clashes, and controversies. Research in social science and disability* (vol. 11, pp. 231–243). Emerald.

Tausig, M., Michello, J., & Subedi, S. (2004). *A sociology of mental illness* (2nd ed.). Pearson.

Taylor, S. (2004). Caught in the continuum: A critical analysis of the principle of the least restrictive environment. *Research and Practice for Persons with Severe Disabilities*, 29(4), 218–230.

Taylor, M. G. (2010). Capturing transitions and trajectories: The role of socioeconomic status in later life disability. *Journals of Gerontology Series B: Psychological Sciences and Social Sciences*, 65(6), 733–743.

Taylor, D. M. (2018). *Americans with disabilities: 2014*. https://www.census.gov/content/dam/Census/library/publications/2018/demo/p70-152.pdf

Taylor, D. B. (2019). 87-year-old killed her disabled grandson with overdose, police say. *New York Times*. https://www.nytimes.com/2019/09/25/us/florida-grandmother-overdose-grandson.html

Taylor, S. J., & Bogdan, R. (1998). *Introduction to qualitative research methods: A guidebook and resource* (3rd ed.). Wiley.

Taylor, S. J., Bogdan, R., & DeVault, M. L. (2016). *Introduction to qualitative research methods: A guidebook and resource* (4th ed.). Wiley.

Taylor, V., & Whittier, N. E. (1999). Collective identity in social movement communities: Lesbian feminist mobilization. In J. Freeman & V. Johnson (Eds.), *Waves of protest: Social movements since the sixties* (pp. 169–194). Rowman & Littlefield.

Teems, Y. R. (2016). 'My body feels old': Seniors' discursive constructions of aging-as-disabling. *Review of Disability Studies*, 12(2), 107–121.

TenBroek, J. (1966). The right to live in the world: The disabled in the law of torts. *California Law Review*, 54(2), 841–919.

Thomas, C. (1999). *Female forms*. Open University Press.

Thomas, C. (2007). *Sociologies of disability and illness: Contested ideas in disability studies and medical sociology*. Palgrave.

Thomas, D. M. (2009). Culture and disability: A Cape Verdean perspective. *Journal of Cultural Diversity*, 16(4), 178–186.

Thomas, D. M. (2017). A Cape Verdean perspective on disability: An invisible minority in New England. In D. M. Thomas (Ed.), *Women's health: Readings on social, economic and political issues* (pp. 442–458). Kendall Hunt.

Thompson, V. (2018, March 26). The overlooked history of black disabled people. *Rewire News*. https://rewire.news/article/2018/03/16/overlooked-history-black-disabled-people

Titchkosky, T. (2003). *Disability, self and society*. University of Toronto Press.

Titchkosky, T. (2011). *The question of access: Disability, space, meaning*. University of Toronto Press.

Torras, M. (2006). The impact of equality, income, and the environment on human health: Some inter-country comparisons. *International Review of Applied Economics*, 20(1), 1–20.

Torrey, E. F., Kennard, A. D., Eslinger, D., Lamb, R., & Pavie, J. (2010). *More mentally ill persons are in jails and prisons than hospitals: A survey of the states*. Treatment Advocacy Center.

Torrey, E. F., Zdanowicz, M. T., Kennard, A. D., Lamb, H. R., Eslinger, D. F., Biasotti, M.C., & Fuller, D. A. (2014). *The treatment of persons with mental illness in prisons and jails: A state survey*. Treatment Advocacy Center.

Totenberg, N. (2020). *Supreme Court allows states to virtually eliminate the insanity defense*. National Public Radio (NPR). https://www.npr.org/2020/03/23/820190552/supreme-court-allows-states-to-virtually-eliminate-the-insanity-defense

Tovey, B. (2016). Kingly impairments in Anglo-Saxon literature: God's curse and God's blessing. In J. R. Eyler (Ed.), *Disability in the Middle Ages* (pp. 135–148). Ashgate.

Trainor, A. A. (2010). Reexamining the promise of parent participation in special education: An analysis of cultural and social capital. *Anthropology & Education Quarterly*, 41(3), 245–263.

Tregaskis, C., & Goodley, D. (2005). Disability research by disabled and non-disabled people: Towards a relational methodology of research production. *International Journal of Social Methodology*, 8(5), 363–374.

Trent, J. W. (1994). *Inventing the feeble mind: A history of mental retardation in the United States*. University of California Press.

Trent, J. W. (2013). *The manliest man: Samuel Gridley Howe and the contours of nineteenth-century American reform*. University of Massachusetts Press.

Tsao, G. (2016). Growing up Asian American with a disability. *Disability Visibility Project*. https://disabilityvisibilityproject.com/2016/02/21/guest-blog-post-growing-up-asian-american-with-a-disability-by-grace-tsao/

Tumin, D. (2016). Marriage trends among Americans with childhood-onset disabilities, 1997–2013. *Disability and Health Journal*, 9(4), 713–718.

Turk, M. A., Landes, S. D., Formica, M. K., & Goss, K. D. (2020). Intellectual and developmental disability and Covid-19 fatality trends: TriNetX analysis. *Disability and Health Journal*. https://www.ncbi.nlm.nih.gov/pmc/articles/PMC7245650/

Unicef. (n.d.). *The legacy of land-mines*. https://www.unicef.org/sowc96/9ldmines.htm

Union of the Physically Impaired Against Segregation (UPIAS), 1976. *Fundamental principles of disability*. UPIAS.

United Nations. (2006). *Convention on the rights of persons with disabilities*. https://www.un.org/development/desa/disabilities/convention-on-the-rights-of-persons-with-disabilities/convention-on-the-rights-of-persons-with-disabilities-2.html

United Nations, Human Rights, Office of the High Commission. (2015). *Committee on the rights of persons with disabilities considered initial report of Brazil*. https://www.ohchr.org/EN/NewsEvents/Pages/DisplayNews.aspx?NewsID=16348&LangID=E

United States Bureau of Labor Statistics. (2020a). Employment situation of veterans news release. *BLS*. bls.gov/news.release/vet.htm

United States Bureau of Labor Statistics. (2020b, December). Highlights of women's earnings in 2019. *BLS*. https://www.bls.gov/opub/reports/womens-earnings/2019/pdf/home.pdf

United States Census Bureau. (2012). *Nearly 1 in 5 people have a disability in the US, Census Bureau reports*. https://www.census.gov/newsroom/releases/archives/miscellaneous/cb12-134.html

United States Census Bureau. (2017a). *Measuring disability in a census: Select topics in international censuses*. US Department of Commerce.

United States Census Bureau. (2017b). *How disability data are collected from the American community survey*. United States Census Bureau. https://www.census.gov/topics/health/disability/guidance/data-collection-acs.html

United States Census Bureau. (2019). *Current population survey: 2019 annual social and economic (ASEC) supplement*. https://www2.census.gov/programs-surveys/cps/techdocs/cpsmar19.pdf

United States Census Bureau. (2020). *Living with disabilities: Number of Americans with a disability by age, sex, and disability type*. https://www.census.gov/content/dam/Census/library/visualizations/2020/comm/living-with-disabilities.pdf

United States Census Bureau. (n.d.a). *How disability data are collected from decennial*. https://www.census.gov/topics/health/disability/guidance/data-collection-decennial.html

United States Census Bureau. (n.d.b). *American community survey: Why we ask questions about… disability?* https://www.census.gov/acs/www/about/why-we-ask-each-question/disability/

United States Department of Education, National Center for Education Statistics. (2019a). *Digest of education statistics, 2018 (NCES 2020-009)*. https://nces.ed.gov/fastfacts/display.asp?id=64

United States Department of Education, National Center for Education Statistics. (2019b). *Status and trends in the education of racial and ethnic groups*. https://nces.ed.gov/programs/race-indicators/indicator_RBD.asp#:~:text=In%20school%20year%202015%E2%80%9316,13%20percent)%2C%20Hispanic%20and%20Pacific

Üstün, T. B., Kostanjsek, N., Chetterji, S., & Rehm, J. (Eds.). (2010). *Measuring health and disability: Manual for WHO disability assessment schedule*. World Health Organization.

Uwumarogie, V. (2020, April 17). "There's beauty in me as a whole and my prosthetic is part of me": Marsh Elle on representing for disabled black women in PLAYBOY. *Madamenoire*. https://madamenoire.com/1147283/marsha-elle-playboy/

Van Dyke, N., & McCammon, H. J. (2010). Introduction. In N. V. Dyke & H. J. McCammon (Eds.), *Strategic alliances: Coalition building and social movements* (pp. xi–xxviii). University of Minnesota.

Van Wyck, N., & Leech, R. (2016). Becoming the mother of a child with a disability: A systematic literature review. *Community, Work & Family*, 19(5), 554–568.

Voulgarides, C. K. (2018). *Does compliance matter in special education? IDEA and the hidden inequities of practice*. Teachers College Press.

Walker, N. (2015). Neuroqueer: An introduction. *Neurocosmopolitan*. https://neurocosmopolitanism.com/neuroqueer-an-introduction/

Wall, G. (2010). Mothers' experiences with intensive parenting and brain development discourse. *Women's Studies International Forum*, 33(3), 253–263.

Wallerstein, I. (1974). *The modern world-system*. Academic Press.

Walsh, S. (2011). 'What does it matter?': A meditation on the social positioning of disability and motherhood. In C. Lewiecki-Wilson & J. Cellio (Eds.), *Disability and mothering: Liminal spaces of embodied knowledge* (pp. 81–87). Syracuse University Press.

Walton, D. R. (2011). *What's a leg got to do with it?: Black, female and disabled in America*. Center for Women Policy Studies. https://www.peacewomen.org/sites/default/files/whatsaleggottodowithit_blackfemaleanddisabledinamerica_donnarwalton_0.pdf

Wang, Q. (2005). *Disability and the American family: 2000*. Bureau of the Census, Department of Commerce. https://www.census.gov/prod/2005pubs/censr-23.pdf

Ware, J. E. (1986). The assessment of health status. In L. H. Aiken & D. Mechanic (Eds.), *Applications of social science to clinical medicine and health policy* (pp. 204–228). Rutgers University.

Ware, S., Rusza, J., & Dias, G. (2014). It can't be fixed because it's not broken: Racism and disability in the prison industrial complex. In L. Ben-Moshe, C. Chapman, & A. C. Carey (Eds.), *Disability incarcerated: Imprisonment and disability in the United States and Canada* (pp. 164–184). Palgrave Macmillan.

Washington Group on Disability Statistics. (2009). *Understanding and interpreting disability as measured using the WG short set of questions*. https://www.cdc.gov/nchs/data/washington_group/meeting8/interpreting_disability.pdf

Wasserberg, M. J. (2014). Stereotype threat effects on African American children in an urban elementary school. *Journal of Experimental Education*, 82(4), 502–517.

Webber, C. B., & Sobal, J. (2007). Physical disability and food access among limited resource households. *Disability Studies Quarterly*, 27(3). https://dsq-sds.org/article/view/20/20

Weber, M. ([1922] 1968). *Economy and society*. Bedminster.

Weiss, G., & Lonnquist, L. E. (2017). *Sociology of health, healing, and illness* (9th ed.). Routledge.

Welsh, M. J. (2016). Back to the future: Irving K. Zola's contributions to the sociology of disability. In S. E. Green & S. N. Barnartt (Eds.), *Sociology looking at disability: What did we know and when did we know it?* (pp. 97–141). Emerald.

Welsh, M. J. (2018). *Decreased visibility: A narrative analysis of episodic disability and contested illness* (Graduate dissertation, University of South Florida). https://scholarcommons.usf.edu/cgi/viewcontent.cgi?article=8575&context=etd

Wendell, S. (2001). Unhealthy disabled: Treating chronic illnesses as disability. *Hypatia*, 16(4), 17–33.

West, S. L., Graham, C. W., & Cifu, D. X. (2009). Rates of alcohol/other drug treatment denials to persons with physical disabilities: Accessibility concerns. *Alcohol Treatment Quarterly*, 27(3), 305–316.

Wheatley, E. (2002). Blindness, discipline, and reward: Louis IX and the foundation of the Hospice des Quinze Vingts. *Disability Studies Quarterly*, 22(4), 194–212.

Wheatley, E. (2010). *Stumbling blocks before the blind: Medieval constructions of a disability*. University of Michigan Press.

Whitesel, J. (2017). Intersections of multiple oppressions: Racism, sizeism, ableism, and the "illimitable etceteras" in encounters with law enforcement. *Sociological Forum*, 32(2), 426–433.

Whitt, T. D. (2014a). My thoughts on applied behavior analysis (ABA) autism. *LovinAdoptin*. http://lovinadoptin.com/2014/03/26/my-thoughts-on-applied-behavior-analysis-aba-autism/

Whitt, T. D. (2014b). More perspectives on applied behavior analysis (ABA) autism. *Lovin Adoptin*. http://lovinadoptin.com/2014/04/09/more-perspectives-on-applied-behavior-analysis-aba-autism/

Wickham, P. (2001). Idiocy and the laws in colonial England. *Mental Retardation*, 39(2), 104–113.

Wilkerson, A. (2011). Disability, sex radicalism, and political agency. In K. Q. Hall (Ed.), *Feminist disability studies* (pp. 193–217). Indiana University Press.

Wilkerson, A. (2020). *Caste: The origins of our discontents*. Random House.

Wilkinson, R. G., & Pickett, K. (2010). *The spirit level: Why equality is better for everyone*. Penguin.

Williams, R. (1970). *American society: A sociological interpretation* (3rd ed.). Alfred Knopf.

Williams, D. R., & Mohammed, S. A. (2013). Racism and health: Pathways and scientific evidence. *American Behavioral Scientist*, S7(8), 1152–1173.

Williamson, B. (2015). Access. In R. Adams, B. Reiss, & D. Serlin (Eds.), *Keywords for disability studies* (pp. 14–16). New York University Press.

Willingham, E. (2013). The five scariest autism treatments. *Forbes*. https://www.forbes.com/sites/emilywillingham/2013/10/29/the-5-scariest-autism-treatments/#3672b7961953

Wilper, A. P., Woolhandler, S., Boyd, J. W., Lasser, K. E., McCormick, D., Bor, D. H., & Himmelstein, D. U. (2009). The health and health care of US prisoners: Results of a nationwide survey. *American Journal of Public Health*, 99(4), 666–672.

Wilson, D. J. (2004). Fighting polio like a man: Intersections of masculinity, disability, and aging. In B. G. Smith & B. Hutchinson (Eds.), *Gendering disability* (pp. 119–133). Rutgers University Press.

Winzer, M. A. (1993). *The history of special education: From isolation to integration*. Gallaudet University Press.

Winzer, M. A. (1997). Disability and society before the 18th century: Dread and despair. In L. J. Davis (Ed.), *The disability studies reader* (pp. 75–109). Routledge.

Wong, A. (2017). Our existence is resistance: Summer fundraiser for @NationalADAPT. *The Visibility Project*. https://disabilityvisibilityproject.com/2017/07/04/our-existence-is-resistance-summer-fundraiser-for-nationaladapt/

Wong, A. (2019). My Medicaid, my life. In P. Catapano & R. Garland-Thomson (Eds.), *About us: Essays from the disability series of the New York Times* (pp. 27–30). Leveright.

Wong, A. (Ed.). (2020). *Disability visibility: First-person stories from the 21st century*. Vintage Books.

Wood, C. (Ed.). (2014). *Criptiques*. Word Press. https://criptiques.files.wordpress.com/2014/05/crip-final-2.pdf

Wood, D. H. (2017a). Staging disability in Renaissance drama. In A. F. Kinney & T. W. Hopper (Eds.), *A new companion to Renaissance drama* (pp. 487–500). Wiley.

Wood, T. (2017b). Rhetorical disclosures: The stakes of disability identity in higher education. In S. L. Kerschbaum, L. T. Eisenman, & J. M. Jones (Eds.), *Negotiating disability: Disclosure and higher education* (pp. 75–91). University of Michigan Press.

World Prison Brief. (n.d.). *Highest to lowest – Prison population rate*. https://www.prisonstudies.org/highest-to-lowest/prison_population_rate?field_region_taxonomy_tid=All

Yong, A. (2007). *Theology and Down syndrome: Reimagining disability in late modernity*. Baylor University Press.

Young, S. (2014). *I'm not your inspiration, thank you very much*. TED: Ideas Worth Spreading. https://www.ted.com/talks/stella_young_i_m_not_your_inspiration_thank_you_very_much/discussion

Young, J. (n.d.). Bullying and students with disabilities. *National Council on Disability*. https://ncd.gov/publications/2011/briefing-paper-bullying-and-students-disabilities

Zald, M. N., & McCarthy, J. D. (1997). *Social movements in an organizational society: Collected essays*. Routledge.

Zola, I. K. (1982). *Missing pieces: A chronicle of living with a disability*. Temple University Press.

Zuvekas, S. H., & Vitiello, B. (2012). Stimulant medication use among US children: A twelve year perspective. *American Journal of Psychiatry*, 169(2), 160–166.

Index

A

Able-disabled, 204
Ableism, 77–78, 88–90, 143
   average (mean) earnings, 1988–2014, 76 (figure)
   average percentage employed, 1988–2014, 77 (figure)
   culture and, 95
   definition of, 77
   everyday interactions, 78
   in higher education, 253
   in parenting, 181–182
   inaccessibility and, 86–88, 87 (photo)
   institutional, 84–86
   racism, 77–78
   sexual ableism, 148
Abraham, L., 118
Access and accessibility, 86
   invalidation of, 118–119
   rights and, 203
   symbols of, 99–100, 203
   to health care, 226–229
Active treatment, 104
Activities of Daily Living (ADLs), 5
Activism, 39, 264–265
   African American, 160–161
   barriers to, 272–273
   definition of, 264
   Disability Justice, 112, 208
   emergence of, 265–269
   feminist, 147
   identity and, 120–121, 124–125, 130
   inequality and, 273–275
   history of, 64–68
   maternal, 174
   sexual rights and, 153
   tactics of, 269–270
Activity limitations, 27
Adulthood, transition to, 176–178
Affirmative activists, 124
African American or Black, 17, 19
   activism, 160–161, 266
   diagnosis of, 155–156
   disability identity and, 158–160
   education and, 156, 248–251
   families and, 167–169
   health care and, 229
   history and, 56, 57
   incarceration and, 256
   representation of, 106
   research and, 35
   statistics regarding, 154, 155, 156
   stereotypes of, 157–158
Agents of socialization, 126
Aging, 184–186, 185 (photo)
Albrecht, G., 15, 206
Alexander, J., 94
Almshouses, 54
Alper, M., 246
Alternative sentencing, 259
Ambivalent medicalization, 173
American Civil War, 58
American Coalition of Citizens with Disabilities (ACCD), 65
American Community Survey, 24–25, 28, 34, 138
American Medical Association (AMA), 58, 216
American Sign Language (ASL), 185
Americans with Disabilities Act (ADA), 6, 25, 65–66, 76–77, 84, 85, 87, 160, 171, 192, 194, 204, 253, 265, 268, 275
Anand, S., 62
Ancient Egypt, 45–46
   social structure in, 46 (table)
Ancient Greece, 46–47
Ancient Rome, social structure in, 48 (table)
Angell, A., 161
Anticipated value of marriage, 180
Applied Behavioral Analysis (ABA), 128, 219
Aristotle, 47
Aronson, A., 94
Asch, A., 141
Asian Americans, 96, 154, 159, 167
   education, 248–249
   employment, 156
   poverty, 155, 169
Autism, 12, 67, 1010, 161
   applied behavioral analysis and, 219
   cure culture and, 105, 212
   diagnosis and, 157, 173, 244–245
   family and, 175
   stereotypes and, 79, 149, 257

B

Backlash, 267
Barnartt, S., 270
Baynton, D., 78
Beethoven, 105
Berger, N.P., 88
Berger, P., 6
Berne, P., 161, 198, 208

Biased sampling, 36
Bible, 47, 52
Bingham, S., 129
Biomedical approach, 212
Black Death, 48
Black Panther Party, 112
Blind work, 127
Blindness and blind people, 8, 9, 30, 46–47, 51, 55, 63, 100, 127, 212
  activism by, 122, 264, 266
  as metaphor, 100
  community, 18, 19, 74, 107
  education of, 235, 245
  in history, 46–47, 49, 50, 51, 52, 55, 59, 60, 62–63, 64
  parenthood, 181, 183
  stereotypes and stigma of, 79, 119–120, 141–142, 181
  socialization and, 126–127
Blum, L., 39
Bogdan, R., 36
Bolden, C., 158
Bonilla-Silva, E., 105, 278
Bourdieu, P., 13, 246
Bowe, Frank, 65, 264
Brahmin, 73
Brazil, 67–68
  social structure in, 68 (table)
Breaking Bad, 106
British colonization, 61
Brown, A. M., 153
Brown, K., 106, 141
Brown, R., 145
Buddhism, 50
Bulgaria, 205–206
Burch, S., 148
Bush, George H.W., 267, 268 (photo), 272 (photo)
Butler, J., 19, 131

C
Calvin, John, 52
Cameron, Thomas, 56
Capital, 109
Capitalism, 190
  Disability Justice critiques of, 112, 265
  global, 199
  materialist theories and, 13–15, 20, 190–191, 276–277
  poverty and, 194, 196
  production of disability caused by, 190–193
  sexuality and, 148
Carceral logic, 256
Carceral responses, 254–255
Caribbean, 57–58
Carrey, J., 107
Carter administration, 65, 267

Cassell, J., 105
Caste system, 72–75
Catholic Church, 48–49, 51, 67–68, 103
Census, 26, 28–29, 32
Cerebral palsy (CP), 27, 106, 116, 119, 129, 157, 212, 264
Cevik, K., 161
Charismatic leaders, 271
Charity, 11, 49
Charles, Ray, 74, 74 (photo)
Children's Health Insurance Program (CHIP), 218
China, 50–51, 275–276
  foot-binding, 73 (photo)
  social structure in, 51 (table)
Christianity, 47, 63
Civil rights, 65, 202–204
  Ableism and, 86, 95, 274
  African American, 160–161
  in China, 276
Civil Rights Act, 65
Civil rights frame, 266
Class systems, 72–75, 73 (photo), 74 (photo)
Cohen, G., 84
Collective disability identity, 120–123
Collective identity, 268
Colonial Caribbean, 57, 58 (table)
Colonization, 54–56, 57–58, 61–63, 198
Color-blind racism, 153, 278
Commodification, 190, 206–207
Community-based care and services, 170, 223–225
Competence, 80
Compulsory able-bodiedness, 96, 143, 263, 270
Concealment, 129–131
Concerted cultivation, 172, 246
Cone, Kitty, 65, 268
Confucianism, 50
Connor, D., 83, 249
Contentious tactics, 269–270
Cooley, C. H., 12, 116
Counterculture, 112
Courtesy stigma, 172
COVID-19, 229–231, 230 (photo)
Cox, P., 131
Criminalization, 254
Criminal justice, 254–255
Crip theories, 19–20
  parenting and, 183
  sexuality and, 151, 153
Crip time, 20
Critical theory, 38
Cross-disability stereotypes, 79
Cultural capital, 109, 174, 246–247
Cultural oppression, 102–110
Cultural resistance, 110–112

Index

Culture
  American values and, 94–97
  definition of, 93
  disability culture, 111
  elements of, 93–102
  material culture, 102, 102 (photo)
  micro and macro levels, 12–13
  norms and rituals, 101
  symbols and language, 98–100
Curative violence, 105
Cure, 10–11, 12–13, 57, 60, 77, 104–105, 117, 172, 212, 220
Cyborgs, 132–134, 133 (photo)

D

Daniels, J., 107
Darling, R., 123–125, 124 (table), 271
Dart, Justin, 268, 268 (photo)
Data literacy, 34
D/deafness and Deaf community
  activism, 264, 272
  criminal justice and, 257–258
  disability, 32
  education and, 245
  history, 46, 47, 52, 55, 59, 60, 64, 100, 148
  representation, 106, 107
Deinstitutionalization, 64, 221–222
  home and community–based services (HCBS), 223–226
  incomplete process of, 222–223
Demographics, 167–169
Dependence, 96
Deserving poor, 50, 61, 200–201
DeVault, M., 35
Developmental mismatch, 252
Deviance, 4, 59–60, 101, 117, 173, 254–256
Diagnostic Statistical Manual (DSM), 29
Digital divide, 277
Dillaway, H., 86
Disability, 2–3
  American values and, 94–97
  as biophysiological conditions/impairments, 29
  carceral responses, 254–255
  cliff, 177
  culture, 93–112
  definitions of, 5–6
  display, 130
  distinguishing illness, 212–213
  economic inequality, 194–199
  health/determinants of, 226–227
  identity, 29–30, 120–125
  incarceration of people with, 255–258
  limitations and difficulties, 26–29, 27 (figure)
  measurments of, 26–33
  medical and social models of, 8–11, 8 (photo), 9 (table)–10 (table)
  as minority group, 75–77
  minority model of, 17
  parenting among people with, 181–184
  production and experience of, 11–20, 190–198
  program eligibility, 31–32
  qualitative research, 32–33, 33 (table)
  quantitative research, 26–32
  relational models of, 18
  social construction of, 6–8
  social disadvantage, 30–31, 31 (photo)
Disability activism, 121, 264–265, 272 (photo)
  barriers to, 272–273
  China, 275–276
  collective identity, 268
  contentious tactics, 269–270
  disability culture, 270
  disability justice, 112, 161, 208, 259
  existence is resistance, 270
  history of, 64–66, 67, 68
  identity and, 120–121, 124–125, 130
  independent living movement, 271
  inequality in, 273–275
  in–system tactics, 269
  never–ending cycle of, 275
  oppositional consciousness, 268
  political backlash, 267
  political opportunity, 266
  resource mobilization theory, 268–269
  social movement frames, 266
  sexual, 153
  tactics, 269–270
Disability Adjusted Life Years (DALY), 197
Disability Business, 15
Disability identity
  collective, 120–121
  development, 122
  embodiment, 128–131
  as fluid, 131–132
  identity politics, 122
  impression management, 128–131
  performativity, 128–131
  self and, 115–116
  socialization, 125–127
  status and roles, 116–125
  Typology of disability orientations, 123–125
Disability Implicit Association tests, 81
Disability industry, 206–207
Disability justice, 112, 161, 208, 259
Disability pride, 120–123
Disability Rights Movement, 65–66, 67, 96, 208, 265, 272–274
Disabled in Action, 271
Disabled Women's Alliance, 147
Discourse, 12–13, 103–105, 200, 204
Discrimination (*See also* Ableism)

education, 83
health care and treatment, 82
labeling theory, 82
workplace, 83–84
Disease, 212
Dis–identification, 123
Dominant discourses, 12
Douglass, F., 118
Down syndrome, 7, 88, 104, 169–170, 171
Drapetomania, 56
Du Bois, W. E. B., 19, 105
Dwarfism, 45, 52, 61

E
Early America, 53–56, 56 (table)
Early Modern Europe, 51–53, 53 (photo)
Economic inequality (*See* socioeconomic status, poverty)
Education, 173–174, 227, 234–253
diagnosis and, 239, 244–245
family, 177–178
higher education, 239, 251–253
history of, 52–53, 55, 60, 64, 220, 235
inclusion, 240–243, 245, 249
Individuals with Disabilities Education Act (IDEA), 235–236
Inequality in, 83, 87–88, 144, 251
intersectionality in, 243–251
labeling, 83, 239–240
race and, 156, 248–251
rates, 25, 156, 237–239
role in health, 227
school–to–prison pipeline, 258–259
segregation, 240–243
socio–economic status and, 246–246
special education. *See* Special education
stigma, 240
sexuality and, 149
Egypt, 45–46
Einstein, Albert, 105
Emancipatory research, 39
Embodiment, 18–19, 18 (photo), 127–131, 140, 218, 226
Employment, 66, 86, 202–204, 218, 230, 278–279
rates, 24, 76–66, 145, 156
inequality in, 83–85, 85–86, 143–144
Engels, F., 102
England, 63
Enwheeled, 218
Erickson, E., 125
Essentialized disability, 3
Europe, 48–50, 73, 98, 104, 190
Eugenics, 59–60, 103–104, 118–119, 148, 200, 220, 235, 264, 59 (photo)
Existence is Resistance, 270

F
Family
advocacy, 174, 264, 271–272
aging in, 184–186
demographics, 167–169
economy and, 103, 192–193, 203 (photo), 207
filicide, 119
history of, 46–51, 54–58, 62, 64, 66
inequality and, 74–75
marriage, 179–181
normalization in, 101
parenting children with disabilities, 171–176
parenting by people with disabilities, 181–184
pregnancy & birth, 169–171
siblings, 176
transition to adulthood, 176–178
values of, 97
Fannon, T., 129
Farber, B., 15
Feebleminded, 59, 98
Feminist disability studies, 17–18, 35, 139
Feminist Intersectional Disability Framework, 139
Feminist methodology, 39, 40
Feminist movement, 147
Ferri, F., 83, 249
Feudalism, 48–50
Fighting Polio Like a Man, 142
Finding Nemo, 107
Fine, M., 141
Finger, A., 147
Foot–binding, 73 (photo)
Foucault, M., 12, 38, 102, 147
Frame (social movement theory), 266
Franklin, Ben, 55
Freak shows, 61

G
Gabel, S., 32
Gallaudet, Thomas, 55, 235
Galton, Francis, 59
Garcia, Kennedy, 141
Garland–Thomson, R., 121
Gender, 137–147
binary, 143–144
disability and, 137–138, 140–147
feminist and intersectional frameworks, 139–140
Feminist movement, 147
identity, 19
queer identities, 143
roles, 140–141
unequal outcomes, 144–146
Generalized other, 125–127
Gill, C., 122

Gill, M., 148, 150
Globalization, 67
Goffman, E., 4, 84, 118, 128
Gould, R., 83
Graying of America, 184
Greece, 46–48, 100
Green, S., 129
Grossman, B., 16

H
Habitus, 13, 110
Hahn, H., 5
Haraway, D., 132
Harris, A., 39
Hawking, Stephen, 74, 105
Health
    capitalism and, 191–192
    conceptualizations of, 5, 29, 59, 211–212
    determinants, 226–229
    differentials, 154, 156–157, 226
Health behaviors, 229
Health care
    ableism in, 82, 86–87
    accessibility in, 66, 75–76, 117–118, 150
    commodification of, 206–207
    COVID–19, 229–231, 230 (photo)
    disability, 211–212
    illness, 211–212
    insurance, 16, 25, 194, 196–197, 201–202, 205, 227–228
    medical model, *See* Medical model
    mental, *See* Mental health
    treatment and rehabilitation, 217–218
    workers, 191, 207
Health, Education and Welfare (HEW), 267
Healthy disabled, 213
Hegemony, 103
Hephaestus, 46
Herzog, A., 89
Heteronormativity, 147, 149, 179
Heterosexism, 78, 175, 274
Heumann, Judy, 267, 270
Hierarchies of disadvantage, 144
Higher education, 251–253
    ableism in, 253
    college accommodations, 251–252
    developmental mismatch, 252
    disability services, differences in, 251–252
    rates of attaining, 25, 83, 155–156, 227, 237, 239
    self–advocacy, 252
Hilfiger, Tommy, 102
Hinduism, 62
Hippocrates, 47
Hispanic (Latino/a), 154, 167, 171, 257
    education, 161, 248–249
    employment, 156
    incarceration, 256
    poverty, 155, 169

Historical comparative analysis, 44–45
Hitselberger, Karen, 141
Home and community–based services (HCBS), 222, 223–226
Howe, Samuel, 55, 235 (photo)
Humanism, 52
Humanitarianism, 95
Human rights, 208, 265
    In UN Convention of the Rights of Persons with Disabilities, 67

I
Identity, 115
    collective disability, 121
    disability, 115–125
    disability identity development, 122–123
    race, disability, and, 158–159
Identity–first language, 98–99
Identity politics, 122
Ideology, 74, 102, 181, 185, 256
Illness, 104, 117, 182, 212
Impairment, 5, 6, 7
Impairment–specific stereotypes, 79
Implicit bias, 81
Impression management, 128–131
Inaccessibility, 9, 86–88, 87 (photo), 100, 150, 177, 180, 228, 269, 273, 277, (*See also* Access)
Independent Living Movement, 65, 96, 177, 271
India, 61–63, 73, 119–120
Individualism, 15, 74, 94–95, 104
Individualized Education Program (IEP), 31, 236, 250–252
Inequality, 16, 132–134, (*See also* Stratification, Ableism)
    cultural oppression and, 102–110
    economic and, 76–77
    forms of, 72–75
    habitus and reproduction of, 109–110, 109 (table)
Ingersoll, I., 251
Inspiration porn, 107
Institutions, 13, 34, 53, 59–60, 64, 66, 68, 84, 119, 193–194, 205, 219–21, 224–225, 235, 256–257, 266, 272
Institutional ableism, 84–86
Institutional bias, 84, 228
Institutional discrimination, 84
Institutional inertia, 243
Institutionalization, 60, 170, 219–221, 225–226
Institutional racism, 153
Institutional Review Boards (IRBs), 35–36
Institutional settings, 225 (table)
Instrumental Activities of Daily Living (IADLs), 5
In–system tactics, 269
Intellectual disability, 6–7, 32, 52, 56, 64, 88, 98, 221, 241, 244–245, 248, 250, 267
Intelligence, 7, 273

Intensive motherhood, 171, 181, 183
International Association of Athletics Federation (IAAF), 133
International Classification of Functioning, Disability and Health (ICF), 27 (figure)
Intersectionality, 16–18, 137
   gender. *See* Gender
   race. *See* Race
   sexuality. *See* Sexuality
Intimate citizenship, 151–152
Invisibility, 88–90
Isolated affirmative activism, 125

J
Jefferson, Thomas, 55
Johnson, Roland, 272, 272 (photo)
Joyner, H., 148
Juette, Melvin, 12
Justifiably excluded type, 88

K
Kafer, A., 18, 20, 105
Kahlo, Frida, 105
Karloff, Boris, 106 (photo)
Karmel, J., 191
Keller, Helen, 107, 108 (photo)
Kennedy, John F., 267
Kim, E., 105
Kimmel, M., 94
Kshatriyas, 73

L
Labeling theory, 7, 82, 239–243
Language, 98–100, 244
Lanier, H.K., 95
Lareau, A., 246
Laughlin, Harry, 59
Leavy, P., 39
Lehrer, Riva, 74
Leiter, V., 252
Leprosy, 48
Lewis, T., 78
Liebowitz, C., 98
Life course,
   adulthood, transition to, 176–178
   aging, 184–186, 185 (photo)
   birth, 169–171
   child with disabilities, 171–173, 175–176
   education, 173–174
   family, 167–169, 178–181
   marriage, 178–181, 179 (photo)
   medical systems, navigating, 173
   parenting by people with disabilities, 181–184
   parenting children with disabilities, 171–175, 172 (photo)
   pregnancy, 169–171
Linton, S., 120
Littlepage, William, 56
#LiveBoldly, 119
Locke, John, 52
Longmore, P., 110, 270
Looking glass self, 116, 119
Louis IX, King, 49
Luckmann, T., 6
Luther, Martin, 52
Lysack, C., 86

M
MacInnes, M., 179
Mad activists, 99, 215
Madhouses, 53 (*See also* Institutions)
Madison, James, 55
Mairs, N., 99, 128
Mama Might Be Better Off Dead, 118
Manning, Lynn., 19
Marital Value, 179–180
Maroto, M., 85
Marriage, 178–181
Marriage Penalty, 149, 180
Martino, A. S., 13, 150
Marx, K., 13–14, 38, 102
Masculinity, 126–127, 140, 142–143
Master status, 82, 118, 225
Material culture, 102, 102 (photo)
Material hardship, 75
Materialist theories, 13–15, 15 (photo), 20, 189–190, 276
Maternal activism, 174, 264, 271–272
Mather, Increase and Cotton, 55
Mauldin, L., 39
McCarthy, I., 123
McGuire, A., 105
McRuer, R., 96
Mead, G.H., 12, 125
Mead's theory of socialization, 125
Means of production, 13
#MeBeforeEuthanasia, 119
Me Before You, 119
Medicaid, 16, 25, 85–86, 126, 180, 182, 198, 202, 207, 218, 223, 224, 227–228
Medical discourse, 104–105
Medicalization, 216
   advantages, 216 (table)
   disadvantages, 216 (table)
Medical model, 8–13, 8 (photo), 9–10 (table), 66, 99, 104, 159, 173, 211
   attention–deficit/hyperactivity disorder (ADHD), 216, 217 (figure)
   deinstitutionalization, 221–222

growing dominance of, 216–217
institutionalization, 219–221, (*See also* Institutions)
medicalization, 58, 62, 148, 170, 173, 216–217, 216 (table), 254
professional sovereignty, 216
rehabilitation, 204, 217–219
treatment, 217–219
Medical sociology, 3
Medicare, 16, 25, 85–86, 126, 180, 182, 198, 202, 207, 218, 223, 224, 227–228
Medieval Era, 98
China, 50–51
Medieval Europe, 48–50, 50 (table)
Mental disability, 29, 78, 101, 138–139, 191, 213–216
activism, 99, 215, 270, 274
families with, 168, 178–179, 183
gender and, 138–139
healthcare, 150, 228
history of, 47–48, 52–61, 64, 66
incarceration and, 81, 101, 254–255, 257–258
institutionalization, 170, 194, 200, 217, 219–222, 272 (*See also* Institutions)
race and, 156–158
research on, 29–30, 35, 37
rights and, 85, 117–119
sexuality and, 144, 147
stigma and, 81–82, 201
violence against persons with, 90, 146
Mental health parity, 228
Mental illness (*See* Mental disability)
Mercantilism, 53
Meritocracy, 16, 74–75, 104–105, 112, 154
Michalko, R., 126–129
Militarism, 193
Million Dollar Baby, 119
Mills, C. W., 3
Ming Dynasty, 51
Minority group, 17, 72, 75–77, 121, 154, 171
Minority model, 17, 21 (table), 72, 74–75
Molloy, E., 83
Moloney, M., 145
Monotheistic religion, 47
Moore, Jr., Leroy F., 40
Moral entrepreneurship, 174
Moral/Religious Model, 11
Morgan, P., 249
Morris, J., 39
Mother blame, 172
Mullins, Aimee, 141
Multidimensional approach to health, 212

N
Nario–Redmond, M., 79, 83
Narratives, 103–105, 107, 112, 120–121, 142, 173

National Institute on Mental Health, 29
Native Americans, 106, 137, 154, 167, 171, 229
education, 157, 248–249
employment, 156
history, 53–54, 66, 199
poverty, 155, 169
Nazis, 35, 61
Negative rights, 202
Neighborhood, 228
Neoliberalism, 196, 204–207
NeoNazis, 112
Neuroqueer movement, 143
New York Times, 119
Nielsen, K., 53
Nigeria, 97
Nishida, A., 159
Nixon administration, 267
Normalization, 101, 147, 172
Norms, 4, 7, 13, 20, 21 (table), 45–46, 94, 100–101, 105, 107, 123, 124 (table), 126, 140, 151, 214, 254
Normality (including abnormality, normative, normalcy, etc), 9–10 (table), 11–13, 18, 20, 21 (table) 61, 77–78, 88, 98, 104–105, 107, 111, 127, 130–131, 134, 140, 144, 147, 149, 151, 170, 172, 175, 212, 214, 253, 263
Normative Time, 20
Norris, William, 53 (photo)

O
Occupational structures, 85–86
Occupy Wall Street, 112
Oliver, M., 4, 14
Olympics, 133
Ong–Dean, C., 83
Operationalization, 26
Oppositional consciousness, 268
Ostrander, N., 87
OToole, C., 145, 147, 153, 274
Overclassification, 249

P
Pakistan, 62
Paralympics, 133
Parenting (*See also* Family)
ableism, 181–182
aging and, 184–186
advocacy, 148, 161, 174, 264, 272, 175,
children with disabilities, 105, 116, 172 (photo), 240, 244–245
cultural capital and, 246–250, 150, 157,
discrimination and, 104, 145–147, 181–182
economic marginality, 182
impact on, 174–175
outcomes, 183

parents with disabilities, 117, 181–183
policy, 95, 182, 226, 36
practices, 183
race and, 159, 161, 250
schools and, 173–174, 246–247
Parsons, T., 4, 117
Participatory Action Research (PAR), 40, 251–252
Passing, 127, 129–130
Paternalism, 80, 151, 199
People Magazine, 107
Performativity, 19, 128–131
Personal activists, 124
Person–centered services, 223, 225, 225 (table)
Person–first language, 98
Pettinicchio, D., 85, 266
Philip, Aaron, 141
Piaget, J., 125
Pity, 61, 78, 80, 97–98, 106–108, 174, 263–264, 269
Plummer, K., 151
Pluralism, 50
Polio, 98, 105, 142, 267, 270
Political economy, 16, 190
  capitalism (*See also* Capitalism), 190–193
  disability industry, 206–207
  economic inequality, 194–197
  production of disability, 190–199
  responses to disability, 199–205
  theories, 189–190
  world systems theory, 197–198
Political opportunity theory, 266
Political theories of disability and the state, 15–16, 193–194, 199–205, 266–267
Politics of Disablement, 14
Polytheistic religion, 45–46
Positive rights, 202
Positivism, 38
Poster child campaigns, 61, 107, 269
Poverty, 194–197
  direct care workers, 207
  Disability Justice and, 112, 265
  family, 169, 170, 182–183, 184
  gender and, 142, 144–145
  global, 195, 197–198, 275–276
  inequality and, 75–76, 86, 95, 109, 150, 167, 194–197, 263, 274
  history, 49, 53–54, 58, 59, 63, 66, 68
  200–201, 204–205, 267
  race and, 155, 157, 167–168, 249–250, 274
  religion, 3, 17, 25, 145, 155, 195
  relationship to disability, 15, 80, 128, 157,
Praxis, 229
Pregnancy
Prejudice, 80, 145, 169–171, 182
Primary causes, 79–82, 130, 145
Prisons, 226

Prison (*See also* incarceration), 15, 66, 194, 197, 220, 222, 254–158
  mental health, 101, 200, 222, 254–255
  school–to–prison pipeline, 258–259
  therapeutic jurisprudence, 259
Prison industrial complex, 256
Productivism, 204
Professional sovereignty, 216
Proletariat, 13
Promising diagnoses, 244–255, 248, 250
Protestant Reformation, 51
Proxy respondents, 37
Psychiatric survivors, 64, 215, 264

Q

Qualitative research, 32–33
Quantitative research, 26–33, 33 (table)

R

Racial distinctiveness, 250
Race, 153–160 (*See also* African Americans, Asian Americans, Native Americans)
  activism, 160–161, 274
  education and, 83, 156 (table), 239, 248–250
  employment and, 156 (table)
  families and, 167, 169
  health and, 229
  history, 56–59, 61, 63, 66
  identity, 158–160
  poverty and, 144, 155, 155 (table), 169
  prevalence of disability by, 137, 154–157, 154 (table), 229
  racialization of diagnosis, 155–156
  stereotypes, 141, 157–158
  theories of, 17–19, 139–140
Racism, 18–19, 57, 78, 94, 105, 112, 118, 143, 229 (*See also* Race)
  institutional racism, 153
  color–blind racism, 153, 278
Reclamation, 99, 141, 214
Re–embodiment, 218
Relational inequality, 149–150
Relationality, 16–18, 21 (table)
Relational model, 18, 86, 118, 149, 166, 178
Relations of production, 13
Representation, 105–108, 111, 152, 158, 179, 250
Research, 24–43, 275
  alliances with researchers, 275
  data literacy, 34
  emancipatory research, 39
  ethical issues in, 34–37
  gatekeepers, 36–37
  measuring disability, 26–33, 33 (table)
  participants, 34–35
  Participatory Action Research (PAR), 40
  power in, 38–40
  sampling, 36

Resignation, 124, 124 (table)
Resource mobilization theory, 268–269
Richard III, King, 50
Richards, P., 56
Richter, Z., 101
Risky mothers, 181
Ritual, 63, 72, 87, 93–94, 97, 101, 116, 172
Roberts, Ed, 96–97, 124–125, 270
Roles, 4, 12, 60, 101, 108, 116–123, 125–126, 132, 172, 212, 221
  disability activist role, 121–122
  gender roles, 138, 140–143, 175
  maternal role, 172, 174
  role disruption, 178
  role-taking, 125
  scholar–activist role, 40
  sick role, 117–118, 213
Rome, 46–47
  social structure in, 48 (table)
Roosevelt, Franklin D., 267
Rooting, 177
Rosenhan, D., 82
Rousso, H., 116

S
504 sit-ins, 65
Sakakibara, K., 30
Sampling, 36
Samuels, E., 20
Sandwich Generation, 186
Sapir–Whorf thesis, 98
Schizophrenia, 82, 156, 178, 214
Scholar–activist, 40
School-to-prison pipeline, 258–259
Scientific motherhood, 173
Scotch, R., 4, 267, 270
Scrooge, Ebenezer, 107 (photo)
Scull, A., 15, 102
Secondary conditions, 226
Section, 504, 65, 266–267
Second shift, 171
Segregation, 4, 80–81, 88–90, 148, 150, 200, 204, 229
  educational, 83, 150, 240–248, 278
  history, 49, 62, 64, 200, 235
  in services, 85, 106, 221, (*See also* Institutions)
  racial, 154, 167
Self-advocacy, 178
  In education, 252
  movements, 264, 272
Self-fulfilling prophecy, 83, 173, 240
Sequin, E., 53
Sexism, 7, 18, 78, 112, 199
Sexuality, 13, 116, 147–153, 225–226 (*See also* Heterosexism, Heteronormativity, LGBT+, Neuroqueer Movement)
  ableism, 116, 120, 145, 148, 172, 228, 274
  activism, 143, 153
  barriers to, 148–150, 179
  community settings, 225
  health, 83, 150
  intimate citizenship, 151–152
  politics, 151–153
  sexual exploration, 150–151
  sexual rights, 153
  victimization, 146
Sheppard, Alice, 74
Sherry, M., 89
Shifrer, Dara, 83, 240, 250–251
Shudras, 73
Siblings, 176, 185
Sickness, 4, 11, 20, 32, 100, 104, 120, 142, 212–213
Sick role, 117–118, 213
Sighted ways, 126–127, 129
Silverman, A., 84
Simmel, G., 118
Singer, P., 118
Sitala, 62
Slavery, 52–53, 56–58, 73–74, 118, 153, 156–158, 199
Smith, D., 19, 35
Smith, S., 105
Snyder, M., 81
Social capital, 109–110, 228–229, 73
Social change
  disability activism, 263–276
  disability rights movement, 65–66, 67, 96, 208, 264–265, 272–274
  social movement theory, 266, 268–269
  structural change, 276–277
Social construction, 3, 6–8, 10–12, 32, 44–46, 127, 140, 147, 153
Social Darwinism, 103–104
Social death, 118
Socialization, 120, 125–127, 166, 178
Social model, 8–11, 8 (photo), 9 (table)–10 (table)
Social movement frames, 266
Social movements (*See* Activism, Social Change)
Social security, 31, 60, 86, 194, 196–197, 201–202, 217–218, 267
Social Security Administration (SSA), 5, 31, 96, 190
Social Security Disability Insurance (SSDI), 144, 201–202, 205
Social stasis, 263
Social structure
  in Ancient Egypt, 46 (table)
  in Ancient Rome, 48 (table)
  in Brazil, 68 (table)
  in China, 51 (table)
  in Colonial Caribbean, 57, 58 (table)
  in Early America, 56 (table)
  in Early Modern–1850 Europe, 54 (table)
  in India, 63 (table)
  in Medieval Europe, 50 (table)

in Rome, 48 (table)
in United States, 62 (table), 66 (table)
Socioeconomic status (SES), 75, 83, 167–168, 174, 194, 229, 246–247, 250–251, 256, 274
(*See also* Poverty, Inequality)
Sociological imagination, 2–3
Sociology, 3–5, 24
Solomon, Olga, 161
Special education (*See also* Education)
educational achievements, 236–239
gender, 138
Individuals with Disabilities Education Act (IDEA), 235
intersectional analysis of, 75, 243–251
diagnoses, 244–246
emergence of, 235–236
history, 60–62
inclusion and segregation, 240–243
labelling in, 239–240
race, 102, 159, 174, 248–251
rates, 237–238
socioeconomic status (SES), 246–247
Standpoint theory, 19
State-centered theories, 15–16
Status, 17, 31, 73–75, 77, 116–118, 120, 125–127, 131–133, 142, 205
master status, 82, 118, 225 (table)
status symbol, 73
Stereotype Content Model, 80, 80 (table)
Stereotypes, 79–80
education, 83, 240
employment, 83–84
gender, 140–143
health, 82, 228
intersectionality, 17
negative, 9, 82, 84, 100, 106, 129–130, 173, 207
race, 19, 96, 141, 155–159
in research, 37
sexuality, 148–149
Stereotype threat, 84
Sterilization, 7, 59–60, 81, 90, 104, 119, 148, 194, 200, 264
Stevens, B., 150–151
Stigma, 10, 26, 30, 118–119
Stiker, H., 50
Stone, D., 15
Stone, E., 50
Stratification, 4, 16–17, 21 (table), 72–75, 73 (photo), 74 (photo), 144, 153
Stuck in Transition, 177
Subculture, 111–112, 123–124
Successful Aging, 185
Superstructure, 14
Supplemental Security Income (SSI), 180, 201–202
Surplus labor, 15
Sweden, 184, 195

Symbolic interactionism, 12, 20 (table), 116
Symbols, 98–100, 99 (figure)

T
Tabula rasa, 52
Tang Dynasty, 51
Taoism, 50
Taylor, S., 36
Temporarily able-bodied, 131
TenBroek, J., 9, 86
Theoretical perspectives, 11–20, 20–21 (table)
Tiny Tim, 107 (photo)
Titchkosky, T., 87–88, 253
Total institutions, 220–221
Transhumanism, 132–134
Transinstitutionalization, 222
Tsao, G., 159
Tubman, Harriet, 105
Tuskegee experiments, 34
Twelve Tables, 47
Typology of Disability Orientations, 123–124

U
Ugly laws, 60–61, 254
Underclassification, 249
Undeserving poor, 50, 200–201
United Nations Convention on the Rights of Persons with Disabilities, 2008, 67, 208, 275

V
Vaishyas, 73
Values, 94–96
Van Gogh, Vincent, 105
Verstehen, 12
Violence, 18, 36, 79, 88–90, 105, 119, 139, 143, 146, 150, 157, 193–194, 197, 215, 257–258
Voulgarides, C., 161, 250
Vulnerable Populations, 35–36

W
Walsh, S., 182
Walton, D., 161
Weber, M., 12, 16, 69
Welsh, M., 117
Wilkerson, A., 147
Williams Jr., R., 94
Wilson, Junius, 148
Wonder, Stevie, 74
Wong, A., 126
World Systems Theory, 197–198
World War II, 61, 64
World Wars I, 60

Y
Young, S., 79, 121 (photo)

Z
Zola, I., 4, 96